HARVARD STUDIES IN CLASSICAL PHILOLOGY

VOLUME 106

HARVARD STUDIES
IN
CLASSICAL PHILOLOGY

VOLUME 106

Department of the Classics, Harvard University
Cambridge, Massachusetts
Distributed by Harvard University Press
2011

THIS BOOK IS PRINTED ON ACID-FREE PAPER, AND ITS
BINDING MATERIALS HAVE BEEN CHOSEN FOR STRENGTH
AND DURABILITY.

LIBRARY OF CONGRESS CATALOGUE NUMBER: 44–32100

ISBN-13: 978-0-674-07201-5

PRINTED IN THE UNITED STATES OF AMERICA

EDITORIAL NOTE

Harvard Studies in Classical Philology is published by the authority of the President and Fellows of Harvard College on behalf of the Department of the Classics. Publication is assisted by the generosity of the Class of 1856, as well as by other gifts and bequests. The guidelines for style and a statement of the editorial policy may be found under Publications on the Department web page at classics.fas.harvard.edu.

CONTENTS

Contents

A PICNIC, A TOMB, AND A CROW

HESIOD'S CULT IN THE *WORKS AND DAYS*

Natasha Bershadsky

I. THE DISCREET CHARM OF HESIOD'S PICNIC

Hesiod's "prescription for the perfect picnic" (to use Martin West's phrase)[1] is one of the most alluring passages in the *Works and Days* (582–596). The voice of the poet conjures an enchanting space that is untroubled by the heat at the height of summer and undisturbed by any pursuit apart from blissfully abundant eating until the point of total contentment. As the passage draws to a close, the only motion left is the gentle stirring of the wind and the flowing of water and wine. The sound effects are exquisite: the fivefold alliterative assonance of *a* in ἀντίον ἀκραέος ἀενάου ἀπορρύτου ἀθόλωτος (596–597) frames a nearly anagrammatic phonetic figure *TRePSanTa PRoSōPa*.[2]

> Ἦμος δὲ σκόλυμός τ' ἀνθεῖ καὶ ἠχέτα τέττιξ
> δενδρέῳ ἐφεζόμενος λιγυρὴν καταχεύετ' ἀοιδὴν

I am very grateful to Laura Slatkin, Christopher Faraone, Albert Henrichs, Anna Bonifazi, and Valeria Sergueenkova for discussions of my argument at different stages of its development. I would also like to thank the anonymous reader of *HSCP*, whose comments helped me to clarify the exposition. I had the pleasure of presenting an earlier version of this paper at the conference "Diachrony," at Duke University, October 2010. Finally, my debt to Gregory Nagy is obvious throughout the paper; it is a joy to thank him.

[1]   West 1978:54.

[2]   The repetition of the *a*-sound is noticed by Petropoulos (1994:87). We can observe a similar sound effect in Sappho *fr.* 2, describing another delightful landscape of shadow and running streams (compared later in the discussion with the passage from the *Works and Days*). In line 5, ἐν δ' ὕδωρ ψῦχρον κελάδει δι' ὔσδων 'herein cold water purls through branches,' the repetition of consonants (*n, d, d, r, r, n, d, d, n*) is overlaid with a recurrent vowel pattern of *u-o*: ὕδωρ, ψῦχρον, ὔσδων. I am grateful to the anonymous reader of *HSCP* for drawing my attention to this parallel.

πυκνὸν ὑπὸ πτερύγων, θέρεος καματώδεος ὥρῃ,
585 τῆμος πιόταταί τ' αἶγες, καὶ οἶνος ἄριστος,
μαχλόταται δὲ γυναῖκες, ἀφαυρότατοι δέ τοι ἄνδρες
εἰσίν, ἐπεὶ κεφαλὴν καὶ γούνατα Σείριος ἄζει,
αὐαλέος δέ τε χρὼς ὑπὸ καύματος· ἀλλὰ τότ' ἤδη
εἴη πετραίη τε σκιὴ καὶ βίβλινος οἶνος
590 μάζα τ' ἀμολγαίη γάλα τ' αἰγῶν σβεννυμενάων
καὶ βοὸς ὑλοφάγοιο κρέας μή πω τετοκυίης
πρωτογόνων τ' ἐρίφων· ἐπὶ δ' αἴθοπα πινέμεν οἶνον,
ἐν σκιῇ ἑζόμενον, κεκορημένον ἦτορ ἐδωδῆς,
ἀντίον ἀκραέος Ζεφύρου τρέψαντα πρόσωπα·
595 κρήνης δ' ἀενάου καὶ ἀπορρύτου ἥ τ' ἀθόλωτος
τρὶς ὕδατος προχέειν, τὸ δὲ τέτρατον ἱέμεν οἴνου.

When the golden thistle is in bloom and the loud-
     sounding cicada,
perched on a tree, pours down his clearly-heard song
585 incessantly from under his wings, in the season of
     summer, with all its labors,
then it is that goats are fattest, wine is best,
women are most wanton, and men are weakest;
for Sirius dries up their heads and their knee-caps,
and the skin gets dry from the heat. At this time, at
     long last,
let there be a shady place under a rock, wine from
     [Thracian] Biblos,
590 barley-cake soaked in milk, the milk of goats that are
     reaching the end of their lactation,
and the meat of a cow fed in the woods, one that has
     not yet calved,
and of first-born kid goats. That is the time to drink
     bright-colored wine,
sitting in the shade, having one's heart sated with food,
turning one's face toward the cooling Zephyr.
595 Then, from an ever-flowing spring that flows down-
     ward, untainted by mud,

> Pour a drink that is three parts water, but make the
> fourth part wine.[3]

As it happens, the charm of this passage is accompanied by some striking peculiarities. The first problem is that the passage disrupts the chronological sequence of agricultural labor. The preceding episode in the poem is harvest (571–581), the subsequent one winnowing/threshing (597–599). However, according to the supplied astral cues the feast should happen *later* in the summer than the threshing. A prompt for the beginning of the threshing is the heliacal rising (i.e. the appearance at dawn) of Orion: "when strong Orion first appears" (εὖτ' ἂν πρῶτα φανῇ σθένος Ὠρίωνος, 598).[4] The feast, on the other hand, takes place in the period around the heliacal rising of Sirius (whose pernicious diurnal presence overhead causes the parching heat), which indicates a date approximately a month later.[5] What is the rationale for moving the feast forward to this untimely position in the poem?

Even more incongruous is the very subject of the passage, repose in a shady location. As we have seen, the episode anomalously appears midway into one of the year's most labor-intensive and strategically important periods. There is heavy emphasis on the necessity of exertion at harvestime.[6] In particular, it is necessary to "avoid sitting down in shady places" (φεύγειν δὲ σκιεροὺς θώκους, 574). West comments: "It seems that the injunction to work hard ... and not to go sitting in the shade (574–576) led the poet's thought straight on to the grateful antithesis ..."[7] Such linking of ideas by opposition, while not impossible, would suggest a lax construction. Can we find a more accurate explanation for the swift shift from labor to leisure?

---

[3]   All translations from the *Works and Days*, unless noted otherwise, are by Gregory Nagy. The text is cited from the edition of Solmsen, Merkelbach, and West.

[4]   West 1978:309.

[5]   The time-span depends on how we define the rising of a constellation. West (1978:309) gives June 20 as the date of the heliacal rising of Betelgeuse, Orion's brightest star. Sirius' heliacal rising is at the end of July. See West 1978:54, 309; Detienne 1994:100–101, nn9, 10; Nicolai 1964:117, Hamilton 1989:49–50. Edwards (2004:152–153) places the feast before the threshing, following Mazon 1914:128; Edwards' view, however, is invalidated by the fact that he ignores Sirius' heliacal rising as a chronological cue.

[6]   See Petropoulos 1994:74–75.

[7]   West 1978:54.

Finally, the summer menu of barley-cakes made with milk, meat of a forest-grazing cow, and the delicate flesh of kid goats (590–592) prompted a tart reaction from a medieval commentator. Tzetzes doubted that Hesiod's brother, the supposed addressee of these cooking suggestions, would be able to afford such a splurge.

> Πῶς δὲ, ὦ Ἡσίοδε, ὁ πρὸ μικροῦ περιλεσχήνευτος σὸς ἀδελφὸς καὶ πένης καὶ ἀγοραῖος ἕξει τοιαύτας τροφὰς, ἃς μόλις ἕξουσι καὶ οἱ τῆς μοίρας ὄντες τῆς κρείττονος; βοὸς ἀγελαίας καὶ ἀτόκου κρέας καὶ πρωτοτόκων ἐρίφων; εἰ μή που αἴφνης αὐτῷ τὰ τοῦ Ἰὼβ παρεσύρησαν θρέμματα, ἢ αἱ τοῦ Ἐριχθονίου ἀγέλαι προσεπεγένοντο, ἢ πᾶσα σχεδὸν ἡ οὐσία Τριταίχμου τοῦ Βαβυλωνίου τοῦ Ἀρταβάζου υἱοῦ ...

> How then, Hesiod, will your brother—who a little while ago was a lounge loafer, a poor man, and a low fellow—have such victuals that even those who are his betters hardly have? The meat of a herd-heifer that has not yet calved, and of the first-born kid-goats? Perhaps the possessions of Job were suddenly swept away to him, or he was credited with the herds of Erichthonius, or possibly with the whole property of Tritaichmus the Babylonian, Artabazus' son ...?

Tzetzes then exhibits both his rancor and his erudition, gained from Herodotus, by enumerating the wealth of Tritaichmus: a copious daily tribute of silver, sixteen thousands mares and eight hundred stallions (not counting the war-horses), and a myriad of hounds.[8]

Tzetzes' surprise, somewhat bitter, helps us to appreciate the gastronomic eccentricity of the passage,[9] an eccentricity obscured by the modern habit of casual meat consumption. We should look for reasons behind this delightful outburst of Hesiodic hedonism.

---

[8] Tzetz. Schol. Hes. *Op.* 591.
[9] The "gourmet" quality of the provisions was noted by Beall 2001:163, Edwards 2004:148.

II. ASSUMPTIONS AND METHODS

The idiosyncrasies of the passage will be my starting points in the exploration of the feast's fare and setting, and of the episode's place in the overall structure of the *Works and Days*. I hope to show that the episode has pervasive ritual and mythical connotations. I will further suggest a previously overlooked source that may offer an insight into the feast scene: the traditions of Hesiod's *vita*.

The point that myths about Hesiod can be germane to our understanding of the feast scene is central for my argument and constitutes a key methodological issue, so a brief exposition of its logic is necessary. We do not possess any direct historical data about the emergence of the *Works and Days*. However, the internal analysis of the text suggests that the poem was composed and performed orally throughout a long period of its development.[10] We can try to make an educated guess about the specifics of this process, namely, about the historical circumstances of the poem's formation and transmission. A milieu of the poet's cult constitutes a plausible candidate for a locus of the poem's perpetuation.[11] There are historically attested cases in which a transmission of the poet's biographical tradition and poetry are tied to the site of the poet's hero cult.[12] Obviously, the framework of a cult is not a neutral setting for the perpetuation of the poem: the myths and rituals of the cult would be immensely important for the audience and would affect the poem's reception. Furthermore, since the oral transmission of the poem involves a constant recomposition-in-performance, we may expect that references to various features of the cult would be incorporated into the poem and could conceivably acquire a great thematic prominence.[13]

---

[10] Nagy 2009:273–274. Stoddard 2004:1–33 provides a good overview of the literature on the subject.

[11] On poets' cult in ancient Greece, see Nagy 1999:279–308; Clay 2004.

[12] Archilochus' cult on Paros is the key example. Nagy 1990b:50–51, 2009:307; Clay 2004:81–82, 95.

[13] Nagy 2009:282–283.

The existence of Hesiod's cult (or, rather, cults) is strongly suggested by our sources.[14] Moreover, Gregory Nagy asserts that "an ideology reflecting the cult of the poet Hesiod is built into the poetry of Hesiod."[15] Several extant accounts of Hesiod's life, death, and burial can be connected to the worship of Hesiod in particular locations. I propose to compare these accounts to the details of the feast scene that (as I hope to show) are likely to have cultic significance. A correspondence between the feast scene and a particular myth about Hesiod would provide an argument for anchoring the poem at a certain stage in its development to the historical reality of one of Hesiod's cults. If the text reveals affinities with the myths traceable to different cult centers, an examination of the relation between such allusions may offer us a glimpse of the poem's diachronic profile and, ultimately, an outline of its history.

III. (EC)CENTRIC LEISURE AND THE GOLDEN AGE

The chronological irregularity, whereby the feast is placed before the threshing, can be contrasted with the symmetrical features of the episodes before and after it. The harvest (571–581) and the threshing/storage (597–608) are united in a ring composition by the recurrence of several words.[16] On a more general level, the feast passage is embedded in two rings: the episodes of the inner one (571–581, 597–608) relate to the harvest of cereals, while those in the outer one (564–570, 609–614) are concerned with vines.[17]

Such a framing of the feast scene—at the expense of the temporal continuity of the narrative—implies that the episode is thematically central. The feast constitutes the apex of the year, the exact opposition to the hardships of the winter scene (504–560).[18] Yet the passage is chronologically deviant, occupationally deviant, even climatically

---

[14] Nagy 2009:304–308; Compton 2006:76–86; Beaulieu 2004; Clay 2004:63, 75; Burkert 1983:203–204; Lefkowitz 1981:4,6,10; Brelich 1958:322.

[15] Nagy 1990b:48.

[16] βοῦς (581, 608), δμώς (573, 608), βίος (577, 601), οἶκος (576, 601): Petropoulos 1994:74–75.

[17] Nicolai 1964:116–117, Riedinger 1992:137.

[18] Nelson 1998:56–57.

deviant, with its sharp shift from the environment that "drains, sears, and emasculates"[19] (586–588) to the comforts of shade and coolness (589–596). Are there any episodes in the poem to which the feast scene can be connected thematically?

Indeed, there are three notable instances of ease and abundance: the Golden Race (109–120), the heroes inhabiting the Isles of the Blessed (167–173), and the city of just men (225–237).[20] The human condition of toil and distress is suspended in these situations, and the people enjoy contentment and leisure (a partial one in the case of the just city). Furthermore, both the Golden Race and the inhabitants of the just city are said to take pleasure in feasts (115, 231). The contrast that we have observed in our passage, between the scorching heat "in the toilsome season of summer" (θέρεος καματώδεος ὥρῃ, 584) and the satisfied relaxation by the stream formally parallels the opposition between the Iron Age, in which people never rest from "toil and distress" (καμάτου καὶ ὀιζύος, 177), and the festive existence of the Golden Race.

The similarity of the feast episode to scenes of the idyllic after-life (and, by extension, to the conditions of the Golden Age[21]) grows stronger if we examine descriptions of blissful posthumous existence beyond the *Works and Days*. They tell of clement weather, beautiful vegetation, a mild breeze. More specifically, it is Zephyr (cf. *Op.* 594) that refreshes men—or, as it has been argued, *reanimates* them[22]—in Elysium (*Od.* 4.567–568).[23] Pindar's Isles of the Blessed feature gusts of wind breathing from Oceanus, flowers of gold (*Ol.* 2.71–72), meadows of red roses, shady trees, and sacrifices of oxen (*fr.* 129.3–4, 12).[24]

---

[19] Lamberton 1988a:128.

[20] These passages are connected by the formula καρπὸν ... ἔφερε/φέρει ζείδωρος ἄρουρα—"the grain-giving earth bore/bears them fruit" (117, 172–173, 237). See Knox 1989:15; Nelson 1998:129, 216n22, with further references. Bonnafé 1984:246 observes the similarity between the feast scene and the just city.

[21] Nagy 1999:168–171 shows that the Hesiodic depiction of the Golden Age is homologous with the traditional descriptions of the Isles of the Blessed as transmitted by Pindar. See also Brown 1998.

[22] Nagy 1999:167–168 (especially §28n2), 196; cf. Bernabé and Jiménez San Cristóbal 2008:31–33.

[23] Zephyr also continually engenders and ripens fruits in the paradisiacal garden of Alcinous on Scheria (*Od.* 7.118–119).

[24] See also a new elegiac fragment by Simonides (22 West²), discussed by Mace 1996.

Aristophanes' *Frogs* portrays the initiates down in Hades dancing in groves and meadows full of flowers (*Ran.* 440–449); descriptions of the afterlife found in the 'Orphic' gold tablets also refer to springs, meadows, groves, and the availability of cool water to the thirsty dead.[25]

The feast scene is situated in the real world: only a golden thistle, rather than the Pindaric fruits and flowers of gold, is blossoming.[26] However, the parallels to the Golden Age/Isles of the Blessed are sufficiently strong for us to presume that such associations are built into the passage. We will return to the discussion of their significance. At the moment let us change our focus and examine the list of the picnic's victuals that so much riled Tzetzes.

IV. MEATS, WATER, AND WINE

Tzetzes' bewilderment appears justified when we consider the Ancient Greek diet. Beef was eaten rarely, and suckling kids, at least in the Classical period, were regarded as an expensive treat.[27] However, the flare-up of opulence in the poem acquires a different hue as soon as we remember that meat-eating in the Greek world was inseparably connected with sacrifice. There was, in the words of Marcel Detienne, an "absolute coincidence of meat-eating and sacrificial practice."[28] Thus, the feast in the *Works and Days* cannot be reduced to an extravagant "picnic:" what is described is a sacrificial meal. Indeed, the specifications about the cow—forest-grazing, not yet calved—are best

[25] On the connection between the gold tablets and Pindar's depictions of the afterlife, see Deonna 1939; Zuntz 1971:370–374; Burkert 1985:293; Lloyd-Jones 1985:245–279; Edmonds 2004:47–48; Calame 2007:45–47; Bernabé and Jiménez San Cristóbal 2008:25–36, 174–177, 196–197.

[26] "Golden thistle" is a standard translation for σκόλυμος (LSJ). However, at least in the later period other thistles could also be called σκόλυμος. For example, Pliny describes σκόλυμος as having a purple flower which then turns white (*HN* 20.262–263). On the possibility of σκόλυμος being a generic name for various edible thistles, see Dawkins 1936:6.

[27] Dalby 1996:60, 2003:213,160. Dalby (1996, 91) also believes μάζα ἀμολγαίη (590) to be analogous to ἄμης 'milk cake,' which he describes as the "most delicate and elaborate" way of preparing cereal. See also Dalby 1996:240.

[28] Detienne 1989:3. See also Casabona 1966:80; Robert and Robert 1970:511; Berthiaume 1982:65; Vernant 1989:25–26; Zaidman and Pantel 1991:23; Pierce 1993:234–240 (and 236n63 for earlier literature); Ekroth 2002:291.

paralleled not by self-indulgent gastronomic suggestions[29] but by common ritual stipulations regarding the gender, age, color, and other characteristics of an animal to be sacrificed on a particular occasion.[30] A familiar example comes from the *Odyssey*. Circe instructs Odysseus concerning a sacrifice to the dead in the Underworld (*Od.* 10.527–528):

ἔνθ' ὄϊν ἀρνειὸν ῥέζειν θῆλύν τε μέλαιναν
εἰς Ἔρεβος στρέψας

Sacrifice a young ram and a black female sheep there,
turning them toward Erebus ...

A few lines earlier, an exact parallel to the Hesiodic cow appears: Odysseus is to promise that, upon his return to Ithaca, he will sacrifice to the dead a cow that has not calved (στεῖραν βοῦν, *Od.* 10.522=11.30).[31]

Another detail that finds its best parallel in the realm of ritual is an instruction concerning the pouring of water and wine (596):

τρὶς ὕδατος προχέειν, τὸ δὲ τέτρατον ἱέμεν οἴνου.

Pour a drink that is three parts water, but make the
fourth part wine.

---

[29] The iambic poet Ananius (conventionally dated to the sixth century BC) recommends a shrimp in a fig-leaf in the spring, she-goat in the fall, and mutton in the summer, when "the cicadas chirp" (ὅταν θέρος τ' ἦι κηχέται βαβράζωσιν, fr. 5.6). He considers a fattened ox to be delicious both night and day (Anan. fr. 5.9–10). Athenaeus, citing Ananius' poem, concludes with the following remark: "I quoted Ananius at length because I believe that he offers this sort of advice to lecherous individuals" (τῶν τοῦ Ἀνανίου πλεόνων ἐμνημόνευσα νομίζων καὶ τοῦτον ὑποθήκας τοῖς λάγνοις τοιαύτας ἐκτεθῆσθαι, Ath. 7.282c, trans. Olson 2008). Dalby 1996:117 is uncertain about Ananius' degree of seriousness; however, the poem's fastidious gluttony seems to be an inversion of normative values characteristic of iambic poetry. Cf. Nagy 1990a:396–400 on Archilochus; particularly relevant for the present discussion is Nagy's observation of the analogy between the notion of *iambic* and Bakhtin's concept of *carnival*, with its desire to recapitulate the Golden Age: Nagy 1990a:398. Fittingly, Teleclides' comic play *Amphictyons* (cited in Ath. 7.268a) portrayed the Golden Age as a glut of self-producing foods, and among rivers of broth and streams of sauces, little milk-cakes (ἀμητίσκων, Telecl. fr. 1.12), flying into people's throats, make an appearance.

[30] See Graf 2002:119.

[31] The meat of kids (ἐρίφων, 592) also twice appears in the *Odyssey* in a formulaic description of a sacrifice (*Od.* 17.242, 19.398).

The verb χέω regularly denotes the pouring of a libation,[32] and προχέω is attested in the same sense (Hdt. 7.192.2). Accordingly, Evelyn-White translated the line as referring to a libation: "thrice pour an offering of water, but make a fourth libation of wine." West rejects this translation for the following reasons. First, the time for libations prescribed in the *Works and Days* is sunrise and sunset (339, 724), not midday. Second, libations are "not such great fun that they deserve a place in this catalogue of pleasures." Finally, the gods would not "want quite so much water, although it appears beside mead and wine in the libation to the dead in *Od.* 11.26–28."[33] This logic is not water-tight. What if this episode is *not* just a catalogue of pleasures? What if the gods do want water sometimes,[34] or the recipient of the libation is not a god but, say, a dead hero?

A passage that bears numerous correspondences with the pattern of drink-pouring in the *Works and Days* is a famous instruction that the chorus gives to Oedipus about his libation to the Eumenides (*OC* 469–484). The Chorus tells Oedipus to fetch sacred drink-offerings from a perennial spring (ἱερὰς ἐξ ἀειρύτου χοὰς / κρήνης, 469–470). Then he should pour the drink-offerings while facing the dawn (χοὰς χέασθαι στάντα πρὸς πρώτην ἔω, 477). Three libations (lit., "three streams"—τρισσάς γε πηγάς, 479)[35] are to be poured: the first two with pure water, the third with a mixture of water and honey (481). When the ground (described as μελάμφυλλος, 'darkened by foliage,' 482) has received the libation, Oedipus is to utter a prayer (484).

This ritual diverges to a degree from the action in the *Works and Days*: the libation in Sophocles is wineless, while the Hesiodic passage mentions wine; Oedipus is told to face East, while the recipient of the instruction in the *Works and Days* is described as "turning his face toward the cooling Zephyr" (ἀντίον ἀκρᾱέος Ζεφύρου τρέψαντα πρόσωπα, 594), i.e. to the West. Nevertheless, the two passages have

---

[32] Casabona 1966:279–297.

[33] West 1978:308. West himself admits that if line 596 is taken as a recipe for wine-mixing (1:3), the resulting drink is oddly weak: νηφάλιος καὶ ἀδρανὴς κρᾶσις, "sober and ineffective mixture," in Plutarch's words (*Quest. Conv.* 657c9). Dalby 1996:243.

[34] See Henrichs 1983:96–97.

[35] Kamerbeek 1984:84.

much in common. In both, the water, drawn from a perennial spring, is poured out a specific number of times, and after that a different liquid is poured. The action is set in a shady location, and the orientation of the actor (East vs. West) is indicated.[36]

The similarity suggests that the pouring of liquids in the *Works and Days* is likely to be a libation. However, a combination of actions that is overtly portrayed as an integrated ritual gesture in the *Oedipus at Colonus* (pouring libations while facing West) is not presented as a unified act in the *Works and Days*. In the same way, no explicit reference to animal sacrifice appears in the Hesiodic passage, and we can only infer its presence from the mention of the meats. We will consider the problem of this opacity later on. Now I would like to address two different questions. If there is a sacrifice and a libation described in the feast scene, what is their occasion? And where do they happen?

V. THE DOG STAR AND THE WIND

In our search for the potential occasion of the feast, let us first examine a fragment by Alcaeus (fr. 347a Campbell), closely related to lines 582–588 of the passage from the *Works and Days*.

τέγγε πλεύμονας οἴνῳ, τὸ γὰρ ἄστρον περιτέλλεται,
ἀ δ' ὤρα χαλέπα, πάντα δὲ δίψαισ' ὑπὰ καύματος,
ἄχει δ' ἐκ πετάλων ἄδεα τέττιξ ...
ἄνθει δὲ σκόλυμος· νῦν δὲ γύναικες μιαρώταται,
λέπτοι δ' ἄνδρες, ἐπεὶ <δὴ> κεφάλαν καὶ γόνα Σείριος
ἄσδει

Drench the lungs with wine, for the star returns,
the season is harsh, all is thirsty from the heat,

[36] For the importance of orientation in a ritual offering compare εἰς Ἔρεβος στρέψας "turning [the sheep] toward Erebus" (*Od.* 10.528), cited above. The action of sitting down (cf. ἐζόμενον in *Op.* 593) also can be incorporated into the prayer act: on Scheria, Odysseus comes to Athena's sacred grove, sits down, and makes a prayer (*Od.* 6.321–323). Another detail that may bear a trace of cultic connotations is Bibline wine (589). It is perhaps significant that the earliest non-fragmentary reference to it (apart from the *Works and Days*) appears in a description of a libation to Apollo (Eur. *Ion* 1195). On the suggested places of origin of the wine, see West 1978:306, Gow 1951:250–251.

the sweet cicada shrills from the leaves,
the golden thistle flowers, and now women are the
  foulest,
and men weak, since Sirius parches the head and
  knees.[37]

The two poems, with their shared diction and metrical variation, have to derive from a common precursor.[38] Petropoulos extends this argument, suggesting that modern Greek harvest songs, featuring motifs of female desire and a singing cicada, are descendants of the same tradition.[39] Petropoulos then retrojects the modern practice into the Hesiodic passage, assuming it to be a harvest celebration.[40] It may seem straightforward to connect the scene with the celebration at the end of harvest,[41] yet, as Lamberton notices in his review of Petropoulos' book, the chronology of the feast episode prevents it: "the Dog Days fall nearly two months after the grain harvest in Hesiod's reckoning."[42] The peculiar order of the episodes, in which the feast anachronistically intrudes between the harvest and the threshing, and the cursory treatment of the threshing in the narrative[43] also argue against perceiving the feast as a happy finale to the regular agricultural sequence.

Richard Martin offers different comparanda for the passages of Hesiod and Alcaeus: seasonal songs in general, and in particular the tradition of Russian calendar-songs (*koljadki*), whose references to seasonal abundance can function as wish-incantations. He proposes that a seasonal song was adapted by the sympotic poetry of Alcaeus and the didactic poetry of Hesiod.[44] The idea that the Hesiodic passage "quotes" a song of an incantatory nature, whose aim is to alleviate the

---

[37] Trans. Martin 1992, modified.

[38] Hooker 1977:80–81; Nagy 1990a:462–463; Martin 1992:23; Petropoulos 1994:17, 81–82. Ar. *Pax* 1159–1171 and *Av.* 1088–1100 are further thematically connected compositions.

[39] Petropoulos 1994.

[40] Petropoulos 1994:75.

[41] Cf. Kledt 2000:1003n6.

[42] Lamberton 1996:79. Nelson 1998:50 emphasizes that haste is normally expected at the transition from harvest to threshing.

[43] Nelson 1998:56.

[44] Martin 1992:23.

hardships and augment the joys of the season, is particularly appealing in light of the sharp atmospheric shift that occurs in the scene. Right after the last image shared by the Hesiodic passage and Alcaeus' song—the parching of the flesh by Sirius—there is a transition, marked by the expression ἀλλὰ τότ' ἤδη, "at this time, at long last" (588), to the portrayal of a "world characterized by extraordinary abundance," a "refuge" from the detrimental influence of the Dog Star.[45] The implicit incantatory force of the seasonal song surfaces in the optative εἴη (589): let there be shade, wine, meat, breeze.

We possess a mythical account (and references to an attendant ritual) that is concerned precisely with mitigating the deleterious effect of Sirius.[46] The tale's season is the Dog Days. Sirius burned in the sky (ἔφλεγε, Ap. Rhod. 2.516), causing a plague. Aristaeus was commanded by Apollo, his father, to go to Ceos. On Ceos, he sacrificed to Sirius and to Zeus. As a result, the cooling Etesian winds started to blow, and the plague stopped. Since then the Etesian winds have blown for forty days after Sirius' rising. The Ceans kept the practice of sacrificing before the heliacal rising of Sirius. They and other Greeks render divine honors to Aristaeus.[47]

The motifs of harmful Sirius, a beneficent wind, and an alleviation of blazing heat all occur in the feast scene. We can hypothesize that the occasion of the animal sacrifice and libation in the Hesiodic passage is a festival similar to the Cean one, whose aim is to bring relief during the Dog Days of summer.

VI. THE JOYS OF *ALSOS*

In what kind of locale does the feast happen? There is a rock that provides shade (589), and a perennial spring (595). Further, if we interpret the reference to the cicada (582–583) not only as a temporal cue but also as a detail of the setting, we can add to our list of landscape

---

[45] Lamberton 1988a:128.

[46] For the list of ancient references to Sirius' fever-inducing quality, see West 1978:262; Detienne 1994:9, 114.

[47] Ap. Rhod. 2.516–527, Diod. Sic. 4.82.1–3; see Burkert 1983:109–111 for a discussion and further references. For the cults of Aristaeus, see Lloyd-Jones 1977.

elements a tree on which the cicada is perching. Perhaps there is more than one tree, since cicadas are commonly associated with wooded locations.[48] In an Iliadic simile, chirping cicadas are situated in the woods (*Il.* 3.151–152):

> τεττίγεσσιν ἐοικότες οἵ τε καθ' ὕλην
> δενδρέῳ ἐφεζόμενοι ὄπα λειριόεσσαν ἱεῖσι

> ... similar to cicadas who, through the woods,
> perching on trees, send out their lily-like voice.[49]

The logic by which a forest sprouts from a casual mention of a cicada can appear precarious. Yet, when we apply the same reasoning in a parallel case, it works accurately. In the *Shield*, the season of a fight between Heracles and Cycnus is described in the following way (*Sc.* 393–397):

> ἦμος δὲ χλοερῷ κυανόπτερος ἠχέτα τέττιξ
> ὄζῳ ἐφεζόμενος θέρος ἀνθρώποισιν ἀείδειν
> ἄρχεται, ᾧ τε πόσις καὶ βρῶσις θῆλυς ἐέρση,
> καί τε πανημέριός τε καὶ ἠῶς χέει αὐδὴν
> ἴδει ἐν αἰνοτάτῳ, ὅτε τε χρόα Σείριος ἄζει

> When a dark-winged *loud-sounding cicada, perched* on a
>   green
> shoot, starts to *sing* to men
> of *summer*—his food and drink the delicate dew—
> and both all day long and at the break of dawn he *pours*
>   his voice
> in the most terrible heat, when *Sirius dries up the skin* ...

Formulaic similarities with our passage are prominent. This description may look just like a seasonal vignette, but the text explicitly identifies the setting of the fight as a sacred grove of Apollo's sanctuary at Pagasae (*Sc.* 70, 99–100). So, at least in this instance it appears that

---

[48] Arist. *Hist. an.* 556a21–22. See Petropoulos 1994:83–84.

[49] Nagy (1994:421n22) suggests that the tradition of a drinking song reflected in our Hesiodic passage and Alc. fr. 347 is also evoked in these lines.

the reference to the cicada can function both as a temporal and local marker, evoking a wooded location in high summer.

The mention of Apollo's sanctuary brings us to our next subject. We have observed some similarities between the feast episode and the descriptions of the Golden Age and the Isles of the Blessed. However, another group of setting descriptions bears a closer resemblance to the Hesiodic scene. One may think of a sheltering shade of roses, and a cold stream purling amid apple branches in Sappho's invocation of Aphrodite (Sapph. fr. 2); green glens, alive with nightingales, in the choral eulogy of the Eumenides' sacred grove (OC 668–693); a verdant resting spot on the bank of Ilissus—a "holy place of some nymphs and of Achelous"—enthusiastically described by Socrates (Phdr. 230b–c). All these beautiful locales happen to be sanctuaries, and I propose that the setting of the feast in the Works and Days is also a sacred precinct.[50]

The nexus of a spring and trees, usually in the form of a sacred grove (alsos), repeatedly appears in conjunction with sanctuaries both in archaic and classical literature and in the reality of the cult.[51] The

---

[50] These descriptions of scenery, as well as the feast scene itself, are typical examples of a locus amoenus (Schönbeck 1962:61–87; Elliger 1975:180–181, 289–290; Thesleff 1981; Bonnafé 1984:247, 1998:6–7, 18, 25–26, 52–56, 81; for the classical definition of locus amoenus, see Curtius 1953:195). Thesleff (1981:31) asserts an association between the locus amoenus and religious experience. Cf. Motte 1973. Kledt (2000:1010) also remarks that "in der Antike die Beschreibung eines locus amoenus quasi automatisch den Gedanken an heilige Plätze hervorrief, an denen man zu Ehren der Götter Feste feierte." However, Thesleff (1981:42) singles out the Hesiodic feast and Archilochus' Cologne Epode as principal examples of "secularized" loci amoeni. Since the publication of Thesleff's article, it has been shown that the setting of the Cologne Epode is a sacred precinct of Hera (Miralles and Pòrtulas 1983:136n16, 17; Nagy 1990a:399–400), which calls for a reassessment of the notion of a "secular" locus amoenus. A comprehensive examination of the relation between loci amoeni and sacred space is beyond the boundaries of this paper, but as a preliminary hypothesis I would like to suggest that the locus amoenus is always a numinous topos in archaic and classical literature. Loci amoeni figure as settings of the Golden Age and of posthumous paradise, a scenery found in the margins of the world, landscapes of myth and sites of sanctuaries. I am particularly interested in shifts of register that often characterize representations of a locus amoenus, such as an alternation of idyllic and ominous (Segal 1974, Petrone 1998:180), or a modulation between seduction and initiation (Calame 1992 and 2007). The locus amoenus appears to have a high potential for multilevel diachronic signification, shuttling between the realms of myth and ritual.

[51] Some literary examples are Il. 2.305–307; Od. 6.291–292, 17.205–211; h. Ap. 3.383–385; Sappho fr. 2; Ibyc. fr. 286; Bacchyl. 11.118–120; Soph. OC 668–693; Eur. Ion 112–127;

connection between sacred precincts and groves was so strong that the word *alsos* was at some point metonymically extended in poetic speech to denote any sanctuary.[52] A lushness of vegetation could serve as a tell-tale sign, identifying the area's sacred status. For example, from the profuse growth of laurel, olive and vine, Antigone deduces that the site to which she has led Oedipus is sacred (*OC* 16–17).[53] Moreover, the natural beauty of a locale could be perceived as a manifestation of its numinous resident.[54] A piece of striking (if late) evidence for such a mentality is Philostratus' *On Heroes*. The setting of the *On Heroes* is the vineyard and gardens around the tomb of the hero Protesilaus. There are springs, whose water is deliciously varied in taste, and tall trees, whose branches intertwine, garland-like (5.3); the site is permeated by the "divine" (θεῖον, 3.4) scent of plants. As the Phoenician visitor (and the reader) is introduced to the mystery of Protesilaus' cult by a vine-dresser who works the land around the tomb, it becomes apparent that the marvelous smell of the flowers derives from the sweetness of the hero's breath (10.2, 11.3). The beauty of the precinct "becomes the ultimate epiphany of the cult hero."[55]

The *On Heroes* brings us back to the topic of the Golden Age. The Phoenician visitor at once discerns that the life-style of the vine-dresser has qualities reminiscent of the existence of the Golden Race (*Her.* 2.1).[56] Similarly, practices and beliefs evocative of the Golden Age are attested in association with some sacred groves.[57] In a recent

---

Pl. *Phdr.* 230b–c; Theoc. 1.1–11, 5.45–59, 7.135–157, 25:18–22. See also Burkert 1985:85–86; Edlund 1987:54; Jost 1994:217; Pedley 2005:39. Water and springs in particular were inherently sacred: Cole 1988:161, Segal 1974:21. The archaeologist John Camp observes: "Wherever there is water one can expect to find a sanctuary." See Hägg, Marinatos, and Nordquist 1988:172. Springs in sanctuaries: Cole 1988. Springs as a habitat of nymphs: Larson 2001:8–10.

[52] οἱ δὲ ποιηταὶ κοσμοῦσιν, ἄλση καλοῦντες τὰ ἱερὰ πάντα κἂν ᾖ ψιλά, Str. 9.2.33 (quoting Pind. fr. 51a as an illustration). *Alsos* is the most common type of sacred place in Homer. See Polignac 1995:16; Sourvinou-Inwood 1993:4–5; Vermeule 1974:105–106, 108. On *alse* in general, see Bonnechere 2007, Birge 1994, Graf 1993, Birge 1982.

[53] On the ways of recognizing a sacred space in antiquity, see Cole 2004:40–44.

[54] Cf. Bonnechere 2007:26.

[55] Nagy 2001:xxvii–xxviii; cf. Whitmarsh 2004:245.

[56] Maclean 2004:254–255, Whitmarsh 2004:242–243.

[57] Graf 1993.

article, Bonnechere argues that the link with the Golden Age should be extended to most Greek sacred groves. He describes the groves as "sites of exceptional purity, irreducible to the nature-culture opposition because their nonculture was that of the Golden Age and its plenty."[58] The environment of an *alsos*, with its pleasures of shade, fresh water,[59] and a leisurely, unproductive pastime, perfectly fits the description of the feast's venue and the scene's associations with the Golden Age. The fact of meat-consumption, as we have discussed, gives an additional indication that the episode is set in a cultic space.[60] Cumulatively, the menu and the venue strongly suggest that the feast takes place in a sanctuary.

VII. *A* ROCK OR *THE* ROCK?
THE SETTING OF THE FEAST AND HESIOD'S VITAE

At this point a new issue arises: is the scene a generic depiction of a stylized festival, or does it portray a specific situation? Let me rephrase the question slightly: the scene has been indubitably perceived as generic for a long period of the poem's existence; but could there have been a particular referent (or referents) at a certain point?

The depiction of the setting lacks strong individuating details. A spring and trees, as we have seen, are typical features of sacred precincts. The only other element of the landscape is a rock or, possibly, a cave, in the shadow of which the feast takes place (πετραίη τε σκιή, 589). Rocks and caves are less common in sanctuaries than are springs and groves, but they are still numerous.[61] The description of the feast's fare, on the other hand, is suggestive precise. How does one decide whether the scene is generic or specific? I propose that this question can be tackled by taking into consideration plausible scenarios of the poem's creation and transmission.

---

[58] Bonnechere 2007:27. Cf. Nagy 1999:189–190 on sacred precincts named Elysium and Isles of the Blessed.

[59] Jacob 1993:43.

[60] See Marinatos 1993:228 on ritual dining in sanctuaries. She argues that sacrificial meals were "the primary activity which took place in sanctuaries."

[61] For example, *Od.* 17.208–211. See Burkert 1985:85, Ustinova 2009.

The feast scene appears to contain a cluster of cultic elements. Hesiod also was a figure of cult, and, as I said earlier, it is probable that the sites of his cult played a crucial role in the formation and dissemination of Hesiodic poetry. A cultic setting would exert a powerful influence on the poetry, making the references in the poem gravitate toward the local sacred realia. Therefore, I suggest that even a relatively broad correspondence between the cultic details of the feast scene and a local myth about Hesiod deserves careful scrutiny, since we could be encountering a potential site of a junction between Hesiodic poetry and Hesiod's cult, and a clue concerning the history of the poem's development.

Let us review what is known about the transmission of the *Works and Days*, and about various locales of Hesiod's cult. We have a few pieces of evidence pointing toward Helicon and the city of Thespiae as sites of perpetuation of the poem. Pausanias was shown a lead tablet with the text of the *Works and Days* (minus the first ten lines) by the Hippocrene spring (Paus. 9.31.4). He also reports that the oldest tripod dedicated on Helicon was the one received by Hesiod for his victory in a poetic contest in Chalcis (Paus. 9.31.3). Sandwiched between the mention of the tripod and the tablet is Pausanias' remark that the people of Thespiae celebrate a festival and games called Musaea in the grove of the Muses. Calame suggests, accordingly, that, in parallel to the Muses, Hesiod was honored at the spring of Hippocrene with a cult focusing on his victory in Chalcis.[62] Nagy further connects the reception and transmission of Hesiodic poetry at Thespiae with the activity of an association called "co-sacrificers (*sunthutai*) to Hesiodic Muses," attested in an inscription (*IG* VII 1785, 3rd c. BC).[63]

These indications that Hesiod's cult on Helicon and in Thespiae was associated with the perpetuation of Hesiodic poetry, and of the *Works*

---

[62] Calame 1996:51, 54; cf. Nagy 1999:296, Brelich 1958:321–322. Calame (1996:51) also observes that the attribution of the foundation of Ascra and the first sacrifice to the Muses to the same characters, Otus and Ephialtes, reinforces the idea of Hesiod's heroic status on Helicon. Lamberton (1988b:493) argues that the Musaea was instrumental in the formation of the persona of Hesiod. He believes, however, that the Musaea originated in the late 3rd c. BC (Lamberton 1988b:496–497).

[63] Nagy 1990a:29n66.

and Days in particular, corroborate the working hypothesis of this paper about the role of a poet's cult in the formation and transmission of his or her poetry. The interface between the cult of Hesiod on Helicon and Hesiodic poetry is, thus, an important question deserving a separate investigation.

The locus of Hesiod's cult on Helicon presents an obvious candidate for the referent of the feast scene. However, can we point to a locale that would fit the setting of the feast in the environs of the Valley of the Muses? There are, certainly, streams, groves and caves there;[64] however, to the best of my knowledge, no ancient source singles out any particular grove, spring, and rock/cave on Helicon as belonging to an integral whole. In particular, no tradition describing Hesiod's life or cult mentions a constellation of a rock, spring, and grove connected to Hesiod on Helicon. We need to extend our search for a referent of the feast scene to other sites of Hesiod's cult.

An important locus of Hesiod's cult was in West (Ozolian) Locris. The myth of his death in Locris is attested as early as Thucydides, who describes the Athenian forces camping in the Locrian "precinct of Nemean Zeus, in which Hesiod the poet is said to have been killed by the people of the district, it having been foretold to him that he should suffer that in Nemea" (ἐν τοῦ Διὸς τοῦ Νεμείου τῷ ἱερῷ, ἐν ᾧ Ἡσίοδος ὁ ποιητὴς λέγεται ὑπὸ τῶν ταύτῃ ἀποθανεῖν, χρησθὲν αὐτῷ ἐν Νεμέᾳ τοῦτο παθεῖν, Thuc. 3.96.1). The *Contest of Homer and Hesiod* preserves a fuller version of the myth. After his victory in the poetic contest in Chalcis, Hesiod sails to Delphi, where the Pythia greets him with an assurance of world-wide fame and an admonition to avoid the grove of Nemean Zeus:

> ὄλβιος οὗτος ἀνὴρ ὃς ἐμὸν δόμον ἀμφιπολεύει,
> Ἡσίοδος Μούσῃσι τετιμένος ἀθανάτῃσιν·
> τοῦ δ' ἦ τοι κλέος ἔσται ὅσην τ' ἐπικίδναται ἠώς.

---

[64] There is the grove of the Muses and Hippocrene (as well as numerous other streams on Helicon). Among other sights on the approach to the grove, Pausanias also mentions a small cave sanctuary of Linus, to whom heroic honors were rendered in conjunction with the cult of the Muses (Paus. 9.29.6). On the connection of the ancient sites in the Valley of the Muses and Helicon with modern topographical and archaeological features, see Wallace 1974 and Aravantinos 1996.

ἀλλὰ Διὸς πεφύλαξο Νεμείου κάλλιμον ἄλσος·
κεῖθι δέ τοι θανάτοιο τέλος πεπρωμένον ἐστίν.

Cert. 219–223

This man is blessed who attends my house,
Hesiod, honored by the immortal Muses;
his fame will reach as far as the Dawn spreads.
But beware the beautiful grove of Nemean Zeus,
For there the fulfillment of death is ordained for you.[65]

To keep away from Nemea, Hesiod goes to Oenoe in Locris, not recognizing that it is a region sacred to Nemean Zeus. There he is suspected by his hosts of seducing their sister; they kill him and throw his body into the sea. Dolphins pick his body up and bring it to the shore at Rhium at the time of a festival.[66] Plutarch's narrative follows the same lines, adding that Hesiod was killed in the vicinity of the temple of Nemean Zeus, and was buried there after the dolphins brought his body ashore.[67] At this point it is pertinent to cite Gregory Nagy's observation that the rescue of Hesiod's body by the dolphins is "a narrative scheme that is particularly appropriate to a cult hero in whose honor a festival is founded."[68]

We gain further information about the Locrian burial place of Hesiod from Pausanias' narrative about the transfer of Hesiod's bones from Locris to Orchomenus (Paus. 9.38.4).[69] The Orchomenians were

---

[65] The oracle abounds in the vocabulary of hero cult. On *olbios*, 'blissful', as a description of a cult hero in an afterlife, *telos* as 'fulfillment' or 'ritual of initiation' and *timē* as the 'honor of cult', see Nagy 1990a:244–249, 1999:118§1n2.

[66] *Cert.* 215–236 Allen, with a reference to Alcidamas' *Museum* as a source in line 240. On the traditional nature of Alcidamas' narrative, see Nagy 2009:299.

[67] Plut. *Conv. sept. sap.* 162d-f.

[68] Nagy 1990b:50, 2009:306. Nagy compares the rescue of Hesiod's body with a myth about dolphins rescuing the body of Melicertes/Palaemon, in whose honor the Isthmian games were instituted. Cf. Burkert 1983:203–204. The suggestion that the story of Hesiod's Locrian death is an aetiology for a ritual is as old as Nilsson 1906:383–384.

[69] Hesiod had a hero cult in Orchomenus, but his tomb was situated in the agora (Tzetz. Proleg. in Hes. *Op.* p. 92 Colonna), so the Orchomenian site of worship is not directly relevant for the analysis of the feast scene. For the discussion of the Orchomenian cult and its relation to the *Works and Days*, see Section X below.

suffering from a plague,[70] and were told by the Delphic oracle that their sole remedy was to bring the bones of Hesiod to Orchomenus from the region of Naupactus.[71] The Pythia stated that the location of the bones would be revealed by a crow. Upon disembarking, the envoys saw a rock (πέτρα) in the vicinity of the road, and on the rock a bird.[72] They found Hesiod's bones in the cleft of the rock (καὶ τοῦ Ἡσιόδου δὲ τὰ ὀστᾶ εὖρον ἐν χηραμῷ τῆς πέτρας).[73]

We have one more text that portrays Hesiod's burial, this time in supernatural terms, and alludes to cultic honors for him in Locris (*Anth. Pal.* 7.55):

Λοκρίδος ἐν <u>νέμεϊ σκιερῷ</u> νέκυν Ἡσιόδοιο
Νύμφαι <u>κρηνίδων</u> λοῦσαν ἀπὸ σφετέρων
καὶ τάφον ὑψώσαντο· γάλακτι δὲ <u>ποιμένες αἰγῶν</u>
ἔρραναν ξανθῷ μιξάμενοι μέλιτι·
τοίην γὰρ καὶ γῆρυν ἀπέπνεεν ἐννέα Μουσέων
ὁ πρέσβυς καθαρῶν γευσάμενος λιβάδων.

In a *shady glade* of Locris the Nymphs bathed
Hesiod's body with water of their *springs*
and raised up a tomb; there *goatherds* sprinkled *milk*

---

[70] Cf. the story of Aristaeus stopping the plague (Ap. Rhod. 2.516–527).

[71] Compton 2006:84 lists analogous instances of the relocation of heroes' bones meant to ward off a catastrophe. Cf. Blomart 2004.

[72] Remarkably, Lucian (*De mort. Peregr.* 41) in painting a picture of a false hero—who is *not* going to be accompanied by signs of heroic status in death—tells that there will be no cicadas or crows at his tomb: Ἐννόει τὸ λοιπὸν οἷα εἰκὸς ἐπ᾽ αὐτῷ γενήσεσθαι, πόιας μὲν οὐ μελίττας ἐπιστήσεσθαι ἐπὶ τὸν τόπον, τίνας δὲ <u>τέττιγας οὐκ ἐπάσεσθαι</u>, τίνας δὲ <u>κορώνας οὐκ ἐπιπτήσεσθαι</u> καθάπερ ἐπὶ τὸν <u>Ἡσιόδου τάφον</u>, καὶ τὰ τοιαῦτα. "Imagine what is likely to happen in his honor hereafter, how many bees will not settle on the place, what *cicadas will not sing upon it*, what *crows will not fly to it*, as they did to the *tomb of Hesiod*, and so forth!" Trans. Harmon 1996, mentioned in Clay 2004:173n105. It is tempting to interpret the juxtaposition of cicadas and crows as an additional indication of the affinity between the feast scene and Hesiod's Locrian tomb.

[73] Pausanias' account belongs to the tradition that situated the (first) tomb of Hesiod in the precinct of Nemean Zeus. Plutarch's narrative provides an explicit connection, portraying a situation in which the Locrians conceal the exact location of Hesiod's tomb in the precinct of Nemean Zeus, in order to thwart the efforts of the Orchomenians, who, according to an oracle that they have received, desire to carry the relics away. Plut. *Conv. sept. sap.* 162e–f. See Section X below for further discussion.

mixing it with yellow honey.
For such voice the old man breathed forth,
having tasted the pure streams of the nine Muses.

The beautiful shady grove of Nemean Zeus, springs of the Nymphs, a rock or a cave keeping Hesiod's bones, and libations of goat milk: this combined description of Hesiod's Locrian tomb tallies well with the feast scene.[74] The elements—the rock, the springs and the grove—coalesce into the landscape of Hesiod's death, entombment and worship. The idyllic setting appears to be carrying Hesiod in its midst.

VIII. HESIOD AT THE FEAST

I have conjectured that the site of Hesiod's tomb in Locris is a referent of the feast scene. The sacrifice and libation that are obliquely invoked in the episode belong, I suggest, to a religious festival honoring Hesiod as a cult hero. Below I provide some evidence strengthening this proposition, and examine how my interpretation resonates with the major themes of the *Works and Days*.

First I would like to substantiate the claim that the feast scene, involving the eating of meat and the libation of wine, fits with our current conceptions regarding the rituals of hero worship. I cite the conclusion of a recent treatise on sacrifice in hero-cults: "The basic ritual in hero-cults was a sacrifice at which the worshippers ate."[75] *Thusia*, a sacrificial banquet, was equally common and central in the worship of both heroes and gods.[76] Wine libations in hero-cults also seem to be the normal practice:[77] wineless libations, usually cited as a

---

[74] The requirement that the cow whose meat is consumed in the feast scene be 'fed in the woods' (ὑλοφάγοιο, 591) can be connected to the wooded surroundings of the temple of Nemean Zeus in Locris, as is suggested by the very term Nemean (from νέμος 'wooded pasture, glade') and by "νέμεϊ σκιερῷ" of the epigram (7.55). For sacrificial animals grazing in the sanctuaries, see Lupu 2005:27–28, with further references.

[75] Ekroth 2002:341.

[76] Ekroth 2002:169, 212–213, 287–301, 303–304; Burkert 1985:205; Nock 1972:575–602.

[77] Examples in Brelich 1958:162–163; Jameson, Jordan, and Kotansky 1993:70; Ekroth 2002:179n213 and 220–221; Lupu 2005:372–373.

sign of a cult with a chthonic character, were rarely poured to heroes.[78] Offerings of cakes (sometimes later consumed by the worshippers) are abundantly attested in hero-cults.[79] Libations of milk in hero-cult are attested relatively rarely,[80] but they are mentioned, for example, in Plutarch's description of the honors to the heroic war dead at Plataea.[81]

The representation of Hesiod as a dead hero finds a counterpart in the corpus of other archaic poets: Nagy shows that, in certain poems of Alcaeus and Theognis, the voice of the poet can be dramatized as speaking out of the tomb.[82] Hesiod's farming expertise may also be linked with his cult hero status: the very ability of Hesiod to give advice concerning the proper ways of working the land can be compared with a special knowledge of agriculture possessed by the hero Protesilaus, who is portrayed by Philostratus as helping and instructing his worshipper in farming (*Her.* 2.8; 11.3–5).

As we have seen, Philostratus describes the devotee of Protesilaus as leading a life comparable to the Golden Age (*Her.* 2.1). The evocation of the Golden Age in the feast scene, with its clement weather and plentiful food, can be understood as a parallel phenomenon: the presence of a hero transforms the Iron Age into the Age of Gold. I construe the anachronistic placement of the feast scene as intentional and iconic, indicating a holiday, a momentary break in the chain of succes-

[78] Henrichs 1983:98–99, esp. n58; Ekroth 2002:317. The semantics of libations to heroes are still not well understood (Ekroth 2002:130), and a study is necessary that would explore the significance of variations in substances and proportions. For example, Henrichs 1983:99 states that unmixed wine was standard for heroes (and for the dead), while Jameson, Jordan, and Kotansky (1993, 72) assume that wine mixed with water was normal in libation to heroes and gods.

[79] Jameson, Jordan, and Kotansky 1993:69; Jameson 1994:36, 37–39, 43, 46; Van Straten 1995:97; Ekroth 2005:276,281,283. μάζα, 'barley-cake', served as a customary offering to Trophonius (Paus. 9.39.11) and Ino (Paus. 3.23.8). On the modes of offering cakes, see Gill 1991:7–15; Jameson 1994:37–39.

[80] On libations of milk see Graf 1980 and Burkert 1983:57n35, both with further references.

[81] Cited in Henrichs 1983:99n58, Ekroth 2002:102. In Philostratos' *On Heroes*, the vinedresser describes his offering milk to Protesilaus at the time of a full moon in the early spring. The vinedresser presents the milk, saying "these are the streams of the season; drink!" (τὸ τῆς ὥρας νᾶμα, σὺ δὲ πῖνε). As soon as he leaves, the milk disappears in the blink of an eye (*Her.* 11.9).

[82] On Theognis: Nagy 1985:68–81, 1990b:273–274. On Alcaeus: Nagy 1993.

sive tasks.[83] The festival cannot stop the cycle of the works and days, restoring the Golden Age forever; but it can suspend the cycle for a short while, giving to the participants a brief glimpse (and a taste) of immortality.

The festival is positioned in the poem at the crucial moment of the agricultural cycle, between harvest and threshing. Such arrangement can indicate the notional importance of the festival for the successful completion of the crop-gathering. The festival also implicitly resolves the neîkos with Perses. At the start of the poem, Hesiod admonishes Perses that there is little time for quarreling until the harvest is stored inside; only when Perses is satiated (κορεσσάμενος, 33), can he start wrangling over others' property (30–34). This advice to postpone the litigation until the harvest is over implies that after reaching prosperity Perses would no longer be interested in instigating a court case.[84] Indeed, the description of the threshing, whose diction echoes the language of Hesiod's admonition,[85] is not followed by the reexamination of the neîkos. Instead, the feast scene portrays a person who is satiated with food (κεκορημένον ἦτορ ἐδωδῆς, 593) and is clearly not in a litigious mood. I submit that the festival scene settles the neîkos with Perses by rendering the fairest possible judgment: the proponent of justice, Hesiod, receives a hero cult. Thus the conflict between dikē and hubris, between Hesiod and Perses,[86] spills over from the poem into the real world, and is settled in the real world. As long as Hesiod receives his fair share, a hero cult (whose focal event is the summer festival), the city (or cities) rendering the cult would remain governed by dikē. The continuation of Hesiod's hero cult is understood to be equivalent to the upholding of dikē—one guarantees the other, and one is impossible without the other.[87]

---

[83] Cf. Burkert's formulation that festivals "interrupt and articulate everyday life." Burkert 1985:225.

[84] Edwards 2004:41.

[85] Compare βίος ἔνδον ἐπηετανὸς and Δημήτερος ἀκτήν (31–32) with Δημήτερος ... ἀκτὴν (597), βίον (601), ἔνδοθι (601), ἐπηετανόν (607).

[86] On Hesiod and Perses as exponents of, respectively, dikē and hubris, see Nagy 1990b:74–75.

[87] Cf. Nagy 1990b:69 on the instructions in the latter part of the Works and Days: "moral and ritual correctness are consistently made parallel."

Nagy makes a case that the *Works and Days* "dramatizes the actual passage of time required for the working of *Dikē*;" ultimately *dikē* prevails in the poem.[88] The triumph of justice, celebrated in the festival scene, is embedded in the fabric of the year. The conception of *dikē* is dynamic and cyclical: the performance of the yearly cycle of works, crowned with the harvest and the festival in honor of Hesiod, brings the Golden Age back; once the round of works and days starts over again, the Iron Age struggle between *dikē* and *hubris* resumes.[89]

Another important theme present in the feast scene is the fraught relationship between men and women. During the Dog Days, male and female desires are out of balance: "women are most wanton, and men are weakest" (μαχλόταται δὲ γυναῖκες, ἀφαυρότατοι δέ τοι ἄνδρες, 586).[90] Detienne and Vernant show that the reference to the parching female desire at the peak of summer is part of Hesiod's systematic representation of the woman as "a fire created by Zeus as a counterpart to the fire stolen by Prometheus."[91] The presence of the cicada is particularly appropriate in this context, since according to one of the myths the cicada is what remains of Tithonus, consort of Eos, "withered counterpart of her eternally renascent desire."[92] However, the feast in the shadow of the rock remedies the situation, providing "a refuge [...] from women, whose lust is represented as an exceptional threat at this brutal season."[93]

[88] Nagy 1990b:66, 67.

[89] *Dikē* vs. *hubris* is a central theme of the Myth of the Generation: the Golden Generation is marked by *dikē*, while the Iron Generation is characterized by an ongoing struggle between *dikē* and *hubris*. Vernant 1965:20, 24–26; Nagy 1999:154–55.

[90] On the subject of balance and measure in the *Works and Days*, see Slatkin 2004.

[91] Vernant 1989:67. A woman can singe her man without a torch (704–705). See Detienne 1994:120–122, 191n111 and 112; Vernant 1966:256n1, 1989:67–68; Oliensis 1991:121; Nagy 1994:421–423.

[92] Oliensis 1991:121. Interestingly, Rosen (1990:107–109) draws a parallel between the cicada and Hesiod.

[93] Lamberton 1988a:128. Pliny reports that ingestion of *scolymos* with wine has an aphrodisiac effect, citing the passages of Hesiod and Alcaeus (fr. 347a) as corroborating evidence (*HN* 22.86–87); thus the drinking song about male impotence during high summer might implicitly contain advice for regaining potency. Lowrie 1991:421; Nagy 1994:422.

It is interesting to juxtapose the protective quality of the feast scene, sheltering men from deleterious female desire, with the story of Hesiod's death. Hesiod dies on account of a woman: the two brothers who host him in Locris kill him in the belief that he has seduced their sister. Different traditions exist concerning Hesiod's culpability: one claims that he was wrongly accused, another holds him responsible.[94] Aristotle's *Constitution of the Orchomenians* (fr. 565 Rose) belongs to the latter strain, reporting that the poet Stesichorus is Hesiod's son from that liaison.[95]

At this point I will revisit the hero Aristaeus, who saves the Ceans from the plague caused by the Dog Star. Aristaeus' son is Actaeon, and Diodorus Siculus makes the following proto-structuralist comment about the significance of the dogs in Aristaeus' life (Diod. Sic. 4.82.3):

> τοῦτο δ' ἄν τις συλλογιζόμενος εἰκότως θαυμάσαι τὸ τῆς περιπετείας ἴδιον· ὁ γὰρ ὑπὸ τῶν κυνῶν ἰδὼν τὸν υἱὸν τετελευτηκότα, οὗτος τῶν κατὰ τὸν οὐρανὸν ἄστρων τὸ τὴν αὐτὴν ἔχον προσηγορίαν καὶ φθείρειν νομιζόμενον τοὺς ἀνθρώπους ἔπαυσε, καὶ τοῖς ἄλλοις αἴτιος ἐγένετο τῆς σωτηρίας.

> Now the man who ponders upon this event may reasonably marvel at the strange turn which fortune took: for the same man who saw his son done to death by the dogs likewise put an end to the influence of that star which, of all the stars of heaven, bears the same name and is thought to bring destruction upon mankind, and by so doing was responsible for saving the lives of the rest.[96]

We can, in the same way, "reasonably marvel" at the theme of women in Hesiod's life, poetry, and cult: the poet is undone by a woman,

---

[94] Paus. 9.31.6, Plut. *Conv. sept. sap.* 162d; *Certamen* 234 Allen. O'Sullivan (1992:98–99) argues that the account acknowledging Hesiod's guilt is a more archaic version of the story; Compton (2006:82n28) disagrees.

[95] Lefkowitz 1981:4–5 notes a correspondence between this account of Stesichorus' birth and *Op.* 270–274.

[96] Trans. Oldfather 2000.

whereas the summer festival helps to keep the destructive feminine power in check.[97]

IX. FURTHER AFIELD IN THE *WORKS AND DAYS*

I have attempted to demonstrate that the biographical tradition concerning Hesiod's death in Locris can be fruitfully considered as a context for the feast scene. Logically the next question is, are there other passages in the *Works and Days* in which connections with the myths about Hesiod may be present? I believe that there are, indeed, such passages. I shall provide a brief outline of my reasons for selecting two episodes of the *Works and Days* as potential foci for further research; I shall consider one more instance of a possible interaction between the poem and narratives of Hesiod's cult in greater detail in the next section.

My first example is a passage from the winter scene (526–535):

> οὐ γάρ οἱ ἠέλιος δείκνυ νομὸν ὁρμηθῆναι,
> ἀλλ' ἐπὶ κυανέων ἀνδρῶν δῆμόν τε πόλιν τε
> στρωφᾶται, βράδιον δὲ <u>Πανελλήνεσσι</u> φαείνει.
> καὶ τότε δὴ κεραοὶ καὶ νήκεροι ὑληκοῖται
> λυγρὸν μυλιόωντες ἀνὰ δρία βησσήεντα,
> φεύγουσιν, καὶ πᾶσιν ἐνὶ φρεσὶ τοῦτο μέμηλεν,
> οἳ σκέπα μαιόμενοι πυκινοὺς κευθμῶνας ἔχουσι
> κὰκ <u>γλάφυ πετρῆεν</u>· τότε δὴ <u>τρίποδι βροτοὶ</u> ἶσοι,

---

[97] Cf. Nagy 1990b:4 on the connection between the catastrophe of a myth and the regularity of a ritual. A particularly interesting parallel to the figure of Hesiod in the *Works and Days* and vitae emerges from the discussion of the hero Lityerses in Karanika 2009. The song of Lityerses, as stylized in Theoc. 10.40–55, contains advice concerning harvest and threshing, and bears numerous similarities to the poetry of the *Works and Days*. In myth, Lityerses is a reaper who kills those who lose in a reaping competition with him. He is killed by Heracles, and lamented in harvest songs (Phot. *Lexicon* λ 227, 228, and scholia to Theoc. 10.41). Particularly interesting is Karanika's suggestion that Lityerses' agricultural advice in Theoc. 10.40–55 contains implicit references to his death. An analogous tradition of harvest songs, lamenting the death of a hero and giving agricultural advice, may be in the background to the episodes of the harvest and the feast in the *Works and Days*. Athenaeus (10.415b) describes Lityerses as a glutton: this mythical detail finds a correspondence on the level of ritual in the abundance characterizing the Hesiodic feast.

οὖ τ' ἐπὶ νῶτα ἔαγε, κάρη δ' εἰς οὖδας ὁρᾶται·
τῷ ἴκελοι φοιτῶσιν, ἀλευόμενοι νίφα λευκήν.

The sun shows him [the octopus] no range to head
    towards.
Instead, it comes and goes over the community and the
    city of dark-skinned men.
But it shines more tardily for *all the Hellenes.*
Then it is that the creatures of the forest, horned and
    unhorned alike,
gnash their teeth pitifully as they flee through the
    woods of the glens.
For all of them there is one thing in their hearts:
how to find some cover in cozy nooks
in a hollow rock. Then, like a *three-legged one,*
whose back is broken down and whose head looks down
    upon the ground,
like such a one they range about, trying to escape the
    white snow.

The depiction of the animal hordes, running through the woods,
gnashing their teeth, is wonderfully strange. But it is their destina-
tion that is really remarkable, in light of the previous discussion: it is
a rocky hollow (γλάφυ πετρῆεν, 533). The shadow-producing rock of
the feast-scene turns out to have a counterpart.[98] It is most appealing
to interpret the rock in line 589 and the rocky hollow in line 533
as relating to the same cave-like structure, apparently enjoying its
own microclimate year round, cool in the summer and warm in the
winter. The cave's ultra-sheltering nature, and its role as the focus of
a centripetal motion, suggest its special status. The occurrence of the
rocky hollow in the winter episode strengthens my interpretation of
the shadow-giving rock in the feast scene as a locus enclosing Hesiod's
bones; furthermore, the description of the animals' flight to the cave

---

[98] On the symmetry between the summer (582–596) and winter (504–563) scenes,
see Nelson 1998:56. I note in particular the mention of first-born kids (πρωτογόνων δ'
ἐρίφων, 543) and of an ox (βοός, 541, 544) in the winter scene, replicating the meats eaten
in the summer feast. Cf. West 1978:295.

gains an unexpected possibility of cultic significance. Interestingly, Bonnechere mentions in his discussion of the Golden Age-like characteristics of the sacred groves that "wild beast were often imagined to live there comfortably instead of struggling for life."[99]

The animals who first run toward the cave are next portrayed as imitating a three-legged man in his wanderings. Hamilton observes that there are only two occurrences of τρίπους in the *Works and Days*: the three-legged man and a tripod that Hesiod wins in the contest in Chalcis (657). A further link between the winter passage and the contest episode is forged by the mention of pan-Hellenes (Πανελλήνεσσι, 528) and Hellas (Ἑλλάδος, 653), the only two references to Greece or Greeks in the poem. Hamilton concludes that the passages must be thematically connected.[100] More specifically, it is attractive to conjecture that the man with a tripod and the wandering three-legged man, emulated by the animals, are one and the same: Hesiod himself.

In my second example my analysis starts off from a very small detail. Introducing the description of the contest in Chalcis, Hesiod claims that he never sailed over the sea in a ship, apart from a short crossing from Aulis to Euboea (650–651). The surprising element is a focus particle γε, following the mention of a ship (650):

οὐ γάρ πώ ποτε νηὶ γ᾽ ἐπέπλων εὐρέα πόντον

for never yet have I sailed in a ship *ge* over the wide sea

West comments that γε cannot have restrictive force in this case, since the statement about never sailing in a *ship* absurdly implies the possibility of a shipless sailing: "as if there were other means of crossing the sea."[101] For usual mortals, indeed, ships are the only option; however, Hesiod's biographical tradition furnishes an episode of his sailing the sea by other means.

---

[99] Bonnechere 2007:28.

[100] Hamilton 1989:72–73.

[101] West 1978:319. On the frequent restrictive force of γε, see Denniston 1954:114–115, 140. Some examples of the restrictive γε in the Homeric epics are *Il.* 4.372, 17.27, 19.218, 20.211, 21.291, 23.77; *Od.* 14.512, 24.251. The particle γε again appears after the word 'ship' in line 660, enclosing in a ring composition the description of Hesiod's victory in the poetic contest in Chalcis.

After Hesiod is killed, his murderers throw his body into the sea. Enter the dolphins: they take the body up and bring it to the shore at Rhium in the Gulf of Corinth.[102] Even more interestingly, the *Contest of Homer and Hesiod* specifies that the corpse was cast into the sea between Locris and Euboea and brought to Rhium by the dolphins on the third day (*Cert.* 232–236).[103] If we follow this tradition, Hesiod's body, before finally coming into the Gulf of Corinth, must have sailed through the Euboean Gulf and around all of the Peloponnese. The dolphins had a long journey to cover in three days.

The biographical tradition reported by Pausanias aligned Hesiod with Poseidon: Hesiod's murderers are said to have "sinned against Poseidon" (ἀσεβήσασιν ἐς Ποσειδῶνα, Paus. 9.31.6).[104] The connection with Poseidon extends to Hesiod's home city: Oeoclus, one of Ascra's mythical founders, is a son of the nymph Ascra and Poseidon.[105] This positive relationship between Hesiod and Poseidon in the biographical traditions can be contrasted with a strikingly negative stance of the *Works and Days* toward sailing:[106] for example, the people of the just city do not travel on ships (236–237). And yet, the *Nautilia* operates on the extended metaphor connecting poetry with sailing.[107] I wonder whether the ambiguities and ironies of the Hesiodic attitude to sailing may perhaps be connected to a pattern of antagonism towards Poseidon during Hesiod's lifetime and a symbiosis with Poseidon in death.[108] Intriguingly, the feast scene features wine from Biblos in Thrace,[109] making Gow comment in disbelief that the imported wine

---

[102] Plut. *Conv. sept. sap.* 162e, *De soll. an.* 984d; *Certamen* 231–232.

[103] West (2003:343n15) considers "between Locris and Euboea" a mistake to be emended; however, see Nagy 2009:306.

[104] A sacrifice to Poseidon is also reported at Rhium (Paus. 10.11.6). See Burkert 1983:203n37.

[105] Paus. 9.29.1–2, quoting a poem of Hegesinus transmitted through Callippus of Corinth.

[106] Nelson 1998:165, 228n43.

[107] Nagy 1990b:77–78; Rosen 1990; Graziozi 2002:169–171; Dougherty 2001:20–25.

[108] On a god-hero antagonism in myth and a symbiosis in cult, see Nagy 1999:118–150. On the sharp shifts of attitude to sailing in the *Nautilia*, see Griffith 1983:60–61; Lamberton 1988a:131; on the *Nautilia* disrupting the orderly sense of a year's cycle see Nelson 1998:167.

[109] West 1978:306.

"seems out of the question" for Hesiod.[110] However, apparently Hesiod's tolerance of overseas journeys has increased greatly in his Locrian afterlife. Fittingly, the season of safe sailing starts just after the feast (663–672).[111]

X. HESIOD'S HOME AND THE TRAVEL OF TRADITION

I have referred before to the peculiar opacity of the cultic allusions in the feast scene. Indeed, if the Locrian festival is central to Hesiod's hero cult and poetry, why are the ritual overtones not more explicit, and why is the geographical location of the feast not indicated? Part of the answer has to be the pan-Hellenic trend, bleaching the local color out of the poetic tradition.[112] Another factor is a mystical obfuscation, typical for the descriptions of hero cults.[113] Finally, a potential third factor emerges from a consideration of another, at first glance unrelated, passage in the *Works and Days*.

Among the painstakingly detailed advice at the end, one piece stands out for its obscurity (746–747):

> μηδὲ δόμον ποιῶν ἀνεπίξεστον καταλείπειν,
> μή τοι ἐφεζομένη κρώξῃ λακέρυζα κορώνη.

> When you are building a house, do not leave it rough-hewn,
> or a cawing crow may settle on it and croak.[114]

West comments: "The roof is to be smoothed off so that the crow cannot easily get a foothold."[115] The recommendation does not sound very practical: it would seem that an attempt to make a house crow-proof by careful smoothing of the roof is bound to prove futile, or at least would involve a massive amount of work. In any case, the aim of such an undertaking is unclear. West conjectures that the crow cawing

---

[110] Gow 1952:250; Lamberton 1988a:128.

[111] West 1978:323.

[112] Nagy 1990a:52–81, esp. 56–57, 1990b:128.

[113] Nagy (2001:xx) comments that "opaque signification is a vital aspect of the traditional essence of hero cults." See also xvi, esp. n4, xixn9.

[114] Trans. Evelyn-White 1982.

[115] West 1978:341.

on the roof forebodes some evil for the house, and muses that "it is typical of the human mind to find comfort in averting an omen of ill, as if the ill itself were thereby averted."[116] Perhaps I can offer a more specific interpretation of the crow's significance.

Pausanias' narrative about the Orchomenians carrying Hesiod's bones off from Locris (Paus. 9.38.3–4) fits the two lines from the *Works and Days* surprisingly well. In Pausanias' story, *a crow* on a rock indicates Hesiod's tomb—his sacred *abode*[117]—to the Orchomenians. As a result, the Locrians suffer the loss of Hesiod's presence.

A further correspondence between the two passages emerges from the consideration of the hapax ἀνεπίξεστον (746). A related (and rare) adjective ἄξεστος appears in *Oedipus at Colonus* in the context of a sanctuary: Antigone offers to Oedipus, whom she led to the sacred grove of Colonus, to sit down on an "unhewn stone" (ἀξέστου πέτρου, *OC* 19). Later in the play a similar description of the same stone is given: "this holy seat, *not shaped by an axe*" (ἀσκέπαρνον, *OC* 101)."[118] Thus, ἄξεστος has an aura of a sacred inviolability. We can hypothesize that ἀνεπίξεστος should express a comparable idea, denoting a pristine natural state; such an adjective seems remarkably appropriate if applied to Hesiod's rock in Locris.

In Orchomenus, according to Paul Wallace's conjecture, Hesiod's bones were held by a Mycenaean tholos.[119] The basis of this suggestion is Pausanias' description of a *tholos*, followed by the mention of Hesiod's grave (Paus. 9.38.2–3):

θησαυρὸς δὲ ὁ Μινύου, θαῦμα ὂν τῶν ἐν Ἑλλάδι αὐτῇ καὶ τῶν ἑτέρωθι οὐδενὸς ὕστερον, πεποίηται τρόπον τοιόνδε·

---

[116] West 1978:341.

[117] The meaning of δόμος as 'house of a god, temple' is widely attested (LSJ): cf. *Od.* 7.81, among many other examples. On a parallel phenomenon of *oikos/oikeō* relating to a hero's precinct, see Nagy 1985:76–77, 1990a:268–269; Edmunds 1981:223n8; Henrichs 1976:278.

[118] The scholiast actually glosses ἀσκέπαρνος as ἄξεστος. *Scholia in Sophoclem, OC* verse 100.

[119] Wallace 1985:167–168. The archaeological data indicate that the tholos was a site of cult in the Roman period, and probably also in the Hellenistic period. Hall 1995:585n55; Alcock 1991:462–463, 1993:183; Antonaccio 1993:67n39; Schliemann 1881:19–25.

λίθου μὲν εἴργασται, σχῆμα δὲ περιφερές ἐστιν αὐτῷ,
κορυφὴ δὲ οὐκ ἐς ἄγαν ὀξὺ ἀνηγμένη· τὸν δὲ ἀνωτάτω τῶν
λίθων φασὶν ἁρμονίαν παντὶ εἶναι τῷ οἰκοδομήματι. τάφοι
δὲ Μινύου τε καὶ Ἡσιόδου·

The treasury of Minyas, a wonder second to none either in
Greece itself or elsewhere, has been built in the following
way. It is made of stone; its shape is round, rising to a
rather blunt apex; they say that the highest stone is the
keystone of the whole building. There are graves of Minyas
and Hesiod.[120]

Immediately following is the story of the transfer of Hesiod's bones
from Locris. The tholos in Pausanias' account is an ultimate feat of
stone construction, a building that would be the very opposite of the
unhewn rock that housed the bones of the poet in Locris. Viewed in
this context, advice not to leave the house that you are building rough-
hewn, lest a crow should settle on it,[121] sounds extremely like a taunt
that the Orchomenians could have addressed to the Locrians after the
transfer of the bones. The insecurity of keeping the bones in the natural
"rough-hewn" rock contrasts with the supreme safety of lodging them
in an architectural tour de force.

If we interpret the advice about the crow and the house as an
Orchomenian taunt incorporated into the *Works and Days*, a variant
reading ἀνεπίρρεκτον 'unconsecrated,' attested in scholia (Schol. vet.
Hes. *Op.* 746 p. 227 Pertusi), acquires a point. Rather than presuming
that the variant is due to a scribal error of copying the word from two
lines below (748), we can perceive the mockery of the resulting line:

μηδὲ δόμον ποιῶν ἀνεπίρρεκτον καταλείπειν ...

---

[120] Trans. Jones 1979.

[121] Rosen (1990:111) suggests that ἐφεζομένη in line 747 (the crow settling on a
house) recalls ἐφεζόμενος in line 583 (a cicada perched on a tree). These are the only
two instances of ἐφέζομαι in the *Works and Days*. The repetition of ἐφεζομένη in line 747
may be taken as the poem's internal evidence of the crow's connection with the feast
scene; it functions as an ironic echo of the feast's description, especially as the participles
ἐφεζόμενος and ἑζόμενον (583, 593) frame the feast scene.

> when you are building a (sacred) abode, do not leave it
> without offerings ...[122]

—or the hero will grow angry with you, and then the communicative
crow will come, followed by the Orchomenians. The taunt implies that
the Locrians are to blame themselves for the loss of Hesiod, since they
neglected to give him his due offerings.

What is the exact relation between the Locrian and Orchomenian
cults of Hesiod? If these two traditions were originally independent of
each other, then the story of the transfer of Hesiod's bones must be a
later attempt to harmonize the contradictory claims of the two cities.
However, it seems to me that the evidence points to the Orchomenian
cult presupposing the existence of the Locrian one. The tradition of
Hesiod's two burials is attested in an epigram transmitted through
Aristotle's *Constitution of the Orchomenians* (fr. 565 Rose):

> χαῖρε δὶς ἡβήσας καὶ δὶς τάφου ἀντιβολήσας,
> Ἡσίοδ᾽, ἀνθρώποις μέτρον ἔχων σοφίης.

> Hail, you who twice were young and twice received a
>   tomb,
> Hesiod, you who hold the measure of wisdom for
>   human beings.[123]

We do not have any reference to the Orchomenian cult of Hesiod
that is incompatible with the idea that Hesiod's tomb first was located
in Locris.[124] All extant narratives of Hesiod's death situate it in Locris;

---

[122] For ἀνεπίρρεκτον as 'lacking offerings' cf. ἐπιρρέζεσκον, 'made offerings', in the
description of the Nymphs' fountain in *Od.* 17.211.

[123] Trans. Most 2006. Tzetzes attributed this epigram to Pindar (Tzetz. Proleg. in Hes.
Op. p. 92 Colonna). For discussion, see Scodel 1980.

[124] An important piece of information, deriving from Plutarch and Aristotle's
Constitution of the Orchomenians, is passed on by the scholia (Plutarch fr. 82 Sandbach
= Schol. vet. Hes. *Op.* 633–40 p. 202 Pertusi, Arist. fr. 565 Rose): ἀοίκητον δὲ αὐτὸ (τὸ
πολίχνιον τὴν Ἄσκραν) ὁ Πλούταρχος ἱστορεῖ καὶ τότε εἶναι, Θεσπιέων ἀνελόντων τοὺς
οἰκοῦντας, Ὀρχομενίων δὲ τοὺς σωθέντας δεξαμένων. ὅθεν καὶ <τὸν θεὸν> Ὀρχομενίοις
<προστάξαι> τὰ Ἡσιόδου <λείψανα λαβεῖν καὶ θάψαι παρ᾽ αὐτοῖς>, ὡς καὶ <Ἀριστοτέλης>
φησὶ γράφων τὴν Ὀρχομενίων πολιτείαν. ("Plutarch narrates that it [the little town of
Ascra] was uninhabited in his time too, because the Thespians killed the inhabitants and
the Orchomenians took in the survivors. For this reason, he said, the god had ordered the

similarly, all extant narratives of Hesiod's death mention the later relocation of the bones by the Orchomenians.[125] The only account that requires comment in this respect is Plutarch's *Dinner of the Seven Wise Men*. It dramatizes a situation in which Hesiod is buried near the Locrian temple of Nemean Zeus, and the location of his grave is kept secret, so that the Orchomenians, who have been prompted by an oracle, would not be able to steal the body (*Conv. sep. sap.* 162f). I believe that in this case we are not dealing with an independent tradition that denies the transfer of the bones to Orchomenus,[126] but rather with Plutarch's narrative device, staging the sages' banquet at the point in the past when the transfer has not yet happened.

Thus, I consider the transfer of Hesiod's bones from Locris to Orchomenus essentially a historical event,[127] whose probable consequence should have been an accompanying shift in the locus of transmission of Hesiodic poetry, with ensuing subtle "Orchomenization" of the *Works and Days*. Wallace identifies a plausible historical context for the transfer of Hesiod's bones in the middle of the fifth century BC.[128] At this date we would expect the tradition of the *Works and Days* to be relatively crystallized,[129] the presence of the "Locrian" feast scene already fixed in the poem. It is possible that at this point the scene was stripped of any reference to the festival's location at the sanctuary of Nemean Zeus in Locris, since such references would have been incongruous at

---

Orchomenians to take Hesiod's remains and bury them in their own city, as Aristotle too says in his *Constitution of the Orchomenians*" [trans. Most 2006, modified]). In this account, it is not clear from *where* the Orchomenians should take Hesiod's bones; indeed, Nagy (1990b:49) interprets ὅθεν as referring to Ascra. However, ὅθεν can also be translated as "in consequence of which" (so West 1978:317), with Apollo ordering the Orchomenians to bring the remains of the poet *from Locris*—a reading perfectly in line with the story in Paus. 9.38.3–4 and Plut. *Conv. sep. sap.* 162f.

[125] Arist. fr. 565 Rose; Paus. 9.31.6, 9.38.3–4; Plut. *Conv. sep. sap.* 162e–f, *Cert.* 224–253 Allen, Tzetz. Proleg. in Hes. *Op.* p. 92 Colonna..

[126] Contra Nagy 2009:305.

[127] For other instances of the hero cult transfer in ancient Greece, see Blomart 2004.

[128] Wallace builds on Larsen's argument that Orchomenus and not Thebes was at the head of the formation of the Boeotian confederacy in 447 BC (Larsen 1960:9–18). "Orkhomenos, as the bulwark and guardian of the old traditions, would have found in that period some advantage in having the old poet's bones" (Wallace 1985:167).

[129] On the crystallization of Hesiodic poetry, see Nagy 1990b:79.

Orchomenus. In addition, the Orchomenian mockery of the Locrians has apparently been incorporated into the canonical body of the *Works and Days*. It is significant that the two lines concerning the crow come from the end of the poem—a part that would be performed less, and accordingly would crystallize more slowly,[130] allowing the incorporation of the new materials at a relatively late date.

XI. FURTHER QUESTIONS

My analysis of the cultic background of the *Works and Days* produces numerous further questions. They concern the history of Hesiod's cults, and its implication for our understanding of Hesiodic poetry. What is the significance of variants existing within the tradition of Hesiod's death in Locris?[131] Plutarch's Hesiod seems different from the Hesiod of the *Constitution of the Orchomenians*: how did the perception of Hesiod as a cult hero change through the ages? What was the ideological and political framework of the transfer of Hesiod's bones from Locris to Orchomenus? What was the relation between the Locrian, Orchomenian and Heliconian/Thespian cultic and poetic traditions, and did it vary though time? What is the relation of these (reconstructed) traditions to our text of the *Works and Days*? Can details of other Hesiodic poems—for example, of the *Theogony*—be connected to Locris or Orchomenus? What was the stance of Athens vis-à-vis different locales of Hesiod's cult?[132]

In his analysis of Hesiodic biographical traditions, Gregory Nagy emphasizes the multiplicity of disparate myths about Hesiod, stemming from rival hero cults: "we cannot speak of any single perspective—not to mention any single truth value inherent in these myths."[133] The poetry of the *Works and Days*, it appears, exhibits a similar multi-

---

[130] Lord 2000:17. The end of the *Odyssey* provides an example of such lesser fixity, with scholia reporting Aristarchus' athetization of the text following *Od.* 23.296, as well as of *Od.* 23.310–43, 24.1–204. See Nagy 1996:182n107.

[131] Cf. Paus. 9.31.6. At least two alternative accounts, by Alcidamas and by Eratosthenes, are attested in *Certamen* 240–244.

[132] On the recomposition-in-performance of Hesiodic poetry in Athens in the sixth century BC, and the Athenian efforts at appropriation of the figure of Hesiod in that period, see Nagy 2009:294–296, 302–303.

[133] Nagy 2009:307.

vocality, joining the personae of Hesiod the Ascraean, Hesiod the Locrian, Hesiod the Orchomenian, the hero of ritual and of myth. The task of clarifying the patterns of agreement and argument played out by these voices remains to be done.

University of Chicago

WORKS CITED

Aitken, E. B., and J. K. B. Maclean, eds. 2004. *Philostratus's* Heroikos: *Religion and Cultural Identity in the Third Century C.E.* Atlanta.

Alcock, S. E. 1991. "Tomb Cult and the Post-Classical Polis." *AJA* 95:447–467.

———. 1993. Graecia Capta: *The Landscapes of Roman Greece.* Cambridge.

Alcock, S. E., and R. Osborne, eds. 1994. *Placing the Gods: Sanctuaries and Sacred Space in Ancient Greece.* Oxford.

Antonaccio, C. 1993. "The Archaeology of Ancestors." In *Cultural Poetics in Archaic Greece: Cult, Performance, Politics,* ed. C. Dougherty and L. Kurke, 46–70. Oxford.

Aravantinos, V. 1996. "Topographical and Archaeological Investigations on the Summit of Helicon." In Hurst and Schachter 1996, 185–192.

Beall, E. F. 2001. "Notes on Hesiod's *Works and Days,* 383–828." *AJP* 122:155–171.

Beaulieu, M.-C. 2004. "L'héroïsation du poète Hésiode en Grèce ancienne." *Kernos* 17:103–117.

Bernabé, A., and A. I. Jiménez San Cristóbal. 2008. *Instructions for the Netherworld: The Orphic Gold Tablets.* Leiden.

Berthiaume, G. 1982. *Les rôles du mágeiros: Étude sur la boucherie, la cuisine et le sacrifice dans la Grèce ancienne.* Mnemosyne Supplement 70. Leiden.

Birge, D. E. 1982. *Sacred Groves in the Ancient Greek World.* PhD diss. University of California at Berkeley.

———. 1994. "Trees in the Landscape of Pausanias' *periegesis.*" In Alcock and Osborne 1994, 231–246.

Blomart, A. 2004. "Transferring the Cults of Heroes in Ancient Greece: A Political and Religious Act." In Aitken and Maclean 2004, 85–98.

Bonnafé, A. 1984. *Poésie, nature et sacré*. Lyons.

Bonnechere, P. 2007. "The Place of the Sacred Grove (*Alsos*) in the Mantic Rituals of Greece: The Example of the *Alsos* of Trophonios at Lebadeia (Boeotia)." In Conan 2007, 17–41.

Brelich, A. 1958. *Gli eroi greci: Un problema storico-religioso*. Rome.

Brown A. S. 1998. "From the Golden Age to the Isles of the Blest." *Mnemosyne* 51:385–410.

Burkert, W. 1983. *Homo Necans*. Berkeley, CA (orig. pub 1972).

———. 1985. *Greek Religion*. Trans. J. Raffan. Cambridge, MA (orig. pub 1977).

Calame, C. 1992. "Prairies intouchées et jardins d'Aphrodite: espaces 'initiatiques' en Grèce." In *L'initiation: Actes du colloque international de Montpellier, 11–14 Avril 1991*. Vol. 2, ed. A. Moreau, 103–118. Montpellier.

———. 1996. "Montagne des Muses et Mouséia: la consécration des *Travaux* et l'héroïsation d'Hésiode." In Hurst and Schachter 1996, 43–56.

———. 2007. "Gardens of Love and Meadows of the Beyond: Ritual Encounters with the Gods and Poetical Performances in Ancient Greece." In Conan 2007, 43–56.

Casabona, J. 1966. *Recherches sur le vocabulaire des sacrifices en Grec des origines à la fin de l'époque classique*. Aix-en-Provence.

Cazanove, O. de, and J. Scheid, eds. 1993. *Les bois sacrés: Actes du Colloque international organisé par le Centre Jean Bérard et l'École pratique des Hautes Études (V^e section), Naples, 23–25 Novembre 1989*. Naples.

Clay, D. 2004. *Archilochos Heros: The Cult of Poets in the Greek Polis*. Washington, DC.

Cole, S. G. 1988. "The Uses of Water in Greek Sanctuaries." In Hägg, Marinatos, and Nordquist 1988, 161–165.

———. 2004. *Landscapes, Gender, and Ritual Space: The Ancient Greek Experience*. Berkeley, CA.

Compton, T. M. 2006. *Victim of the Muses: The Poet as Scapegoat, Warrior, and Hero in Greco-Roman and Indo-European Myth and History*. Washington, DC.

Conan, M., ed. 2007. *Sacred Gardens and Landscapes: Ritual and Agency*. Washington, DC.

Curtius, E. R. 1953. *European Literature and the Latin Middle Ages.* Trans. W. R. Trask. New York (orig. pub. as *Europäische Literatur und lateinisches Mittelalter*, Bern 1948).

Dalby, A. 1996. *Siren Feasts: A History of Food and Gastronomy in Greece.* London.

———. 2003. *Food in the Ancient World: From A to Z.* London.

Dawkins, R. M. 1936. "The Semantics of Greek Names for Plants." *JHS* 56:1–11.

Denniston, J. D. 1954. *The Greek Particles.* 2nd ed. Oxford.

Deonna, W. 1939. "Croyances funéraires: La soif des morts." *Revue de l'histoire des religions* 119:53–81.

Detienne, M. 1994. *The Gardens of Adonis: Spices in Greek Mythology.* Trans. J. Lloyd. 2nd ed. Princeton (orig. pub. as *Les jardins d'Adonis*, Paris 1972).

———. 1989. "Culinary Practices and the Spirit of Sacrifice." In Detienne and Vernant 1989, 1–20.

Detienne, M., and J.-P. Vernant, eds. 1989. *The Cuisine of Sacrifice among the Greeks.* Trans. P. Wissing. Chicago (orig. pub. as *La cuisine du sacrifice en pays grec*, Paris 1979).

Dougherty, C. 2001. *The Raft of Odysseus: The Ethnographic Imagination of Homer's* Odyssey. Oxford.

Edlund, I. E. M. 1987. *The Gods and the Place: Location and Function of Sanctuaries in the Countryside of Etruria and Magna Graecia (700–400 BC).* Stockholm.

Edmonds, R. G. 2004. *Myths of the Underworld Journey: Plato, Aristophanes and the "Orphic" Gold Tablets.* Cambridge.

Edmunds, L. 1981. "The Cults and the Legend of Oedipus." *HSCP* 85:221–238.

Edwards, A. T. 2004. *Hesiod's Ascra.* Berkeley, CA.

Ekroth, G. 2002. *The Sacrificial Rituals of Greek Hero-Cults in the Archaic to the Early Hellenistic Periods.* Kernos Supplément 12. Liège.

Elliger, W. 1975. *Die Darstellung der Landschaft in der griechischen Dichtung.* Berlin.

Evans, J. 1998. *The History and Practice of Ancient Astronomy.* Oxford.

Evelyn-White, H. G. 1982. *Hesiod. The Homeric Hymns and Homerica.* Cambridge, MA.

Gill, D. 1991. *Greek Cult Tables.* New York.

Gow, A. S. F. 1952. *Theocritus.* 2nd ed. Vol. 2. Cambridge.

Graf, F. 1980. "Milch, Honig und Wein: Zum Verständnis der Libation im griechischen Ritual." In *Perennitas: Studi in onore di Angelo Brelich,* ed. U. Bianchi et al., 209–221. Rome.

———. 1993. "Bois sacrés et oracles en Asie Mineure." In Cazanove and Scheid 1993, 23–29.

———. 2002. "What is New about Greek Sacrifice?" In *Kykeon: Studies in Honour of H. S. Versnel,* ed. H. F. J. Horstmanshoff et al., 113–126. Leiden.

Graziosi, B. 2002. *Inventing Homer: The Early Reception of Epic.* Cambridge.

Griffith, M. 1983. "Personality in Hesiod." *Classical Antiquity* 2:37–65.

Hägg, R., N. Marinatos, and G. C. Nordquist, eds. 1988. *Early Greek Cult Practice: Proceedings of the Fifth International Symposium at the Swedish Institute at Athens, 26–29 June, 1986.* Stockholm.

Hall, J. M. 1995. "How Argive Was the 'Argive' Heraion? The Political and Cultic Geography of the Argive Plain, 900–400 B.C." *AJA* 99:577–613.

Hamilton, R. 1989. *The Architecture of Hesiodic Poetry.* Baltimore.

Harmon, A. M. 1996. *Lucian.* Vol. 5. Cambridge, MA (orig. pub. 1936).

Haß, P. 1998. *Der locus amoenus in der antiken Literatur: Zu Theorie und Geschichte eines literarischen Motivs.* Bamberg.

Henrichs, A. 1976. "Despoina Kybele: Ein Beitrag zur religiösen Namenkunde." *HSCP* 80:253–286.

———. 1983. "The 'Sobriety' of Oedipus: Sophocles *OC* 100 Misunderstood." *HSCP* 87:87–100.

Hooker, J. T. 1977. *The Language and Text of the Lesbian Poets.* Innsbruck.

Hurst, A., and A. Schachter, eds. 1996. *La montagne des Muses: Recherches et recontres: Publications de la faculté des lettres de Genève.* Geneva.

Jacob, C. 1993. "Paysage et bois sacré: ἄλσος dans la *Periègèse de la Grèce* de Pausanias." In Cazanove and Scheid 1993, 31–44.

Jameson, M. H. 1994. "Theoxenia." In *Ancient Greek Cult Practice from the Epigraphical Evidence: Proceedings from the Second International Seminar on Ancient Greek Cult, organized by the Swedish Institute at Athens, 22–24 November 1991,* ed. R. Hägg, 35–57. Stockholm.

Jameson, M. H., D. R. Jordan, and R. D. Kotansky. 1993. *A Lex Sacra from Selinous*. Durham, NC.

Jones, W. H. S. 1979. *Pausanias. Description of Greece*. Vol. 4, *Books VIII (XXII)-X.* Cambridge, MA.

Jost, M. 1994. "The Distribution of Sanctuaries in Civic Space in Arkadia." In Alcock and Osborne 1994, 217–230.

Kamerbeek, J. C. 1984. *The Plays of Sophocles: Commentaries*. Part VII, *The Oedipus Coloneus*. Leiden.

Karanika, A. 2009. "Reaping a Rich Harvest: A Diachronic Perspective on the *Lityerses* Work-Song Tradition." Paper given at the conference *Diachrony: Diachronic Aspects of Ancient Greek Literature and Culture*, Duke University, Durham, NC, October 24, 2009.

Kledt, A. 2000. Review of Haß 1998. *Göttinger Forum für Altertumswissenschaft* 3:1001–1011.

Knox, B. 1989. "Work and Justice in Archaic Greece: Hesiod's *Works and Days*." In *Essays: Ancient and Modern*, 3–22. Baltimore.

Lamberton, R. 1988a. *Hesiod*. New Haven, CT.

———. 1988b. "Plutarch, Hesiod, and the Mouseia of Thespiai." *Illinois Classical Studies* 13:491–504.

———. 1996. Review of Petropoulos 1994. *CP* 91:78–79.

Larsen, J. A. O. 1960. "Orchomenos and the Formation of the Boeotian Confederacy in 447 B.C." *CP* 55: 9–18.

Larson, J. 2001. *Greek Nymphs: Myth, Cult, Lore*. Oxford.

Lefkowitz, M. R. 1981. *The Lives of the Greek Poets*. Baltimore.

Lloyd-Jones, H. 1977. "Aristaios in Boeotia?" *Zeitschrift für Papyrologie und Epigraphik* 25:135–136.

———. 1985. "Pindar and the After-Life." In *Pindare: Huit exposés suivis de discussions*, ed. A. Hurst, 245–279. Vandoeuvres–Geneve.

Lord, A. B. 2000. *The Singer of Tales*. 2nd ed. Ed. S. Mitchell and G. Nagy. Cambridge, MA.

Lowrie, M. 1991. Review of *Polyhymnia: The Rhetoric of Horatian Lyric Discourse* by G. Davis. *BMCR* 2:417–22.

Lupu, E. 2005. *Greek Sacred Law: A Collection of New Documents*. Leiden.

Mace, S. 1996. "Utopian and Erotic Fusion in a New Elegy by Simonides (22 West²)." *Zeitschrift für Papyrologie und Epigraphik* 1996:233–247.

Maclean, J. K. B. 2004. "The αἶνοι of the *Heroikos* and the Unfolding Transformation of the Phoenician Merchant." In Aitken and Maclean 2004, 251–266.

Maclean, J. K. B., and E. B. Aitken. 2001. *Flavius Philostratus. Heroikos.* Atlanta.

Marinatos, N. 1993. "What Were Greek Sanctuaries? A Synthesis." In Marinatos and Hägg 1993, 228–233.

Marinatos, N., and R. Hägg, eds. 1993. *Greek Sanctuaries: New Approaches.* London.

Marsilio, M. S. 2000. *Farming and Poetry in Hesiod's* Works and Days. Lanham, MD.

Martin, R. P. 1992. "Hesiod's Metanastic Poetics." *Ramus* 21:11–33.

Mazon, P. 1914. *Les travaux et les jours.* Paris.

Miralles, C., and Pòrtulas, J. 1983. *Archilochus and the Iambic Poetry.* Rome.

Most, G. W. 2006. *Hesiod. Theogony, Works and Days, Testimonia.* Cambridge, MA.

Motte, A. 1973. *Prairies et jardins de la Grèce antique: De la religion à la philosophie.* Brussels.

Nagy, G. 1985. "Theognis and Megara: A Poet's Vision of His City." In *Theognis of Megara: Poetry and the Polis,* ed. T. J. Figueira and G. Nagy, 22–81. Baltimore.

———. 1990a. *Pindar's Homer: The Lyric Possession of an Epic Past.* Baltimore.

———. 1990b. *Greek Mythology and Poetics.* Ithaca, NY.

———. 1993. "Alcaeus in Sacred Space." In *Tradizione e innovazione nella cultura greca da Omero all'età ellenistica: Scritti in onore de Bruno Gentili,* ed. R. Pretagostini, 221–225. Rome.

———. 1994. "Copies and Models in Horace *Odes* 4.1 and 4.2." *Classical World* 87:415–426.

———. 1996. *Poetry as Performance: Homer and Beyond.* Cambridge.

———. 1999. *The Best of the Achaeans: Concepts of the Hero in Archaic Greek Poetry.* Rev. ed. Baltimore (orig. pub. 1979).

———. 2001. "The Sign of the Hero: A Prologue." In Maclean and Aitken 2001, xv–xxxv. Atlanta.

———. 2009. "Hesiod and the Ancient Biographical Traditions." In

Brill's Companion to Hesiod, ed. F. Montanari, A. Rengakos, and C. Tsagalis, 271–311. Leiden.

Nelson, S. A. 1998. *God and the Land: The Metaphysics of Farming in Hesiod and Vergil*. Oxford.

Nicolai, W. 1964. *Hesiods Erga: Beobachtungen zum Aufbau*. Heidelberg.

Nilsson, M. P. 1906. *Griechische Feste von religiöser Bedeutung mit Ausschluss der attischen*. Berlin.

Nock, A. D. 1972. *Essays on Religion and the Ancient World*. Ed. Z. Stewart. 2 vols. Cambridge, MA.

Oldfather, C. H. 2000. *Diodorus of Sicily. The Library of History*. Vol. 3, *Books 4.59–8*. Cambridge, MA (orig. pub. 1939).

Oliensis, E. 1991. "Canidia, Canicula, and the Decorum of Horace's *Epodes*." *Arethusa* 24:107–138.

Olson, S. D. 2008. *Athenaeus. The Learned Banqueters*. Vol. 3, *Books 6–7*. Cambridge, MA.

O'Sullivan, N. 1992. *Alcidamas, Aristophanes and the Beginnings of Greek Stylistic Theory*. Hermes Einzelschriften 60. Stuttgart.

Pedley, J. 2005. *Sanctuaries and the Sacred in the Ancient Greek World*. Cambridge.

Petrone, G. 1998. "*Locus amoenus/locus horridus*: Due modi di pensare la natura." In *L'uomo antico e la natura*, ed. R. Uglione, 177–195. Turin.

Petropoulos, J. C. B. 1994. *Heat and Lust: Hesiod's Midsummer Festival Scene Revisited*. Lanham, MD.

Pierce, S. 1993. "Death, Revelry and *Thysia*." *Classical Antiquity* 12:219–266.

Polignac, F. de 1995. *Cults, Territory, and the Origins of the Greek City-State*. Trans. J. Lloyd. Chicago (orig. pub. as *Naissance de la cité grecque*, Paris 1984).

Riedinger, J.-C. 1992. "Structure et signification du 'calendrier du paysan' d'Hésiode (*Travaux* vv. 383–617)." *Revue de philologie, de littérature et d'histoire anciennes* 66:121–141.

Robert, J., and L. Robert. 1970. "Bulletin épigraphique." *Revue des études grecques* 83:362–488.

Rosen, R. M. 1990. "Poetry and Sailing in Hesiod's *Works and Days*." *Classical Antiquity* 9:99–113.

Schliemann, H. 1881. *Orchomenos. Bericht über meine Ausgrabungen im böotischen Orchomenos.* Leipzig.

Schönbeck, G. 1962. *Der locus amoenus von Homer bis Horaz.* PhD Diss. Heidelberg.

Scodel, R. 1980. "Hesiod Redivivus." *Greek, Roman and Byzantine Studies* 21:301–20.

Segal, C. 1974. "Death by Water: A Narrative Pattern in Theocritus (*Idylls* 1, 13, 22, 23)." *Hermes* 102:20–38.

Slatkin, L. M. 2004. "Measuring Authority, Authoritative Measures: Hesiod's *Works and Days.*" In *The Moral Authority of Nature,* ed. L. Daston and F. Vidal, 25–49. Chicago.

Solmsen, F., R. Merkelbach, and M. L. West, eds. 1990. *Hesiodi Theogonia, Opera et Dies, Scutum.* 3rd ed. Oxford.

Sourvinou-Inwood, C. 1993. "Early Sanctuaries, the Eighth Century and Ritual Space: Fragments of a Discourse." In Marinatos and Hägg 1993, 1–17.

Stoddard, K. 2004. *The Narrative Voice in the Theogony of Hesiod.* Mnemosyne Supplement 225. Leiden.

Thesleff, H. 1981. "Man and *Locus Amoenus* in Early Greek Poetry." In *Gnomosyne: Menschliches Denken und Handeln in der frühgriechischen Literatur; Festschrift für Walter Marg zum 70. Geburtstag,* ed. G. Kurz, D. Müller, and W. Nicolai, 31–45. Munich.

Ustinova, Y. 2009. *Caves and the Ancient Greek Mind: Descending Underground in the Search for Ultimate Truth.* Oxford.

Van Straten, F. T. 1995. *Hierà kalá: Images of Animal Sacrifice in Archaic and Classical Greece.* Leiden.

Vermeule, E. T. 1974. "Der Götterkult bei Homer." In *Götterkult,* 76–132. Archaeologia Homerica 3, V. Göttingen.

Vernant, J.-P. 1965. *Mythe et pensée chez les Grecs: Études de psychologie historique.* Paris.

———. 1966. "Le mythe hésiodique des races: Sur un essai de mise au point." *Revue de philologie, de littérature et d'histoire anciennes* 40:247–276.

———. 1989. "At Man's Table: Hesiod's Foundation Myth of Sacrifice." In Detienne and Vernant 1989, 21–86.

Wallace, P. W. 1974. "Hesiod and the Valley of the Muses." *Greek, Roman and Byzantine Studies* 15:5–24.

———. 1985. "The Tomb of Hesiod and the Treasury of Minyas at Orkhomenos." In *Proceedings of the Third International Conference on Boiotian Antiquities, Montreal, Quebec, 31.X.1979–4.XI.1979,* ed. J. M. Fossey and H. Giroux, 165–179. Amsterdam.

West, M. L. 1978. *Hesiod. Works and Days.* Oxford.

———. 2003. *Homeric Hymns, Homeric Apocrypha, Lives of Homer.* Cambridge, MA.

Whitmarsh, T. 2004. "The Harvest of Wisdom: Landscape, Description, and Identity in the *Heroikos.*" In Aitken and Maclean 2004, 237–250.

Zaidman, L. B., and P. Schmitt Pantel. 1989. *La religion grecque.* Paris.

Zuntz, G. 1971. *Persephone: Three Essays on Religion and Thought in Magna Graecia.* Oxford.

SAPPHICA

ALEXANDER DALE

I. IAMBICS BY SAPPHO?

THE SUDA (4.322 Adler = fr. 235 V) lists iambics among the works of Sappho: Σαπφώ ... ἔγραψε δὲ μελῶν λυρικῶν βιβλία θ´ ... ἔγραψε δὲ καὶ ἐπιγράμματα καὶ ἐλεγεῖα καὶ ἰάμβους καὶ μονῳδίας ("Sappho ... wrote nine books of lyric poetry ... she also wrote epigrams, elegies, iambics, and monodies"). Corroboration for this statement is sometimes sought[1] in two other attestations, Philodemus *De poem.* 1.117.10–11 Janko: καὶ Σαπφώ τινα ἰαμβικῶς ποιεῖ ("and even Sappho composed something 'iambic'") and Julian *Ep.* 10, pp. 12–13 Bidez–Cumont: τοὺς ἰάμβους ... οἵους ἡ καλὴ Σαπφὼ βούλεται τοῖς ὕμνοις ἁρμόττειν ("the iambics ... which fair Sappho accommodated to her hymns"). Add to this the anonymous and corrupt line fr. 117, which is tantalizingly close to a syncopated iambic trimeter †χαίροις ἀ νύμφα†, χαιρέτω δ᾽ ὁ γάμβρος[2] ("farewell, bride, and farewell to the groom"), and we have the notion of iambics by, or attributed to, Sappho solidly embedded in the scholarly tradition.

If the statement of the Suda is accepted, it would mean that Sappho wrote iambic poetry—specifically stichic iambic trimeters—and not simply that iambics occurred as isolated cola in her poetry.[3] It is

Sappho is cited from Voigt's edition, and equivalence with the numeration of Lobel-Page should be assumed unless otherwise stated. I am grateful to the anonymous referee for many insightful comments and suggestions, and to Ivy Livingston at *HSCP* for invaluable help in preparing the manuscript.

[1] See Yatromanolakis 1999:179–195.

[2] ἀ νύμφα χαίροις Lobel; χαίροις ⟨σ⟩υ νύμφα, Yatromanolakis, *alii alia*.

[3] Ancient metricians, when discussing a meter, will often observe that it is to be found as an isolated colon in a certain poet, but when we encounter a metrical term in a non-metrical source, it always implies compositions in that metrically determined εἶδος.

highly improbable that Sappho (or Alcaeus, for that matter) composed iambic poetry[4] such as that associated with the great iambographers Archilochus, Semonides, and Hipponax. Dactylic hexameters do occur in Sappho, but otherwise the Aeolic tradition remains metrically and generically distinct from its Ionian neighbours in Asia Minor and the Aegean islands. We would no more expect Sappho or Alcaeus to compose iambus than we would expect Archilochus to write sapphic stanzas. One explanation for the ascription of iambics to Sappho might be postulated, only to be rejected.[5] Three epigrams are ascribed to her in the *Palatine Anthology* (*AP* 6.269, 7.489, 7.505, 'Sappho' 1–3 *FGE*), and doubtless more were circulated under her name in antiquity,[6] which might well account for the Suda's statement that Sappho wrote epigrams. Furthermore, in the Hellenistic and Imperial periods iambic trimeters were not an overly rare meter for epigram.[7] One might wonder whether there was a body of iambic epigrams ascribed to Sappho which, transmitted along with elegiac epigrams, lasted long enough to get recorded as iambics in a source used by the Suda. This hypothesis is unlikely; there is much to suggest that in the Imperial and Byzantine periods poems that were not epigrams came to be classified as such,[8] and nothing to suggest that something which could have been classified as an epigram was classified differently. If the Suda's source knew of iambic epigrams ascribed to Sappho, we would expect them to have been subsumed under the ἐπιγράμματα in the Suda entry.[9] Thus, if we are to explain the attestations for iambics by Sappho, we will need to look further than the explanations outlined above.

---

[4]   And here we mean not only trimeters, but tetrameters and the epodic forms found in Ionian iambus; cf. West 1974:22.

[5]   Cf. Yatromanolakis 1999:185–187, who does not however make the exact argument suggested here.

[6]   We have no fewer than twenty-two ascribed to Alcaeus.

[7]   See Dale 2010.

[8]   For example, various items in the polymetric *AP* 13 probably do not come from epigrams; cf. Gow-Page (*HE* 2.218) on *AP* 13.10 = Call. fr. 400 Pfeiffer.

[9]   A Byzantine lexicographer is more likely to have used ἐπιγράμματα, and not ἴαμβοι, to refer to epigrams in iambics.

As noted already, there are two further attestations for iambic poetry associated with Sappho. The first, from Philodemus, should be quoted in full (*De poem.* 1.117.7–13 Janko):

> οἱ γ[ὰρ ἰ]αμβοποιοὶ τραγικὰ ποιοῦσιν, καὶ οἱ τραγῳδοποιοὶ πάλιν ἰαμβικά, καὶ Σαπφώ τινα ἰαμβικῶς ποιεῖ, καὶ Ἀρχίλοχος οὐκ ἰαμβικῶς.

For the iambic poets compose 'tragic' [serious or elevated] poetry, and the tragic poets compose 'iambic' [scurrilous or invective] poetry, and even Sappho composed something 'iambic', and Archilochus something un-'iambic.'

The important point here is that ἰαμβικῶς means not iambic poetry as a strict eidographic description, but poetry in an *iambic manner*.[10] Likewise, when he says that iambic poets wrote τραγικά, he means not that they wrote tragedies, but that they wrote serious or elevated poetry, not scurrilous iambic poetry.[11] However, before we can draw any conclusions from this, we need to look at the passage from Julian cited above.

Julian is writing to Alypius of Antioch:

> Ἤδη μὲν ἐτύγχανον ἀνειμένος τῆς νόσου, τὴν γεωγραφίαν ὅτε ἀπέστειλας ... ἔχει γὰρ καὶ τὰ διαγράμματα τῶν πρόσθεν βέλτιον, καὶ κατεμούσωσας αὐτὸ προσθεὶς τοὺς ἰάμβους, οὐ μάχην ἀείδοντας τὴν Βουπάλειον κατὰ τὸν Κυρηναῖον

---

[10] ἰαμβικῶς only here before Eustathius, but cf. the uses of the verb ἰαμβίζω, which often means simply to lampoon, and not to lampoon in iambic verse, e.g. Phot. *Lex.* ι 4 Theodoridis: ἰαμβίζειν· τὸ χλευάζειν ("ἰαμβίζειν 'to jest'"); Arist. Quint. *De musica* 1.16.25: ἴαμβος μὲν οὖν ἐκλήθη ἀπὸ τοῦ ἰαμβίζειν, ὅ ἐστι λοιδορεῖν ("ἴαμβος was so named from the verb ἰαμβίζειν, which means 'to rebuke'"). According to George Choeroboscus, one can ἰαμβίζειν in the galliambic meter, Hephaestion p. 246.1 Consbruch. Catullus uses the term 'iambic' in non-iambic poetry in the sense of invective, e.g. 36.5, 40.2, 54.6.

[11] For τραγικός in the sense 'elevated, serious', cf. Hermogenes Περὶ μεθόδου δεινότητος 33.1–2, p. 450 Rabe: τὸ τραγικῶς λέγειν Ὅμηρος μὲν ἐδίδαξε, Δημοσθένης δὲ ἐμιμήσατο ("in 'tragic speaking' Homer was the teacher, and Demosthenes the disciple"). One might think that Semonides fr. 1 *IEG*² 1–2, ὦ παῖ, τέλος μὲν Ζεὺς ἔχει βαρύκτυπος | πάντων ὅσ᾽ ἐστὶ καὶ τίθησ᾽ ὅκῃ θέλει κτλ ("My son, the outcome does Zeus the far-thunderer hold of all that is, and makes distribution according to his will ..."), would be a good example of an iambic poet writing something τραγικά.

ποιητήν, ἀλλ᾽ οἵους ἡ καλὴ Σαπφὼ βούλεται τοῖς ὕμνοις
ἁρμόττειν.

I was already recovering from my illness when you sent
the geographical treatise ... the diagrams are better than
the previous ones, and you further embellished it by
adding the iambics, not "singing the fight with Boupalus,"
as the Cyrenaean poet [Callimachus] would put it, but such
as those the fair Sappho accommodated to her hymns.

Alypius had sent Julian a geographical treatise, which he seems to have
prefaced with some iambic verses. This makes it sound like a dedication,
possibly to Julian himself. Iambic prefaces were not at all uncommon at
this period, either to prose works or to other forms of poetry, such as
hexameters.[12] Two further points emerge. First, that the iambic lines
were obviously simply iambic trimeters,[13] without any connotations
of the subject-matter common to Ionian iambus in the archaic period,
or its Hellenistic imitators; we would not expect Alypius to preface a
geographical treatise, possibly dedicated to Julian, with scurrilous
verse. Secondly, Julian is not saying that Sappho wrote ἴαμβοι, rather
that she accommodated them (ἁρμόττειν) to her poetry. What this
suggests is that Julian knew poems where iambic trimeters, or perhaps
a colon that appeared almost identical to trimeters, occurred *as isolated
cola* in her poetry. Books 1–3 of Sappho were metrically homogeneous,
but all the evidence we have for the remaining books suggests that a
great variety of meters were to be found. We have a line from Sappho
that is nearly a trimeter (fr. 117, quoted above), which obviously came
from an epithalamium, and the *Epithalamia* seem to have been very
varied in meter, including some polymetric poems. Furthermore, Julian
and his circle were very familiar with Sappho's *Epithalamia* (see further
discussion below). It was probably in just such an epithalamium that
Julian found iambic lines, and it is these that he praises Alypius for
imitating.[14] Thus neither Philodemus nor Julian attest iambic poetry

---

[12] See in particular Cameron 1970.

[13] For ἴαμβος = ἰαμβεῖον in late Greek, see West 1974:22n2.

[14] Whether Alypius' iambics did recall Sappho in any way is another matter. Julian
is being kind (and demonstrating his learning); rhetors often recommended Sappho as

as we understand it for Sappho; furthermore, each refers to a separate and distinct phenomenon, as they observed it, in Sappho's poetry. However, we still have to account for exactly what Philodemus meant by ἰαμβικῶς.

II. SAPPHO ἸΑΜΒΙΣΔΟΙΣΑ

The vast majority of Sappho's surviving poetry can hardly be described as scurrilous, let alone iambic.[15] However a few of the *Epithalamia* reveal traces of the bawdy and scurrilous content often associated with the genre.[16] Most famous is Sappho fr. 111:

> ἴψοι δὴ τὸ μέλαθρον,
> ὑμήναον,
> ἀέρρετε τέκτονες ἄνδρες·
> ὑμήναον.
> γάμβρος †(εἰσ)έρχεται ἴσος Ἄρευι†,
> ⟨ὑμήναον,⟩
> ἄνδρος μεγάλω πόλυ μέσδων.
> ⟨ὑμήναον.⟩

> 5 εἶσ' ἴσ' Ἄρευι Lobel–Page

High the rafters—Hymenaeus!—raise, ye carpenters;—
Hymenaeus!—here comes the bridegroom equal to Ares—
⟨Hymenaeus!⟩—far bigger than a big man—⟨Hymenaeus!⟩

---

a model for sublimity of expression (pseudo-Longinus *De sublimitate* 10.1–3; Menander Rhetor 402.17). Thus what Julian is really doing is paying Alypius a great compliment (after all, he had charged him, or was about to, with the thankless task of rebuilding the great temple in Jerusalem).

[15] I find nothing persuasive in the attempt of Aloni 2001 to find an iambic nature in fr. 31; exploring the boundaries of genre is one matter, stretching them beyond all recognition is quite different. Cf. Morrison's review (2003).

[16] *Contra* Page 1955:120, who categorically states that "There is no trace ... in Sappho of that ribaldry which was characteristic of the songs recited at this and other stages of Greek wedding-ceremonies." For epithalamia generally, see Contiades-Tsitsoni 1990.

This is hardly a formal and heavy-handed compliment to the bridegroom on account of his stature.[17] Rather, as Geoffrey Kirk first saw,[18] the reference is to the bridegroom's fantastically erect penis, too large to be accommodated by the confines of the house.[19] As Kirk says (1963:52), Sappho is "conscientiously improper." This sort of scurrilous content is not alien to iambic poetry.

Fr. 110 V (= 110a L–P) was probably in the same vein:

θυρώρῳ πόδες ἐπτορόγυιοι,
τὰ δὲ σάμβαλα πεμπεβόεια,
πίσσυγγοι δὲ δέκ' ἐξεπόνησαν

Seven cubits long are the door-keeper's feet, five ox-hides thick his sandals, ten cobblers worked hard to make them.

The fragment is addressed by a chorus to the door-keeper of the bridal chamber, whose duty was to prevent friends from coming to the bride's rescue at the last moment.[20] The lines emphasize the immovability of the door-keeper and, though not malicious, are light-heartedly abusive in the manner that we often find in epithalamia. Furthermore, there is most likely innuendo of the kind found in fr. 111. The foot as metaphor for genitals is found in various places,[21] most notably Eubulus fr. 107 *PCG*: ἐν θαλάμῳ μαλακῶς κατακείμενον· ἐν δὲ κύκλῳ νιν | παρθενικὰ τρυφερὰ †χλανιδανα μαλακὰ κατάθρυπτοι | τὸν πόδ' ἀμαρακίνοισι μύροις τρίψουσι τὸντ ἐμόν ("lying softly in a bed-chamber … [they] will rub my foot with marjoram-oils"). Equally revealing for this fragment of Sappho is Ar. *Lys.* 414–419:

---

[17] Thus Page 1955:120.

[18] Kirk 1963. See further the endorsement and enhancement of Lloyd-Jones 1967.

[19] For μέγας meaning 'erect', see Henderson 1991:115–116.

[20] Pollux 3.42, καλεῖται δέ τις τῶν τοῦ νυμφίου φίλων καὶ θυρωρός, ὃς ταῖς θύραις ἐφεστηκὼς εἴργει τὰς γυναῖκας τῇ νύμφῃ βοώσῃ βοηθεῖν ("One of the bridegroom's friends was also called θυρωρός, who stood before the doors [of the bridal chamber] and prevented the women from coming to the bride's aid"). Hesychius θ 957 Latte, θυρωρός· ὁ παράνυμφος, ὁ τὴν θύραν τοῦ θαλάμου κλείων ("θυρωρός: the best-man who kept shut the door of the bedroom"). On the epic quality of the language, which would add to the humor of the lines, see Murgatroyd 1987:224.

[21] See Henderson 1991:129–130.

ἕτερος δέ τις πρὸς σκυτοτόμον ταδὶ λέγει
νεανίαν καὶ πέος ἔχοντ' οὐ παιδικόν·
"ὦ σκυτοτόμε, τῆς μου γυναικὸς τοῦ ποδὸς
τὸ δακτυλίδιον πιέζει τὸ ζυγόν,
ἄθ' ἁπαλὸν ὄν· τοῦτ' οὖν σὺ τῆς μεσημβρίας
ἐλθὼν χάλασον, ὅπως ἂν εὐρυτέρως ἔχῃ."

Someone else says to a leatherworker—a young man, but with no boy's penis, "Hey cobbler, my wife's sandal-strap is pinching her little toe—it's sensitive, you see. Go around at noon and stretch it out, so that it's a bit more wide."

In fr. 111 it was the bridegroom who was the focus; here it is the best man. Though perhaps not as obvious a target for this kind of sexual humor, the general context of scurrilous abuse that we find in the *Epithalamia* makes the address to the door-keeper perfectly understandable.

Fr. 115 might also provide a clue:

τίῳ σ', ὦ φίλε γάμβρε, κάλως ἐικάσδω;
ὄρπακι βραδίνῳ σε μάλιστ' ἐικάσδω.

To what, dear bridegroom, shall I best compare thee? I liken you most of all to a slender shoot.

No one seems to have taken exception to the bridegroom being compared to a slender shoot or sapling.[22] However, it is hardly an innocent compliment. First of all, in antiquity men were often thirty or more at the time of marriage—hardly saplings.[23] Furthermore, the

---

[22] 'Slender shoot', 'branch' seems to be the primary meaning, cf. LSJ s.v.; at Pind. *Parth.* 2.7–8 (fr. 94b Maehler) a female chorus carries a ὄρπακ' ἀγλαόν | δάφνας ("a splendid shoot of laurel"). Campbell (1967 ad loc.) compares *Il.* 18.56, where Thetis says of Achilles ὁ δ' ἀνέδραμεν ἔρνεϊ ἶσος ("he sprang up like a shoot"). But the point is that he grew up like a sapling, i.e. quickly. She is hardly comparing the best of the Achaeans to a twig. The speed with which a hero grows up is a common *topos* in Greek and other Indo-European traditions; cf. West 2007:149–150 and 427–429.

[23] Though we do not have direct evidence for Lesbos at the turn of the sixth century, thirty is specified as the appropriate age from Hesiod on, *Op.* 695–697, ὡραῖος δὲ γυναῖκα τεὸν ποτὶ οἶκον ἄγεσθαι, | μήτε τριηκόντων ἐτέων μάλα πόλλ' ἀπολείπων | μήτ' ἐπιθεὶς μάλα πολλά ("lead a wife to your house in due season, being neither short of thirty by

adjective βραδίνος occurs in only one other place in Sappho (fr. 102.2) of Aphrodite, βραδίναν δι' Ἀφροδίταν.[24] Soft or slender is perfectly suitable for Aphrodite, hardly for the praise of a grown man and bride-groom; elsewhere in the *Epithalamia* Sappho compared a bridegroom to Achilles, which of course would have been a compliment.[25] The lines are surely pointed, and various possibilities might suggest themselves. I think the most likely is that a comparison which would be perfectly suitable for a bride is instead used of the groom. At *Od.* 6.163 Nausicaa, in a passage imbued with erotic and nuptial imagery, is likened to a φοίνικος νέον ἔρνος ("a young shoot of palm"), while in Theocritus' epithalamium for Helen and Menelaus (18.29–30) Helen is compared to a tall cypress, πιείρᾳ μεγάλα ἅτ' ἀνέδραμε κόσμος ἀρούρᾳ | ἢ κάπῳ κυπάρισσος ("as a tall cypress adorns the fertile field or garden where it springs up"). Thus in fr. 115 we would once again have playful abuse directed at the bridegroom.[26]

In conclusion we can add fr. 103.8 V (= 103.11 L–P):

γά]μβρον, ἄσαροι γὰρ ὑμαλικ[

br]idegroom, for chiding are ?your frien[ds

The line is one among a list of incipits preserved in *P. Oxy.* 2294.[27] γά]μβρον suggests it is from an epithalamium, while ἄσαροι suggests mockery of the bridegroom. Presumably Lobel is right in reading ἄσαροι γὰρ ὑμάλικ[ες, where the taunting might be similar to that directed towards the bridegroom at Theoc. 18.9–15. The masculine

---

many years, nor having added many"). See further West 1978 ad loc., who cites e.g. Sol. fr. 27.9 *IEG*[2], Pl. R. 460e.

[24] Once in Alcaeus, fr. 304 col. ii. 9 L–P, unless the fragment is to be ascribed to Sappho; cf. Treu 1968:161–164. The text is too fragmentary for us to be sure of the context or reference; the Muses and perhaps Graces seem to be mentioned in the previous lines.

[25] Fr. 218 V = 105(b) L–P = Himerius *Or.* 9.16. Himerius had read the poem in question; see further below.

[26] The comparison here is of a kind with the games of wit played at symposia and elsewhere, where participants are subjected to ridicule through absurd compari-sons, as at Ar. *Birds* 804–805 οἶσθ' ᾧ μάλιστ' ἔοικας ἐπτερωμένος; | εἰς εὐτέλειαν χηνὶ συγγεγραμμένῳ ("Do you know what you look like fitted out with feathers? Like a cheaply painted goose") with Dunbar 1995 ad loc., Dover 1980 on Pl. *Symp.* 215a4.

[27] On this papyrus, the so-called 'new bibliographical fragment,' see further below.

form (no doubt indicating performance by a male chorus) is not problematic; Greek wedding songs usually involved mixed choruses, cf. [Hes.] *Sc.* 276–280.[28]

From Sappho's *Epithalamia* we have roughly fifteen verbatim fragments, totalling some thirty-five lines.[29] That four of these fragments, totalling fourteen lines, show the same scurrilous and jocular abuse that we find in other examples of the genre should suggest that this was in fact a fairly prominent feature of the *Epithalamia*. For all the differences between Sappho's address to the best man in fr. 110, or teasing of the bridegroom in fr. 111, and Hipponax' invective against Bupalus, it is not difficult to see how Philodemus considered Sappho to have written τινα ἰαμβικῶς. It is no great step from this to a grammarian in a less enlightened age listing iambics among her works.

III. *LIBER EPITHALAMIORUM?*

What place the *Epithalamia* occupied in the collected works of Sappho has long been a matter of debate.[30] It will not do to rehearse the argument here, but a few points are worth making. It is often stated that a separate book entitled *Epithalamia* stood at the end of the Alexandrian edition of Sappho, bringing the total number of books to nine.[31] For a nine-book edition of Sappho there are two pieces of evidence: the first is an epigram by Tullius Laurea (*AP* 7.17 = Laurea 1 *GP*), which says that Sappho wrote nine books of poetry. I am, however, inclined to agree with Yatromanolakis, who suggests[32] that Laurea's motive is essentially poetic—nine books of poetry corresponding to nine Muses.[33] The second is the Suda entry on Sappho (quoted above), which tells us

---

[28] See further the evidence for mixed choruses in wedding songs assembled by Swift 2006:125–140.

[29] A conservative estimate. I discount frr. 27, 30, 44 (on which see below) and 141, on which see Page 1955:123–125.

[30] In particular Page 1955:112–126, Yatromanolakis 1999.

[31] Page 1955:123–125.

[32] Yatromanolakis 1999:181–184.

[33] *AP* 7.17.5–7, ἢν δέ με Μουσάων ἐτάσῃς χάριν, ὧν ἀφ' ἑκάστης | δαίμονος ἄνθος ἐμῇ θῆκα παρ' ἐννεάδι, | γνώσεαι ὡς Ἀΐδεω σκότον ἔκφυγον ("But if you judge me by the Muses, from each of whom I have taken a flower to set beside my nine, you will know that I escaped the darkness of Hades").

that Sappho wrote θ', nine, books. Lobel observed that elsewhere the
Suda makes use of Laurea's epigram, and thus that the Suda's statement might well be derived from Laurea.[34] In addition to these two
testimonia, we have a passage in Servius where he refers to a book of
Sappho entitled *Epithalamia*.[35] This, however, would be the only testimony for a book with a title *Epithalamia*, as all other sources that
quote fragments which are assigned to the *Epithalamia* do so without
either a book title or number. In addition to this we have *P. Oxy.* 2294,
the 'new bibliographical fragment' (= fr. 103 V), which Page argued
indicated that Book Eight consisted of 130 lines, and was followed by
a book entitled *Epithalamia*. Page's reconstruction has understandably
attracted criticism,[36] and has been dealt with in detail by Yatromanolakis (1999:187–192), who suggests that the papyrus is a list of incipits,
130 lines of which were taken from Sappho's eighth book, and all of
which are epithalamia. Though uncertainty regarding the interpretation of the papyrus remains,[37] Yatromanolakis' reconstruction is the
most plausible so far proposed, and furthermore receives independent
support from the arguments advanced below. Thus before positing, on
slender evidence, a ninth book of Sappho with a separate title, perhaps
we should ask whether any other solutions present themselves.

It is generally assumed that Sappho's *Epithalamia* were distributed
among the various books of the Alexandrian edition where meter
allowed their placement in one of the earlier books. This assumption,
however, rests solely on three fragments, 27, 30, and 44. In fr. 27 the
only thing to suggest an epithalamium is line 8 σ]τείχομεν γὰρ ἐς γάμον,
which is inconclusive. Page (1955:125) says there is 'no doubt whatever'

[34] Lobel 1925:xiv; see also Yatromanolakis 1999:181–184. Lobel also observes that
Laurea might have been misled by θ', which can stand for either eight or nine in a series
of books.

[35] On *Georg.* 1.31 (= fr. 234 V) *generum vero pro marito positum multi accipiunt iuxta
Sappho, quae in libro qui inscribitur* Ἐπιθαλάμια *ait.*

[36] Cf. Lasserre 1955; Treu 1968:167–168.

[37] For example, we cannot be certain about the number of missing letters, and thus it
is impossible to determine what relation επιγεγρα[in line 15 has to]λαμια in 16 (from the
beginning of which at least ten to twelve letters are missing). Likewise the traces in 14
could be η, i.e. book 8, or could be ι, picking up the number in line 3 and referring to the
number of incipits in the papyrus.

that fr. 30 is from an epithalamium. Here is the text with only minor supplements:

νύκτ[. . .].[

πάρθενοι δ[
παννυχίσδοι[σ]αι[
σὰν ἀείδοισ[ι]ν φ[
5 φας ἰοκόλπω·

ἀλλ' ἐγέρθεις ἠϊθ[ε
στεῖχε σοὶς ὑμάλικ[ας
ἤπερ ὄσσον ἀ λιγύφω[νος
ὔπνον [ἴ]δωμεν

4 φ[ιλότατα καὶ νύμ- Wilamowitz

night ... maidens ... revelling through the night ... in song
... violet-robed ... come, wake up ... go to your peers ... that
we may see less sleep ?than the clear-voiced ?

The language and imagery here are not incompatible with wedding-songs,[38] but it does not follow that the fragment must then be from an epithalamium. *Pannychis* celebrations, which could accompany both religious and secular observances, often included female choruses, and we do not need to assume a wedding context for their occurrence here.[39] Furthermore, symposia and drinking through the night were generally associated with the *pannychis*, which could equally account for ἠϊθ[and ὑμαλικ[in the text, however they might be supplemented. Yet, even if the poem does suggest an epithalamiac context, other scenarios could be envisaged. We might have a mythological narrative with direct speech, or the lines we have could be a future projection, such as we find in fr. 1. This is not to say that fr. 30 cannot have been from an epithalamium, only that we might wish to be on firmer ground

---

[38] Accepting Wilamowitz' appealing supplement would certainly strengthen the case for an epithalamium, though other supplements are possible, such as e.g. μορ]φᾶς ἰοκόλπω.

[39] On *pannychides* generally, see Bravo 1997.

before stating categorically that it was and thus that Sappho's epithalamia were distributed amongst her various books.

Lastly there is fr. 44, the Wedding of Hector and Andromache.
It has long been suggested that the poem was performed as part of a
wedding ceremony, and thus is an epithalamium.[40] There are many
reasons to doubt this ascription.[41] To begin with, the poem as we have
it is an extended narrative, without any indication of performance at
an actual wedding. None of the fragments that can safely be ascribed to
the *Epithalamia* show any indication of the sort of narrative we see here.
Furthermore, while the wedding of Hector and Andromache is unques-
tionably suitable material for poetry, it is hardly appropriate for a
mythological exemplum in a wedding song—Hector is later to be slain,
Andromache enslaved, and their infant son Astyanax thrown from the
walls of Troy, his head shattering on the rocks below. In light of this,
the foreshadowing of Hector's death throughout the poem strongly
argues against an epithalamic function.[42] In the *Iliad*, at the moment
when Andromache learns of Hector's death, the poet says (22.468–472):

> τῆλε δ᾽ ἀπὸ κρατὸς βάλε δέσματα σιγαλόεντα,
> ἄμπυκα κεκρύφαλόν τε ἰδὲ πλεκτὴν ἀναδέσμην
> κρήδεμνόν θ᾽, ὅ ῥά οἱ δῶκε χρυσῆ Ἀφροδίτη
> ἤματι τῷ ὅτε μιν κορυθαίολος ἠγάγεθ᾽ Ἕκτωρ
> ἐκ δόμου Ἠετίωνος, ἐπεὶ πόρε μυρία ἕδνα.

> From her head she threw the glittering head-dress far
> away, the band and net and woven wreath, and the veil
> which golden Aphrodite gave her on the day when Hector
> of the flashing helmet brought her from the house of
> Eëtion, after he had given countless wedding-gifts.

---

[40] See Wilamowitz 1914:228–229, Page 1955:71–72.

[41] Wilamowitz' classification of the poem as an epithalamium was first seriously
questioned by Lesky 1966:142.

[42] Parallels and correspondences between fr. 44 and the *Iliad*—particularly with
regard to Hector's death and the ransoming of his body—are discussed by Kakridis 1966
and Schrenk 1994. We should further note that the dactylic meter and features of epic
dialect and prosody in this poem (features admitted in only a small number of Sappho's
poems; see Lobel 1925:xxv–xxvii) would automatically invite comparison with the
Homeric portrayal of Hector.

As Griffin (1980:2) notes, Homer's description of Andromache's casting off of her head-dress here is not mentioned as a mere fact. The recollection of the wedding of Hector and Andromache at this point, as symbolized by her head-dress, serves to heighten the pathos of the scene.[43] This Homeric association of the death of Hector with his wedding to Andromache clearly informs Sappho's narrative. In fr. 44 we also find a description of Hector conveying Andromache to Troy from Eëtion's household in Thebe, followed by mention of the wedding gifts (5–10):

> Ἔκτωρ καὶ συνέταιρ[ο]ι ἄγοισ' ἐλικώπιδα
> Θήβας ἐξ ἰέρας Πλακίας τ' ἀπ' [ἀϊ]ν⟨ν⟩άω
> ἄβραν Ἀνδρομάχαν ἐνὶ ναῦσιν ἐπ' ἄλμυρον
> πόντον· πόλλα δ' [ἐλί]γματα χρύσια κἄμματα
> πορφύρ[α] καταὔτ[με]να, ποίκιλ' ἀθύρματα,
> ἀργύρα τ' ἀνάριιιθμα ιποτήιριιαι κἀλέφαις.

Hector and his companions are bringing from holy Thebe and ever-flowing Plakia the bright-eyed and graceful Andromache in their ships over the salt-sea; and there is an abundance of gold bracelets and purple perfumed robes, and wondrous adornments and countless silver drinking-cups and ivory.

This juxtaposition of voyage and wedding gifts can only point to the Iliadic passage quoted above. Schrenk (1994:147) observes that Andromache's dowry in Sappho also seems to refer to the treasures that Priam used to ransom Hector's body at *Il.* 24.229–234: "Sappho seems to be suggesting (through guilt by association) that Andromache's dowry becomes part of Hector's ransom."[44]

---

[43] Thus ΣT on *Il.* 22.468.

[44] Schrenk 1994:145–146 also observes that, prior to Andromache's discovery of Hector's death, she is seen weaving a purple robe (22.441, δίπλακα πορφυρέην) which foreshadows Hector's funereal shroud (24.796, πορφυρέοις πέπλοισι), both of which might be picked up by κἄμματα πορφύρ[α] καταὔτ[με]να.

There is a further striking example of interaction between fr. 44 and the *Iliad*. In the last two lines of the poem the narrator represents the men of Troy invoking Apollo and praising the happy couple (33–34):

ˌΠάον' ὀνκαλέοντεϛˌ ἐκάβολον εὐλύραν
ˌὔμνην δ' Ἔκτορα κ' Αˌνδρομάχαν θεο⟨ε⟩ικέλο[ιϛ.

Calling upon Paian the far shooter, god of the fair lyre,̓
they sang Hector and Andromache like unto the gods.

Some time ago Gregory Nagy observed two points.[45] Firstly, there is bitter irony in the invocation of Apollo here. In the *Iliad* Apollo is, along with Ares and Aphrodite, the patron of Troy and of Hector. When Hector finally meets his fate at the hands of Achilles, Homer says (*Il.* 22.212–213) ῥέπε δ' Ἔκτορος αἴσιμον ἦμαρ | ᾤχετο δ' εἰς Ἀΐδαο, λίπεν δέ ἑ Φοῖβος Ἀπόλλων ("and so fell Hector's fated day, and he went off to Hades, and Phoebus Apollo left him"). The man whose marriage Apollo is called upon to celebrate in Sappho is the same man whose death is heralded by Apollo deserting him in the *Iliad*. The most telling feature of these lines, however, is the epithet θεοείκελος, used of Hector and Andromache. This epithet occurs twice in the *Iliad* (1.131 and 19.155), in both instances in the same position after the hephthemimeral caesura, in both instances used of Achilles: θεοείκελ' Ἀχιλλεῦ. Thus in the *Iliad* the slayer of Hector is described as θεοείκελος at line-end, while in Sappho Hector and Andromache are so described. Furthermore, the position of the epithet in Sappho (whose meter here is dactylic pentameter) is equivalent to its position in Homer before Ἀχιλλεῦ; someone hearing the line being delivered would almost certainly recall the epic θεοείκελ' Ἀχιλλεῦ (⏑ ⏑ – ⏑ ⏑ – –), only to hear it truncated and left hanging as θεοεικέλοις (⏑ ⏑ – ⏑ –). It is hard to believe that Sappho or her audience could have thought the song as it stands appropriate for a wedding.

Schrenk (1994:149–150n16) neatly sums up the situation, as applicable to its original audience as it is to modern readers: "[t]his is an ironic poem which gathers its force from the juxtaposition of the

---

[45] Nagy 1974:135–139. I am indebted to Annette Teffeteller for bringing this to my attention.

increasing naive joy of the participants with the building horror of the enlightened reader." The influence of the *Iliad* on later portrayals of Hector is all-pervasive, more so than in the case of many figures in the epic cycle.[46] It is difficult to reconcile this influence of the epic tradition, as well as Sappho's subtlety and skill as a poet, with the notion that a poem which so deftly and directly invokes the *Iliad* and foreshadows Hector's death—and by implication the enslavement of Andromache—could have been intended to celebrate a wedding on archaic Lesbos.[47]

It has long been recognized that the organization of, and distribution of poems among, the Alexandrian books of Sappho was broadly along metrical lines; Book One consisted of poems in the Sapphic stanza, Book Two in Aeolic dactylic pentameters, and so forth. By Book Four or Five, however, the uniformity of meter begins to break down, and we have various metrical forms ascribed to, e.g., Book Five.[48] From here on, from the evidence that we have, there is nothing to suggest

---

[46] See Wathelet 1988:466–506. The anonymous reviewer observes that a number of characters in Greek myth had checkered careers, and that a poet can focus on one aspect from that career without having extraneous considerations affect the audience's appreciation of the portrayal. This might be the case with Heracles, Odysseus, Agamemnon, and many others (even Paris' career was multi-faceted, involving not only the Judgement, but the story of his exposure at birth and return to Troy as recounted in e.g. Euripides' *Alexander*, frr. 42–64 *TrGF*). Hector, however, was inextricably tied to the fate of Troy through his death—as Griffin 1980:1 notes, the death of Hector stands for the fall of Troy itself. This influence of the epic tradition can be seen in later accounts; the only tragedy in which we know Hector to have figured in any way is Aeschylus' *Phrygians*, frr. 263–272 *TrGF*, which deals with the ransoming of the corpse (see West 2000:340–343). Thus in Hector's case we would expect that any treatment by a later poet would of necessity be colored by awareness of his ultimate fate, let alone fr. 44 with such overt reference to the Iliadic treatment of his death.

[47] Pallantza 2005:79–88, in an analysis that draws heavily upon Rissman 1983:119–141, argues that the Iliadic allusions of fr. 44, as well as the application of the epithet θεοείκελος to Andromache, serve to elevate the female sphere to equal that of the male, and place Andromache on a par with Achilles, providing "ein siegreiches Gegenbild zu Krieg und Tod." It seems incredible to imagine that Sappho could have written what she has for a joyous celebration, let alone expected the intended audience (on Pallantza's interpretation) to have interpreted it as appropriate. Pallantza's interpretation is furthermore predicated upon the assumption of a monolithic function for all of Sappho's poetry, based on extrapolating notions about Sappho and her 'circle' from a select number of poems.

[48] Hendecasyllables, asclepiads, glyconics, etc. See Page 1955:114–116.

that the remaining books were metrically uniform, and furthermore it would make *prima facie* sense that if meter was an organizing principle in Sappho's collected works, and that if by Book Four or Five we get various meters attested for the same book, this is because there were not enough representative examples of the meter to comprise a book. Thus we would not expect Book Six or Seven to be metrically homogeneous, if Book Five was not.

As noted earlier, the *Epithalamia* exhibit a great deal of metrical variety. No fewer than ten different metrical forms are found in the fifteen verbatim quotations.[49] For Book Six we have no evidence whatsoever—no quotation from or reference to it; the only clues as to its existence are references to a seventh and eighth book, which necessarily presuppose a sixth. As for Book Seven, we only have one attestation, Hephaestion p. 34.9 Consbruch, who quotes two lines from it.[50] Book Eight is attested in only one place, Photius *Bib.* cod. 161, p. 103a40 Bekker (= fr. 233 V). We have no quotations ascribed to it, but Photius tells us that it was excerpted by one Sopater the Sophist.

There are several people with this name attested for the fourth to fifth centuries AD, and Page, in dismissing Wilamowitz' suggestion[51] that the book that Sopater excerpted was the *Epithalamia*, says it is uncertain which Sopater is meant. We can, however, be more confident than Page allows. It seems fairly certain that a Sopater the Sophist was active in Athens in the mid-fourth century AD,[52] in Himerius' circle, and perhaps even his pupil.[53] Furthermore it is this Sopater to whom Photius devotes considerable attention,[54] the author of the Διαίρεσις Ζητημάτων and excerptor of various works, Sappho's eighth book among them. Now Himerius, a bulwark against the encroaching

---

[49] See above, with n29.

[50] Fr. 102. The text of Hephaestion is, as so often, corrupt at this point. See Page 1955:115.

[51] Wilamowitz 1900:73.

[52] To be distinguished from the Apamean Neoplatonist disciple of Iamblichus, who might, however, be our Sopater's grandfather; cf. Russell 1983:7.

[53] At issue is whether to read ὁ μέντοι σοφιστὴς Ἰμέριος or ὁ σοφὸς ὁ ἡμέτερος Ἰμέριος at 8.318.29 Waltz; see Innes and Winterbottom 1988:1 and 246; Weißenberger in *Der neue Pauly*, s.v. Sopatros.

[54] Cf. Cribiore 2007:50.

tide of Christianity, was a great admirer of archaic lyric, and particularly Sappho. However, the only Sappho he ever quotes from are the *Epithalamia*,[55] various allusions are also obviously to the *Epithalamia*,[56] and nowhere does he quote from or allude to a poem that is obviously not from the *Epithalamia*.[57] Incidentally, Himerius is one of only two authors from later antiquity to have written a prose epithalamium (we shall encounter the other below).[58] Furthermore, that other great fourth-century pagan and disciple of Himerius, Julian the Apostate, had a great fondness for Sappho, and quotes from and alludes to her several times, including the enigmatic reference to her iambics that stands at the beginning of this article. Julian was well read in Greek literature, but we might wonder whether his regard for Sappho was inherited from his old teacher and later companion Himerius. Julian certainly knew the *Epithalamia*—as Yatromanolakis points out (1999:187), he paraphrases fr. 34 in the manner of an epithalamium (*Or.* 3.109c), while ps.-Julian uses the phrase χαῖρε πολλά found in fr. 116 (*Ep.*183, p. 242.20 Bidez–Cumont).

We might then envisage the following scenario. Sappho was a highly regarded poet in Himerius' circle. One of these figures, Sopater, makes an excerpt of Sappho's eighth book. What were the contents of this book? Himerius shows a great fondness for Sappho's *Epithalamia*, perhaps to the exclusion of all her other poetry. The rhetoricians dug freely and deeply in earlier poetry, not primarily out of fondness for it as literature, but to adorn their writings with learned allusions and elegant turns of phrase. If Sopater were acquainted with, and perhaps even a student of, Himerius, we might expect him to make an excerpt from the master's favorite book, the *Epithalamia*. And the reason for this excerpt, like so many collections of *Eclogae* in late antiquity, would have been to serve a practical purpose. It would have been intended

---

[55] 104(b), 108.

[56] 105a TEST, 194 V, and 218 V = 105(b) L–P.

[57] 208 V, 221 V.

[58] Surprising perhaps, given the popularity from the Antonine period on of reworking archaic and classical lyric genres in prose forms; the prescriptions in Menander Rhetor come to mind here, as do the prose hymns of Aelius Aristides.

as a handbook for the use of rhetors, a collection of the most beautiful language and best turns of phrase to be found in Sappho's eighth book.

The question now becomes, can we find any evidence that the book which Sopater excerpted for a rhetorical handbook, Sappho's eighth book, was in fact the *Epithalamia*? Yes, we can. Syrianus, the fifth-century Neoplatonist commentator on Hermogenes, gives us two verbatim quotations from Sappho. The first is fr. 2.5–6, which, however, is quoted by Hermogenes, and it is obvious that Syrianus found the lines that he quotes in Hermogenes and nowhere else. Immediately afterwards, he quotes three lines for which he is our only source, fr. 105a:

οἶον τὸ γλυκύμαλον ἐρεύθεται ἄκρῳ ἐπ' ὔσδῳ,
ἄκρον ἐπ' ἀκροτάτῳ, λελάθοντο δὲ μαλοδρόπηες·
οὐ μὰν ἐκλελάθοντ', ἀλλ' οὐκ ἐδύναντ' ἐπίκεσθαι.

Like the sweet-apple which reddens on the high bough,
high upon the highest branch, which the apple-pickers
have missed—yet they did not miss it, but rather were
unable to reach it.

Incidentally, these are three of the most beautiful lines in Greek poetry. Perhaps Himerius, the teacher of the excerptor in whose work Syrianus must have found these lines, thought so too, for he alludes to them and more besides from undoubtedly the same poem, and gives us the clue that they are from an epithalamium.[59]

After the fourth century, quotations of, and allusions to, Sappho begin to dry up.[60] While we do have a small number scattered among authors of the following centuries, in many instances these are quotations of or allusions to fragments preserved in texts that were widely copied and read in the Byzantine period, and thus are not evidence for the independent transmission of Sappho's text. I give a few exam-

---

[59] Himerius *Or.* 9.16 (p. 82 Colonna) = fr. 218 V (= 105(b) L–P) Σαπφοῦς ἦν ἄρα μήλῳ μὲν εἰκάσαι τὴν κόρην ... τὸν νυμφίον τε Ἀχιλλεῖ παρομοιῶσαι καὶ εἰς ταὐτὸν ἀγαγεῖν τῷ ἥρῳ τὸν νεάνισκον ταῖς πράξεσι ("It was Sappho who compared the bride to an apple ... and likened the bridegroom to Achilles and put him on a par with the hero in his achievements").

[60] For familiarity with Sappho's poetry in the later Byzantine period, see Garzya 1971.

ples. Stobaeus preserves four lines of fr. 55, but the first three lines are quoted at Plutarch *Quaest. Conviv.* 646e–f, and it is most likely that Stobaeus found the last line in a text of Plutarch that contained it.[61] Anna Comnena (*Alex.*15.9, 3.223.12 Leib) alludes to fr. 137, but is more likely to have found the fragment in Aristotle (our source for the text) than anywhere else. Even Eustathius only preserves one unique fragment of Sappho (fr. 34), and this is alluded to twice by Julian,[62] and thus Eustathius (and perhaps Julian as well) might have found the passage somewhere other than in a text of Sappho.[63] We do have the occasional pleasant surprise, however; fr. 96.6–9 seems to be echoed at Nicetas Eugenianus 3.336 (twelfth century).[64]

Given the paucity of unique quotations from and allusions to Sappho in writers after the fourth century, the awareness we find of the epithalamia is that much more telling. We noted above the fragment from Syrianus (fr. 105a). We can add more. Choricius (19, p. 86 Förster-Richtst) quotes fr. 112.3–5. Lines 1–2 are preserved in Hephaestion (55.24–5 Consbruch), and thus it is possible that Choricius found the remaining lines there. However, it is not normally Hephaestion's practice to quote five lines when one or two will do.[65] The poem is again an epithalamium, and Choricius might instead have found them in Sopater's handbook. Choricius was a rhetor (from the Gaza school), and thus might have been more interested in rhetorical handbooks than metrical handbooks. Furthermore, Choricius is, apart from Himerius, the author of the only other prose epithalamia from later antiquity to have come down to us.[66] Fr. 117 is quoted by Hephaestion (p. 13.7 Consbruch), but without an attribution. Nicetas Choniates, however,

---

[61] For all his anthologizing, Stobaeus only preserves one unique fragment of Sappho (fr. 121).

[62] *Or.* 3.109c (1.140 Hertlein), *Ep.* 194, p. 264 Bidez–Cumont.

[63] Most of Eustathius' references to Sappho come from Athenaeus.

[64] Perhaps it is no coincidence that the papyrus that preserves fr. 96, *P. Berol.* 9722, from the seventh century AD, is the latest Sappho papyrus that we have.

[65] Cf. Cameron 1993:138. The meter is stichic (although the text was probably written in two-line stanzas separated by paragraphoi in the Alexandrian edition, cf. Lobel 1925:xvi), and lines 1–2 are a complete sentence.

[66] On Choricius' epithalamia, see Penella 2005.

tells us that it is by Sappho;[67] once again, he might have found the attribution in a better text of Hephaestion, or he could have found it in Sopater.

We have one last clue. In 1960 Robert Browning[68] published a notice of an unpublished, anonymous panegyric (subsequently attributed to Michael of Italy[69]) on the consecration of Michael II Oxites, patriarch of Constantinople, and the emperor Manuel I Comnenus, thus dating the work to July 1143 or shortly after. The panegyrist refers to Sappho's songs (= fr. 194A V):

> οἷον ᾄδει Σαπφὼ ἡ ποιήτρια μαλακοῖς τισι ῥυθμοῖς καὶ
> μέλεσιν ἐκλελυμένοις τὰς ᾠδὰς διαπλέκουσα, καὶ ἵπποις
> μὲν ἀθλοφόροις ἀπεικάζουσα τοὺς νυμφίους, ῥόδων δ'
> ἁβρότητι παραβάλλουσα τὰς νυμφευομένας παρθένους,
> καὶ τὸ φθέγμα πηκτίδος ἐμμελέστερον ποιοῦσα.

> Such as the poetess Sappho sings, weaving her songs with
> soft rhythms and licentious melodies, likening the bride-
> grooms to prize-winning horses and the brides to the
> softness of roses, making her voice more tuneful than the
> lyre.[70]

The allusion is obviously to an epithalamium. And, as Browning says (1960:192), "Our panegyrist will have got his citation not from an anthology, still less from a text of Sappho, but from a rhetorical handbook." Knowledge of Sappho, like knowledge of most Greek lyric poetry, would have been quickly vanishing in the early Byzantine period. We would expect that such a work could only have been compiled long before the iconoclastic controversy put a stop to any serious scholar-

---

[67] *Or.*5.43.25–8. Nicetas' brother Michael Choniates was also a student of classical poetry, and might have owned the last copy of Callimachus' *Hecale*; cf. Hollis 2009:38–40.

[68] Browning 1960. See further Wirth 1963.

[69] Wirth 1962; cf. Browning 1960:192n2.

[70] Cf. fr. 156 πόλυ πάκτιδος ἀδυμελεστέρα ("more sweet-sounding than a lyre"). Michael might have been familiar with the phrase from [Demetrius] *Eloc.* 162 (our source for the fragment) or his commentators. Equally possible, however, is that he chanced upon it in Sopater.

ship.[71] It is surprising that Sappho's eighth book lasted long enough to be read by Himerius and excerpted by Sopater. Syrianus, Choricius, and Michael of Italy all seem to have used a handbook drawing on Sappho's *Epithalamia*; this can only be what Photius tells us Sopater excerpted from Sappho's eighth book, the last book in the Alexandrian edition, the *Epithalamia*.[72]

IV. SAPPHO AND HER BROTHERS

One piece of information about Sappho handed down to us in the biographical tradition is that she had less than harmonious relations with her brother Charaxus. We are told that while in Naucratis as a wine merchant he took up with a prostitute, identified as either Doricha or Rhodopis. On account of this Sappho railed against him in verse. The main testimonia for Charaxus, and Sappho's invective against him, are Herodotus 2.135, Strabo 17.1.33, and Athenaeus 13.596b–c (= fr. 254 V, 202 L–P), as well as *P. Oxy.* 1800 (= fr. 252 V), and Ovid *Her.* 15.63–70, 117–120. In addition to this we have three fragments of Sappho which might have dealt with her errant brother and his insalubrious consort, frr. 5, 7, and 15.[73]

---

[71] For scholarship and education during the iconoclastic period, see Lemerle 1971:97–104; Wilson 1983:63–78.

[72] The existence of such a work so late is astonishing indeed, and one can only wonder whether it lasted as long as this in a Constantinopolitan library just to be lost in the conflagration wrought by the Franks and Venetians sixty years later.

[73] Lidov 2002:203–237 has mounted a sustained argument against the veracity of all accounts concerning Sappho, Charaxus, and Doricha/Rhodopis, tracing all later versions of the story back to Herodotus, and positing as Herodotus' source not Sappho but a fifth-century comedy (possibly Cratinus). I applaud his scepticism concerning the biographical tradition in antiquity as well as the acceptance of this tradition and the proclivity for biographical readings in modern scholarship. However, I find his methods and conclusions unconvincing. It can in no way be proved, and is not nearly as plausible as he implies, that later sources are reliant on Herodotus—Athenaeus in fact corrects the account in Herodotus. Lidov furthermore places too much emphasis on Posidippus' epigram on Doricha (122 A–B), which is open to various readings. Lidov's ultimate suggestion, that Sappho wrote an epithalamium for Charaxus and Doricha, carries little conviction. It is, however, not my intention to refute his argument here, and thus I will only engage with his approach where it seems particularly important for the present purpose.

Fr. 5 begins with a prayer to Aphrodite and the Nereids for her brother's safe return, presumably from Egypt, before going on to hope that he will atone for past mistakes, 5.5 ὅσσα δὲ πρ]όσθ' ἄμβροτε πάντα λῦσα[ι ("to atone for all past sins ...") and bring honor to her (Sappho), 5.9–10 τὰν κασιγ]νήταν δὲ θέλοι πόησθαι | – ‿ –] τίμας ("may he wish to do honor to his sister").[74] Line endings go on to suggest hardship and suffering, as well as the possibility of public reproach, 5.14 ἐπαγ[ορί]αι πολίταν. Doricha is mentioned by name in the scrappy fr. 7, and again in a hostile context at fr. 15.9–12.[75]

From the various references we can build up a more complete picture. Charaxus became involved with a prostitute, which resulted in financial hardship for him.[76] According to Ovid, he was reduced to a shameful existence on the seas.[77] Public shame seems to have been an important factor, cf. fr. 5.14 ἐπαγ[ορί]αι πολίταν and Ovid *Her.* 15.64 *turpi ... pudore*. Sappho seems to have offered advice, which was not warmly received, Ovid *Her.* 15.67 *me quoque, quod monui bene multa fideliter, odit.* As a result of everything, Sappho resorted to upbraiding her brother in verse, Herodtous 2.135.6 ἐν μέλει Σαπφὼ πολλὰ κατεκερτόμησέ μιν ("Sappho greatly reviled him in song"); cf. Athenaeus 13.596c.

---

[74] Lidov 2002 casts doubt on the supplements κασί]γνητον at line 2 and κασιγ]νήταν at line 9, and thus questions whether the poem was even about Sappho or her brother. True, we should always guard against being too quick to accept supplements, and it is not impossible that other words stood in the gaps. However, sense and meter, along with the coordinated masculine and feminine]γνητον and]νηταν, make the supplements almost certain.

[75] Note also the close resemblance of 15.5 ὅσσα δὲ πρ]όσθ' [ἄμ]βροτε κῆ[να λῦσαι to 5.5 quoted above.

[76] Herodotus says that Charaxus paid a great sum of money to the Samian Xanthes to obtain Rhodopis. Ovid and Athenaeus make no mention of a ransom, but agree that the end result of the association was penury for Charaxus.

[77] Perhaps as a pirate? *Her.* 15.65–66 *factus inops agili peragit freta caerula remo,* | *quasque male amisit, nunc male quaerit opes.* In the archaic period, however, being reduced to a life on the sea was often simply emblematic of abject poverty, as in the case of Hesiod's father at *Op.* 633–638, who πλωίζεσκ' ἐν νηυσὶ βίου κεχρημένος ἐσθλοῦ ... φεύγων ... κακὴν πενίην ("used to sail in ships in want of a decent life ... fleeing ... harsh poverty") or one of the wretched enumerated in Sem. fr. 1 *IEG²* at 15–17, who take to sea εὖτ' ἂν μὴ δυνήσωνται ζόειν ("when they are unable to make a living [on land]"); cf. also *Op.* 236–237.

These accounts are often taken at face value as evidence of, and a glimpse into, domestic life on Lesbos around the turn of the sixth century BC.[78] Sappho's concern for public opinion has even been seen as evidence for her own impeccable morals.[79] Rather than seeing this as simply an incident of domestic disharmony elevated to high poetry, we would do better to locate these songs and references in the context of wisdom poetry, familiar above all else in Greek from Hesiod's instruction of and admonition to his brother Perses.

The parallels with Hesiod are striking indeed. A wayward brother is exhorted, often with mockery and abuse, to make right his wrongs;[80] a dispute over finances is involved, in the case of Hesiod and Perses over the division of an estate.[81] Later, Perses has fallen on hardship, and must eke out a living.[82] He is advised to avoid an evil reputation.[83] Likewise, Sappho's greatest concern seems to have been the financial ruin occasioned by Doricha/Rhodopis.[84] Sappho advises Charaxus,[85] and presumably the advice concerned how he should conduct himself and tend to his estate (an estate that Sappho would presumably have had an interest in). In this context we should perhaps recall fr. 203 V, quoted by Athenaeus (10.425a), Σαπφώ τε ἡ καλὴ πολλαχοῦ Λάριχον τὸν ἀδελφὸν ἐπαινεῖ ὡς οἰνοχοοῦντα ἐν τῷ πρυτανείῳ τοῖς Μυτιληναίοις ("The fair Sappho often praised her brother Larichus for being a wine-pourer in the prytaneion at Mytilene"). I suspect that what we have here is not a reference to a poem that extolled the virtues of her brother Larichus, but rather that Sappho held Larichus up to Charaxus as an example

---

[78] Page 1955:45–51 offers a fairly straightforward biographical reading.

[79] As perhaps most extremely stated by Smyth 1900:252: "Sappho's sensitiveness to the voice of public reproach occasioned by her brother's ill-fame is morally inconceivable had she herself not been innocent of the turpitude with which she was charged by the Athenian writers of comedy."

[80] *Op.* 397 ἐργάζεο, νήπιε Πέρση ("work, foolish Perses!").

[81] *Op.* 35–41.

[82] *Op.* 396.

[83] *Op.* 760 δειλὴν δὲ βροτῶν ὑπαλεύεο φήμην ("avoid the wretched talk of men").

[84] In the Akkadian *Counsels of Wisdom* (ca. 1500–1200 BC) a man, possibly the vizier to a king, advises his son against, among other things, marrying slaves and prostitutes; see Lambert 1960:96–106.

[85] Cf. the passage from Ovid cited above.

of how a virtuous man should conduct himself.[86] An honorific position such as this would be the last thing to attract public reproach. Charaxus, like Perses, is forced to make a living by any means possible, and is perhaps warned against invoking public censure. But what about Sappho's abuse of her brother? Ideally, wisdom poetry should not end by giving up hope and resorting to invective. We are not, however, told anywhere that Sappho resorted to attack when all else failed, simply that she reproached him. The reproach was most likely, just as in Hesiod, interspersed amidst admonition.

If we accept the Charaxus motif in Sappho as an example of wisdom poetry, we are then presented with a further question: is there any truth behind the poems, or are they simply generic types? Did Sappho even have a brother named Charaxus, or any brothers at all? All the evidence we have, from Herodotus, Ovid, Athenaeus, and the Oxyrhynchus *Life*, was obviously gleaned solely from Sappho's text. Charaxus' name might present a clue. It is exceptionally rare, attested elsewhere only once, from Roman Italy (*IGUR* II 694). The noun χάραξ, however, is used of a vine-prop, while in the passive the cognate verb χαράσσω can mean 'to be angry or exasperated'. As a speaking-name for a wine merchant who is the object of censure it is perhaps not overly inappropriate. Perhaps Sappho did have three brothers, and perhaps Doricha[87] too was real. The only thing we can be reasonably certain of is that they all featured in Sappho's poetry. If Charaxus

---

[86] *Mutatis mutandis*, that is; a wine-pourer was the job of a boy, whereas Charaxus was a grown man in trade (the Oxyrhynchus *Life* tells us that Charaxus was the eldest). The point would have been to shame Charaxus, who was unable to match the standard set by his younger brother.

[87] At the margin of *P. Oxy.* 1231 col. i. 11 (= fr. 15 V) there is a spot of ink on a line with the bottom of the bowl of ρ which does not appear to be incompatible with ω, *pace* Lidov 2002:203 and 224 (I have not been able to examine the papyrus; the plate in Turner 1987:46–47, no. 17, is better than that in *P. Oxy.* XII). The scribe is inconsistent in the formation of ω; sometimes the upper right side of the bowl curves to the left, e.g. later in line 11, again in line 13, but sometimes is almost vertical, as at e.g. line 30 in προσωπω. Thus the spot of ink could be the upper part of the second bowl of ω, with the lower part lost through abrasion, which is not uncommon at the margin where text has been lost. Add to this the need for a long single syllable at the beginning of the line which ends in -ριχα, and the supplement Δ]ωρίχα is inescapable (a difficulty acknowledged by Lidov 2002:224n48).

and Doricha (and possibly Larichus) did figure in a complex of songs in the paraenetic tradition, then we are at least justified in suspicion regarding their historical veracity. In the case of Hesiod and Perses, one of the arguments in favor of some truth behind the dispute, and at the very least the actual existence of Perses, is the latter's name. As West says (1978:34), "Hesiod would not have called an invented poltroon by the name of a minor deity distinguished for knowingness ..., whereas Hesiod's father might have had a religious reason for so naming a son." This particular argument is not available to us.[88]

The preceding argument should not be seen to suggest the direct influence of Hesiod on Sappho. In the archaic period wisdom or paraenetic poetry is found not only in Hesiod but also in Theognis, Semonides, Mimnermus, and Archilochus.[89] All (and this includes Sappho) are presumably drawing on a common literary tradition that has antecedents in the wisdom poetry of the Ancient Near East. It furthermore seems likely that Sappho's invectives against her brother would have contributed to Philodemus' impression, discussed at the beginning of this article, that Sappho composed songs in an iambic manner.

NEW YORK UNIVERSITY,
INSTITUTE FOR THE STUDY OF THE ANCIENT WORLD

ABBREVIATIONS

A–B   *Posidippi Pellaei quae supersunt omnia*, ed. C. Austin and G. Bastianini. Milan 2004.

FGE   *Further Greek Epigrams*, ed. D. L. Page. Cambridge 1981.

G–P   *The Greek Anthology: The Garland of Philip*, ed. A. S. F. Gow and D. L. Page. 2 vols. Cambridge 1968.

---

[88] Though there are other arguments in favor of some truth behind the figure and dispute in the *Works and Days*; see West 1978:33–40.

[89] Perhaps we should speak more specifically about an East Aegean/West Anatolian koine? Though Hesiod tells us that he has the Muses alone to thank for his poetic training, perhaps it is not insignificant that his father was from Aeolian Cyme.

HE   *The Greek Anthology: Hellenistic Epigrams*, ed. A. S. F. Gow and D. L.
       Page. 2 vols. Cambridge 1965.
IEG²   *Iambi et elegi Graeci*, ed. M. L. West. 2nd ed. 2 vols. Oxford 1990.
L–P   *Poetarum Lesbiorum fragmenta*, ed. E. Lobel and D. L. Page. Oxford
       1955.
PCG   *Poetae comici Graeci*, ed. R. Kassel and C. Austin. Berlin and New
       York 1983–.
Pf.   *Callimachus*, ed. R. Pfeiffer, 2 vols. Oxford 1949–1953.
TrGF   *Tragicorum Graecorum fragmenta*, ed. B. Snell et al. 5 vols.
       Göttingen 1977–2005.
V   *Sappho et Alcaeus*, ed. A.-M. Voigt. Amsterdam 1971.

WORKS CITED

Aloni, A. 2001. "What is That Man Doing in Sappho, fr. 31 V.?" In *Iambic
    Ideas: Essays on a Poetic Tradition from Archaic Greece to the Late
    Roman Empire*, ed. A. Cavarzere et al., 29–40. Lanham, MD.
Bravo, B. 1997. *Pannychis e Simposio: Feste private notturne di donne e
    uomini nei testi letterari e nel culto.* Pisa.
Browning, R. 1960. "An Unnoticed Fragment of Sappho?" *CR*, n.s.,
    10:192–193.
Cameron, A. 1970. "*Pap. Ant.* III. 115 and the Iambic Prologue in Late
    Greek Poetry." *CQ*, n.s., 20:119–129.
———. 1993. *The Greek Anthology: From Meleager to Planudes.* Oxford.
Campbell, D. A. 1967. *Greek Lyric Poetry: A Selection of Early Greek Lyric,
    Elegiac, and Iambic Poetry.* London.
Contiades-Tsitsoni, E. 1990. *Hymenaios und Epithalamion: das Hochzeitslied
    in der frühgriechischen Lyrik.* Stuttgart.
Cribiore, R. 2007. *The School of Libanius in Late Antique Antioch.* Princeton.
Dale, A. 2010. "Lyric Epigrams in Meleager's *Garland*, the *Anthologia
    Palatina*, and the *Anthologia Planudea*." *Greek, Roman and Byzantine
    Studies* 50:193–213.
Dover, K. J. 1980. *Plato. Symposium.* Cambridge.
Dunbar, N. 1995. *Aristophanes. Birds.* Edited with Introduction and
    Commentary. Oxford.

Garzya, A. 1971. "Per la fortuna di Sappho a Bisanzio." *Jahrbuch der öster-reichischen Byzantinistik* 20:1–5.

Griffin, J. 1980. *Homer on Life and Death*. Oxford.

Henderson, J. 1991. *The Maculate Muse: Obscene Language in Attic Comedy*. 2nd ed. Oxford.

Hollis, A. S. 2009. *Callimachus. Hecale*. 2nd ed. Oxford.

Innes, D., and M. Winterbottom. 1988. *Sopatros the Rhetor: Studies in the Text of the Διαίρεσις Ζητημάτων*. BICS Supplement 48. London.

Kakridis, J. T. 1966. "Zu Sappho 44 LP." *Wiener Studien* 79:21–26.

Kirk, G. S. 1963. "A Fragment of Sappho Reinterpreted." *CQ*, n.s., 13:51–52.

Lambert, W. G. 1960. *Babylonian Wisdom Literature*. Oxford.

Lasserre, F. 1955. Review of *Sappho and Alcaeus: An Introduction to the Study of Ancient Lesbian Poetry*, by D. L. Page, and *Poetarum Lesbiorum fragmenta*, by E. Lobel and D. L. Page. *L'antiquité classique* 24:470.

Lemerle, P. 1971. *Le premier humanisme byzantin: Notes et remarques sur enseignement et culture à Byzance des origines au Xe siècle*. Paris.

Lesky, A. 1966. *A History of Greek Literature*. Trans J. Wills and C. Heer. London.

Lidov, J. B. 2002. "Sappho, Herodotus, and the *Hetaira*." *CP* 97:203–237.

Lloyd-Jones, H. 1967. "Sappho Fr. 111." *CQ*, n.s., 17:168.

Lobel, E. 1925. Σαπφοῦς μέλη: *The Fragments of the Lyrical Poems of Sappho*. Oxford.

Morrison, A. D. 2003. Review of *Iambic Ideas: Essays on a Poetic Tradition from Archaic Greece to the Late Roman Empire*, by A. Cavarzere et al. *JRS* 93:340–341.

Murgatroyd, P. 1987. "Sappho 110aLP: a Footnote." *CQ*, n.s., 37:224.

Nagy, G. 1974. *Comparative Studies in Greek and Indic Meter*. Cambridge, MA.

Page, D. L. 1955. *Sappho and Alcaeus: An Introduction to the Study of Ancient Lesbian Poetry*. Oxford.

Pallantza, E. 2005. *Der troische Krieg in der nachhomerischen Literatur bis zum 5. Jahrhundert v. Chr.* Hermes Einzelschriften 94. Stuttgart.

Penella, R. J. 2005. "From the Muses to Eros: Choricius's Epithalamia for Student Bridegrooms." In *Gaza dans l'Antiquité Tardive: Archéologie, rhétorique et histoire*, ed. C. Saliou, 135–148. Salerno.

Rissman, L. 1983. *Love as War: Homeric Allusion in the Poetry of Sappho.* Königstein.

Russell, D. A. 1983. *Greek Declamation.* Cambridge.

Schrenk, L. P. 1994. "Sappho Frag. 44 and the 'Iliad.'" *Hermes* 122:144–150.

Smyth, H. W. 1900. *Greek Melic Poets.* New York.

Swift, L. A. 2006. "Mixed Choruses and Marriage Songs: A New Interpretation of the Third Stasimon of the *Hippolytos.*" *JHS* 126:125–140.

Treu, M. 1968. *Sappho.* 4th ed. Munich.

Turner, E. G. 1987. *Greek Manuscripts of the Ancient World.* 2nd ed., ed. P. J. Parsons. BICS Supplement 46. London.

Wathelet, P. 1988. *Dictionnaire des Troyens de l'Iliade.* 2 vols. Liège.

West, M. L. 1974. *Studies in Greek Elegy and Iambus.* Berlin.

———. 1978. *Hesiod. Works and Days.* Edited with Prolegomena and Commentary. Oxford.

———. 2000. "*Iliad* and *Aethiopis* on the Stage: Aeschylus and Son." *CQ,* n.s., 50:338–352.

———. 2007. *Indo-European Poetry and Myth.* Oxford.

Wilamowitz-Moellendorff, U. von. 1900. *Die Textgeschichte der griechischen Lyriker.* Berlin.

———. 1914. "Neue lesbische Lyrik (Oxyrhynchos-Papyri X)." *Neue Jahrbücher für das klassische Altertum* 33:225–247. (Repr. as *Kleine Schriften.* Vol. 1, 384–414. Berlin, 1935.)

Wilson, N. G. 1983. *Scholars of Byzantium.* London.

Wirth, P. 1962. "Wer ist der Verfasser der Rede auf den Patriarchen Michael II. Kurkuas Oxeites?" *Byzantinische Zeitschrift* 55:269–273.

———. 1963. "Neue Spuren eines Sapphobruchstücks." *Hermes* 91:115–117.

Yatromanolakis, D. 1999. "Alexandrian Sappho Revisited." *HSCP* 99:179–195.

FAST, FAMINE, AND FEAST

FOOD FOR THOUGHT IN CALLIMACHUS' *HYMN TO DEMETER*

ANDREW FAULKNER

I. DIGRESSION AND TRANSGRESSION:
THE HYMN AND ITS MODELS

τρὶς δ' ἐπὶ Καλλιχόρῳ χαμάδις ἐκαθίσσαο φρητί
αὐσταλέα ἄποτός τε καὶ οὐ φάγες οὐδὲ λόεσσα.
μὴ μὴ ταῦτα λέγωμες ἃ δάκρυον ἄγαγε Δηοῖ·
κάλλιον, ὡς πολίεσσιν ἑαδότα τέθμια δῶκε,
κάλλιον, ὡς καλάμαν τε καὶ ἱερὰ δράγματα πράτα
ἀσταχύων ἀπέκοψε καὶ ἐν βόας ἧκε πατῆσαι,
ἁνίκα Τριπτόλεμος ἀγαθὰν ἐδιδάσκετο τέχναν·
κάλλιον, ὡς (ἵνα καί τις ὑπερβασίας ἀλέηται)
π[   ]ἰδέσθαι.

Callim. Hymn 6.15–23

IN THESE LINES of Callimachus' *Hymn to Demeter* the narrative voice suggests that attention be turned from those events that brought tears to Demeter,[1] the goddess's privations and sorrow during the search for her abducted daughter Persephone, towards something more positive. Three alternatives are introduced by repetition of κάλλιον, 'better' (18, 19, 22). The first two are brief accounts of Demeter's gifts of laws to cities and agrarian skills to mankind, which Triptolemus first

---

[1] The plural λέγωμες (6.17) first suggests the collective voice of the women taking part in the festival, but the poet, in the guise of a leading female celebrant, directs the narrative. Cf. Hopkinson 1984:3–4, "Here [the poet] lurks apart behind the insubstantial voice, and we are left with a poem *in uacuo*, a narrative whose obvious emotion and subjectivity have no definable referent." On the female voice of the hymn, see Bing 1995:37–42.

learned. Such aetiological firsts are common elements in Greek hymns,[2] and at first the switch to more positive praise of the goddess seems genuine. However, the claim to move to subject matter more pleasing to Demeter is ultimately somewhat misleading: the third and most important item introduced by κάλλιον is the story of Erysichthon's transgression against Demeter in her sacred grove, another vexing event for the goddess. One is confronted with the question: how does this choice of subject matter for the main narrative of the hymn reflect the climax of the thrice repeated κάλλιον?

This apparent contradiction has been explained in a number of ways. We are told in line 22 that the myth is introduced as a cautionary tale, lest we ourselves transgress,[3] such that the story of Erysichthon offers moral instruction, as does the didactic poetry of Hesiod.[4] Demeter will ultimately have her revenge in the case of Erysichthon, making the tale an inverse example pleasing to the pious celebrants of the goddess, whose procession opens the poem. Another view sees the introduction of the Erysichthon myth as a comic twist, a story "in the lighthearted spirit of those who have already mourned and fasted with the goddess, and now release their emotions."[5] Quite apart, however, from whether the myth is uplifting for the goddess, her celebrants, and the audience, the repetition of κάλλιον seems to build to a point about the literary nature of the subsequent narrative. Hopkinson notes: "enjoyed for its own sake, the tale of Erysichthon will be κάλλιστον."[6] This superlative is undoubtedly the eventual conclusion, but the specific claim that it will be κάλλιον ('better') to treat the Erysichthon myth expressly contrasts Callimachus' narrative with the myth of Persephone's abduc-

---

[2]   Cf. Clay 1996:494 and Faulkner 2005:66–71.

[3]   Line 23 must have further introduced the story of Erysichthon's crime and punishment. Wilamowitz supplied π[αῖδα κακὸν Τριόπα σκιοειδέα θῆκεν] ἰδέσθαι and Ardizzoni π[εινάοντα πόησ' Ἐρυσίχθονα δειλὸν] ἰδέσθαι; see further Hopkinson 1984:99.

[4]   Hopkinson 1984:4–5, 99; ὑπερβασίας ἀλέηται (6.22) recalls Hes. *Op.* 828 (ὑπερβασίας ἀλεείων), significantly the last line of that poem. See Van Tress 2004:170–171.

[5]   McKay 1962b:64.

[6]   Hopkinson 1984:5. Cf. Spanoudakis 2002:295, "The goddess' unreserved approval of the novel treatment is demonstrated by her fascination with the novel ambience in which Callim. places her."

tion, which was cut short in line 17.[7] As Haslam and Bing have shown, following from this announced departure, Callimachus' treatment of the Erysichthon myth both recalls and distances his hymn from the *Homeric Hymn to Demeter* (*Hom. Hymn* 2):[8] the description of Demeter's sacred trees recalls the *Homeric Hymn* through verbal reminiscence,[9] while thematically the violation of the tree parallels the violation of Persephone—both cry out and are heard by Demeter, but in the latter case the goddess exacts immediate revenge on the transgressor.[10] Also, Demeter takes the disguise of a mortal woman and affects the fortunes of a son of noble parents in both narratives,[11] though in the *Homeric Hymn* it is the mother who transgresses by spying upon Demeter, while in Callimachus' tale the mother is an innocent victim of her hapless son. And the two narratives share the theme of a vengeful λιμός brought by the goddess—in the *Homeric Hymn* Demeter brings a famine upon humanity, while Erysichthon is afflicted by an unending personal hunger.[12]

The abrupt rejection of the story of Demeter's search for her daughter might also signal Callimachus' departure from the narrative of his predecessor Philitas' elegiac hymn to Demeter, which seems to have dealt with Demeter's wanderings in search of Persephone.[13] It has been suggested that the exhortation in line 17 to turn away from subject matter which brings tears to Demeter (μὴ μὴ ταῦτα λέγωμες ἃ

---

[7] See Fuhrer 1988:67–68, Hunter 1992:9–11.

[8] Haslam 1993:119n14, and Bing 1995:29–33. Cf. Depew 1993:70.

[9] Line 37 (μέγα δένδρεον αἰθέρι κῦρον) recalls the description of Demeter's epiphany at *Hom. Hymn* 2.188–189 (ἡ δ' ἄρ' ἐπ' οὐδὸν ἔβη ποσὶ καί ῥα μελάθρου | κῦρε κάρη), as perhaps also do lines 57–58 (Δαμάτηρ δ' ἄφατόν τι κοτέσσατο, γείνατο δ' αὖ θεός· | ἵματα μὲν χέρσω, κεφαλὰ δέ οἱ ἅψατ' Ὀλύμπω). See further Richardson 1974:208, Bulloch 1977:117n27, Hopkinson 1984:131, and Faulkner 2008:241.

[10] Line 39 (κακὸν μέλος ἴαχεν ἄλλαις) and *Hom. Hymn* 2.20 (ἰάχησε δ' ἄρ' ὄρθια φωνῇ).

[11] Haslam (1993:119n14) notes that Erysichthon is called πολύθεστε in line 47, while Demophon is πολυάρητος at *Hom. Hymn* 2.220. Hopkinson (1984:122) and Bing (1995:32) also point to the parallelism of Demeter's first address in disguise to Erysichthon in line 47 (τέκνον πολύθεστε τοκεῦσι) and her first words to the daughters of Celeus at *Hom. Hymn* 2.136–137 ([sc. θεοὶ] δοῖεν κουριδίους ἄνδρας καὶ τέκνα τεκέσθαι | ὡς ἐθέλουσι τοκῆες).

[12] See further below, pp88–89.

[13] See Spanoudakis 2002:142–243.

δάκρυον ἄγαγε Δηοῖ) may allude directly to Philitas' poem.[14] In support
of the hypothesis that Callimachus is turning away from the treatment
of the narrative by Philitas, Heyworth points to the likelihood that
Philitas was the model for the description of Demeter's sacred grove
in Callimachus *Hymn* 6.25–30, as well as the *locus amoenus* in Theocritus
Id. 7.3–9 and the description of bees carrying holy water to Demeter
in Callimachus *Hymn* 2.110–112.[15] He suggests that in Philitas' narrative Demeter breaks her fast in the grove: fasting would be a point of
connection, for Callimachus emphasizes Demeter's fasting in the short
account of her wanderings before the rejection of this story in line
17, and hunger is the central theme of the subsequent Erysichthon
narrative. Callimachus praises Philitas' *Demeter*, probably over one
of Philitas' longer poems,[16] in *Aetia* fr. 1.9–12 Pfeiffer, but rejection of
the well-used narrative need not coincide with censure of Philitas'
poetic treatment. Müller and others following him have argued that
Callimachus' sixth *Hymn* functions as a narrative metaphor for poetic
composition:[17] the fasting Demeter and her grove represent the new
poetic aesthetic of Callimachus, while Erysichthon represents the
old. There is much to recommend this reading, but the opposition of
Demeter (new poetics) and Erysichthon (old poetics) is complicated by
the fact that Callimachus presents his Erysichthon narrative in a positive light as κάλλιον. If the Erysichthon narrative is representative of

---

[14] Spanoudakis (2002:173–174, 294–295), following Cessi (1908:124–125), compares
Philitas fr. 12 = fr. 2.3–4 Powell (καὶ γάρ τις μελέοιο κορεσσάμενος κλαυθμοῖο | κήδεα
δειλαίων εἷλεν ἀπὸ πραπίδων), on the grounds that it is Demeter who has had her fill
of weeping. He also (307–308) thinks that Philicus' mention of tears in *SH* 680.40 (σοῖς
προσανήσεις δακρύοισι πηγήν) draws on Philitas; see, however, Heyworth 2004:152–153.

[15] Heyworth 2004:146–153. Spanoudakis 2002:244–303 provides a detailed discussion of possible influence. The groves of Callimachus and Philitas are later linked by
Propertius 3.1.1–2 (*Callimachi Manes et Coi sacra Philitae,* | *in uestrum, quaeso, me sinite ire
nemus*).

[16] See Cameron 1995:303–320, who identifies the long poem (τὴν μακρήν) that is
unfavorably compared to the *Demeter* as Philitas' *Bittis*. An alternative interpretation sees
Philitas' *Demeter* praised in contrast to Antimachus' *Lyde*. See also Hopkinson 1988:93–94
and Krevans 1993:154–156.

[17] Müller 1987, Bing 1995:40, Murray 2004:212–223, the latter also on the metapoetic
dimensions of the comparable Phineus–Paraibius episode in Ap. Rhod. *Argon.* 2.456–499,
which very probably draws on Callimachus' Erysichthon narrative; on the relative dates
of the two, see Bulloch 1977.

literary transgression, it is at the same time treated well by Callimachus in his poetry. Moreover, the rejection of the Demeter narrative also complicates Callimachus' stance towards other poets. Even a good poet aligned with the new aesthetic, such as Philitas, must be cautious about which narrative he chooses.

The story of Demeter's wandering was clearly popular, and Callimachus may have had other accounts of Demeter's search for Persephone in mind too.[18] The myth is treated by Philicus, a contemporary of Callimachus, in his hymn to Demeter.[19] It also appears to have been taken up by Antimachus in his *Lyde*,[20] a poem to which Callimachus signalled his antipathy in an epigram (fr. 398 Pfeiffer, Λύδη καὶ παχὺ γράμμα καὶ οὐ τορόν). The *Lyde* is of particular importance here, for in addition to the story of Demeter's wandering, Antimachus may have narrated the tale of Erysichthon in the poem: the detail of the future flight of the Pelasgians from Dotium to Cnidus mentioned by Callimachus at the beginning of the Erysichthon story in *Hymn* 6.24 (οὔπω τὰν Κνιδίαν, ἔτι Δώτιον ἱρὸν ἔναιον) is paralleled in the *Lyde* (fr. 85 Matthews, φεύγοντας γαίης ἔκτοθι Δωτιάδος), and it has been suggested that Callimachus is responding to Antimachus in his choice of narrative.[21] A number of verbal and thematic allusions in the hymn to the tale of Cydippe and Acontius in *Aetia* fr. 75 Pfeiffer may also serve to recall earlier Hellenistic comparison of Callimachus and Antimachus: *Hymn* 6.63 (ναὶ ναί, τεύχεο δῶμα, κύον, κύον) evokes *Aetia* fr. 75.4–5 Pfeiffer (Ἥρην γάρ κοτέ φασι—κύον, κύον, ἴσχεο, λαιδρέ | θυμέ, σύ γ' ἀείσῃ καὶ τά περ οὐχ ὁσίη), an allusion which, as Durbec points out,[22] recalls the poet's self-conscious avoidance of transgressing poetic

---

[18] Heyworth (2004:153) suggests that the repetition of the number three in Callim. *Hymn* 6.13–15 may indicate that three texts are rejected as models. On the significance of the number three in the poem see below, n62.

[19] *SH* 676–680. See most recently Furley (2010), with bibliography. Callimachus himself seems to have alluded to the story in the *Aetia* (frr. 21.10; 63; and 611 Pfeiffer), but perhaps did not treat it at length; see Montanari 1974:113–115, Hinds 1987:54n11.

[20] Fr. 78 Matthews, also frr. 31 (*Thebaid*) and 145 (*incertae sedis*); see Richardson 1974:69 and Matthews 1996 ad loc. on parallels between Antimachus and *Hom. Hymn* 2.

[21] See McKay 1962a:105n1 and Matthews 1996:242–245. Cf. Ap. Rhod. fr. 10 Powell. The parallel is also noted in Hopkinson 1984 ad loc.

[22] Durbec 2005. He also directs attention to the subsequent mention of possible transgression by the revelation of Demeter's mysteries in *Aetia* fr. 75.6–7 (ὤναο κάρτ' ἕνεκ'

boundaries. On the thematic level, both Erysichthon and Cydippe are young persons who offend a goddess and are punished with physical suffering that has social consequences: Erysichthon's grieving mother fibs that Erysichthon is unable to attend, among other social events, the wedding of Polyxo's son Actorion (*Hymn* 6.77–82), due to a wound inflicted by a boar while her son was hunting. In fr. 75 Pfeiffer, Cydippe is unable to attend her own wedding, arranged by her father, due to the divine illness brought on by Artemis because of Cydippe's unwitting oath to marry Acontius. The language used to describe the disease of Erysichthon at *Hymn* 6.92 καὶ τούτων ἔτι μέζον ἐτάκετο μέστ' ἐπὶ νευράς is also similar to that used of Cydippe's malady at fr. 75.14–15 ἦ τότ' ἀνιγρή | τὴν κούρην Ἀ[ίδ]εω μέχρις ἔτηξε δόμων.[23] Now, the Cydippe tale may have been at the heart of Callimachus' polemic against the *Lyde* in fr. 398 Pfeiffer, mentioned above. That line was very likely written in response to an epigram of Asclepiades, which praises the *Lyde*:[24]

> Λύδη καὶ γένος εἰμὶ καὶ οὔνομα· τῶν δ' ἀπὸ Κόδρου
> σεμνοτέρη πασῶν εἰμι δι' Ἀντίμαχον
> τίς γὰρ ἔμ' οὐκ ἤεισε; τίς οὐκ ἀνελέξατο Λύδην,
> τὸ ξυνὸν Μουσῶν γράμμα καὶ Ἀντιμάχου;

> AP 9.63, 32 Gow–Page, adapted

Cameron has suggested that the opening lines of this epigram implicitly contrast Antimachus' *Lyde* with Callimachus' *Cydippe*: the claim that Lyde is σεμνοτέρη τῶν ἀπὸ Κόδρου may refer to Cydippe, one of only two female descendants of Codros notable in literature.[25] If this is the case, the shared themes and language of the Cydippe and Erysichthon narratives may intentionally recall literary polemic

---

οὔ τι θεῆς ἴδες ἱερὰ φρικτῆς, | ἐξ ἂν ἐπεὶ καὶ τῶν ἤρυγες ἱστορίην) as a point of contact between the two passages.

[23] Cf. Hopkinson 1984:154.

[24] See Gow–Page 1965, vol. 2:217 and Gutzwiller 1998:219–220.

[25] See Cameron 1995:303–307; this view depends upon Cameron's dating of the *Cydippe* to sometime between 279 and 274 BC, before *Aetia* 1–2 and in the lifetime of Asclepiades (Cameron 1995:247–262). The descent of Cydippe's father Promethus from Codrus is mentioned at fr. 75.32. The other Codrid, Leimonis, was treated by Callimachus in frr. 94–95 Pfeiffer.

against the *Lyde*, a poem which itself may have narrated both the wanderings of Demeter and the tale of Erysichthon.

In what follows, I will attempt to show that the motif of hunger and thirst (whether imposed by an external agent or voluntarily adopted through fasting) that is shared by the stories of Demeter's search for Persephone and Erysichthon's transgression is more central to the opposition of the two tales than has previously been thought. In particular, I will examine further how Erysichthon's ultimate fate, as a beggar starving at the crossroads, invites comparison with Demeter's fasting during her search for Persephone. Several individual instances of the motif of hunger and thirst in the hymn have been noted in previous scholarship, but no study has yet provided a comprehensive reading of how the theme functions within the progression of the poem. In the next two sections (II and III) I will examine how hunger and thirst play a role in all three major transitions in the hymn: the transition from the opening ritual setting to the story of Demeter's search for Persephone, the transition to the Erysichthon narrative discussed above, and the transition back to the ritual setting at the end of the narrative. It will be shown how, as the poem develops, the motif brings cohesion to the poem's different parts. Finally, I will return in the last section (IV) to the question of Callimachus' engagement with his poetic predecessors, discussed above, to explore further how the invitation to compare the two narratives in the sixth *Hymn* impacts upon the metaliterary implications of the Erysichthon story, and reflects upon Callimachus' posture towards Hellenistic poetic aesthetics.

II. FAST AND FAMINE IN THE TALE OF DEMETER'S WANDERINGS

Hunger and thirst traditionally play a prominent role in the story of Demeter's search for her daughter Persephone. In the *Homeric Hymn to Demeter*, fast and famine are at issue in three main phases of the story. First, in her initial grief at the loss of her daughter, Demeter removes herself from the company of the gods and for nine days wanders the earth without eating, drinking, or bathing (*Hom. Hymn* 2.49–50, οὐδέ ποτ' ἀμβροσίης καὶ νέκταρος ἡδυπότοιο | πάσσατ' ἀκηχεμένη, οὐδὲ χρόα βάλλετο λουτροῖς). Her fast is only broken after her arrival at the house of Celeus, where Iambe's jests lighten her mood (*Hom. Hymn* 2.198–211): after Iambe's jests (202–205), Metaneira pours the cyceon and gives it to Demeter to drink.[26] Second, Demeter in her anger brings a great famine upon mankind, leaving the fields barren and unproductive (*Hom. Hymn* 2.305–333). The race of man would have perished because of the famine, had it not been for the intervention of Zeus (*Hom. Hymn* 2.310–313, καί νύ κε πάμπαν ὄλεσσε γένος μερόπων ἀνθρώπων | λιμοῦ ἀπ᾽ ἀργαλέης | εἰ μὴ Ζεὺς ἐνόησεν, ἑῷ τ᾽ ἐφράσσατο θυμῷ).[27] Third, the breaking of Persephone's fast by the unwilling ingestion of a pomegranate seed requires her to remain with Hades for one third of the year (*Hom. Hymn* 2.371–374, 393–404, 411–413).[28]

Later Greek accounts do not always treat fast and famine together, whereas the *Hymn to Demeter* combines the story of Demeter's gift of the Mysteries or agriculture to the Eleusinians with the famine motif.[29] But fasting and hunger seem to have been prominent in Hellenistic accounts of Demeter's wanderings, including Philitas' and Philicus' versions.[30] Nicander refers to Demeter's fast in the *Alexipharmaca* apropos of the *cyceon*,[31] as well as in the parallel tales of Ascalabus and Ambas related in the fourth book of the *Heteroeumena* and the *Theriaca*:[32] both Ascalabus and Ambas, the sons of Misme and Metaneira respec-

---

[26] For more on the *cyceon*, a mixture of grains and liquid, and its use after ritual fasting in Demeter cult, see Richardson 1974:344–348. On fasting in the Thesmophoria, see Kledt 2004:132–133.

[27] See Kledt 2004:91–100.

[28] On the lacunose 387–404, in which Demeter asks Persephone if she has eaten anything while in the underworld, see Richardson 1974:282. For the symbolism of the pomegranate seed, see Kledt 2004:52–53.

[29] See Richardson 1974:258–260. Demeter's own fast is not mentioned as part of her wanderings at Eur. *Hel.* 1301–1368, but the famine she brings to mortals and gods is described in detail (1327–1337). The famine is not part of Orphic accounts.

[30] For Philitas, see above, pp77–79, and below, n40. For Philicus, see *SH* 680.37 ( ]τε πολλ[ὴ] πολὺν ἐγδεξαμένη τὸμ παρὰ κῦμα νήστην, of the devotees of the Eleusinian procession) and 56–57 (μὴ βάλλετε χόρτον αἰγῶν, | οὐ τόδε πεινῶντι θεῶι, of the fasting Demeter). Cf. Callim. fr. 21.10 Pfeiffer: νήστ[ι]ες ἐν Δηοῦς ἤμασι Ῥαριάδος.

[31] Nic. *Alex.* 128–132.

[32] Antoninus Liberalis 24, citing Nicander as the source for the tale of Ascalabus, and Nic. *Ther.* 484–487. See Jacques 2002:143–144. On the disputed date of these poems, see Cameron 1995:194–205, who argues for their attribution to the elder Nicander, a contem-

tively, mock Demeter for drinking the *cyceon* so fervently after her fast. The goddess punishes the young men by pouring the remains of her drink on them, thereby turning them into geckos. This story, later recounted by Ovid,[33] links the motifs of hunger and youthful transgression against Demeter. The combination of fasting and famine is also later reflected in Ovid's accounts of the myth in *Metamorphoses* 5 and *Fasti* 4, which may, along with imitating Hellenistic models, have drawn directly on the *Homeric Hymn to Demeter*:[34] Ceres fasts while searching for her daughter (*Met.* 5.446–447, *Fast.* 4.533–536, 547–548), she brings a famine on mankind because of the abduction (*Met.* 5. 474–486, *Fast.* 4.617–618), and Proserpina breaks a fast by ingesting pomegranate seeds (*Met.* 5.529–538, *Fast.* 4.603–608).[35]

When Callimachus' sixth *Hymn* enters upon the myth of Demeter's search for her daughter Persephone, the theme of abstinence from food and drink links the myth to the ritual procession of female celebrants with which the poem opens. The transition to the myth is effected rather suddenly in line 8 by the epic relative ὅς τε:

τὸν κάλαθον κατιόντα χαμαὶ θασεῖσθε, βέβαλοι,
μηδ' ἀπὸ τῶ τέγεος μηδ' ὑψόθεν αὐγάσσησθε
μὴ παῖς μηδὲ γυνὰ μηδ' ἃ κατεχεύατο χαίταν
μηδ' ὅκ' ἀφ' αὐαλέων στομάτων πτύωμες ἄπαστοι.
Ἕσπερος ἐκ νεφέων ἐσκέψατο (πανίκα νεῖται;),
Ἕσπερος, ὅς τε πιεῖν Δαμάτερα μῶνος ἔπεισεν
ἁρπαγίμας ὅκ' ἄπυστα μετέστιχεν ἴχνια κώρας.

Callim. *Hymn* 6.3–9

---

porary of Callimachus. Jacques (2002:xiii n1) retains the view that they are the work of a younger poet of the second century.

[33] Ov. *Met.* 5.446–461. For the influence of Nicander on Ovid, see Bömer 1976:341–342. For Ovid's treatment of the Erysichthon myth in *Met.* 8.725–884 and his engagement with Callimachus, see Murray 2004:223–240 and Van Tress 2004:185–188.

[34] For the likelihood that Ovid responds directly to the *Homeric Hymn to Demeter*, see Hinds 1987:51–98.

[35] In the case of Proserpina, Ovid makes it explicit that the girl broke a fast 'ieiunium' (*Met.* 5.534–535, *ieiunia uirgo | soluerat*; *Fast.* 4.603, *siquidem ieiuna remansit*; 607, "*rapta tribus*" *dixit* "*soluit ieiunia granis*"). In the *Homeric Hymn to Demeter* she is given the seed by Hades (371–372, 411–412), whereas at *Met.* 5.534–538 she plucks the fruit herself. See further Hinds 1987:88–90.

Hesperus, the personified evening about to bring an end to the ritual procession and fasting of Demeter's devotees, was the only one able to persuade Demeter to end her fast when she was searching for her daughter. The relative often introduces expanded attributive praise of a deity at the beginning of hymns,[36] but when it marks a transition to narrative digression one does not expect the generalizing particle.[37] ὅς τε has lost this predominately generalizing force already in Pindar and fifth-century tragedy,[38] but for one familiar with the model of the *Homeric Hymns* ὅς τε would more naturally introduce expanded attributive praise of Hesperus than a narrative digression.[39] Hesperus is in any case a unique choice as the cause of the end of Demeter's fast,[40] and Callimachus seems to be contradicting expectations on both thematic and structural levels.

In many ways this is not a usual transition to narrative. The same ritual voice continues to speak, addressing Demeter directly in the second person,[41] and the movement to the story of Demeter's search for Persephone is closely tied to what has come before. The repetition of Hesperus' name in lines 7–8 acts as a bridge between the two sections, which are further linked by the theme of hunger. The image of the

[36] See Clay 1996:494 and Furley and Bremer 2001:56.

[37] Where a unique past action (narrative, apportionment, or birth) is introduced by a relative clause in the *Homeric Hymns*, epic τε is not present; cf. *Hom. Hymn* 2.2; 6.2; 8.3; 12.1; 15.1, 4; 17.2; 18.3; 19.6; 29.1. On the attributive nature of the aorists ὦρσε and ἐδαμάσσατο, introduced by ἥ τε in *Hom. Hymn* 5.2–3, see Faulkner 2005:66–68. For the generalizing force of the epic relative, see Denniston 1950:521–523 and Ruijgh 1971, *passim*. On the relative introducing narrative digression in epic and choral lyric, see also West 1966:161.

[38] See Denniston 1954:523–524. Ruijgh (1971:970) concludes that Callimachus' use of epic τε often retains at least part of its original 'digressif-permanent' value, but notes a number of irregular examples.

[39] Cf. *Hom. Hymn* 22.3 ([Ποσειδάων], ὅς θ' Ἑλικῶνα καὶ εὐρείας ἔχει Αἰγάς) and 23.2–3 ([Ζεύς], ὅς τε Θέμιστι | ἐγκλιδὸν ἑζομένη πυκινοὺς ὀάρους ὀαρίζει).

[40] In *Hom. Hymn* 2 it is Iambe who ends Demeter's fast through her jesting, a role played by Baubo in the Orphic version. See Richardson 1974:215, Hopkinson 1984:87, and Kledt 2004:64–65. Spanoudakis (2002:293–294) argues that this detail could allude to the account by Philitas, in which Demeter may have broken her fast in the evening at Chalcon's palace. Heyworth (2004:146–153; see above, pp77–79) instead suggests that Philitas' Demeter breaks her fast in a sacred grove. Cf. Ov. *Fast.* 4.535–536 *quae quia principio posuit ieiunia noctis,* | *tempus habent mystae sidera uisa cibi.*

[41] This *Du-Stil* is typical of cult hymns and appropriate to the imagined ritual context; see Race 1990:102–106.

fasting celebrants spitting from dry mouths in line 6 is answered by the figure of Demeter taking her first drink in line 8, such that the story of Demeter serves as a hopeful *exemplum* for the thirsty, fatigued women taking part in the festival: [42] understood in this way, the generalizing force of ὅς τε can be felt in the myth's role as an *aition* for cult practice. The arrival of evening at the end of the festival of Demeter will always, in the reality of cult worship, bring an end to abstinence from food and drink, just as it once in the past brought an end to Demeter's long fast. [43]

The fact of Demeter's abstinence from food and drink during her search for Persephone is then repeated twice more in quick succession: as Demeter travels across the earth she does not eat, drink, or bathe (line 12, οὐ πίες οὔτ' ἄρ' ἔδες τῆνον χρόνον οὐδὲ λοέσσα), nor does she eat, drink, or bathe as she sits three times at the well of Callichorus (line 16, αὐσταλέα ἄποτός τε καὶ οὐ φάγες οὐδὲ λοέσσα). Once again, Demeter's actions are apposite to the fasting of her devotees, a point that is signaled by the similarity of αὐσταλέα (line 16) to the earlier αὐαλέων (line 6). [44] But this emphasis on her fasting is also, as Bing has argued, an echo of the *Homeric Hymn to Demeter*: [45] both poems twice mention Demeter's fast in parallel contexts, first when Demeter is searching for her daughter and then when she is sitting down. [46] Callimachus' version departs in small ways from the *Homeric Hymn*, [47] but the broad parallelism undoubtedly invites comparison

---

[42] Cf. Hopkinson 1984:4.

[43] Similarly, the historical narrative of Demeter's purification and fasting in *Hom. Hymn* 2.192–211 acts as an *aition* for cult practice. See Richardson 1974:211–217 and cf. Faulkner 2005:66–68. Ruijgh (1971:969) labels this case "un exemple de ὅς τε digressif introduisant un fait mythique du passé."

[44] See Hopkinson 1984:95: αὐσταλέα is a Homeric *hapax*, which highlights the deliberateness of the echo.

[45] Bing 1995:30–31.

[46] Cf. *Hom. Hymn* 2.49–50 (οὐδέ ποτ' ἀμβροσίης καὶ νέκταρος ἡδυπότοιο | πάσσατ' ἀκηχεμένη, οὐδὲ χρόα βάλλετο λουτροῖς) and 200–201 (ἀλλ' ἀγέλαστος ἄπαστος ἐδητύος ἠδὲ ποτῆτος | ἧστο). The more compressed Callimachean version of course places the two instances far closer together.

[47] The vocabulary is largely different, as is the order of the mention of food and drink. The only term of fasting taken directly from *Hom. Hymn* 2, line 200 ἄπαστος, is applied by Callimachus to the female worshippers in line 6, ἄπαστοι. See further Hopkinson 1984:84 and Bing 1995:31.

with the earlier model, which sets the tone for the comparison of the Erysichthon myth with the story of Demeter's search for Persephone. For hunger and thirst are also at the centre of the second major transition in the hymn.

The movement to the main narrative of the poem, discussed at the outset of this article, emphasizes the theme of eating and drinking as a link between the stories of Demeter's search and Erysichthon's *hubris*. Structurally, a full line describing the fasting of Demeter immediately precedes the sudden transition to the Erysichthon narrative in line 17. This not only underlines the motif in what has come before but also announces its importance for the upcoming narrative. Erysichthon's insatiable appetite, although the inversion of Demeter's fast, provides the central point of comparison between the two stories and appropriately contrasts also with the pious fasting of the female devotees of Demeter.[48] Accordingly, the passage of transition to the Erysichthon myth in lines 17–23 itself continues to treat the theme of eating. The second of the three alternative subjects introduced by κάλλιον is Demeter's gift of agriculture to mankind (lines 19–21). She teaches Triptolemus the civilized arts of cultivating crops, the cutting of straw and corn, and the skill of threshing with oxen. This contrasts with the preceding fasting of Demeter and is suggestive of the plenty that awaits the female celebrants at the end of the festival. Such ordered agriculture, along with Demeter's gift of laws to cities, also stands in direct opposition to the grotesque, socially destructive appetite of Erysichthon that is soon to be introduced, and thereby acts as an appropriate pivot on which to turn toward the narrative.[49]

---

[48] On the latter point cf. Hopkinson 1984:5n2 and Bulloch 1984:220.

[49] A clever selection of vocabulary for the description of threshing in lines 19–20 (ἱερὰ δράγματα πράτα | ἀσταχύων ἀπέκοψε καὶ ἐν βόας ἧκε πατῆσαι) might even hint playfully at the narrative to come. Threshing with oxen is described as early as *Il.* 20.495–497, but the usual words for this process are τρίβειν and ἀλοᾶν, whereas Callimachus uses πατῆσαι, a Homeric *hapax* (used by Homer only at *Il.* 4.157): see Hopkinson 1984:98, who does, however, note Eust. 575.41–42 ἀλωή ... ὁ τόπος ἐν ᾧ πατεῖται ὁ πυρός. The similarity of πατέω 'to trample' and πατέομαι 'to eat' could be suggestive of Erysichthon's hunger to come when placed beside βόας: he later in line 108 eats the bull that his mother was raising for sacrifice to Hestia, and the verb πατέομαι describes his hunger at line 68 (ὅσσα πάσαιτο τόσων ἔχεν ἵμερος αὐτίς).

Furthermore, the language of line 18 (ἑαδότα τέθμια δῶκε) suggests an etymology for Demeter's title Θεσμοφόρος.[50] This title and Demeter's establishment of laws for cities, along with her gift of agriculture, should be understood in direct opposition to cannibalism. There is a general opposition of civilisation and cannibalism in Greek literature, certainly present already in the fourth century BC.[51] Pausanias 8.42.6 reports a Pythian oracle that told the Phigalians that Demeter had made them nomads again after having given them the arts of agriculture and warned them that she would also again make them cannibals if they did not appease and honor her. In the well-known Isis aretalogy found at Cyme, Isis, who is in the inscription called Θεσμοφόρος,[52] proclaims that she has given laws to man, provided food, and with the help of her brother Osiris put a stop to cannibalism (8–9: ἐγὼ νόμους ἀνθρώποις ἐθέμην, | καὶ ἐνομοθέτησα ἃ οὐθεὶς δύναται μεταθεῖναι, 11–12: ἐγώ εἰμι ἡ καρπὸν | ἀνθρώποις εὑροῦσα, 23–24: ἐγὼ μετὰ τοῦ ἀδελφοῦ Ὀσίριδος τὰς ἀνθρωποφα- | γίας ἔπαυσα).[53] Now, the end result of Erysichthon's uncontrollable hunger according to Ovid *Met.* 8.875–878 is cannibalism, a conclusion to the story of which, as Bulloch has argued, Callimachus was very probably aware:[54] Erysichthon's autophagy is not directly attested before Ovid,[55] but a parallel for the grotesque punishment is found in the story of Cleomenes recounted in Herodotus 6.75. Cleomenes, having gone mad, dismembers himself from the legs up, until he reaches his stomach, at which point he dies. According to the Athenians, this madness was inflicted as a punishment for Cleomenes' cutting down the τέμενος of Demeter and Persephone. Autophagy itself is not mentioned in Herodotus' account, but the detail that Cleomenus dismembers himself until he reaches his stomach is suggestive. One might also compare the myth of Tantalus

[50] See Hopkinson 1984:96–97.
[51] See Festugière 1972:145–149.
[52] See Witt 1997:106 on the syncretism of Isis and Demeter.
[53] Text from Engelmann 1976:98–99, no. 41. On this and other versions of the Isaic aretalogy, see Fowden 1993:45–52. The Isis hymn discovered at Maroneia specifically mentions Triptolemus and the gift of agriculture alongside Isis' establishment of laws for cities; see Grandjean 1975.
[54] Bulloch 1984:220–222.
[55] Hes. fr. 43 mentions only hunger (λιμός) (43[a].5, λιμοῦ and 7, λιμὸν).

and Pelops, mentioned in Pindar *Ol.* 1.36–51, in which the father cooks his son and then feeds him to the gods. Demeter, distracted by the loss of her daughter, is the only one of the gods to be tricked into eating the grotesque meal.[56] This may have been a precursor to stories in which Demeter imposes cannibalism as a punishment. If autophagy was known to Callimachus' audience as a possible fate for Erysichthon, the opposition of Demeter Thesmophoros to cannibalism sets the mention of her role as the bringer of laws at this point in the poem in playful contrast to the upcoming narrative.

III. ERYSICHTHON AND DEMETER

Thus far we have seen how the motif of hunger and thirst plays an important role in the transition from the opening ritual setting to the story of Demeter's search for Persephone in lines 6–9 of the *Hymn*, as well as in the transition in lines 17–23 from this story to the main narrative of the poem. The subsequent tale of Erysichthon's transgression in many obvious ways furthers this motif: Erysichthon intends to cut down the sacred tree in order to build a banquet hall for his companions to feast in continuously (lines 54–55), a desire that is ironically turned back upon him in the form of an unending personal appetite.

The narrative therefore acts as an appropriate tale of caution for the devotees who have been fasting.[57] But we have also noted how Callimachus seems to use the theme of fasting within the narrative in a pointed way to compare and distance the tale from the story of Persephone's abduction. Both Haslam and Bing have pointed out how, among other themes, the two tales are linked by λιμός:[58] in the *Homeric Hymn*, Demeter is the cause of a famine (λιμός), which threatens to starve humanity, whereas Erysichthon is struck by an insatiable hunger

---

[56] On the connection of the Tantalus–Pelops myth to Demeter's search for Persephone, see Griffith 1989.

[57] Cf. Hopkinson 1984:5n2 on the appropriateness of the narrative for what has preceded, "linked of course with the theme of eating, uppermost in the celebrants' minds after a day's fast."

[58] Haslam 1993:119n14 and Bing 1995:32. Cf. above, p77.

(λιμός).[59] The inversion is pointedly ironic, for not even an endless crop would satisfy the hunger of Erysichthon.

Such pointed allusion to the tale of Demeter's search for Persephone through the motif of food does not, I believe, end here. There seems to be a further invitation to compare Erysichthon's fate directly with the fasting of Demeter, which is so emphasized at the beginning of the poem. In the last two lines of the narrative, we are told that Erysichthon, the king's son, sits at the crossroads begging for the refuse of feasts (lines 114–115, καὶ τόχ' ὁ τῶ βασιλῆος ἐνὶ τριόδοισι καθῆστο | αἰτίζων ἀκόλως τε καὶ ἔκβολα λύματα δαιτός). These lines certainly allude to the royal beggar Odysseus,[60] whose dirty appearance and social position, like Erysichthon's, do not reflect his noble birth. Ultimately, this allusion illuminates a striking contrast between the two characters, for Odysseus' appearance is only a disguise, whereas Erysichthon has fallen into true ruin because of his *hubris*.[61] However, Erysichthon's squalid fate also recalls the earlier description of Demeter fasting in lines 15–16 (τρὶς δ' ἐπὶ Καλλιχόρῳ χαμάδις ἐκαθίσσαο φρητὶ | αὐσταλέα ἄποτός τε καὶ οὐ φάγες οὐδὲ λοέσσα). He sits (καθῆστο, 114) at the crossroads in a state of filth and hunger, just as Demeter sits (ἐκαθίσσαο, 5) at the well of Callichorus, unwashed and hungry.

Significantly, these parallel actions come at the very end of their respective sections: immediately following the description of the fasting Demeter sitting by the well in lines 15–16, the narrator abruptly begins the transition to the main narrative. Similarly, immediately after the description of the starving Erysichthon sitting at the crossroads, the narrator transitions suddenly out of the narrative, addressing Demeter directly with the vocative Δάματερ at the beginning of line 116. Also parallel in these two passages is the focus on the number three: Demeter sits three times at the well of Callichorus, after

---

[59] See line 66, αὐτίκα οἱ χαλεπόν τε καὶ ἄγριον ἔμβαλε λιμὸν and *Hom. Hymn* 2.310–311, καί νύ κε πάμπαν ὄλεσσε γένος μερόπων ἀνθρώπων | λιμοῦ ὑπ' ἀργαλέης. Cf. λιμός used of Erysichthon's hunger at Hes. fr. 43.5–7.

[60] The language recalls *Od.* 17.219–222; see Bulloch 1977:108–112, Hopkinson 1984:170, Murray 2004:214–216, and Van Tress 2004:176–177.

[61] See Hopkinson 1984:10.

having thrice crossed the Achelous, while Erysichthon sits at the cross-roads (τρίοδοισι, 114).[62]

This echo underlines the role of Demeter in Erysichthon's ruin and seems to emphasize further the contrast between Callimachus' choice of the Erysichthon narrative and the traditional tale of Demeter's search for Persephone.[63] Moreover, the motif of eating and drinking once again plays a significant role in a major transition in the poem, the final return back to the ritual setting that opened the hymn. It has been noted by others that the language of lines 118–119 deliberately recalls the first lines of the poem.[64] Before this, however, the allusion to Demeter's actions at the well of Callichorus at the very end of the narrative paves the road for the transition back to the theme of fasting, which is of direct concern to the female celebrants about to conclude their abstinence from food and drink. It is also a reminder that the goddess can bring both good fortune and ruin.[65] Erysichthon's appetite is the inversion of the women's ritual abstinence, just as his *hubris* is the inversion of their piety. The recollection of Demeter's fasting highlights his role as a negative *exemplum* and helps to bring the poem full circle.

IV. CONCLUSIONS:
ERYSICHTHON AND CALLIMACHEAN POETICS

In what has preceded, I hope to have shown the extent to which the motif of hunger is integral to the progression and cohesion of Callima-chus' sixth *Hymn* to Demeter. The theme plays an important role in all three main transitions in the poem. Fasting provides a link between the

---

[62] Cf. Hopkinson 1984:11n2, "The number three might almost be thematic in the poem: triple anaphora passim in the ritual sections, τρίς 13–15, Τριόπας, Τριπτόλεμος, τρίτον (γένος) 98, τριόδοισι 114, τρίλλιστε 138."

[63] As noted previously by Bing (1995:30–31) and discussed above on pp85–86, the description of Demeter seated while fasting already echoes the *Homeric Hymn*.

[64] See Hopkinson 1984:173: line 118 is very similar to line 1 and line 119 equals line 2.

[65] A double edge also felt in the epithet πολύτροφος, used of Demeter for the second time in the poem in line 119 (= line 2): see Cahen 1930:261, "la déesse πολύτροφος est celle qui nourrit, et c'est celle qui, courroucée, affame," Hopkinson 1984:10, and Vamvouri Ruffy 2004:123–124.

opening ritual setting, in which the female celebrants are abstaining from food and drink, and the story of Demeter's search for her daughter Persephone, during which the goddess does not eat, drink, or wash. Hunger is also at the centre of the transition to the main narrative, whose tale of Erysichthon stands in direct opposition to the story of Demeter's search for her daughter. This opposition is signalled by the threefold repetition of κάλλιον in lines 17–23, rising to the climax of the narrative, but also by an echo of Demeter's fasting in the final two lines: the image of the starving Erysichthon sitting at the crossroads in lines 114–115 recalls the hungry Demeter sitting at the well of Callichorus. Hunger therefore plays an important internal role in the development of the poem: it prepares for the final transition back to the ritual setting that opened the hymn, highlighting the opposition between Erysichthon's appetite and the pious fasting of Demeter and her celebrants.

The figures of the ravenous Erysichthon and the fasting Demeter are also, as explored at the outset of the article,[66] linked to Hellenistic polemic about literary aesthetics. I have argued that parallels between the Erysichthon narrative and the Acontius–Cydippe episode in the *Aetia*, combined with links to the *Lyde*, bring to mind Callimachus' criticism of Antimachus' poem as a παχὺ γράμμα (fr. 398), an apparent response to an epigram of Asclepiades (*AP* 9.63 = 32 Gow–Page). At the same time, as has been pointed out by Durbec,[67] the verbal allusions to the Acontius–Cydippe episode, specifically *Aetia* fr. 75.4–5 recalled at *Hymn* 6.63, highlight the dangers of transgressing poetic boundaries. Erysichthon can, as Müller has argued,[68] be seen as a negative representation of literary aesthetic, in contrast to the fasting Demeter, who represents the new Callimachean poetics.

The parallelism of the sitting Demeter and Erysichthon suggested above furthers this contrast. However, the Erysichthon narrative cannot be viewed only in negative opposition to the narrative of Demeter's search for Persephone. Firstly, Callimachus, while signalling his aware-

---

[66] See above, pp76–81.
[67] Durbec 2005. See above, n22.
[68] Müller 1987. See above, n17.

ness of transgressing poetic boundaries, chooses the Erysichthon narrative over the more traditional tale and treats it with typical Callimachean virtuosity. Secondly, Erysichthon's poverty as a beggar and his emaciated figure, despite his immense appetite (*Hymn* 6.89–93), link him to the Callimachean aesthetic: Callimachus elsewhere refers to his poverty as a poet, a motif which is common in Hellenistic and Latin poetry,[69] while the metaphor of slim/fat for poetic composition is central to the programmatic *Aetia* prologue and Callimachus' criticism of the *Lyde*. As Murray points out, "Demeter's appropriate punishment, which transforms Erysichthon into a perpetually hungry emaciated beggar, transforms him on a metapoetic level into a grotesque hybrid of an old and new poet."[70] The contrasting images of Demeter and Erysichthon are therefore ultimately destabilizing rather than confirmatory of a sharp distinction between the two.

Within the ritual frame, then, the invited comparison of Demeter and Erysichthon at the end of the narrative functions for the celebrants as a warning of how similar religious transgression and piety can appear: one would not, in a grotesque inversion of fasting, want to end up like Erysichthon. Beyond the ritual frame, however, the female narrative voice overlaps with Callimachus' poetic voice. On this level, the tale serves as a warning not just of narrative transgression, but also of the fine line between competing poetic aesthetics. Callimachus' poetic metaphor is more nuanced than a comparison of old and new: he has managed Erysichthon well, but his fellow Hellenistic poets should be as careful as his pious celebrants.[71]

UNIVERSITY OF WATERLOO

---

[69] See Kerkhecker 1999:70n41 on *Iambi* fr. 193 for a list of instances and Bulloch 1970 on the *Aetia* fragment *SH* 239.

[70] Murray 2004:214. She goes on, however, to maintain a strong distinction between Demeter as a symbol of Callimachus' aesthetic and Erysichthon as a symbol of opposition to those new poetics.

[71] Versions of this article were read at the University of Western Ontario, the University of Toronto, and Université Laval. I am grateful to the audiences on all these occasions for their helpful comments and criticism. I am particularly indebted to the anonymous referee for *HSCP* and to Professor William Furley, who read the original manuscript with care and offered insightful critique.

WORKS CITED

Bing, P. 1996. "Callimachus and the *Hymn to Demeter.*" *Syllecta Classica* 6:29–42.

Bömer, F. 1976. *P. Ovidius Naso. Metamorphosen.* Vol. 2, *Buch IV–V.* Heidelberg.

Bulloch, A. W. 1970. "A New Interpretation of a Fragment of Callimachus' *Aetia*: Antinoopolis Papyrus 113 fr. I (b)." *CQ*, n.s., 20:269–276.

———. 1977. "Callimachus' *Erysichthon*, Homer and Apollonius Rhodius." *AJP* 98:97–123.

———. 1984. "The Future of a Hellenistic Illusion: Some Observations on Callimachus and Religion." *Museum Helveticum* 41:209–230.

Cahen, É. 1930. *Les hymnes de Callimaque: Commentaire explicatif et critique.* Paris.

Cameron, A. 1995. *Callimachus and His Critics.* Princeton.

Cessi, C. 1908. "De Philitae carminibus quaestiones." *Eranos* 8:117–43.

Clay, J. S. 1996. "The *Homeric Hymns.*" In *A New Companion to Homer* (Mnemosyne Suppl. 163), ed. I. Morris and B. Powell, 489–507. Leiden.

Denniston, J. D. 1954. *The Greek Particles.* 2nd ed. Oxford.

Depew, M. 1993. "Mimesis and Aetiology in Callimachus' *Hymns.*" In Harder, Regtuit, and Wakker 1993, 57–78.

Durbec, Y. 2005. "<<KYON, KYON>>: Lectures métapoétiques d'une apostrophe (Callimaque, *Aitia*, fr. 75, 4 Pfeiffer et *Hymne* à Déméter 63)." *REG* 118:600–604.

Engelmann, H. 1976. *Die Inschriften von Kyme.* Bonn.

Faulkner, A. 2005. "Aphrodite's Aorists: Attributive Sections in the Homeric *Hymns.*" *Glotta* 81:60–79.

———. 2008. *The Homeric Hymn to Aphrodite.* Oxford.

Festugière, A. J. 1972. *Études de religion grecque et hellénistique.* Paris.

Fowden, G. 1993. *The Egyptian Hermes: A Historical Approach to the Late Pagan Mind.* Princeton.

Fuhrer, T. 1988. "A Pindaric Feature of the Poems of Callimachus." *AJP* 109:53–68.

Furley, W. D., and J. M. Bremer. 2001. *Greek Hymns.* Vol. 1, *The Texts in Translation.* Tübingen.

———. 2010. "'Philikos' *Hymn to Demeter.*" *Paideia* 64:483–508.

Gow, A. S. F., and D. L. Page. 1965. *The Greek Anthology: Hellenistic Epigrams.* 2 vols. Cambridge.

Grandjean, Y. 1975. *Une nouvelle arétalogie d'Isis à Maronée.* Leiden.

Griffith, R. D. 1989. "Pelops and Sicily: The Myth of Pindar *Ol.* 1." *JHS* 109:171–173.

Gutzwiller, K. J. 1998. *Poetic Garlands: Hellenistic Epigrams in Context.* Berkeley.

Harder, M. A. , R. F. Regtuit, and G. C. Wakker, eds. 1993. *Hellenistica Groningana: Proceedings of the Groningen Workshops on Hellenistic Poetry.* Vol. 1, *Callimachus.* Leuven.

———, eds. 2004. *Hellenistica Groningana: Proceedings of the Groningen Workshops on Hellenistic Poetry.* Vol. 7, *Callimachus II.* Leuven.

Haslam, M. W. 1993. "Callimachus' *Hymns.*" In Harder, Regtuit, and Wakker 1993, 111–125.

Heyworth, S. 2004. "Looking into the River: Literary History and Interpretation in Callimachus, *Hymns* 5 and 6." In Harder, Regtuit, and Wakker 2004, 139–159.

Hinds, S. 1987. *The Metamorphosis of Persephone: Ovid and the Self-Conscious Muse.* Cambridge.

Hopkinson, N. 1984. *Callimachus. Hymn to Demeter.* Cambridge.

———. 1988. *A Hellenistic Anthology.* Cambridge.

Hunter, R. 1992. "Writing the God: Form and Meaning in Callimachus, *Hymn to Athena.*" *Materiali e discussioni per l'analisi dei testi classici* 29:9–34.

Jacques, J.-M. 2002. *Nicandre. Oeuvres.* Vol. 2, *Les thériaques: Fragments iologiques antérieurs à Nicandre.* Paris.

Kerkhecker, A. 1999. *Callimachus' Book of* Iambi. Oxford.

Kledt, A. 2004. *Die Entführung Kores: Studien zur athenisch-eleusinischen Demeterreligion.* Stuttgart.

Krevans, N. 1993. "Fighting Against Antimachus: The *Lyde* and the *Aetia* Reconsidered." In Harder, Regtuit, and Wakker 1993, 149–160.

Matthews, V. J. 1996. *Antimachus of Colophon: Text and Commentary.* Mnemosyne Suppl. 155. Leiden.

McKay, K. J. 1962a. *The Poet at Play: Kallimachos,* The Bath of Pallas. Mnemosyne Suppl. 6. Leiden.

———. 1962b. *Erysichthon: A Callimachean Comedy.* Mnemosyne Suppl. 7. Leiden.

Montanari, F. 1974. "L'episodio Eleusino delle peregrinazioni di Demetra: a proposito delle fonti di Ovidio, *Fast.* IV. 502–62 e *Metam.* V. 446–61." *Annali della Scuola Normale Superiore di Pisa, Classe di lettere e filosofia,* 3rd ser., 4:109–137.

Müller, C. W. 1987. *Erysichthon: Der Mythos als narrative Metapher im Demeterhymnos des Kallimachos.* Stuttgart.

Murray, J. 2004. "The Metamorphoses of Erysichthon: Callimachus, Apollonius, and Ovid." In Harder, Regtuit, and Wakker 2004, 207–241.

Race, W. H. 1990. *Style and Rhetoric in Pindar's Odes.* Atlanta.

Richardson, N. J. 1974. *The Homeric Hymn to Demeter.* Oxford.

Ruijgh, C. J. 1971. *Autour de "τε épique": Études sur la syntaxe grecque.* Amsterdam.

Spanoudakis, K. 2002. *Philitas of Cos.* Mnemosyne Suppl. 229. Leiden.

Tress, H. van. 2004. *Poetic Memory: Allusion in the Poetry of Callimachus and the Metamorphoses of Ovid.* Mnemosyne Suppl. 258. Leiden.

Vamvouri Ruffy, M. 2004. *La fabrique du divin: Les* Hymnes *de Callimaque à la lumière des* Hymnes *homériques* et *des* Hymnes *épigraphiques.* Liège.

West, M. L. 1966. *Hesiod. Theogony.* Oxford.

Witt, R. E. 1997. *Isis in the Ancient World.* Baltimore (orig. pub. as *Isis in the Greco-Roman World.* Ithaca, NY, 1971).

A NEW MANUSCRIPT
OF CLASSICAL AUTHORS IN SPAIN

Guillermo Galán Vioque

M ATRITENSIS 4697 (= M),[1] bound in 1883 in red leather, is a manuscript of 292 pages measuring 218 x 148 mm and paginated in
the upper right corner of the recto by a recent hand.[2] It came into
the Spanish National Library in 1878, purchased from the Librería
de Mariano Murillo. It is obviously absent, therefore, from Iriarte's
catalog of Greek codices,[3] and, although it is included in Vieillefond's
article on additions to the collection of Greek manuscripts[4] and there
is a full description of its contents in Andrés' catalog,[5] it remains
completely unknown to those who have dealt with the textual transmission of the texts it contains, except as far as the *Batrachomyomachia*
is concerned.[6]

The manuscript has two different sections. In the first one an
unidentified copyist transcribed on thick paper, around the middle of
the fifteenth century, Niphon's treatise *Synopsis Palamiticae haereseos*,
better known as *Adversus Gregorium Palamam* (ff1–10v),[7] erroneously
attributed to Demetrius Kydones,[8] and the epistle of the Latin Patriarch
of Constantinople Paulus to Pope Urban V and his cardinals concerning

---

[1] *Olim* N. 159 (Andrés 1987:146).
[2] It was not paginated when Vieillefond mentioned it in print (see Vieillefond
1935:301).
[3] Iriarte 1769.
[4] Vieillefond 1935:201–202.
[5] Andrés 1987:258–260
[6] Torné Teixido 2001:280–285.
[7] The standard edition, with Latin translation, is *PG* 154, 837–864.
[8] On the erroneous attribution to Cydones, see Mercati 1931:62–77, and Rigo
1988:59n9 and 60n10.

the Palamite errors defended by the emperor John Kantakouzenos ca. 1368–1369 (ff11r–v).[9]

This copy appears to be unknown to the editors of these texts. They are usually copied together, such as in ms. Vaticanus gr. 1093, ff1–12v (epistle at f12)[10] and Vaticanus gr. 677, ff15–22v (epistle at f22) (sixteenth century), an apograph of the former copied by Giorgio Tribizias, and they were also published together, but in reverse order and with a Latin translation, by P. Arcudius,[11] where the treatise is already attributed to Demetrius Kydones.[12] The treatise is also present in the first quaternion of Vaticanus gr. 1095, this time attributed to Niphon, though crossed through.[13] The epistle is present in Vaticanus gr. 604, f50v (XIV ex.), where it is rightly dated to 6877 (= 1368–1369).

As in the case of Vaticanus gr. 677, the copy of M is an apograph of Vaticanus gr. 1093, since they share exclusive readings: at 844D M has προτέλειον instead of ὑπερτέλειον, the reading of Vaticanus gr. 1095, f2, while Vaticanus gr. 677 has a lacuna here [καὶ προτέλειον καὶ ἄχρονον τοῦ],[14] and at 849d it has between τόμῳ and οὐσιώδη, added as a correction as in Vaticanus gr. 1093, ἀλλὰ τὴν ἐνέργειαν αὐτὴν (Vaticanus gr. 667 has an omission and the first hand of Vaticanus gr. 1095 ἀλλὰ αὐ[τὴν]).[15] Besides, M follows almost all the readings pointed to by Laemmer in his collation of Vaticanus gr. 1093,[16] and presents the same corrections to the text pointed out by Mercati in Vaticanus gr.

---

[9]   See *PG* 154, 836–837. This epistle is fully cited at Voordeckers 1967–1968:476–478.

[10]   There is a full collation at Laemmer 1875:108–109 (on its failings, see Mercati 1931:63n3).

[11]   *Opuscula aurea theologica* (Rome) 1630:404–407 (epistle), 408–443 (treatise).

[12]   In this the editor follows the testimony of Vaticanus gr. 677, where it is attributed to τοῦ αὐτοῦ, referring to the author of the preceding document, Demetrius Cydones (see Mercati 1931:65).

[13]   Mercati reads the title as follows: Τοῦ σοφωτάτου καὶ λογιωτάτου ... κῦρ Νύφωνος ἱερομονάχου | τοῦ καλουμένου ὑποψερίου· σύνοψις τῆς τοῦ Παλαμᾶ αἱρέσεως (see Mercati 1931:72).

[14]   See Mercati 1931:64n1, who explains the misreading "per trascorso degli ochi o per isvanimento di parecchie lettere nelle esemplare da cui deriva."

[15]   See Mercati 1931:64n9.

[16]   Laemmer 1875:108–109. It diverges only at 408.4 διέλθωμεν Vaticanus gr. 1093 : διεξέλθωμεν M, 410.3 σχήμασιν Vaticanus gr. 1093 : σχήμασιν πέφυκεν M, and 412.7–8 om. περὶ φωτός Vaticanus gr. 1093 : περὶ φωτός M.

1093, also *supra lineam* or *in margine* (these are omitted in Vaticanus gr. 677 and are perfectly readable in Vaticanus gr. 1095): αὕτη after θεότης and ἔστιν (καὶ) συν(αΐδος) τῇ οὐσίᾳ τοῦ θεοῦ at *PG* 845b, 3–4 (f3v), as well as φάμεν before προέρχεσθαι at *PG* 849d, 5 (f5v).[17]

The second section extends from f12 to f292v, and was copied in the last quarter of the fifteenth century by Ludovicus de Puppio,[18] as can be seen in the *subscriptio* written in red ink at the end of the codex (f292v): *Ludovici Presbyteri de Puppio manu propria scriptus.*

Ludovicus de Puppio is well known as the editor of the only Renaissance commentary on the very influential *Carmina differentialia* by Guarino of Verona, probably the result of notes taken in his classes, his *In differentias Guarini Veronensis interpretatio*, Impressum Pisis: P[er] Gregorium de Ge[n]te, 1485.[19] This is a small volume in quarto with only fifty-eight pages, unpaginated. In the preface Ludovicus states that he wrote it in response to demand from his students: *Efflagitaverunt plerique et generosi adolescentuli ut Guarini Veronensis clari rhetoris quaedam carmina quae in se verborum differentias continent eis interpretarer* (f A).[20] Later he confirms its didactic purpose: *Nam ego non adultis sed initiatis in sacris litterarum has elaboravi* (f A).

Ludovicus is also the author of one of the best Renaissance commentaries on the *Carmina Priapea*, his *Commentarius in Priapea Virgilii aliaque opuscula critica*, which was edited in Rome, ca. 1500, along with two other minor grammatical works, *Ordo ac doctrina in Kalendis ac Idibus* (ff59–65v) and *In comparationes variorum auctorum ordo et utilitas legentium quam componebat et opus* (ff66v–92v).[21]

In addition, we have some other manuscripts copied by the same Ludovicus. Being a commentator on the *Priapea*, he left a copy of this text attributed, as usual in this age, to Virgil, the Berolinensis

[17] See Mercati 1931:66n2.

[18] He is also known as Ludovicus Pretinus Alaster. The most complete biography is to be found at Hausmann 1980:441–442.

[19] See Reichling 1905–1911: vol. 4, 42. It was republished at least in 1492, in Parma, by Angelus Ugoletus, and in 1493, in Brescia, by Thomas Ferrandus. See Grafton and Jardine 1982:65–66, Percival 2004:155–177.

[20] The prologue is published in Garin 1958:499–500.

[21] Hain 1826–1838: vol. 2, 152n13343, Reichling 1907: vol. 3, 156–157. For a full description, see Hausmann 1980:428, 439–442.

Hamiltonianus 479, dated in Siena in 1469.[22] It is preceded by a copy
of the famous *Hermaphroditus* of Antonio Beccadelli, known as the
Panormita, with an elegy to Pietro Lunense, an epistle in verse from
Lorenzo Valla to Andrea Contrario,[23] and some letters exchanged
between humanists of his age which are usually transmitted along with
Panormita's treatise as witness to the reaction this work caused.[24]

There is another manuscript signed by Ludovicus in the Royal
Library in Brussels, ms. Bruxellensis II 1485. It is dated in Florence in
1472, and contains a copy of an anonymous grammatical treatise and
some excerpts.[25] The manuscript Vaticanus Ottob. Lat. 2255, dated in
Rome in 1516, is also attributed to him. It contains an *Epithetorum ex
poetis latinis collectio* with a short appendix on *Animalium voces*.[26] Finally,
at the Communal Library of Perugia there is an undated manuscript,
Perusinus F 68, which contains a short prose treatise on legal logic
dedicated to Pope Julius II, probably in an attempt to seek patronage.[27]

---

[22] *Subscriptio* at f19: *Hic liber est meus Ludovici Laurentii de Puppio florentino agro et sic
scriptum per me ipsum Senis 1469 die 25 0[ctobris]* and 42v: *Hic liber est meus Ludovici Pretini
filli Laurentii de Puppio.* See Hamilton 1882:81, Boese 1966:222–224, Kristeller 1963–1997:
vol. 3, 362. A full description at Coppini 1990:xiii–xiv and cxlvii–cxlix (*stemma codicum*
at ccxxxvii). Information on this copy of the *Priapea* was supplied by Hausmann, on
the authority of M. D. Reeve: see Hausmann 1980:425n9, Reeve 1983:323n4. The *Priapea*
and the *Hermaphroditus* are transcribed together at least in mss. Oxoniensis D'Orville
167, Guelferbytanus 371, Laurentianus 33.22, Parisinus lat. 8206, and Perusinus 740.
The *Priapea* are preceded by some original Latin poems which were published in Boese
1966:223.

[23] See Bertalot 1985:254 (n254) and 38 (n822) (this manuscript is not recorded).

[24] The letters are edited as appendices by Coppini 1990:144–159 (Guarino of Verona to
Giovanni Lamola, pp145–150; and Antonio Beccadelli to Poggio Bracciolini, pp151–159).

[25] *Subscriptio* on f158v: *He regule scripte sunt a me Lodovico de Mugello filio Laurentii
Christofori de Pupio Florentie die XXIIII novembris 1472.* See Kristeller 1963–1997: vol. 3, 123a.

[26] *Subscriptio* on f352 (originally 439): *Ludovici pretini alastri florentini nati et oriundi in
oppido casentinati Puppio | Aretine diecesis et educati Florentię Senis et Pisis et Romę epithetorum
finis | bono omine, bonis avibus, diis felicibus deo apolline et musis et ad | utilitatem omnium Romę
anno quarto pape Leonis X florentini MDXVI | Mensis Julii vel Quintiliis die lune 21 ho. 18 nubilo
et ... | Solis ho. 7 m. 16 coni ...* See Kristeller 1963–1997: vol. 2, 436, Mercati 1938:249n38,
Ruysschaert 1997: vol. 1, 192–193n435.

[27] It is entitled *Ludovici Pretini alias Triflorentini iudicialis dialectica et modi omnes dispu-
tationis. Quoniam ad celum efferantur,* and is ascribed to the sixteenth century (Julius II was
Pope from 1503 to 1513). See Kristeller 1963–1997: vol. 2, 56.

Ludovicus de Puppio was thus a professor of Latin grammar and a minor protagonist of the Italian Renaissance in the last quarter of the fifteenth century who lived between Florence, Siena, Pisa, and Rome.

This second part of M contains a selection of 144 fables of Aesop (ff13–58v), with three *Tetrasticha iambica* attributed to Ignatius Diaconus on f38r–v, the *Batrachomyomachia* (ff59–65), Theocritus' first seventeen *Idylls* with prolegomena, hypotheses to *Idylls* 2 to 15, and an interlinear Latin translation for the first three *Idylls* and lines 1 to 9 and 50 to 63 of the fourth (ff69–161v), and the first two comedies of Aristophanes in the Byzantine triad, *Plutus*, with a Latin translation (166–225v), and *Clouds* (ff229–292v), the latter with prolegomena and *index personarum* (ff226–228v). There are some blank pages before the texts of Theocritus (ff66–71v) and the Aristophanes texts (ff162–165). Since it is an almost unknown manuscript, I shall now go on to study its entire contents, pointing out their value and position in the textual tradition of each author.

I. AESOP'S FABLES

The collection of Aesop's fables in this manuscript is not mentioned in the bibliography on Aesop and the transmission of his works.[28] This is another witness to Aesop's fables in Spain that should be added to the three mentioned by E. Chambry (two in Salamanca, mss. 48 and 230, and one in Toledo, ms. 101–12),[29] and to Escorialensis Y III 10, which contains a brief selection of the fables.

M contains 144 fables of Aesop that have never been collated or studied.[30] They are copied in the same order as in the *recensio Accursiana*, and the codex contains fables only present in this Byzantine recension, such as 268–269, 272–273, and 283–289. It also includes the three *Tetrasticha iambica* of Ignatius Diaconus that usually appear in

---

[28] It is not mentioned among the ninety-four mss. cited by Chambry 1925:1–28, or among those added by Marc 1910:398, Hausrath 1927:1541–1543, or Perry 1981:71n71.

[29] See Chambry 1925:1 and 24.

[30] They are carefully listed at Andrés 1987:258. Andrés mistakenly mentions that this manuscript contains 114 fables.

manuscripts of this recension.[31] A full collation reveals that the collection follows the characteristic textual features of this recension, in particular of family α. In fact, it is an accurate copy of the *editio princeps*, edited by Bonus Accursius around 1480.[32] As is the case of the *editio princeps*, this manuscript omits fable 96, which is truncated at μητὴρ πρὸς ταῦτα in Laurentianus 89.79 and in the manuscripts influenced by it, such as Riccardianus 27, Laurentianus conv. soppr. 97, and Salmanticensis 230. Luccensis 1426 (= L) alone likewise omits fable 96 and has the same number of fables, 147, not 148 as stated by Hausrath,[33] but in more than one reading M diverges from this witness, which in fact is very close to the *editio princeps*.[34] The text of M coincides almost verbatim with the *editio princeps*, with the exception of 250, 1 (f35v), where M has ἀλλήλος instead of the expected ἀλλήλους, a mistake not corrected *in margine* as was the copyist's practice elsewhere, for instance at *Tetr.* 22 (f38v), where he wrote κοινωνίας but added *in margine* the correction -αις.[35] M is the copy and not vice versa, because the copyist of M omitted by mistake ὀρχήσωμαι ... τῆς ἐρίφου at *fab.* 99,

---

[31] See ff. 38r–v. I refer to Ign. *Tetr.* 8, 19, and 22.

[32] *Aesopi fabulae graece et latine*, Mediolani 1480. Another manuscript copy of this edition is to be found in the second part of ms. Parisinus gr. 2825, which contains 61 fables with Latin translation by Rinuccio Aretino, also included at the end of the *editio princeps* (ff103–130) (see Lockwood 1913:51–109, esp. 61–72, Achelis 1928:55–88, and Perry 1934:53–62), and later (ff79–148) the *Vita Aesopi* and 147 fables copied from the *editio princeps*, according to Chambry 1925:15.

[33] See p xiv. Mioni 1964:129 counts 144 fables but makes no mention at all of the three *Tetrasticha iambica*. There are also several mistakes in the identification of the fables (I put Mioni's numbers first, and in parentheses the correct ones): 24 (23), 286 (268), 206 (207), 286 (272), 226 (224), 272 (286), and 164 (163).

[34] See Hausrath 1957:XVI: *itaque Pisanum editorem codice Luccensi usum esse veri similius*. However, L diverges from M, for instance, at 4.3 τοῦ ἱέρακος γάστερα (τοῦ ἱέρακος); 9.8 ἀνασπάσω ἐκεῖθεν πηδήσασα, καὶ σὲ με τοῦ δὲ (ἀνασπάσω ἐντεῦθεν. τοῦ δὲ); 17.3–4 om. τῷ κοινῷ ... καί; 23.2 μίμεσθαι (νέμεσθαι); 29.1 om. οἰκῶν; 33.3–4 πεπηδηκέναι χώραις ἐκόπηδημα (πεπηδηκέναι πήδημα); 42.3 αὐτοῦ (αὐτοὺς); 42.7 τοῦ πατρὸς ἄμπελου (τοῦ πατρὸς); 116.7 om. φίλους; 190.3 om. ἑτέρῳ ... Διός, 188.4 καὶ ὀστὰ (ὀστὰ), 253.8–9 om. ἰδὼν ... οὗτος, 77.8–9 om. δοκοῦντα ... βλαβερά, 11.4–5 om. ἥνυεν ... ἀποθέμενος, 213.5–6 om. πρότερον ... τοῖς, 289.3 ἀπέκτονα (along with Parisinus gr. suppl. 690 and Vindobonensis ph. gr. 178, and 192) (ἀπέκτεινα) (I transcribe first the reading of L and in brackets the reading of M, which coincides with the *editio princeps*).

[35] The readings of the *editio princeps* in Hausrath's apparatus are misreported at 57 (it has [3] δώσειν, [5] ὀφθαλμοὺς αὐτῇ, [6] ἀναβλέπειν) and 169 (Acc. has τίνες, not τίνες τε).

4–5 (f44v). Omissions like this occur in other passages but the copyist usually added the missing words *in margine*.[36] The copyist must have had a manuscript at hand since, for instance, at 17, 8 προσέφερεν he wrote *supra lineam* συν-, the reading of the III β family.[37]

II. THE *BATRACHOMYOMACHIA*

This copy of the *Batrachomyomachia* does not appear in the list of manuscripts of A. Ludwich, and neither is it included by T. W. Allen in his edition, nor mentioned by H. Wölke or R. Glei.[38] It has been studied and fully collated by R. Torné Teixido.[39] Torné Teixido is right in ascribing this witness to the second family of the first group pointed to by Ludwich, due to its coincidence with this group of manuscripts and because it does not follow the characteristic features of the other families.[40] As regards the absence of 255–288, the first possibility pointed to by Torné Teixido should be disregarded.[41] It is more than likely that the copyist was using an antigraph with a page missing and that it had sixteen lines per page, or two pages in the case of a witness with eight lines per page, a number of lines by no means rare, or else that he turned over two pages at once, missing the verso of one page and the recto of the other, in total thirty-two lines.

III. THEOCRITUS' *IDYLLS*

This copy of Theocritus' *Idylls* is not mentioned in Wendel's exhaustive list of testimonies, and it is still omitted from Gallavotti's studies and edition and even from Peter Hicks' relatively recent survey of the

---

[36] See, for instance, f17v, 17, 3–4 ὡς ἂν … αἶσχος, f20, 36, 5–6 ἐστὶν … εἴποι add. *in margine.*

[37] It is also preferred at Korais 1810.

[38] See Ludwich 1894:1–11, later reprinted with only one addition (number 46, Perusinus E 48), in Ludwich 1896:40–52, Allen 1983: vol. 5, 164–167, Wölke 1978, and Glei 1984.

[39] Torné Teixido 2001:280–285.

[40] These are the criteria already established by Ludwich 1894:15, 1896:57–58.

[41] He suggested that the history of the deeds of Meridarpax (256–288) was perhaps a later addition not present in the old manuscripts of the family (see p. 281). In that case this would certainly not be the only witness.

textual transmission of Theocritus.[42] In fact, I have found no trace of it in the bibliography on Theocritus' *Idylls* and their transmission.

Studies of the textual transmission of Theocritus mention only five manuscript witnesses to his text in Spanish libraries. These are Barcinonensis 399, Escorialensis R III 5 and Y II 15, Matritensis 4607, and Salmanticensis 230.[43] And although they are not strictly witnesses of his text, we should add to these a very interesting manuscript, the Salmanticensis 295, which contains critical notes by the Spanish humanist Fernán Núñez de Guzmán, known as Pintianus, the owner of the Salmanticensis 230 mentioned above,[44] some excerpts from his *Idylls* reproduced on f309 of Escorialensis X I 13, and Matritensis 4629 (ff72–88), which contains notes on Theocritus by Konstantinus Laskaris. All of these, with the exception of the last-mentioned, have received the attention they deserve.

To this scanty list we should now add M, which is an unknown witness of the recension called by Wendel the Anonymus Parisinus. Neither he nor Gallavotti mentioned it in the list of manuscripts belonging to this family, even though the latter states "quorum codicum recentiorum en habes indicem, quantum potui, diligentissimum"[45] In this family Gallavotti includes the manuscripts Parisinus gr. 2758, 2833, and 2763, Ambrosianus 37, Oxoniensis Can. 86, Cantabrigensis 600, and Laurentianus 32.43.[46] The first two printed editions, the *editio princeps* of Milan (1480)[47] and the Aldine (1496 and

---

[42] Wendel 1920:170–205, Gallavotti 1993:372–380, Hicks 1993. Nor is it studied by Hiller 1888 or Wilamowitz 1906, and it is not mentioned by Ahrens 1855 (list of Spanish manuscripts used or known on p. XLI) or Gow 1950.

[43] See Wendel 1920:172–174 and 182, Gallavotti 1993:375, and Hicks 1993:221.

[44] He also translated into Latin the first six *Idylls* (ms. Salmanticensis M 71, ff144–180).

[45] Wendel 1920:26–28, Gallavotti 1993:334–335, esp. 334. Nor did Gallavotti mention it in the article he wrote about this family of manuscripts (Gallavotti 1936:45–59).

[46] From this family is derived the so-called Valliana (Ambr. 631, Marcianus 480, Piacenza, Bibl. Comun. N. 6, Gotha, Membr. II, 64, Laurentianus 32.46, Vaticanus gr. 1380, Salmanticensis 230, Parisinus gr. 2834, 2596 and 2726, ff173–180 [*Id.* 17, 18 and 15]), and the Lascariana (Matr. 4607, Mutin. 146, Ambrosianus 427, Berol. Phil. 1602, Mosquensis 471); see Gallavotti 1936:47; 1993:335–338.

[47] *Theocritus, Idyllia. Hesiodus. Opera et dies* (Mediolani, apud Bonum Accursium, 1480).

1496[2]),[48] are also witnesses to this family, since they were printed using a manuscript belonging to this group of codices, and therefore many of its peculiar readings went to print and influenced later editions.[49]

M coincides with the manuscripts of this late family in the prolegomena and the hypotheses, although it transcribes fewer prolegomena than the other witnesses of this family, since it only presents Aa, Ba, and VIIC Ahrens, and it has hypotheses only for *Id.* 2 to 15, as in Parisinus gr. 2833, though the copyist of this last ms. left a blank space before *Id.* 16, 17, and 18, as if he intended to transcribe the hypotheses later.[50] It has the characteristic ending of this family of manuscripts for VIA (οἱ δὲ ἀγροῖκοι τούτου χάριν δῶρα κομίσαντες γεγηθότες ὕμνησαν τὴν θεὰν διὰ τῶν συνήθων αὐτοῖς ἀγροικικῶν ᾠδῶν· καὶ οὕτως ἔλαθεν ἔθος γινέσθαι κἀν τοῖς ἐφεξῆς),[51] and, as mentioned above, it presents the prolegomena VIIC, exclusive to this family. The text of the hypotheses of M coincides with the manuscripts of this family, following all the exclusive readings, including the omissions, attributed by Ahrens to Parisinus gr. 2833 (N)[52] and printed by Valckenaer in his edition.

As regards the text, and as is the case with the other manuscripts of this family, M follows the Moschopulean recension as far as *Idyll 8* and later accepts readings from the Planudean manuscripts.[53] M also follows the characteristic readings of the manuscripts that belong to the so-called Parisina family,[54] such as 2.80 λιπόντι, 83 κοὐδὲ, 146 τᾶς γε ἐμᾶς, 9.2 ἐφεψάσθω, 6 ὑποκρίνοιτο, 14.1 τοὶ αὐτῷ, 23 ἄψαις, 34 ἴσης, 15.4 ἀδεμάτου *in margine* (ἀδειμάντου *in textu*), 10 ἐμεῖο, 11 Δίκωνα τοιαῦτα, 15 πρῶαν, 23 θασόμεθ' ἄρ, 25 ὦν ἴδες χ' ὦν, 32 παῦσαι ὀκοία,

---

[48] Τάδε ἔνεστι ἐν τῆδε τῇ βιβλῶ· Θεοκρίτου εἰδύλλια τοῦτ' ἐστὶ μικρὰ ποιήματα τριάκοντα. τοῦ αὐτοῦ Γένος καὶ περὶ εὑρέσεως τῶν βουκολικῶν (Venitiis, apud Aldum Manutium, 1496 and 1496[2]).

[49] Gallavotti 1936:59.

[50] M has no scholia at all, only a very few marginal corrections.

[51] Ahrens 1855–1859: vol. 2, 5n4.

[52] The Parisinus was copied *circa* 1484 for the Medici by Demetrius Damilas. Later it became the property of Janus Lascaris, Cardinal Niccolò Ridolfi, and Caterina de Medici, after which, along with the rest of her library, it became part of the collection of the National Library of France (see Jackson 1999–2000: 77–81, 95–96).

[53] For instance, 9.2 ἐφεψάσθω, 32 ἐμὶν δ' ἁ μῶσα, 35 μὲν ὁρῶντι. See Ruipérez 1950:77–78.

[54] See Gallavotti 1936:45–59, Ruipérez 1950:77–88, and Gallavotti 1993:336–337.

38 τοῦτο καλὸν εἶπες, 60 ὦ τέκνα, 72 φυλαξοῦμαι, 73 ὥστε ῥύες, 76 θλίβεται, 112 φέροντι, 115 ποιεῦνται, 119 βρίθουσαι, 121 ἐφεζόμενοι, 16.1 εἴ τοι τοῦτο, 44 εἰ μὴ δεινός, 106 ἔγωγε μένοιμί, 17.36 τῆς, 37 ἐπεμάξατο, 42 βαῖνειν, 126 ἐπὶ.

With regard to the position of M in this family of manuscripts, M is in no way a copy of any of the first printed editions mentioned above, since it has prolegomena *recentiora* which did not get into print until L. C. Valckenaer's and Fr. Dübner's editions,[55] and on more than one occasion it does not follow their readings.[56] Especially significant is the fact that it does not have the lacuna at *Id.* 15.22–23 [Πτολεμαίω, | θάσωμαι τὸν Ἄδωνιν· ἀκούω] characteristic of both the *editio princeps* and the Aldine, and that it does not coincide with them at *Id.* 2.58, where M has κακὸν ποτόν, while both editions, and also the later edition of Zacharias Kallierges (1516),[57] and the manuscripts copied from them, such as Marcianus 619 and Vaticanus Ottob. gr. 280, have ποτὸν κακόν.[58]

A full collation reveals that M is closer to Laurentianus 32.43 (La), dated *circa* 1470, than to other manuscripts of this family.[59] It shares with it, and also with Cantabrigensis 600 (Ca), several readings distinct from the Parisinus gr. 2833 (Pa) and the first two printed editions.[60] See, for instance, the following passages:

---

[55] See L. C. Valckenaer, *Theocriti, Bionis et Moschi carmina bucolica* (Leiden, 1779) and F. Dübner, *Scholia in Theocritum auctiora reddidit et annotatione critica* (Paris, 1849).

[56] See *infra*.

[57] Τάδε ἔνεστιν, ἐν τῇ παρουσῇ βίβλῳ. Θεοκρίτου Εἰδύλλια, ἕξ καὶ τριακόντα. Rome, 1516.

[58] Gallavotti 1936:55.

[59] Garin (1914:276–277) thought that it was owned and commented on by Polizianus, but this has been refuted by Perosa 1952, 71; 1955, 28, and 2000:89n14. See also Gallavotti 1993:335n1. See in favor of Garin's proposal Fryde 1996:2, 539, 582–583.

[60] Ahrens 1874: 592, and Hiller 1888:9 erroneously postulated the dependence of La on the Aldine. See Gallavotti 1936:51n2.

	M La Ca	Pa Med Ald
3.29	ποτεμάξατο τὸ πλατάγημα (ποτιμαξάμενον πλατάγησεν M La Ca *in marg.*)	ποτιμαξάμενον πλατάγησεν
5.57	τᾶν (τῶν *supra lineam*)	τῶν
5.65	ἐστὶ	ἐντὶ
5.86	εἴκοτι	εἴκατι
6.10	τῶν	τᾶν
6.22	ποθορῶμαι	ποθορῆμι
6.25	κνίζων ποθορῶμαι	κνίσδων ποθορῆμι
6.27	θάλασσης	θάλασσας
7.2	ἁμῖν	ἄμμιν
7.3	καὶ	ὁ
7.54	ἴσχῃ	ἴσχει
7.57	θάλατταν	θάλασσαν
7.64	ἢ ἐλευκοίων	ἢ καὶ λευκοίων
7.70	αὐτοῖσι	αὐταῖσιν
7.71	*om.* μοι	μοι
7.80	λειμωνόθεν	λειμωνόθε
7.85	ἐξεπόνασας	ἐξετέλασας
7.106	κεῖ μὲν	κῆν μὲν
7.124	νάρκησιν	νάρκαισιν
7.128	γελάξας	γελάσσας
7.131	ἐγών	ἐγὼ
7.136	τὸ τ᾽ ἔγγυθεν (τὸ δ᾽ ἔγγυθεν La *in marg.*)	τὸ δ᾽ ἔγγυθεν
7.137	κελάρυζε	κελάρυσδεν
7.150	κρατῆρ᾽	κρητῆρ᾽

	M La Ca	Pa Med Ald
7.155	παρὰ	πὰρ
8.7	φημί	φαμί
8.11	χρήσδεις τοῦτ᾽ ἐσιδεῖν (*ex* l. 12)	χρήσδεις δ᾽ ὦν᾽ ἐσιδεῖν
8.20	τοῦ	τῶ
8.28, 29	χ᾽ ὢ … χ᾽ ὢ	χ᾽ οἱ … χ᾽ οἱ
8.40	ἀγάγη	ἀγάγοι
8.41	πάντ᾽ ἔαρ	πάντα ἔαρ
8.42	πλήθουσι	πλήθουσιν
8.58	ὄρνισι	ὄρνισιν
8.87	κεφαλῆς	κεφαλᾶς
8.91	οὕτω	ὥς
9.3	βουσὶν	βωσὶν
9.6	ἄλλοθε δ᾽ αὖτις (αὖθις Ca)	ἄλλωθεν δὲ γ᾽
9.18	ποσσὶ	πρὸς ποσσὶ
9.27	κόγχῳ (κόχλῳ *in marg.*)	κόχλῳ
9.33	πλεῖος εἴη	εἴη πλεῖος
9.35	μὲν ὁρῶντι (γὰρ ὁρῶσαι Ca *in marg.*) κίρκη	γὰρ ὁρῶσαι (μὲν ὁρῶντι Pa *in marg.*) κίρκα
10.1	ὦζυρέ	οἰζυρέ
10.2	οὔθ᾽ ἐὸν	οὔτε τὸν
10.7	τεράμνῳ (ου *supra* ω La)	τεράμνου
10.8	συνέβα	συνέβη
10.11	χορίῳ	χορίων
10.15	τᾶν	τῶν
10.16	πρὶν	πρὰν
10.34	ἤ μᾶλον τὺ	ἤ τύγε μᾶλον

	M La Ca	Pa Med Ald
10.38	ἄμμε … ἐλελήθει	ἄμμι … ἐλελήθη
10.54	τὸν	τὼς
11.2	ἐμὶν	ἐμοὶ
11.8	Πολύφημος ὄκκ' (ὄτ' La supra lineam et in marg.)	Πολύφαμος ὄτ'
11.10	κικίννοις	κικίνοις
11.16	κύπριδος … πῆξε	κύπριος … πᾶξε
11.20	ἀπαλλωτέρα δ' ἀρνὸς ἀώρου	ἀπαλωτέρα δ' ἀρνὸς
11.23	ὄκκα	ὄκα
11.29	μέλλει	μέλει
11.32	θάτερον	θώτερον
11.42	ποτ' ἐμὲ	ποτὶ μὲ
11.53	ὦ μοι	τῷ μοι
11.64	ἐγὼ	ἐγὼν
12.3–4	ὅσον … ὅσον … ὅσον	ὅσσον … ὅσον … ὅσσον
12.33	ἐς	πρὸς
13.1	μούνοις	μόνοις
13.5	ὠμφι-	ἀμφι-
13.19	ἀνὴρ	om. ἀνὴρ
13.20	Ἀλκμήνης	Ἀλκμήνας
13.22	νηῦς	ναῦς
13.40	ἐν χώρῳ (ἐν χόρτῳ La in marg.)	ἐν χόρτῳ
13.50	ἐξαίφνης in marg.	
14.6	ὑποδήτος	ὑποδάτος
14.9	ποκα μανεὶς	μανεὶς ποκα
14.17	τις	om. τις

	M La Ca	Pa Med Ald
14.25	ἀπαλὸς (καλὸς *in marg.*)	καλὸς
14.29	οὖν	δ᾽ οὖν
14.48	θνατοί	θνητοί
14.54	ἁλικιώτας	ἡλικιώτας
14.55	κἠγὼν	κἠγὼ
14.60	τὰ δ᾽ ἄλλ᾽ ἀνὴρ	τἄλλα δ᾽ ἀνὴρ
14.68	κρατάφω	κροτάφων
15.4	ἀδειμάντου (ἀδειμάτου *in marg.*)	ἀδειμάτου
15.11	Δικῶνα τοιαῦτα	τοιαῦτα Δικῶνα (Διῶνα Med Ald)
15.17	ἦνθε	κἦνθε
15.21	τἄμπέχονον	τὤμπέχονον
15.44	ὅσος	ὅσσος
15.78	πρῶτον	πρᾶτον
15.84	ἀργυρέας	ἀργυρέῳ
15.85	κλισμοῦ	κλισμῷ
15.92	ὦ καὶ (ὡς καὶ *in marg.*) Βελλερεφόντης Πελλοπαναστὶ (βελλεροφῶν Πελοποννασιστὶ La *in marg.*)	ὡς καὶ βελλεροφῶν Πελοποννησιστὶ
15.104	βράδισται	βάρδισται
15.106	διωναίη ἀθάνατον (-αν *supra* -ον La)	διωναία ἀθάναταν
15.107	ἀνθρώπων	ὠνθρώπων
15.114	συρίου ... μύρου	συρίω ... μύρω
15.115	δ᾽	θ᾽

	M La Ca	Pa Med Ald
15.120	ὑπερποτῶνται	ὑπερποτοῶνται
15.146	γλυκύφωνος (γλυκὺ φωνεῖ *in marg.*)	γλυκύφωνος
15.149	χαῖρ' ... ἀφίκευ (ἀφίκευ M Ca *in marg.*)	χαῖρε ... ἀφίκνευ

Elsewhere, M coincides only with La against Ca, Pa, and both the *editio princeps* and the Aldina:

	M La	Ca Pa Med Ald
6.44	*om.* δὲ	δὲ
8.30	πρῶτος	πρᾶτος
9.9	ἐστὶ *om.* δέ μοι (δέ μοι La *in marg.*)	ἐντὶ δέ μοι
9.13	πρὸς πατρὸς	πατρὸς
10.9	δὲ	κὰ
10.33	κἀνεκείμεθα	τἀνακείμεθα
11.18	ἄειδε τοιαῦτα	τοιαῦτ' ἄειδεν
11.26	ἐμοὶ	ἐμᾷ
11.64	ἐγὼ	ἐγὼν
13.7	τοῦ ... τοῦ	τῶ ... τῶ
13.28	καθιδρυθέντες	καθιδρυνθέντες
13.40	θρύα (ι *supra* υ La)	θρία
14.20	δὲ (μὲν M *supra lineam*)	μὲν
14.64	βασιλῆα	βασιλῆ'
15.38	τοῦτο (ναὶ La *in marg.*)	ναὶ

Among the whole family of the Anonymus Parisinus, M and La undoubtedly have a special relationship. They are both related firstly to Ca and secondly to the other codices of this family and the first two printed editions. Pa, for its part, appears to be particularly closely related to these first two editions.

The number of coincidences between M and La is so high that it seems that M is in fact an apograph of La. They have very few discrepancies[61] and almost all of them can be explained as a consequence of a lack of care on the part of the copyist of M. This is the case with misspellings and omissions of words and lines, and with common mistakes such as confusion between o/ω, λ/λλ, and the absence or presence of ephelcystic -ν.

However, the copyist of M was no doubt using another manuscript as well, since for instance there is divergence in the hypothesis to *Id.* 11, where the copyist of La includes an allusion to Callimachus' epigram 46.1 and 3 (= *AP* 12.150.1 and 3), usually mentioned in the scholium to 11.2b.[62]

The interlinear Latin version is a word-for-word translation of no literary value.[63] It stops suddenly at the end of the fourth *Idyll* (f65v), although the remaining *Idylls* also have a blank interlinear space to accommodate the translation. Besides some sporadic omissions of words, there is a lacuna at *Id.* 2.136–137 [σὺν δὲ κακαῖς μανίαις ... ὡς ὁ μὲν εἶπεν], probably due to the fact that it is a reference to adultery, or because the omission of μανίαις in 136 makes the verse meaningless, and another at 4.10–49. Its first three lines run as follows:

> Dulce quodam sibilus et pinus, caprarie, illa
> quae iuxta fontes dulce sonat. Dulce autem et tu
> tibia canis. Post Pana secundum premium asportabis.

---

[61] For instance, at 5.57 M reads πολλάκις, while La and Ca have τετράκις. However, in La πολλάκις is added *in margine* as a correction twice, once by the same copyist of the main text, the other by another more recent hand (see f12v); at 7.40 La alone reads Σάμου, while the other witnesses, including M, have Σάμω, although M has ου *supra* ω as a correction.

[62] Also present in Ca, but absent from M and Pa.

[63] There are other manuscript translations still unpublished, such as those which can be read in mss. Ambrosianus C 274 inf., D 465 inf., Paduensis (Biblioteca del Seminario Vescovile) 598, Salmanticensis 71, Estensis lat. 1077, Marcianus lat. XIV 10 (4659), Herzog August Bib. 318, Universitatsbiblio. Basel f VI 40 , f VI 40b, Zurich Zentral Biblio. C 86.

They may be compared with Martinus Phileticus' version, published *circa* 1480 but composed several decades earlier:[64]

> Aepole dulce sonat patulis quod discolor aura
> commovet arboribus gelido quae fonte virescunt.
> Et tu dulce sonas grata resupinus in umbra:
> Mellifluo quotiens permulces aethera cantu.
> quo munus tu nempe feres post Pana secundum.

Ludovicus de Puppio's version appears to be an erudite exercise along the lines of those habitually done in class by pupils learning Greek. This is probably why it has some parallelism with the later versions by Joannes Trimaninus, dating from 1539 and also the fruit of his Greek exercises,[65] and that of the Venetian Andreas Divus (1539).[66] It shares with both some striking parallelisms which undoubtedly stem from a common origin, a Greek class where the learning method was word-for-word translation. These interlinear translations can also be detected in the translation by Vitus Winshemius, first published in 1558[67] but dating from several decades earlier,[68] which was to become the vulgate of Latin translations of Theocritus.

---

[64] See Arbizzoni 1993:25–31. This incunable appeared with no date or place of publication, but is usually dated to around the year 1482. An autograph manuscript copy of the first version is preserved in Paduensis (Biblioteca del Seminario Vescovile) 84, ff6v–9v, which is very different from the version that was finally printed. There are other manuscript copies which have the final version (ms. Vaticanus Urbinas Latinus 369 [olim 776] ff2–26, and Londinensis Harleianus 2578 ff95–123). It was reedited several times, at least in Milan (1483), by Simon Magniagus; in Venice (1499), by Bernardinus de Vitalibus; and twice in Paris with commentary (1503 and 1510), by Badius Ascensius.

[65] *Theocriti Syracusani opera latine a Ioanne Trimanino ad verbum diligentissime expressa* (Venetiis, 1539). The first three lines are as follows (f4v): *Iucundum quid susurrus, et pinus caprarie illa,* | *Quae iuxta fontes canit, iocundum avem et tu,* | *Canis: post Pana secundum praemium auferes.* See Castro 1998:116–117.

[66] *Theocriti Syracusani poetae clarissimi Idyllia trigintasex, recens e graeco in latinum, ad verbum translata,* Venetiis 1539. The first three lines are as follows (I follow the Basel edition of 1554, pp11–12): *Dulcem quendam susurrum et pinus caprarie illa* | *Quae apud fontes canit, dulce autem et tu* | *Fistula canis, post Pana secundum praemium auferes.*

[67] *Interpretatio Eidylliorum Theocriti dictata in Academia Witebergensi,* Francoforti, 1558. The first three lines are as follows (p. 6): *Dulcis hic susurrus est, et pinus ista, o pastor caprarie,* | *Quae iuxta fontes resonat, suaviter vero et tu* | *Fistula canis secundum Pana proximum praemium feres.*

[68] On a possible *editio princeps* of this translation *circa* 1536, see Castro 1998:121.

IV. ARISTOPHANES' *PLUTUS* AND *CLOUDS*

The presence of Aristophanes in this manuscript is not mentioned either by J. W. White or any of those who have added new witnesses to his list of manuscripts.[69] It should be added to the eight witnesses that White attributes to Spanish libraries.[70]

Plutus, with interlinear Latin translation (ff166–225v), has neither prolegomena nor scholia. It is preceded only by the epigram [Plato] 14, with original Latin translation below (f165v). This poem is often present at the end of the *Vitae Aristophanis*.[71] The copyist was probably using a manuscript with prolegomena which had this epigram at the end, and either he decided not to copy the *Vitae*, or they were by that time missing. Perhaps the copyist simply put off copying the prolegomena and for that reason left some blank pages before the *Plutus* (ff162–165). There are very few marginal glosses, and most of them are tags to assist with the Latin translation.

The text follows all the readings pointed to by M. R. di Blassi as characteristic of the *recentiores*, such as manuscripts Parisinus gr. 2712 (ca. 1300) (A), Ambrosianus L 39 sup. (ca. 1320) (M), Vaticanus Urb. Lat. 141 (U), and Laurentianus 31.16 (Δ),[72] and even coincides with them in the repetition of 260 after 280.[73] It is somehow more closely related to Δ, transcribed partly by Ioannes Skutariotes.[74] It shares with Δ some peculiar and exclusive readings: 230 δαιμόνων πάντων Πλοῦτε instead

---

[69] See White 1906:1–20. Gelzer 1961:28–29n9, Eberline 1980, Chantry 1996, and Galán Vioque 2009 add new witnesses to White's lists. Following White's accepted way of naming the numerous manuscripts of Aristophanes, this one should be Md5.

[70] White 1906:19–20. He mentions three manuscripts in the Royal Library of the Monastery of El Escorial (mss. Φ III 6, Y III 16, and Ω IV 7), two in the National Library (mss. 4677 and 4683), and another three in the University Library of Salamanca (mss. M 71, M 243 and M 284).

[71] It is found at the end of the *Vita* 29a, the *Vita Tzetziana*[2], and the *Vita Thomana* (see Van Leeuwen 1908:174, Koster 1957:140, 145, and 147).

[72] Blasi 1997:371–373.

[73] To this list of *recentiores*, Neapolitanus 184 (N) could also be added, since it shares all the readings pointed out by Blasi except 216, where N has κἄν. Curiously, at 454 it has καθάρματα, but the same copyist added an ε *supra* the last α, the reading of Marcianus gr. 474 (V), Ambrosianus C 222 inf (K), and Oxoniensis Holkhamensis gr. 88 (L).

[74] Skutariotes is responsible for ff1–154 (*Plutus* is on ff1–28; *Clouds*, with prolegomena, on ff28–60v). See Meyier 1958:285n5, Eberline 1980:9–10, Blasi 1994:125.

of Πλοῦτε πάντων δαιμόνων, 238 om. τῆς, 252 πρὸς σὲ οὐχὶ instead of οὐχὶ πρὸς σέ, 257 ἡμᾶς ὁρμωμένους instead of ὁρμωμένους ἡμᾶς, 284 om. γάρ, 300 om. δὲ, 946 τὸν ἰσχυρὸν τοῦτον θεὸν instead of τοῦτον τὸν ἰσχυρὸν θεὸν.[75]

In addition, this manuscript has been influenced by the Thoman–Triclinian recension,[76] though it is by no means a servile copy and more than once it does not accept Thoman–Triclinian readings.[77] Curiously, at *Pl.* 581 λήμαις there is a gloss with the reading of the Triclinian recension, γνώμαις, just as happens at Marcianus gr. 474 (V).

There also are in M peculiar and, as far as I know, exclusive mistakes, such as the transposition of 16 *post* 12 (with ὅστις instead of οὗτος), and the omission of αἰγῶν τε at 294, ἔπειτ' ... | ... ὁπὸν at 718–719, though ἔπειτ' ἔφλα is added later in another, darker ink.

---

[75] It has in common with A ταῦτα πάντα instead of πάντα ταῦτα, and with U 314 ὡς Ἀρίστυλος instead of Ἀρίστυλος. I have taken the data from Blasi 1997:367–371. M does not share any of these readings with N, except the omission of τῆς at 238.

[76] The distinction between both Byzantine recensions is difficult to establish, especially as regards the Thoman one (see Wilson 2007b:7–8). A short list of its traces in this manuscript will show that it is in fact full of Thoman–Triclinian readings (I have pointed out only the Thoman readings unanimously or almost unanimously accepted as such; I take the readings from Holzinger 1940:140, Coulon 1952, Koster 1957, and Wilson 2007a): 4 ταυτὰ (Th.), 90 ἐποίησεν (Th.), 119 τὰ τούτων μῶρ', ἔμ' εἰ, 176 ἀργύριος, 397 om. λέγω, 438 τίς οὖν φύγοι, 447 φευξούμεθα, 450 om. δ', 456 λοιδορεῖ, 465 ἀνθρώπους, 485 πράττοντ' ἢ τί γ' ἄν, 498–499 οὗτις· ἐγώ σοι τούτου μάρτυς· μηδὲν ταύτην γ' ἀνερώτα, 505 φήμ' ἤ, 586 κοτινῷ στεφάνῳ, 631 τρόπων, 673 ἀθάρης, 681 ταῦθ' ἥγιζεν, 688 δή μου, 707 ταῦτα δ' εὐθὺς ἐγὼ μὲν συνεκαλυψάμην, 765 σ' ἐκ κριβανωτῶν, 920 γ' ἄρα, 946 τὸν ἰσχυρὸν τοῦτον θεὸν, 957 ὡς, 964 ἔνδοθι (-εν supra ι), 983 ἱμάτιον γ', 993 νῦν γ' (om. ἔτι), 1011 νιττάριον, 1018 μ' ἔχειν, 1029 γ' ἀντευποιεῖν, 1044 ὕβρεος, 1055 παῖσαι, 1062 μέν γ' ἄν, 1096 προσίσχεται, 1099 σέ τοι σέ τοι, 1100 λέγω Καρίων, 1107 τί ἐστιν, 1147 ἀλλ' οὖν, 1205 ἄλλαις γάρ.

[77] See, for instance (in parentheses I add the Thoman–Triclinian reading), 77 ἦν (ἤ), 119 εἰδὼς (οἶδ' ὡς), 126 ἐὰν (ἐὰν γ'), 197 βιωτὸν αὐτῷ (βιωτὸν), 260 ὁ (γ' ὁ), 340 θαυμαστὸν (θαυμαστὸν γ'), 431 σοι τὸ βάραθρόν (τὸ βάραθρόν σοι), 452 οὗτος οἶδ' ὁ θεὸς (οὗτος ὁ θεὸς οἶδ'), 482 αὐτό (αὐτό γ'), 485 φθάνοιτε (φθάνοιτον), 504 πεινῶσι (πεινῶσιν), 511 οὔτ' ἄν τέχνην (οὔτε τέχνην ἄν), 528 οὔτ' ἐν (οὔτε), 547 πᾶσι (πᾶσιν), 550 φάτε εἶναι ὅμοιον (εἶναι ὅμοιον), 566 λαθεῖν αὐτὸν δεῖ (δεῖ λαθεῖν αὐτούς), 592 σ' (γε σ'), 598 γρύζης (γρύζειν), 607 χρή (χρήν), 707 μετὰ ταῦτα δ' εὐθὺς ἐγὼ (μετὰ ταῦτα γ' ἐγώ), 736 ὡς γ' (ὡς), 805a πρᾶγμά που (πρᾶγμά τι), 852 καὶ ἰοὺ (ἰοὺ), 892 πεπλησμένος (ἐμπεπλησμένος), 999 ἄμητα γε (ἄμητα τε), 1012 ἥτησ' ἄν (ἥτησεν ἄν σ'), 1018 παγκάλας (παγκάλους), 1111 om. δὴ (γε) 1161 τοίνυν (τοίνυν γ'), 1191 μάλ' (om. μάλ') and 1208 τοίνυν (τοίνυν γ').

As regards the interlinear Latin translation of *Plutus*, almost unknown until now,[78] it is one of the first complete translations of this play after that preserved in ms. Vindobonensis ph. gr. 204, dated 1458 and signed by Alexander of Otranto,[79] and perhaps the translation, still in manuscript form, by Pietro de Montagnana.[80] Previously, Rinuccio Aretino and Leonardo Bruni, the latter probably in collaboration with Giovanni Tortelli, had made partial translations, the first of 400-629, the so-called *fabula Penia*, written *circa* 1414–1416 and a recreation rather than an actual translation, and the second of 1-239, *circa* 1439.[81] Later, the Latin translations of this comedy enjoyed great fortune, being published more than fifty times before 1550.[82]

Ludovicus' version is a word-for-word translation and it is apparently not indebted to its predecessors. The first two lines run as follows: *Quam molesta res est, o Iuppiter et dii,* | *servum fieri insani heri.* They may be compared with Bruni's translation, *Ut permolesta res est, o Ζεῦ, o dei, servum fieri disipientis domini,* and Alexander of Otranto's, *Valde dura res est, Iuppiter et o dii,* | *servum fieri insipientis domini.*[83] There are some curious parallels between this translation and the later one by Andrea Divus, published in Basel in 1539. Compare, for instance, the first two lines (the rest continues in a similar vein): *Quam molesta res est, o Iuppiter et Dij,* | *servum fieri desipientis heri.*[84]

[78] I have found no mention of this translation in the bibliography either on Aristophanes and his transmission or on translation in the Renaissance. It is not even mentioned in Kristeller's famous survey of Renaissance manuscripts (Kristeller 1963–1997). There is only a brief mention in Vieillefond's article (1935) and Andrés' catalogue (1987).

[79] Subscriptio on f110v. See Holzinger 1912:69–76, Hunger 1961:113, Chirico 1991.

[80] Marcianus lat. XIV 10 [4659], ff41–65v. See Wilson 1992:115, 2007:11. For bibliography on this humanist, see Porro 1992:343n1 (with a reproduction of f67 of this manuscript at 362).

[81] See Creizenach 1904:385–386; Lockwood 1909:lvi, 1913:57–76, 1931:163–172; Cecchini and Cecchini 1965; Cecchini and Cassio 1972; Ludwig 1979:667–674; and Wilson 1992:30–31, 2007b:11.

[82] See Süss 1911:23n13, Giannopoulou 2007:309–342 (an exhaustive list on pp312–340), and Van Kerchove 1974:42–127.

[83] See Cecchini and Cecchini 1965:5, Chirico 1991:81.

[84] See Divus 1539:7.

Clouds is preceded by prolegomena and an *index personarum* (ff226–292v). It belongs to the second group pointed to by K. J. Dover, particularly group (a) (i), alongside Neapolitanus 184 (N)[85] and Vindobonensis ph. gr. 227 (Z).[86] Especially remarkable is the coincidence of the *Clouds* of this manuscript with N, a Farnesian manuscript of the second half of the fifteenth century attributed to the hand of Ioannes Skutariotes, the copyist of Δ.[87] They both have the same prolegomena, A1 and A5, with exactly the same readings, including the omissions. Besides, they present the characters in the same order and with the same words. In the text there are striking coincidences that are by no means fortuitous. In fact, M follows all the readings pointed out by Dover as exclusive to N, including the curious addition of a line after 1301 and the positioning of 1188 *post* 1190, except for 172 κεχηνότος (κεχηνάτος),[88] 267 καταβραχῶ (καταβρεχῶ), 604 λαγεῖς (σελαγεῖς), and 1083 πιθόμενός (πυθόμενός). Thus, they probably share the same ancestor, or if one was copied from the other, M is the apographon because it transposes lines into the wrong order (330–331 [331–330 M], 58–59 [59–58 M], and 1327–1328 [1328–1327 M]), it includes mistakes absent from N (1326 μάλα codd. : τοιχωρύχε M *ex* 1327), and it omits lines present in N (538–540, 597–599 om. ἤ τ' ... | ... οἶκον, 851, 901).

As is the case with the *Plutus*, the *Clouds* of this codex has traces of the Thoman–Triclinian recension, though not to the same extent.[89] There are very few readings peculiar to the Thoman–Triclinian recension, certainly fewer than in the *Plutus*. A quick look at Wilson's *apparatus* reveals that there are some instances in which N, and thus also M, coincides with Oxoniensis Holkhamensis gr. 88 (L) exclusively. However, a full collation shows that M follows neither any of the Thoman read-

---

[85] Its signature is II F 27 (Np2 in White). I have found no references, either in the catalogs or in the editions, to the fact that this manuscript has one quire misbound, so that ff31–40v, containing 508–1007, mistakenly come before ff41–50v, with 30–507.

[86] See Dover 1968:cxxiv.

[87] See Blasi 1994:125. Dover erroneously assigned it to the fourteenth century (1968:ciii).

[88] In parentheses I add the reading of N.

[89] On the presence of different recensions in one and the same manuscript, see Dover 1968:cix n1: "Since many manuscripts demonstrably change their affinities in the course of the same play, a fortiori one cannot argue from play to play."

ings pointed out by Wilson in his edition nor the Triclinian readings mentioned in his 1962 article: 115 τἀδικώτερα (τἀδικώτατα),[90] 274 ὑπακούσατε (ἐπακούσατε), 287 μαρμαρέαις ἐν (μαρμαρέαισιν ἐν), 471 εἰς λόγους (ἐς λόγον), 786 om. νῦν, 1029 οἵ τε ζῶντες, τότ' ἐπὶ τῶν προτέρον (τότε ζῶντες ἡνίκ' ἧς τῶν προτέρον), 1231 ἄλλο γ' ἄν (ἀλλ' ἄν). This tendency is confirmed throughout the comedy and shows that it follows Triclinian readings in only a very few passages. Not for nothing did Dover state that N, whose relation with our codex has already been pointed out, "shows no trace of Thoman or Triclinian influence."[91]

In conclusion, this hitherto neglected codex should be taken into account in future studies on the Palamas controversy and on the manuscript reception of Aesop, the *Batrachomyomachia*, Theocritus, and Aristophanes, in order at least to obtain a full perspective of their transmission, including their late witnesses. The manuscript is especially interesting because of the Latin translations it contains, since they appear to be among the first ever done of both Aristophanes' *Nubes* and Theocritus' first four *Idylls*. In fact, the Ludovicus de Puppio section seems to be a fifteenth-century Italian humanist textbook for the study of Greek, since it focuses on the texts used in schools, where the practice of interlinear translation into Latin was highly recommended to improve students' command of both Greek and Latin. It is no doubt a witness to its author's interest in learning Greek, and the only testimony of his Greek writing.

UNIVERSITY OF HUELVA

---

[90] In parentheses I add the reading of the Triclinian edition, following Wilson's *apparatus*.

[91] Dover 1968:cvii n1.

This article was written during a research stay at Clare Hall, University of Cambridge. It forms part of the Research Project "Edición crítica y traducción anotada de los *Idilios* de Teócrito, II" (FFI2008–00940) and P09–HUM 4534 de la Junta de Andalucía. I would like to thank Professor Richard Hunter for his amiability, the librarians of the Mss. Department of the National Library of Spain and those of the Vatican Apostolic Library for their kindness and cooperation, and Mr. J. J. Zoltowski for revising the English version.

WORKS CITED

Achelis, T. 1928. "Die hundert Fabeln des Rinucci da Castiglione." *Philologus* 83:55–88.

Ahrens, H. L. 1855–1859. *Bucolicorum Graecorum Theocriti Bionis Moschi reliquiae.* 2 vols. Leipzig.

———. 1874. "Über einige alte Sammlungen der theokritischen Gedichte." *Philologus* 33:577–609.

Allen, T. W. 1983. *Homeri Opera.* 5 vols. Oxford (orig. pub. 1912).

Andrés, G. de. 1987. *Catálogo de los códices griegos de la Biblioteca Nacional.* Madrid.

Arbizzoni, G. 1993. "Note su Martino Filetico traduttore di Teocrito." *Studi umanistici piceni* 13:25–31.

Bertalot, L. 1985. *Initia humanistica latina.* Vol. 1, *Poesie.* Tübingen.

Blasi, M. R. di. 1994. "Studi sulla tradizione manoscritta di Aristofane [I]." *Bolletino dei classici* 15:123–141.

———. 1997. "Studi sulla tradizione manoscritta del *Pluto* di Aristofane. Parte II: I codici recentiores." *Maia* 49:367–380.

Boese, H. 1966. *Die lateinischen Handschriften der Sammlung Hamilton zu Berlin.* Wiesbaden.

Castro de Castro, D. 1998. *La traducción latina de los "Idilios de Teócrito" de Vicente Mariner.* PhD diss., University of Murcia.

Cecchini, E., and A. C. Cassio. 1972. "Due contributi sulla traduzione di Leonardo Bruni del *Pluto* di Aristofane." *Giornale italiano di filologia* 24:472–482.

Cecchini, M., and E. Cecchini. 1965. *Leonardo Bruni. Versione del Pluto di Aristofane.* Florence.

Chambry, E. 1925–1926. *Aesopi fabulae.* 2 vols. Paris.

Chantry, M. 1996. *Scholia in Aristophanem.* Vol. 3, Fasc 4b., *Scholia recentiora in Aristophanis Plutum.* Groningen.

Chirico, M. L. 1991. *Aristofane in terra d'Otranto.* Naples.

Coppini, D. 1990. *Antonii Panhormitae Hermaphroditus.* Rome.

Coulon, V. 1952. *Aristophane.* Vol. 1, *Les acharniens, Les cavaliers, Les nuées.* 5th ed. Paris.

Creizenach, W. 1904. "Die Aristophanes-Übersetzung des Leonardo Aretino." *Studien zur vergleichenden Literaturgeschichte* 4:385–386.

Divus, A. 1539. *Aristophanis comœdiæ undecim e Grœco in Latinum ad uerbum translatæ.* Basel.

Dover, K. J. 1968. *Aristophanes. Clouds.* Oxford.

Eberline, C. N. 1980. *Studies in the Manuscript Tradition of the Ranae of Aristophanes.* Meisenheim am Glan.

Fryde, E. B. 1996. *Greek Manuscripts in the Private Library of the Medici 1469–1510.* 2 vols. Aberystwyth.

Galán Vioque, G. 2009. "Notes on an Unknown Witness of the Mixed Thoman–Triclinian Recension of Aristophanes." *Hermes* 137:252–259.

Gallavotti, C. 1936. "Da Planude e Moscopulo alla prima edizione a stampa di Teocrito." *Studi italiani di filologia classica* 13:45–59.

———. 1993. *Theocritus quique feruntur bucolici Graeci.* 3rd ed. Rome (orig. pub. 1946).

Garin, E. 1914. "La *expositio Theocriti* di Angelo Poliziano nello Studio Fiorentino (1482–83?)." *Rivista di filologia e di istruzione classica* 42:275–282.

———. 1958. *Il pensiero pedagogico dello Umanesimo.* Florence.

Gelzer, T. 1961. Review of Koster 1957. *Gnomon* 33:26–34.

Giannopoulou, V. 2007. "Aristophanes in Translation before 1920." In *Aristophanes in Performance*, ed. E. Hall and A. Wrigley, 309–342. Oxford.

Glei, R. 1984. *Die Batrachomyomachie: Synoptische Edition und Kommentar.* Frankfurt.

Gow, A. S. F. 1950. *Theocritus.* 2 vols. Cambridge.

Grafton, A. T., and L. Jardine. 1982. "Humanism and the School of Guarino: A Problem of Evaluation." *Past and Present* 96:51–80.

Hain, L. 1826–1838. *Repertorium bibliographicum, in quo libri omnes ab arte typographica inventa usque ad annum MD.* 4 vols. Stuttgart.

Hamilton, W. A. 1882. *Catalogue of the Magnificent Collection of Manuscripts from Hamilton Palace.* London.

Hausmann, F. R. 1980. "*Carmina priapea.*" In *Catalogus translationum et commentariorum*, ed. F. R. Cranz and P. O. Kristeller, vol. 4, 423–450. Washington.

Hausrath, A. 1927. Review of Chambry 1925–1926. *Philologische Wochenschrift* 47:1537–1546, 1569–1575.

———. 1957. *Corpus fabularum Aesopicarum.* 2 vols. Leipzig.

Hicks, P. G. 1993. *Studies in the Manuscript Tradition of Theocritus.* PhD diss., University of Cambridge.

Hiller, E. 1888. *Beiträge zur Textgeschichte der griechischen Bukoliker.* Leipzig.

Holzinger, K. 1912. *Die Aristophaneshandschriften der Wiener Hofbibliothek: Ein Beitrag zur Systematik der Aristophaneshandschriften.* Vol. 2. *Sitzungsberichte der kaiserlichen Akademie der Wissenschaften in Wien, philosophisch-historische Klasse* 169.4. Vienna.

———. 1940. *Kritisch-exegetischer Kommentar zu Aristophanes'* Plutos. *Sitzungsberichte der Akademie der Wissenschaften in Wien, philosophisch-historische Klasse* 218.3. Vienna.

Hunger, H. 1961. *Katalog der griechischen Handschriften der österreichischen Nationalbibliothek.* Vol. 1, *Codices historici, codices philosophici et philologici.* Vienna.

Iriarte, J. de. 1769. *Regiae bibliothecae Matritensis codices Graeci manuscripti.* Madrid.

Jackson, D. F. 1999–2000. "An Old Book List Revisited: Greek Manuscripts of Janus Lascaris from the Library of Cardinal Niccolò Ridolfi." *Manuscripta* 43/44:77–134.

Kerchove, D. van 1974. "The Latin Translation of Aristophanes' *Plutus* by Hadrianus Chilius, 1533." *Humanistica Lovaniensia* 23:42–127.

Korais, A. 1810. *Μύθων Αἰσωπείων συναγωγή.* Paris.

Koster, W. J. W. 1957. *Autour d'un manuscrit d'Aristophane écrit par Démetrius Triclinius.* Groningen.

Kristeller, P. O. 1963–1997. *Iter Italicum: A Finding List of Uncatalogued or Incompletely Catalogued Humanistic Manuscripts.* 7 vols. London.

Laemmer, H. 1875. *Meletematum Romanorum mantissa.* Regensburg.

Leeuwen, J. van. 1908. *Prolegomena ad Aristophanem.* Leiden.

Lockwood, D. P. 1909. "Aristophanes in the XVth century." *TAPA* 40:lvi.

———. 1913. "*De Rinucio Aretino Graecarum litterarum interprete.*" *HSCP* 24:51–109.

———. 1931. "Leonardo Bruni's Translation of Act I of the *Plutus* of Aristophanes." In *Classical Studies in Honor of John C. Rolfe,* ed. G. D. Hadzsits, 163–172. Philadelphia.

Ludwich, A. 1894. *De codicibus Batrachomachiae dissertatio.* Kaliningrad.

———. 1896. *Die Homerische Batrachomachia des Karers Pigre: Nebst Scholien und Paraphrase.* Leipzig.

Ludwig, W. 1979. "Die 'Penia fabula' des Rinuccio da Castiglione: Ein Beitrag zur Rezeption des Aristophanes und Theokrit in der Renaissance." In *Acta conventus neo-latini amstelodamensis: Proceedings of the Second International Congress of Neo-Latin Studies, Amsterdam, 19–24 August 1973,* ed. P. Tuynman, G. C. Kuiper, and E. Kessler, 667–674. Munich.

Marc, P. 1910. "Die Überlieferung des Äsopromans." *Byzantinische Zeitschrift* 19:383–421.

Mercati, G. 1931. *Notizie di Procoro e Demetrio Cidone, Manuele Caleca e Teodoro Melitiniota: Ed altri appunti per la storia della teologia e della letteratura bizantina del secolo XIV.* Vatican City.

———. 1938. *Codici latini Pico Grimani Pio e di altra biblioteca ignota del secolo XVI esistenti nell'Ottoboniana e i codici greci Pio di Modena.* Vatican City.

Meyier, K. A. de. 1958. "Une contribution importante à l'histoire du texte du *De mysteriis* de Jamblique." *Scriptorium* 12:284–289.

Mioni, E. 1964. *Catalogo di manoscritti greci esistenti nelle biblioteche italiane.* Rome.

Percival, W. K. 2004. "A Working Edition of the *Carmina Differentialia* by Guarino Veronese." In *Studies in Renaissance Grammar,* 155–177. Aldershot (= 1994. *Res Publica Litterarum* 17:153–177).

Perosa, A. 1952. Review of *Poliziano, Epigrammi greci,* by A. Ardizzoni. *Parola del passato* 7:66–80.

———. 1955. *Mostra del Poliziano nella Biblioteca Medicea Laurenziana: Manoscritti, libri rari, autografi e documenti; Firenze 23 settembre–30 novembre 1954, Catalogo.* Florence.

———. 2000. "Sugli epigrammi greci del Poliziano." In *Studi di filologia umanistica: I. Angelo Poliziano,* ed. P. Viti, 83–101. Rome.

Perry, B. E. 1934. "The Greek Source of Rinuccio's Aesop." *CP* 29:53–62.

———. 1981. *Studies in the Text History of the Life and Fables of Aesop.* Ann Arbor (orig. pub. Oxford, 1936).

Porro, A. 1992. "La versione latina dell' Ecuba euripidea attribuita a Pietro da Montagnana." In *Dotti bizantini e libri greci nell' Italia del* secolo XV: Atti del convegno internazionale Trento 22-23 ottobre 1990, ed. M. Cortesi, E. V. Maltese, 343–353. Naples.

Reeve, M. D. 1983. "*Priapea*." In *Texts and Transmission: A Survey of the Latin Classics*, ed. L. D. Reynolds and N. G. Wilson, 322–323. Oxford.

Reichling, D. 1905–1911, *Appendices ad Hainii-Copingeri Repertorium bibliographicum*. 7 vols. Munich.

Rigo, A. 1988. "L'epistola a Menas di Gregorio Palamas e gli effetti dell' orazione." *Cristianesimo nella storia* 9:57–80.

Ruipérez, M. S. 1950. "El manuscrito de Teócrito del Códice griego núm. 230 de la Universidad de Salamanca." *Emerita* 18:70–88.

Ruysschaert, J., et al. 1997. *I codici latini datati della Biblioteca apostolica vaticana: Nei fondi Archivio S. Pietro, Barberini, Boncompagni, Borghese, Borgia, Capponi, Chigi, Ferrajoli, Ottoboni*. Vatican City.

Süss, W. 1911. *Aristophanes und die Nachwelt*. Leipzig.

Torné Teixido, R. 2001. "El Matritense B. N. 4697: Estudio del texto de la Batracomiomaquia." *Cuadernos de filología clásica (Estudios griegos e indoeuropeos)* 11:280–285.

Vieillefond, J. R. 1935. "Complemento al catálogo de manuscritos griegos de la Biblioteca Nacional de Madrid." *Emerita* 3:193–213.

Voordeckers, E. 1967–1968. *Johannes VI Kantakuzenos, Kaiser (1347-1354) en monnik (1354-1383). Bijdrage tot de geschiedenis van de Byzantijnse Kerk in de XIVe eeuw*. PhD diss., Ghent University.

Wendel, C. 1920. *Überlieferung und Entstehung der Theokrit-Scholien*. Berlin.

White, J. W. 1906. "The Manuscripts of Aristophanes. I." *CP* 1:1–20.

Wilamowitz, U. von. 1906. *Die Textgeschichte der griechischen Bukoliker*. Berlin.

Wilson, N. G. 1962. "The Triclinian Edition of Aristophanes." *CQ*, n.s., 12:32–47.

———. 1992. *From Byzantium to Italy: Greek Studies in the Italian Renaissance*. London.

———. 2007a. *Aristophanis fabulae*. 2 vols. Oxford.

———. 2007b. *Aristophanea: Studies on the Text of Aristophanes*. Oxford.

Wölke, H. 1978. *Untersuchungen zur Batrachomyomachie*. Meisenheim am Glan.

THE DATES OF THE DRAMATISTS
OF THE *FABULA TOGATA*

Jarrett T. Welsh

V ery little information survives from antiquity about the lives and careers of the three republican dramatists who composed *fabulae togatae*. Their names—Titinius, L. Afranius, and T. Quinctius Atta—are preserved, but for not one of the three are we told a year of birth, a city of origin, or a period of especial celebrity. We are almost as completely uninformed about their deaths; only for Atta can we state that he died at Rome in 77 BC and was buried near the second milestone on the Via Praenestina.[1] Faced with this lack of information, students of the genre have extracted evidence about the poets from vague synchronisms, textual corruptions, alleged references to contemporary events, and silence. Over the past two centuries, dates that were advanced as guesses have acquired an authority that far exceeds what their merits permit. Scholars convinced of the greater reliability of one piece of evidence or another have proposed divergent estimates for the periods in which Titinius and Afranius worked, while the date of Atta's death has passed as sufficient evidence for his career, prompting no further discussion.

Settling the question of when the three dramatists were writing is important to several inquiries about the history of the genre. Principal

Fragments of republican comedy are cited according to Ribbeck 1898. I am grateful to R. J. Tarrant, R. F. Thomas, and E. Dench, who read early versions of the arguments in this paper and provided helpful comments and guidance. The journal's anonymous reader and the editor provided valuable criticism.

[1] Jerome *Chron.* ad 77 BC: *olympiade CLXXV, anno tertio, T. Quinticius Atta scriptor togatarum Romae moritur, sepultusque via Praenestina ad miliarium II.* (Not born in 77 BC, a mistake in the entries in *Der neue Pauly* s.vv. *Quinctius* [I 4] and *Togata.*) The circular tomb known as the *Torr(i)one prenestino* was once regularly identified as the tomb of Atta, but it belongs to a later date; see Ashby 1902:152–153 and Pietrangeli 1940.

among these has been the question of the origin of the *togata* and what relationship it had to the *palliata*.[2] Chronological problems are also crucial to our understanding of the continued development of the genre after its debut. The ability to situate the comedies of Titinius, Afranius, and Atta in their historical contexts and to understand their relationship to developments at Rome in the second century BC would be of equal interest and importance. Voices of imposing authority have rightly forbidden such attempts in the past,[3] but establishing the chronology of the dramatists as securely as possible would provide a basis for investigating the *togata* and its cultural contexts.

This paper therefore aims to reexamine the evidence that has piled up haphazardly concerning the chronologies of Titinius, Afranius, and Atta. Its attitude is radically skeptical. Little of that evidence has anything to do with chronologically precise statements about the lives or careers of the dramatists, and, further, many popular interpretations of that evidence are plainly wrong. This paper seeks progress by setting the chronology of the dramatists on as stable a foundation as possible. The conclusions it reaches are more vague and expansive than the exact statements that currently prevail; false precision has been sacrificed for the sake of what I hope will be judged greater reliability.

I. TITINIUS

We will never know very much about Titinius,[4] owing to the silence of ancient authorities about his life and place of birth.[5] Opinions about the

---

[2]   Pociña and López (2001:178–182) summarize the highlights of past contributions to this debate. Donatus' claim (*De comoedia* 5.4) that Livius Andronicus invented the *togata* is unreliable, as are the suspicions (of, e.g., Leo [1913:92]) that Naevius' *Ariolus* was a *togata*. These suspicions were based on references to Roman, Latin, or Italian customs in the Naevian fragments, but Plautus also made such comments (e.g., *Bacch.* 12; *Cas.* 71–72; *Trin.* 545–546, 609; *Truc.* 690–691). Daviault (1981:17–19), however, states that either Livius or Naevius undoubtedly invented the *togata*.

[3]   Jocelyn 1982:156–157 and 1986:609; cf. Gratwick 1982:726–727.

[4]   Older scholarship identified his name as Vectius or Vettius Titinius, a mistake based on Serenus Sammonicus *De medicina* 1046 (*alia praecepit Titini sententia necti*), where *vecti* was read for *necti*. Neukirch (1833:97–98) provides a convenient doxography.

[5]   Two speculative theories about the playwright's birthplace enjoy some currency. Less plausibly, Neukirch (1833:100) and Daviault (1981:31–32) claims that Titinius was

chronology of the dramatist are deeply divided. According to current theories he was active either as early as 219 BC, and a radical[6] innovator in the field of Roman drama; or around the middle of the second century BC, less radical but still the inventor of a new genre of scenic performance; or at the end of the second century BC, following in the footsteps of Afranius and no innovator at all, but rather an incorrigible archaist.[7] Three passages have been interpreted to provide support for each of the three theories: (i) Lydus *De magistratibus* 1.40; (ii) Charisius p. 315.3–6; and (iii) Fronto 1.7.4. I treat these passages in detail because their significance for the playwright's chronology is regularly overstated, while a skeptical reconsideration shows that the first and third are irrelevant, and that the second has been given credit for a greater degree of precision than it deserves.

According to a widely accepted interpretation of his account of the Roman censorship (*De magistratibus* 1.39–43), Johannes Laurentius Lydus thought that Titinius presented a comedy in 219 BC. Lydus' history of the censorship is, even on a charitable interpretation, bizarre; it includes digressions on Roman drama (1.40–41) and on the etymology of *nepos* (1.42), which are flanked by two conflicting accounts of the censorship. At the head of the digression on Roman drama occurs the following sentence in the earliest manuscript (1.40):

---

born in Rome because we are not told otherwise, in contrast to other early authors. The silence of ancient authorities about the birthplaces of Titinius, Afranius, and Atta tells us less about their cities of origin than it does about how uninterested late republican scholars were in investigating the lives of the dramatists. Rather more worthy of consideration, although ultimately no less speculative (cf. n64), is the idea of Mommsen (1850:319) that Titinius came from the area of southern Latium in which lay Setia, Ferentinum, and Velitrae (which gave rise to titles of his plays). That idea is expanded upon but not proven by Rawson (1985:106–107 = 1991:479–480). Mommsen's suggestion that behind †ilarubra† (Nonius p. 476.32) lies *Ulubrana* would, if correct, add a fourth title connected to the same region.

  [6] Those who put Titinius' debut so early do not always appreciate what that dating implies; cf. Gratwick 1982:726–727: Titinius would be the "first to specialize in a single genre and the first to have a consistent and unflamboyant policy in naming his plays with simple adjectives, ethnics, and nouns like a New Comedy dramatist."

  [7] For the chronological claims, contrast *OCD*[3] s.v. *Titinius* (P. G. McC. Brown) with *Der neue Pauly* s.v. *Titinius* [1] (P. L. Schmidt) and Beare 1964:120.

τό τετίνιος ὁ Ῥωμαῖος κωμικὸς μῦθον ἐπεδείξατο ἐν τῇ Ῥώμῃ.

Several conjectures have been proposed to heal the garbled τό τετίνιος. Students of Lydus' text have generally hewn closely to the paradosis in reading τότε Τίνιος or τότε Τιτίνιος,[8] while students of Roman literature have regarded those readings with greater skepticism.[9] J. H. Neukirch (1833:98–99) bluntly rejected the restoration of Titinius to Lydus' text, certain instead that it referred to Livius Andronicus; this opinion remained dominant in the nineteenth century.[10]

The opening years of the twentieth century saw a vigorous defense of the reading τότε Τιτίνιος and of Lydus' reliability. Wünsch connected τότε and the beginning of Titinius' dramatic activity to the invasion of Hannibal in 219 BC.[11] He argued that Lydus had inserted material into an original framework in which τότε referred back to the discussion of the dictatorship, and specifically to the creation of an ἀντιδικτάτωρ and an ἀνθιππάρχης (allegedly to balance the powers of the *dictator* and the *magister equitum*), when Hannibal was preparing to invade Italy (Ἀννίβου ἐνσκήψαντος τῇ Ἰταλίᾳ, διὰ τὸν ὄγκον τοῦ πολέμου οὐ μόνον δικτάτωρ ἀλλὰ καὶ ἀντιδικτάτωρ, ἱππάρχης τε καὶ ἀνθιππάρχης προεχειρίσθησαν, 1.38.12); when he expanded that original chrono-logical framework, Lydus inadvertently separated τότε from its precise referent, the invasion of Hannibal, and thereby caused the obscu-rity. Such an explanation of Lydus' account seems strained. One may ask why τότε should refer to that point, when Hannibal's invasion is followed by discussion of Caesar's dictatorship (1.38.13), and when, in turning to the censorship, Lydus starts anew from the beginning of Roman history (ἀνέκαθεν, 1.39.1). No connection to the selection of a

---

[8] τότε Τίνιος Fuss 1812 and Bekker 1837; the former (1812:69n4) suggested the possi-bility of reading τότε Τιτίνιος while acknowledging that Lydus would have been in error; cf. Zorzetti 1975:434–435.

[9] τότε Λίβιος, Reuvens 1815:27–29 and Osannus 1816:44; Marx (1888–1889:13) suspected that Lydus was in error. Bandy (1983:279) misreports what Marx meant.

[10] See Ritschl 1845:194–196 and Courbaud 1899:29–31.

[11] Wünsch (1903:xxxv), expanding on a suggestion made by Reuvens (1815:26). Weinstock (1937:1541), Vereecke (1968:63 and 1971:156–157), Carney (1971), Pociña Pérez (1975:87), Daviault (1981:32–33), Bandy (1983), López López (1983:165), and Karakasis (2005:222) follow Wünsch's Hannibalic dating.

dictator to fight Hannibal is made or implied; that a reader would be expected to make such a connection seems implausible. The question is at something of an impasse; no emendation can be persuasive without also explaining the logic of this passage and the year meant by τότε, if τότε is to be read.

A neglected detail in Lydus' account may yet solve this puzzle. I would argue that the answer was suggested long ago by the students of Roman literature who made Lydus refer to Livius Andronicus, but that we can improve upon the arguments from probability offered by Neukirch and by Zorzetti.[12] Lydus' account of the censorship opens with this compressed synopsis:

> ὁ δῆμος ἀνέκαθεν καὶ σύμπαν ἁπλῶς τὸ πολίτευμα
> ἐστρατεύετο, καὶ αὐτῶν τῶν ἱερέων τοῖς πολεμίοις
> ἐπεξιόντων· καὶ πάντες ἀπέτρεφον ἑαυτούς. ἐδέησε τοίνυν
> Ῥωμαίοις προβαλέσθαι τοὺς λεγομένους παρ' αὐτοῖς
> κήνσορας, οἳ τὰς τῶν πολιτῶν οὐσίας ἀπεγράφοντο διὰ
> τὰς ἐν πολέμῳ δαπάνας· οὔπω γάρ, ὡς νῦν, τὸ δημόσιον
> ἐχορήγει τοῖς στρατιώταις, οἷα οὐκ ὄντων αὐτοῖς τέως
> ὑποτελῶν. ὅθεν τοὺς κήνσορας Ἕλληνες τιμητὰς καθ'
> ἑρμηνείαν ἐκάλεσαν. (1.40) Τότε Τιτίνιος

De magistratibus 1.39–40

The time referred to by τότε (1.40.1) may perhaps be recovered with a simpler explanation than that proposed by Wünsch. Lydus states that the censors were appointed to supervise the collection of revenue in time of war, since Rome up to that time had not had tribute-paying subjects (1.39.2, οἷα οὐκ ὄντων αὐτοῖς τέως ὑποτελῶν). Several centuries of history have been run together and the resulting account is compressed, but that detail about the tribute seems important. It suggests that Lydus had in mind the treatment of Sicily as a Roman

---

[12] Zorzetti (1975), following a suggestion of Tanaşoca (1969), offers other reasons for doubting Wünsch's interpretation and for suspecting that Lydus could only refer to Livius Andronicus, but proposes no solution for the synchronism; Guardì (1984:18 with n22) follows his lead.

province after 241 BC and the tributes extracted from it,[13] which would clarify what prompted his digression on Roman drama. He followed the standard history of Roman drama that identified its origin in Livius Andronicus' premiere in 240 BC. It is therefore probably best to restore τότε Λίβιος, but it is also possible that Lydus simply had the wrong name.

The second passage made to offer evidence about Titinius' chronology is preserved by Charisius and descends ultimately from Varro (Charisius p. 315.3–6):

> ἤθη, ut ait Varro de Latino sermone libro V, nullis aliis (*Ritschl*: nullus ali *N*) servare convenit, inquit, quam Titinio Terentio Attae; πάθη (*Keil*: atte pathe *N*: at τὰ πάθη *C*) vero Trabea, inquit, Atilius Caecilius facile moverunt.

Nowhere, admittedly, do Varro or his followers state anything about the chronology of the poets listed. Neukirch (1833:99) was the first to speculate that Varro's lists were ordered chronologically, thereby making Titinius earlier than Terence. He could imagine no reason why Titinius should be placed ahead of Terence, unless Varro had been guided by chronology. This guess was less secure than it might even now appear, for Neukirch could not point to the priority of Terence to Atta to bolster his claim about Titinius. The edition of Charisius that he knew did not print *Attae* at all, but omitted the corrupted text between *Terentio* and πάθη.[14]

The only new evidence for Neukirch's theory came from Keil's restoration, at *Gramm. Lat.* I 241.28, of the name of Atta. That Atta was named after Terence, yielding the sole chronological relationship known from other evidence, accorded with, but did not prove, Neukirch's theory. But the same pattern is evident in the second list of dramatists, and the argument applies to it as well. Trabea and Atilius are shadowy figures in the history of the *palliata* and no other evidence about the periods in which they wrote survives.[15] There is little reason

---

[13] Serrati (2000) offers a good *point d'entrée* to the taxation of Sicily after 241 BC.

[14] Neukirch 1833:99, quoting the text from Van Putschen 1605: col. 215.

[15] See Wright 1974:67 and 70.

to put the two obscure dramatists ahead of Caecilius Statius, who was widely revered in the second and first centuries BC.[16]

Neukirch (1833:99–100), however, took his speculation further. He claimed that the tense of the verb that he read in Charisius (πάθη *vero Trabea, inquit, Atilius Caecilius facile moverant*, taken from Van Putschen 1605) implied that the careers of these three dramatists preceded those in the first triad, which would effectively confine Titinius' career to the short period between Caecilius Statius and Terence. This argument proceeded from an error in the *editio princeps* of Charisius that was replicated in subsequent editions; the manuscripts read *moverunt*.[17] But Neukirch's argument is also wrong on other grounds, for it misses Varro's point. These two lists contrast comic dramatists who paid attention to and preserved consistent characterization with those who easily stirred emotions and thereby created inconsistency. Varro was pointing out differences in language and style, and how they were used to dramatic effect; the traces of the continuation of Varro's discussion, now represented by four quotations from Terence and by two quotations from unknown tragic scripts (Charisius p. 315.7–23), show that Varro was not, in this instance, concerned with presenting a unified chronology of republican dramatists. He was focused, as the title of *De Latino sermone* suggests, on language and on the representation of character and emotion through language. Therefore, although one must reject the second step of Neukirch's argument, the first remains unaffected, so that only the sequence *Titinio Terentio Attae* bears upon the chronology of Titinius.

A general chronological arrangement therefore seems to prevail in Varro's lists of dramatists, making Titinius somehow anterior to Terence. But in what way? We are not told whether the dramatists are arranged by age, making Titinius older than Terence, or by the order in which their plays were first presented, so that Titinius had his debut before 166 BC. In each case a good deal of chronological overlap is possible. In keeping with his theory that the *togata* developed as a

---

[16] Cf. the canon of Volcacius Sedigitus (= Gell. *NA* 15.24), Varro *Sat. Men.* fr. 399.

[17] See Martina 1978:7. Before Neukirch, Bothe (1824:127) had already doubted *moverant*, printing the simple *moverunt* instead (as would Keil *Gramm. Lat.* I 241.29). The doubts of Ritschl (1845:194n) about *moverunt* seem misplaced.

reaction against an over-Hellenizing *palliata*, Courbaud assumed that Titinius was older than Terence but did not begin writing plays until after his younger contemporary's death.[18] Such assumptions are unnecessary, and are not consistent with the kind of research about early dramatists that late-republican scholars could conduct. The archival materials available to Varro were not normally concerned with the birth-dates of republican dramatists, but instead recorded the festival and consular year when a play was performed.[19] The most plausible interpretation of these lists and of the information upon which they were based suggests that Varro had seen evidence that Titinius had presented one or more comedies before Terence's *Andria* debuted in 166 BC. How long before, and whether he was still writing during or even after Terence's career, cannot now be known.[20]

The third piece of alleged external evidence comes from another conjecture that put the name of Titinius into a chronologically arranged list. In this passage, Fronto rejoices that the glory accruing to his speech will be even greater than the glory accruing to authors whose works were copied by noted scholars, since Marcus Aurelius himself has copied out Fronto's speech with his own hand (Fronto 1.7.4 = p. 15.11 Van den Hout):

> quid tale M. Porcio aut Quinto Ennio, C. Graccho aut Titio poetae, quid Scipioni aut Numidico, quid M. Tullio tale usuvenit? quorum libri pretiosiores habentur et summam gloriam retinent, si sunt Lampadionis aut Staberii, Plautii aut D. Aurelii, Autriconis aut Aelii manu scripta e<xem>pla aut a Tirone emendata aut a Domitio Balbo descripta aut ab Attico aut Nepote. mea oratio extabit M. Caesaris manu scripta.

---

[18] Courbaud 1899:30. Bardon (1952:39) dismisses Courbaud's theory and follows the interpretation that puts Titinius earlier than Terence on the basis of Varro's first list.

[19] Jocelyn 1969b:32–33.

[20] Martina (1978:12–13), temporarily granting the chronological interpretation of the list, reached a similar conclusion about the priority of Titinius' career before Terence's, but then rejected this interpretation in favor of making Titinius' priority in this list depend on his greater respect for consistency of characterization than Varro found in the plays of Terence and Atta.

Doubts have occasionally been expressed about the reading *Titio* printed by Mai after his discovery of the palimpsest of Fronto's letters. Lucian Müller (1867:752) preferred *Titinio*, objecting that Titius was far too obscure, and that Fronto must have meant the more famous author of *togatae*. This argument will not withstand scrutiny. In the second century AD the comic poet Titinius was not commonly cited even by readers who were enthusiastic about republican drama.[21] The identification of Titius with the orator and tragedian of the *Brutus* seems sound, and is doubted now only in order to make this passage offer evidence about Titinius.[22] Fronto's list of authors bears signs of chronological arrangement, and the pairing of Titius with C. Gracchus fits that pattern well.[23] Conjecturing the name of Titinius in order to down-date the dramatist radically to the late second century BC is no more effective than forcing him into Johannes Lydus' discussion of Roman drama and, thereby, into the late third century BC.

Neither a sixth-century Byzantine administrator nor a second-century orator can tell us anything about the career of Titinius. Only the Varronian passage offers any probable evidence on this question, but that evidence is rather more imprecise than has been recognized. It gives the impression that Titinius' career belongs to the first half of the second century BC, inasmuch as he had begun presenting plays at least before 166 BC. It is not possible to delimit his career more precisely, and he could have been writing on either side of that period.

So far goes the external evidence; the fragments of Titinius are even less compliant. Scholars convinced that the fragments will yield clues about the chronology of the dramatist have attempted to identify allusions to contemporary events, and have taken them as evidence that this or that play must have soon followed upon those events. In 1922

[21] For the limited readership of the *fabula togata* after 77 BC, see Jocelyn 1991 and Welsh 2010:256–257. Neither Gellius nor Fronto quotes Titinius. Attempts to find in Fronto *Eloq.* 2.14 a specific echo of Titinius 3 seem misguided; see Martina 1978:20n68 for references. Titius, however, enjoyed a good reputation as an orator, and just possibly as a dramatist too (see Novius 67–68).

[22] Bücheler recognized Titius' identity some years before he first published the suggestion in 1868 (see most conveniently Bücheler 1915:626–628). Müller's emendation is defended by Martina (1978:20).

[23] For closer examination of the chronology of Titius, see below, pp142–143.

Przychocki argued that certain fragments belonging to the play generally known as *Barbatus* were redolent of the debates over the repeal of the *Lex Oppia* in 195 BC.[24] Daviault similarly suggested that the title of Titinius' *Psaltria sive Ferentinatis* meant that the play was staged around the time Manlius Vulso returned to Rome from Asia Minor in 187 BC, ineradicably introducing to the city, it was alleged, professional musicians, including *psaltriae*, and other luxuries.[25] Attempts to extract dates from alleged topical references in complete (or very nearly complete) scripts have often come under fire, and their validity as a method of scholarship is dubious.[26] In the case of fragmentary plays, there are even greater reasons to be skeptical that we know enough about the play to understand the context of what survives and how that comic material related to contemporary events.

Such connections to events outside the theater are tenuous at best. The introduction and adoption of cultural practices was never unproblematic; these novelties were met with varying degrees of enthusiasm, indifference, and opposition. Nor are narratives about the introduction of luxuries reliable accounts of cultural developments, set apart from polemic and politics.[27] That the debates crop up only intermittently in our evidence should not suggest that concerns about these issues arose only periodically and died away as quickly as they emerged. The paths of cultural change are never so direct. It is unwise to think that the only time when *psaltriae* were a topic of conversation was immediately on the heels of Vulso's return, and therefore that Titinius' *Psaltria*

---

[24] Przychocki (1922), comparing Titinius 1, 2, 3 and Festus p. 500.2 with Livy 34.1–8; he is followed by Bardon (1952:39), García Jurado (1997:544), and also Daviault (1981:33–34, 109–110), who further claims that the title character of Titinius' *Iurisperita* echoes the intervention of women in public affairs in 195 BC. Gratwick (1982:726–727) rightly rejects the claim that a nascent women's movement in the 190s BC terrified Roman men and was condemned by them (to which Guardì [1984:131–132] is nevertheless still sympathetic), and cautions (1982:727) that these allusions are "individually extremely weak and acquire no extra strength collectively."

[25] Daviault 1981:33–34; his suggestion about Vulso's return seems to be taken as a *terminus post quem* also by Guardì (1984:139).

[26] For such attempts, see, e.g., Buck 1940 and Schutter 1952. Harvey (1986) gives an important refutation of such attempts.

[27] Grainger (1995:24–25) reminds us that one of the probable sources of Livy's account of Vulso's campaign relied on polemic generated by Vulso's enemies.

sive Ferentinatis must have been presented in or shortly after 187 BC.[28] A comedy involving a *psaltria* need not respond immediately to the debut of such individuals at Rome, as Terence's *Adelphoe*, presented in 160 BC, demonstrates,[29] nor, we shall see, does it even need to postdate Vulso's return at all.

The question of the Greek original lingers in the background of any attempt to identify topical allusions in the comedies of Plautus, for it is not always clear whether the allusion is the work of the Greek or the Roman playwright. At first glance, the situation would seem to be more straightforward in the case of Titinius' plays, which ostensibly had no Greek model. However, what seem to be topical allusions could well have derived from other Roman plays, instead of Roman history. For that reason, evidence such as the account of Vulso's return cannot be used to date Titinius' *Psaltria sive Ferentinatis*. To illustrate the general problems of this method with an example specifically relevant to the *Psaltria*, let us imagine that traces of the *didascaliae* to Plautus' *Stichus* had not survived, and that the play had been subjected to the hunt for historical allusions without preconceptions about its date.[30] In one scene, the slave Pinacium reports to Panegyris (and to Gelasimus) what he has spotted on the ship of her husband Epignomus, who has just returned from Asia Minor:

> PIN. venit inquam. PAN. tutin ipsus ipsum vidisti? PIN.
>   lubens.
> argenti aurique advexit nimium. GEL. nimis factum
>   bene.
> hercle vero capiam scopas atque hoc convorram lubens.
> PIN. lanam purpuramque multam. GEL. est qui ventrem
>   vestiam.
> PIN. lectos eburatos, auratos. GEL. accubabo regie.
> PIN. tum Babylonica et peristroma, tonsilia et tappetia

---

[28] The instruments of the professional musicians mentioned by Livy as novelties reappear in the context of public debate almost 60 years later, when Scipio Aemilianus Africanus lambasted a perceived decline in morals, pointing out that free-born Roman children were learning immodest arts (*ORF* 21.30 = Macrob. *Sat.* 3.14.7).

[29] See Ter. *Ad.* 388, 405, 451, 476, 558, 600, 616, 724, 743, 759.

[30] Buck (1940) did not apply his methods to the scripts of *Stich.* and *Pseud.*

advexit, nimium bonae rei. GEL. hercle rem gestam bene.
PIN. poste, ut occepi narrare, fidicinas, tibicinas,
sambucas advexit secum forma exumia ...

Stich. 373–381

Epignomus, after a three-year trip abroad (*Stich.* 29–30), returns with gold, silver, expensive cloth, couches gilded or inlaid with ivory, exquisite tapestries, and shapely exotic musicians. Were we to lack precise information about the date of the *Stichus*, someone would have pointed out the specific connections between this passage and the account of Vulso's return given by Livy (39.6.7–8):

> luxuriae enim peregrinae origo ab exercitu Asiatico
> invecta in urbem est. ii primum lectos aeratos, vestem
> stragulam pretiosam, plagulas et alia textilia, et quae tum
> magnificae supellectilis habebantur, monopodia et abacos
> Romam advexerunt. tunc psaltriae sambucistriaeque et
> convivalia alia ludorum oblectamenta addita epulis.[31]

That observation would have led to the suggestion that Pinacium's description alludes to Vulso's return after his own three-year campaign,[32] and thence to the conclusion that the *Stichus* must be a late play of Plautus, first performed sometime between 187 and 184 BC. Leaving these hypotheticals aside: the Ambrosian palimpsest showed that the *Stichus* premiered in November of 200 BC, over twelve years before Vulso's return.[33] Attempts to connect individual fragments with specific contemporary developments, then, are almost always unpersuasive. None of the allusions allegedly glimpsed in the fragments of Titinius can provide convincing evidence about his career.[34]

---

[31] Cf. Pliny *HN* 37.12; August. *De civ. D.* 3.21. Similar language at L. Calpurnius Piso Frugi fr. 34 (= Pliny *HN* 34.14).

[32] For Vulso in 189–187 BC, see Broughton, *MRR* i.360, 366, 369.

[33] Boutemy (1936) in fact attempted to use the description of the goods on Epignomus' ship as evidence that the *Stichus* was redacted and revived in 187 or 186 BC.

[34] Martina (1978:20–21) attempts to support a radically late date for Titinius (somewhere between 120 and 100 BC) by claiming that Titinius 7–10 refers to the failures of Spurius Postumius Albinus in the war against Jugurtha, but neither the text of the fragment nor this interpretation are guaranteed. It is at least possible that the frag-

Other attempts to extract chronological information from the fragments are equally unsuccessful. Many have tried to make the style of Titinius' language reveal information about the period in which he worked.[35] Scholars comparing the fragments of Titinius to the corpus of extant republican comic verse (which, statistically, means Plautus and Terence), have concluded that the language of Titinius is more Plautine than Terentian. That observation is accurate, as far as the fragments allow us to see, but it tells us nothing about Titinius' dates. If we press the implications of this argument, we could claim that the first-century dramatists Pomponius and Novius, whose styles stand closer to that of Plautus than to that of Terence,[36] must have been active in the late third and early second century BC. Indeed, one would have to rewrite the history of republican comedy: Plautus would have been faced with tremendous competition in multiple comic genres, and some thirty years would have witnessed the full flourishing of republican comedy; after the death of Plautus, nothing new would have been written for the comic stage apart from Terence's six comedies. Such arguments assume that the language of Roman comedy developed in a linear fashion, that Plautus and Terence represent two points in that development, and that the chronology of a fragmentary author can be deduced from the similarity between his style and that of Plautus or Terence. That argument is quite mistaken. The stylized language of the Roman comic stage, of which Plautus offers our fullest example, endured for over a century; Terence mostly stands apart from that tradition. No linear development existed, and no sturdy chronological arguments can be based upon such observations.[37] Attempts to extract chronology from alleged developments in metrical practices are also misleading,

---

ment belongs to a historian rather than to Titinius; see Ribbeck 1898:158 and Martina 1978:21n70. I am not persuaded that Titinius 104 belongs to a polemic against Pomponius, the author of *Atellanae*, that is reflected at Pomponius 191 (see Martina 1978:22–23).

[35] Suggested by Bardon (1952:39n8), explored in fuller detail by Vereecke (1971) and Guardì (1981); cf. Minarini 1997:52–55.

[36] For the language of Pomponius and Novius, see Karakasis 2005:234–246.

[37] Gratwick (1982:727–728) offers a superb sketch of the issue. On the style of comic verse, see Wright 1974 and Karakasis 2005, especially 204–233, on the *togata*.

for they rely on extrapolating information from a pattern of development that did not exist.[38]

The meager details thought to be known about the chronology of
Titinius have dwindled in this investigation. Only Varro's list of poets
looks to offer any reliable information about his dates, but that information is not precise. It suggests that Titinius had begun presenting
plays before 166 BC but tells us nothing about the duration of his career;
without doing any violence to the evidence, one could argue that Titinius
died long before Terence's *Andria* was first presented, or that Titinius'
career began in the early 160s and continued long after Terence died.

II. AFRANIUS

Antiquity preserved no information about the birthplace of Afranius,[39]
nor any detail about the years in which he was born or died. The general
period in which he wrote has been extracted from three synchronisms,
each of which raises further problems. In the first, Velleius Paterculus
appears to link Afranius closely in time with Caecilius Statius and
Terence:

> nam nisi aspera ac rudia repetas et inventi laudanda nomine,
> in Accio circaque eum Romana tragoedia est; dulcesque
> Latini leporis facetiae per Caecilium Terentiumque et
> Afranium suppari aetate nituerunt.

> Vell. Pat. 1.17.1

---

[38] Bardon (1952:39) suggested that Titinius was more likely to be a contemporary of
Plautus than of Terence, since his fragments reveal "la polymétrie plautinienne." Guardì
(1984:19) argues, from the fact that Titinius has (i) a hiatus at the caesura in a senarius
(Titinius 165; Guardì prints the paradosis), (ii) anapaestic verses, and (iii) three cases of
loci Jacobsohniani (Titinius 45, 58, 105; in all three we may reject Ribbeck's unnecessary
supplements), that Titinius is chronologically nearer to Plautus, who has these features,
than to Terence, who seems to avoid them; the argument is reasserted without modification at Guardì (1993:275), despite the objections of Jocelyn (1986:609). To rebut only the
final point, Guardì does not take into account the *loci Jacobsohniani* in Afranius 176, Novius
70, and Pomponius 96; see Questa 1968:378–379 and 2007:295.

[39] The silence of ancient sources on this subject does not suggest that Afranius
was born at Rome, as is argued by Neukirch (1833:167), Courbaud (1899:36), Cacciaglia
(1972:216), and Daviault (1981:38). See above, n5.

Velleius is here not concerned with strict chronologies, however; he is making an argument about the tendency of literary achievements to cluster in the same period. On his own criteria, and by excluding certain "rough" pioneers, he was able to make the leading figures of several literary genres contemporary with each other. He occasionally stretches the limits of what could reasonably be called contemporaneity; the most striking example is to be found in the same discussion, where Livy is linked with the historians of the second century BC, so that he identifies as the zenith of historiography a period of some eighty years (*historicos et<iam>, ut Livium quoque priorum aetati adstruas, praeter Catonem et quosdam veteres et obscuros minus LXXX annis circumdatum aevum tulit,* Vell. Pat. 1.17.2). Attempting to support this argument could have induced him to compress the chronology of the playwrights more than one might otherwise allow.[40] The lack of precision makes it impossible to rely upon this synchronism for anything more than a rather vague indication that Afranius was an author of the second century BC, which has never been in doubt.

A second synchronism provided by Velleius offers a seemingly greater level of detail but, ultimately, no greater chronological precision, since it is plagued by the same problems:

> eodem tractu temporum nituerunt oratores Scipio Aemilianus Laeliusque, Ser. Galba, duo Gracchi, C. Fannius, Carbo Papirius; nec praetereundus Metellus Numidicus et Scaurus, et ante omnes L. Crassus et M. Antonius: quorum aetati ingeniisque successere C. Caesar Strabo, P. Sulpicius; nam Q. Mucius iuris scientia quam proprie eloquentiae nomine celebrior fuit. clara etiam per idem aevi spatium fuere ingenia in togatis Afranii, in tragoediis Pacuvii atque Accii usque in Graecorum ingeniorum comparationem evecti.

> Vell. Pat. 2.9.1–3

---

[40] The argument is found at Vell. Pat. 1.16.2–1.18.1.

Selective interpretation has extracted from Velleius' lists of luminaries greater specificity than they can provide. Students of Roman drama innocent of the chronology of Roman orators have seized upon Scipio Aemilianus and Laelius, in order to put Afranius around the middle of the second century BC (ignoring the famous orators who were active throughout the rest of the century), or they have disregarded the orators entirely and, by running together all the hints about the dramatists from this passage and its counterpart at Velleius 1.17.1, make Afranius a miraculously long-lived contemporary of Pacuvius, Caecilius Statius, Terence, and Accius.[41] All of this depends on ready credence about our abilities to infer chronological relationships from one list to another, and from orators to dramatists.

As in his earlier discussion of literary achievements, Velleius embraces a longer period than we should comfortably accept when constructing the chronology of Roman dramatists. Among orators, Velleius moves from Scipio Aemilianus and Laelius (born ca. 185/184 and 190 BC, respectively) down to Crassus and Antonius, born forty to fifty years later; he then appends a comment about the later successes of C. Iulius Caesar Strabo Vopiscus (curule aedile in 90 BC, who sought the consulship in 88) and P. Sulpicius Rufus (tribune of the plebs in 88 BC). Here, as in 1.17, Velleius is speaking about long periods that simply will not yield the kind of precision needed. His comments about Roman drama are equally difficult to pin down. It is unclear from his language (*per idem aevi spatium*) whether he imagined the dramatists contemporary with only the latter group of orators (C. Caesar Strabo, P. Sulpicius, and Q. Mucius), or with the entire assemblage extending from Scipio Aemilianus down to the luminaries of the early first century BC. It is no more certain, on the basis of this passage, whether Velleius thought Afranius more nearly contemporary with Pacuvius[42] or with Accius,

---

[41] See Beare 1940:37 and 1964:120; Cacciaglia (1972:216) does both. Stankiewicz (1984:209) uses Vell. Pat. 1.17.1 to argue that Afranius wrote in the first half of the second century BC.

[42] It is also not clear whether Velleius followed the lower chronology for Pacuvius, attested by Jerome *Chron. ad* 154 BC (and possibly by Gell. *NA* 17.21.49), which made him the son of Ennius' daughter, or the higher chronology that made him Ennius' nephew (Plin. *HN* 35.19), if the conflicting testimony is not based upon just a simple misinterpre-

who was some fifty years younger. The only certain statement that can emerge is that Velleius thought that Afranius belonged to the flourishing of Roman literary culture in the second century BC that spanned a period of some eighty years.

The third piece of external evidence for the dating of Afranius' career is provided by Cicero, who reports a belief that Afranius sought to imitate the orator C. Titius. That connection gives a little surer foundation for identifying the period in which Afranius wrote:

> eiusdem fere temporis fuit eques Romanus C. Titius, qui meo iudicio eo pervenisse videtur quo potuit fere Latinus orator sine Graecis litteris et sine multo usu pervenire. huius orationes tantum argutiarum tantum exemplorum tantum urbanitatis habent, ut paene Attico stilo scriptae esse videantur. easdem argutias in tragoedias satis ille quidem acute sed parum tragice transtulit. quem studebat imitari L. Afranius poeta, homo perargutus, in fabulis quidem etiam, ut scitis, disertus.[43]

> Cic. *Brut.* 167

The nature of the relationship between Afranius and Titius is vague, and Cicero in fact says nothing about whether the two knew each other personally. His use of *imitari* in literary contexts shows that there need not have been a personal connection between them at all.[44] He could have used the same language to describe Afranius' relationship with Menander or Terence.[45] The connection is therefore of less value for making positive statements about the chronology of Afranius than it is for providing a further *terminus post quem*.

---

tation of *nepos*; see Schierl 2006:2. Given Velleius' broad definition of synchronicity, there is no need to make him follow the lower chronology.

[43] The claim that makes Afranius an orator as well as a playwright (e.g. Leo 1913:375n4) on the basis of this passage must be rejected; see Douglas 1966:129.

[44] Cic. *Rep.* 1.56; *Acad.* 1.10; cf. *Fam.* 2.16.6.

[45] For the notion that Afranius was influenced by Menander's scripts directly and that his comedies bore the imprint of that influence, see Cic. *Fin.* 1.7; Hor. *Epist.* 2.1.57; Macrob. *Sat.* 6.1.4.

Titius, though, poses his own set of chronological problems. With *eiusdem fere temporis* (*Brut.* 167), Cicero makes him roughly contemporary with Crassus and Antonius. He is described by Macrobius as a *vir aetatis Lucilianae* (*Sat.* 3.16.14); we are not now in a position to assess the strength of the evidence on which Macrobius or his source based that claim.[46] Two other pieces of evidence are difficult. Macrobius cites an excerpt from the orator's speech in support of the *Lex Fannia*; the consular sumptuary law was passed in 161 BC.[47] Fronto, describing Titius as a *poeta*, may have made him coeval with C. Gracchus.[48] Taken together those points would suggest an especially long career,[49] and each has been separately discounted so as to define more narrowly the period in which he wrote. Those who dismiss the connection to Gracchus and put Titius' career early in the lifetime of Lucilius draw support from the theory that the orator spoke in favor of the *Lex Fannia* in 161 BC and from the more vague synchronism implied by Velleius Paterculus that links Afranius and Scipio Aemilianus.[50] There is, then, a tremendous circularity in this argument. The evidence that Titius delivered his speech in 161 BC is equally problematic, and many have been persuaded by Cichorius' solution, which makes Titius' speech in support of the law belong not to the debates surrounding its original passage, but to a time when its repeal seemed dangerously immi-

---

[46] But the argument, suggested by Cichorius (1908:265), that Lucilius borrowed a phrase (*... pontes Tiberinus duo inter captus catillo*, 1195 Krenkel; cf. Macrob. *Sat.* 3.16.17) nearly verbatim from Titius (*bonumque piscem lupum germanum, qui inter duos pontes captus fuit*, ORF 51.2.15 = Macrob. *Sat.* 3.16.16) will not hold water. The expression *inter duos pontes* was in common use during this period for the stretch of the Tiber between the *pons Sublicius* and the *pons Aemilius*; see Le Gall (1953:84–85). (Only later would the same name be applied exclusively to the *insula Tiberina*.) It is not certain that Lucilius borrowed the phrase from Titius; rather, the satirist knew the name of the bend in the river where the best fish were said to be caught.

[47] On the law and speeches, see Sauerwein 1970:79–89 and Baltrusch 1989:81–85.

[48] Fronto 1.7.4; see above, p133.

[49] Malcovati (1967:201–202) considers the possibility that Titius' lifetime encompassed the debates over the *Lex Fannia* in 161 BC and the dates implied by *vir Lucilianae aetatis*.

[50] Sumner 1973:101; cf. Douglas (1966:129), who gives the orator a *floruit* not later than 130 BC.

nent.[51] The debates over either the *Lex Didia* (143 BC) or the *Lex Licinia* (of uncertain date[52]) would offer a suitable context for such a speech. All this evidence is imprecise and has only an indirect impact upon Afranius, since we cannot be precise about the nature of the connection between Titius and Afranius. A cool-headed assessment of Cicero's words allows for nothing more than that Afranius was writing plays at the same time as Titius or after him, and that Titius was active most probably in the second half of the second century BC. The alleged connection suggests that Afranius belongs to the second half of the second century BC, and possibly to the latter decades of that period.

What has been taken as external evidence for the chronology of Afranius is thus far too vague to allow any precise statements about the career of the dramatist. Many students of the fragments have nevertheless confidently declared that Afranius was at the height of fame between 104 and 94 BC. We may track that claim back from López López and Bardon to Courbaud, who in turn relied on Neukirch.[53] Neukirch (1833:165–166) surveyed the chronologies of the various individuals mentioned in the passages of Velleius and Cicero before suggesting that Afranius' *floruit* was to be put at 94 BC; for this date he expressed agreement with the judgment of Bothe. In Bothe's first edition of the fragments of Roman drama, however, the date seems to have been pulled out of the air. He reprinted the life of Afranius as it was presented by Petrus Crinitus (who in fact had made Afranius' career contemporary with Caecilius Statius and Terence) before asserting, in a brief aside, the date of 94 BC.[54] There is nothing improbable about putting the height of Afranius' career in the period 104–94 BC, but those dates are not secure.

The arguments extracting a chronology for Afranius from the evidence of Velleius Paterculus and Cicero run aground on the basic problem that neither author wrote with the express purpose of

---

[51] Cichorius 1908:264–266, accepted by Leo (1913:375n4) and Münzer (1937). Gell. *NA* 2.24, and the extracts of Lucilius there cited, suggest that the provisions of the *Lex Fannia* were still very much a topic of debate later in the second century BC.

[52] See Sauerwein 1970:94–104.

[53] López López 1983:25 and Bardon 1952:138, both citing Courbaud 1899:36.

[54] Bothe 1824:156–157, reprinted without modification in Bothe 1834:156–157.

pinpointing the chronology of Afranius. Velleius' chronologies are not precise, and Cicero's testimony is too vague to be of much use. The farthest we may press their statements is to say that Afranius was probably active in the last several decades of the second century BC, and that his career could well have continued into the early years of the subsequent century.

The internal evidence provided by the fragments of Afranius is consistent with that range. Both Terence and Pacuvius are mentioned by name in the fragments, which generally supports a date in the latter part of the second century but does not allow greater precision.[55] Other arguments about the dates of individual plays will not withstand scrutiny. Daviault claimed to find historically topical allusions in fragments of Afranius' *Vopiscus* and *Materterae*. He took the content of Afranius 360–362 to refer to the emphasis that the censor Q. Caecilius Metellus Macedonicus in 131–130 BC placed upon marriage as a means to increase the birth-rate:[56]

> antiquitas petenda in principio est mihi:
> maioris vestri incupidioris liberum
> fuere.

Neither the interpretation of the verses nor a sudden resurgence of interest in marriage as a traditional value in Macedonicus' censorship is secure. To make Afranius' verses match up with a censorial campaign to increase the birth rate, Daviault postulates that the adjective *incupidus* was formed from an intensive prefix *in-* ('very desirous'), rather than from the negative prefix.[57] But there are good reasons to think that the individual who spoke these verses was offering special pleading in defense of his decision not to acknowledge a child, compelling it to die by exposure.[58] But, in any case, even if these verses could be made to

---

[55] Afranius 29 and Afranius 7, respectively, on which see Zorzetti 1973 and Schierl 2006:530–531.

[56] See Daviault 1981:39, 236n4, followed by Guardì 1991:212 and Suerbaum 2002:263.

[57] Daviault 1981:236n4. *In-* as an intensifying verbal prefix is common in Roman tragedy (see Jocelyn 1969a:201 *ad* Enn. *trag.* 26), but it is never found with adjectives.

[58] Ribbeck 1873:209 and 1898:250. Exposure of the infant is mentioned in Afranius 346–347; for appeals to customs of the ancestors, cf. Afranius 363–364.

harmonize with the message of a campaign to increase reproduction, we should not imagine that only a censor's speech could prompt discussions of children and the birth rate. Macedonicus was probably not the only censor to deliver such a speech in Afranius' lifetime; it is very likely that, in 102–101 BC, the censor Q. Caecilius Metellus Numidicus gave a haranguing speech urging Roman men to marry.[59] It is therefore impossible to state that Afranius' *Vopiscus* must have followed closely upon the events of Q. Caecilius Metellus Macedonicus' censorship.[60]

Any claims to a precise date for the career of Afranius need to be regarded with great skepticism. The only reliable evidence from the fragments is the naming of Terence and Pacuvius. No attempts to link fragments or plays with specific events outside the theater can be convincing. The language and meter of this stage-poet, who wrote firmly within the long-standing traditions of Latin comic verse, are, as with Titinius, excluded as grounds for establishing his chronology. Taken together, Velleius and Cicero give good evidence that situates the career of Afranius certainly in the second half of the second century BC and probably in the latter several decades of that period; nothing can prove or disprove whether he continued to write for the stage into the early years of the first century BC.

III. ATTA

In recording the death of Atta in 77 BC, Jerome provides the sole fixed point of chronology for the entire genre.[61] The chronicler made a few serious errors about the lives and deaths of republican poets, but his dates are on the whole accurate, and we are in no position to argue with this one.[62] Admiration of Atta as a dramatist may be inferred from Varro's judgment about his character-drawing, from the reac-

---

[59] See Gell. *NA* 1.6 with McDonnell 1987.

[60] The same problems affect the suggestion by Daviault (1981:39n2, 196n3) that Afranius 214 refers to the *Lex Coelia Tabellaria* of 107 BC. The fragment (*perii! lacrimae linguam saepiunt*) has nothing to do with the use of written ballots in trials for *perduellio*; if it did, the *leges tabellariae* of 139 BC, 137 BC, and 131 BC would have been equally plausible referents. But the speaker simply lays tragic pathos on his or her inability to speak.

[61] For the text, see above, n1.

[62] For references to Jerome's mistakes, see Herbert-Brown 1999:536n6.

tions Horace imagines to his own quibbles with Atta's comedies, and from later commentary about his representation of women's speech.[63] Nothing certain can be stated about his origin in Rome or elsewhere, for it requires one or another of two speculative inferences to make him a *"Romano di Roma,"* although neither is obviously incorrect.[64] Attempts to infer connections between the playwright and renowned actors are guesses.[65]

Atta is the only poet of the three for whom ancient scholars preserved the *tria nomina*.[66] His cognomen was sufficiently obscure that it merited glossing within a century of his death. Verrius Flaccus evidently reported that 'Atta' was applied to individuals who, because of some defect in their feet or legs, walked on the tips of their toes (Paulus p. 11.17–19): *"attae" appellantur, qui propter vitium crurum aut pedum plantis insistunt et adtingunt terram magis quam ambulant, quod cognomen Quintio poetae adhaesit.*[67] Horace is made by many to refer to this etymology in his judgment of the merits of Atta's comedy, expressed at *Epist.* 2.1.79–82:

> recte necne crocum floresque perambulet Attae
> fabula si dubitem, clament periisse pudorem

---

[63] Varro fr. 40 Funaioli (quoted above, p130); Hor. *Epist.* 2.1.79–82 (discussed below, pp146–147); Fronto 4.3.2.

[64] *"Romano di Roma"* is the convenient formulation of Rawson (1985:108 = 1991:481), who suggests that Atta was born in Rome because his *Megalensia* was the one *togata* most likely to have been set there, since the cult of the Magna Mater was not then widely diffused in Italy. This is the other side of Mommsen's argument about Titinius (see above, n5), but it runs afoul of Afranius' *Megalensia* and of the fact that there is no reason to doubt that all *togatae* were performed in Rome, whatever the city represented on stage. In any case, a play's Roman setting tells us nothing about its author's origins. The assertion of Daviault (1981:48) that Atta was Roman because he wrote *togatae* is unconvincing.

[65] The assumption of Guardì (1984:20) that Atta worked with the actor Roscius Gallus has nothing to support it besides the fact that the two men were alive at the same time. Neukirch (1833:156) is more skeptical. Hor. *Epist.* 2.1.82 is not precise enough to support such assumptions.

[66] The praenomen Titus is recorded by Jerome (*Chron.* ad 77 BC); Diomedes (*Gramm. Lat.* I 490.17) records Atta's name as 'G. Quintius' but there is little reason to follow this garbled passage.

[67] For the meaning of *adtingunt terram*, cf. Nepos *Eumenes* 5.5.5: *substringebat caput loro altius, quam ut prioribus pedibus plane terram posset attingere, dein post verberibus cogebat exsultare et calces remittere.*

cuncti paene patres, ea cum reprehendere coner
quae gravis Aesopus, quae doctus Roscius egit.[68]

It is at least worth asking whether Verrius instead invented the explanation of the cognomen from Horace's verses. There is another possible meaning of the poet's cognomen; in the next lemma, Paulus p. 11.20 preserves a second definition for the word: *"attam" pro reverentia seni cuilibet dicimus, quasi eum avi nomine appellemus*.[69] The cognomen *Atta* is not attested for other members of the *gens Quinctia*, and it seems just possible that the name was acquired after a long life.[70]

The only detail recorded about Atta's life is the date of his death, which tells us nothing about the period in which he actively wrote for the stage. Ancient scholars investigating the careers of early dramatists could often only extrapolate the details of their lives from the records of festivals at which plays were performed, and sometimes constructed convenient fictions which made the deaths of those playwrights occur not long after the last recorded performance of a play.[71] But if those scholars were compelled to invent facts about the deaths of early figures like Naevius or Plautus, the situation would have been obviously less hopeless in the case of Atta, who died when Varro was nearly forty years old. In short, then, we may know when Atta died, but attempting to relate his dramatic production to that date remains somewhat hopeless. Given that he held a relatively minor position in the canons of *veteres* established by Augustan-era grammarians and lexicographers, it is perhaps unlikely that he preceded Afranius, and the first two decades of the first century BC provide ample time for the production of his twelve known plays. Probability would therefore incline towards situ-

---

[68] Daviault 1981:48n2. Courbaud (1899:32) expressly denies that Horace referred jestingly either to Verrius' interpretation of the cognomen or, at *Epist.* 2.1.168–176, to "Plautus" in the sense of *scaurus*. For consideration of the literary critiques in *Epist.* 2.1.168–176, see Jocelyn 1995:230–239.

[69] Cf. Paulus p. 13.1: *"atavus," quia atta est avi, id est pater, ut pueri usurpare solent.*

[70] I recognize that I am, on this point, adding a speculative answer founded upon no certain evidence. My point is not to add to the confusion, but rather to suggest that even scholars in the Augustan period may have contributed, in their own way, to the metamorphosis of speculation into received truth.

[71] Jocelyn 1969b:32–34. The case of Naevius' death illustrates the point, for which see Jocelyn 1969b:34n17, 41–42. For further bibliography, see Suerbaum 2002:106.

ating Atta's dramatic career entirely within the first century BC, but not one shred of evidence corroborates that speculation. Only the date of his death, and with it the latest date for the end of the genre as a living tradition, can be known from Jerome's biographical notice.[72]

IV. CONCLUSION

A careful reexamination of what ancient historians, antiquarians, and literary scholars said about the three dramatists who wrote *fabulae togatae* shows how little we know for certain about the periods in which those plays were first performed. Some details and synchronisms are more reliable than others, but the entire picture is vague, and more so than has been admitted. Much of the overly precise fiction that has in the past two centuries grown up around these dramatists needs to be rejected. Titinius was the pioneer of the genre, but we need to abandon once and for all the tidy statements that make him a contemporary of Plautus. In all likelihood he had begun presenting plays before 166 BC; how long before, and whether he continued to present plays during or after the short career of Terence are questions that remain, as they must, unanswered. All evidence points to the conclusion that Afranius was active at some time in the last several decades of the second century BC, but no limits for the beginning or end of his career can be established. There is no reason to doubt that Atta was dead in 77 BC, but the length of his career and its proximity to his death cannot be pinned down with any reliability.

UNIVERSITY OF TORONTO

---

[72] The evidence for the life of the genre after Atta is brittle. No weight should be attached to ps.-Acro *ad* Hor. *Ars P.* 288 (*praetextas et togatas scripserunt Aelius Lamia, Antonius Rufus, Gneus Melissus, Africanus, Pomponius*), for it is not clear that the scholiast has the story right, nor, even if he did, that we could single out Aelius Lamia specifically as a later reviver of the *togata*, *pace* Rawson 1985:108 = 1991:481. C. Melissus' experiment at writing *fabulae trabeatae*, called a *novum genus togatarum* by Suet. *Gramm.* 21.4, was apparently singular; see Kaster 1995:214–222.

WORKS CITED

Ashby, T., Jr. 1902. "The Classical Topography of the Roman Campagna: Part I." *Papers of the British School at Rome* 1:125–285.

Baltrusch, E. 1989. *Regimen morum: Die Reglementierung des Privatlebens der Senatoren und Ritter in der römischen Republik und frühen Kaiserzeit.* Munich.

Bandy, A. C. 1983. *Ioannes Lydus. On Powers, or the Magistracies of the Roman State.* Philadelphia.

Bardon, H. 1952. *La littérature latine inconnue.* Vol. 1, *L'époque républicaine.* Paris.

Beare, W. 1940. "The Fabula Togata." *Hermathena* 55:35–55.

———. 1964. *The Roman Stage: A Short History of Latin Drama in the Time of the Republic.* 3rd ed., rev. London.

Bekker, I. 1837. *Ioannes Lydus.* Bonn.

Bothe, F. H. 1824. *Poetarum Latii scenicorum fragmenta.* Vol. 2 (= Vol. 5.2 of *Poetae scenici Latinorum*). Halberstadt.

———. 1834. *Poetarum Latii scenicorum fragmenta.* Vol. 2 (= Vol. 6 of *Poetae scenici Latinorum*). Leipzig.

Boutemy, A. 1936. "Quelques allusions historiques dans le Stichus de Plaute." *Revue des études anciennes* 38:29–34.

Broughton, T. R. S. 1951–1952. *The Magistrates of the Roman Republic.* New York.

Bücheler, F. 1915. *Kleine Schriften.* Vol. 1. Leipzig.

Buck, C. H., Jr. 1940. *A Chronology of the Plays of Plautus.* Baltimore.

Cacciaglia, M. 1972. "Ricerche sulla fabula togata." *Rivista di cultura classica e medioevale* 14:207–245.

Carney, T. F. 1971. *Bureaucracy in Traditional Society: Romano-Byzantine Bureaucracies, Viewed from Within.* 3 vols. Lawrence, KS.

Cichorius, C. 1908. *Untersuchungen zu Lucilius.* Berlin.

Courbaud, E. 1899. *De comoedia togata.* Paris.

Daviault, A. 1981. *Comoedia Togata: Fragments.* Paris.

Douglas, A. E. 1966. *M. Tulli Ciceronis Brutus.* Oxford.

Fuss, J. D. 1812. *Joannis Laurentii Lydi Philadelpheni De magistratibus reipublicae Romanae libri tres, nunc primum in lucem editi, et versione, notis indicibusque aucti.* Paris.

García Jurado, F. 1997. "Comentario a Titin., *com.* 1 (Ribb.): *inauratae atque inlautae mulieris.*" *Latomus* 56:544–550.

Grainger, J. D. 1995. "The Campaign of Cn. Manlius Vulso in Asia Minor." *Anatolian Studies* 45:23–42.

Gratwick, A. S. 1982. Review of Daviault 1981. *Gnomon* 54:725–733.

Guardì, T. 1981. "Note sulla lingua di Titinio." *Pan* 7:145–165.

———. 1984. *Fabula Togata: I frammenti.* Vol. 1, *Titinio e Atta.* Milan.

———. 1991. "La *togata.*" *Dioniso* 61:209–220.

———. 1993. "La *fabula togata*: Moduli formali ed evoluzione del genere." In *Cultura e lingue classiche,* vol. 3, 3º Convegno di aggiornamento e di didattica, Palermo, 29 ottobre–1 novembre 1989, ed. B. Amata, 271–277. Rome.

Harvey, P. B., Jr. 1986. "Historical Topicality in Plautus." *CW* 79:297–304.

Herbert-Brown, G. 1999. "Jerome's Dates for Gaius Lucilius, *satyrarum scriptor.*" *CQ,* n.s, 49:535–543.

Hout, M. P. J. van den. 1988. *M. Cornelius Fronto: Epistulae.* 2nd ed. Leipzig.

Jocelyn, H. D. 1969a. *The Tragedies of Ennius.* Corr. ed. Cambridge.

———. 1969b. "The Poet Cn. Naevius, P. Cornelius Scipio, and Q. Caecilius Metellus." *Antichthon* 3:32–47.

———. 1982. Review of Daviault 1981. *CR,* n.s, 32:154–157.

———. 1986. Review of Guardì 1984. *Gnomon* 58:608–611.

———. 1991. "The Status of the 'fabula togata' in the Roman Theatre and the Fortune of the Scripts." *Dioniso* 61.2:277–281.

———. 1995. "Horace and the Reputation of Plautus in the Late First Century BC." In *Homage to Horace: A Bimillenary Celebration,* ed. S. J. Harrison, 228–247. Oxford.

Karakasis, E. 2005. *Terence and the Language of Roman Comedy.* Cambridge.

Kaster, R. A. 1995. *C. Suetonius Tranquillus. De grammaticis et rhetoribus.* Oxford.

Keil, H. 1857–1880. *Grammatici Latini.* Leipzig.

Le Gall, J. 1953. *Le Tibre: Fleuve de Rome dans l'antiquité.* Paris.

Leo, F. 1895–1896. *Plauti Comoediae.* Berlin.

———. 1913. *Geschichte der römischen Literatur.* Vol. 1, *Die archaische Literatur.* Berlin.

López López, A. 1983. *Fabularum togatarum fragmenta (Edición crítica).* Acta Salmanticensia: Filosofia y letras 141. Salamanca.

López [López], A., and A. Pociña [Pérez]. 2000. *Estudios sobre comedia romana*. Frankfurt am Main.

Malcovati, E. 1967. *Oratorum Romanorum fragmenta liberae rei publicae*. 3rd ed. Turin.

Martina, M. 1978. "Sulla cronologia di Titinio." *Quaderni di filologia classica* 1:5–25.

Marx, F. 1888–1889. In *Index lectionum in academia Rostochiensi semestre hiberno*, 13. Rostock.

McDonnell, M. 1987. "The Speech of Numidicus at Gellius, *N.A.* 1.6." *AJP* 108:81–94.

Minarini, A. 1997. "Il linguaggio della *togata* fra innovazione e tradizione: Considerazioni sullo stile." *Bollettino di studi latini* 27:34–55.

Mommsen, T. 1850. *Die Unteritalischen Dialekte*. Leipzig.

Müller, L. 1867. "Oesypa Oesopa. Ptolomaeus Neoptolemus Triptolemus. Frontoniana." *Fleckeisens Jahrbücher für classische Philologie* 13 (= *Neue Jahrbücher für Philologie und Paedagogik* 95):750–752.

Münzer, F. 1937. "C. Titius (7)." In *RE* 2A.6/2.1555–1556.

Neukirch, J. H. 1833. *De fabula togata Romanorum: Accedunt fabularum togatarum reliquiae*. Leipzig.

Ossanus, F. G. 1816. *Analecta critica poesis Romanorum scaenicae reliquias illustrantia*. Berlin.

Pietrangeli, C. 1940. "Via Praenestina, 'il Torrione'." *Bolletino della Commissione archeologica comunale di Roma* 68:239–243.

Pociña Pérez, A. 1975. "Naissance et originalité de la comédie *togata*." *L'Antiquité classique* 44:79–88. (= "Nacimiento y originalidad de la comedia *togata*." In López [López] and Pociña [Pérez] 2000, 355–365.)

Pociña [Pérez], A., and A. López [López]. 2001. "Pour une vision globale de la comédie *togata*." *Cahiers du Groupe interdisciplinaire du théâtre antique* 14:177–199.

Przychocki, G. 1922. "De Titinii aetate." In *Charisteria Casimiro de Morawski septuagenario oblata ab amicis, collegis, discipulis*, no editor, 180–188. Krakow.

Putschen, H. van. 1605. *Grammaticae latinae auctores antiqui*. Hanau.

Questa, C. 1968. "Ancora sui 'loci Jacobsohniani.'" *Maia* 20:373–389.

————. 2007. *La metrica di Plauto e di Terenzio*. Urbino.

Rawson, E. 1985. "Theatrical Life in Republican Rome and Italy." *Papers of the British School at Rome* 53:97–113. (= 1991. *Roman Culture and Society: Collected Papers*, 468–487. Oxford.)

Reuvens, C. J. C. 1815. *Collectanea litteraria*. Leiden.

Ribbeck, O. 1873. *Scaenicae Romanorum poesis fragmenta*. 2nd. ed. Vol. 2, *Comicorum Romanorum praeter Plautum et Terentium fragmenta*. Leipzig.

————. 1898. *Scaenicae Romanorum poesis fragmenta*. 3rd. ed. Vol. 2, *Comicorum Romanorum praeter Plautum et Syri quae feruntur sententias fragmenta*. Leipzig.

Ritschl, F. W. 1845. *Parerga zu Plautus und Terenz* [*Parergon Plautinorum Terentiorumque*]. Vol. 1. Leipzig.

Sauerwein, I. 1970. *Die leges sumptuariae als römische Maßnahme gegen den Sittenverfall*. Hamburg.

Schierl, P. 2006. *Die Tragödien des Pacuvius: Ein Kommentar zu den Fragmenten mit Einleitung, Text, und Übersetzung*. Berlin.

Schutter, K. H. E. 1952. *Quibus annis comoediae Plautinae primum actae sint quaeritur*. Groningen.

Serrati, J. 2000. "Garrisons and Grain: Sicily between the Punic Wars." In *Sicily from Aeneas to Augustus: New Approaches in Archaeology and History*, ed. C. Smith and J. Serrati, 115–133. Edinburgh.

Stankiewicz, L. 1984. "Źródła antyczne o Titiniuszu – Przyczynek do chronologii togaty." *Meander* 39:207–212.

Suerbaum, W. 2002. *Die archaische Literatur: Von Anfängen bis Sullas Tod; die vorliterarische Periode und die Zeit von 240 bis 78 v. Chr.* Munich.

Sumner, G. V. 1973. *The Orators in Cicero's* Brutus: *Prosopography and Chronology*. Phoenix Suppl. 11. Toronto.

Tanaşoca, N.-Ş. 1969. "J. Lydos et la *fabula* latine." *Revue des études sud-est européenes* 7:231–237.

Vereecke, E. 1968. "Titinius, témoin de son époque." *Recherches de philologie et de linguistique* 2:63–92.

————. 1971. "Titinius, Plaute et les origines de la fabula togata." *L'Antiquité classique* 40:156–185.

Watt, W. S. 1988. *Vellei Paterculi Historiarum ad M. Vinicium Consulem libri duo*. Leipzig.

Weinstock, S. 1937. "Titinius (I)." In *RE* 2A.6/2.1540–1546.

Welsh, J. T. 2010. "The Grammarian C. Iulius Romanus and the *Fabula Togata*." *HSCP* 105:255–285.

Wright, J. 1974. *Dancing in Chains: The Stylistic Unity of the Comoedia Palliata*. Papers and Monographs of the American Academy in Rome 25. Rome.

Wünsch, R. 1903. *Joannis Lydi De magistratibus populi Romani libri tres.* Leipzig.

Zorzetti, N. 1973. "Una citazione di Pacuvio in Afranio." *Quaderni Triestini sul teatro antico* 3:71–75.

———. 1975. "Problemi di letteratura latina arcaica." *La parola del passato* 30:434–453.

IVY AND LAUREL

DIVINE MODELS IN VIRGIL'S *ECLOGUES*

Andrea Cucchiarelli

A FUNDAMENTAL CONCERN of cultural language is the use of divine models: through the gods they portray, ancient texts produce ideological and political messages. In this paper I will attempt to show how Virgil develops one such language in his *Eclogues*, as he moves from one eclogue to the next, modeling the gods as he goes. The result is a specific divine language that is dominated especially by two great gods, Apollo and Dionysus. I will show that, already in his *Eclogues*, as subsequently in his *Georgics* and *Aeneid*, Virgil shows himself an active contributor to the definition of an "Augustan" ideology, and that he can be thought to play this crucial role by attributing to the gods and their relationships to one another specific, and highly marked, cultural and political valences.[1]

Interest in this sort of approach to Augustan poetry, especially to Virgil, has increased greatly also in the wake of Paul Zanker's celebrated book, *Augustus und die Macht der Bilder*.[2] But I think that the topic

I have had several opportunities to present the core ideas of this paper in lecture form: in Rome, in May 2000, in the seminar directed by the late Luigi Enrico Rossi; in Milan in December 2006, at a conference on pastoral poetry organized by Marina Cavalli and Massimo Gioseffi; and at Yale and Harvard in the fall of 2009. I would like here to record my debt of gratitude to those who, attending my lectures or reading previous versions of my paper, offered helpful suggestions, especially to Alessandro Barchiesi, Sergio Casali, Kirk Freudenburg (with extra thanks for helping with the English translation), Luigi Galasso, David Quint, E. Victoria Rimell, Alessandro Schiesaro, Richard F. Thomas, John B. Van Sickle. Finally I would like to thank Salvatore Settis, to whom, rather many years ago now, I first presented the basic lines of my argument, receiving from him encouragement that I still greatly value.

[1] See, generally, Feeney 1998.

[2] Zanker 1987; further bibliography in notes 5–7.

is far from exausted, and that Zanker's approach needs especially to be applied to the poems I propose to study here: *Ecl.* 1–7. An initial move in this direction has already been made. I refer to a recent article by Michael Sullivan[3] which draws a contrast between the Dionysiac pose of Thyrsis and the Apolline (and "Augustan") pose of his competitor, Corydon. In keeping with this idea, I would like to show that Sullivan's Apolline/Dionysiac antithesis is part of a larger discourse of divine figuration in the *Eclogues*.

I do not wish to propose yet another solution to the question of "why" Corydon wins and Thyrsis loses. Instead I will limit myself to detailing those qualities that characterize the winning poet against those that describe the loser. By so doing I hope to show that Corydon, besides putting us in mind of Apollo, deliberately includes in his poetry features that one more commonly associates with the god Dionysus: Corydon is not, in other words, the exclusively Apolline poet that Sullivan hypothesized. But I want to avoid making any crude allegorical equivalencies: for example, between Dionysus and Antony or, even more problematic, between Apollo and Octavian. Rather, I would like to show that Virgil's divine models allow him to engage dialogically with a wider cultural and ideological context. The result is that the *Eclogues* speak more fully and forcefully, but without being locked into a specific, and necessarily partial, political orientation. My basic aim is to show that Virgil persistently, and therefore intentionally, uses a particular divine vocabulary. And on this basis I would like to suggest that the *Eclogues* demonstrate their participation in a language that resonated more broadly within the contemporary cultural scene wherein they were produced. And it is precisely here that one can underscore, and make something of, the differences that separate the contest's winner, Corydon, from its loser, Thyrsis. But before getting into the details of their contest, we will first look at what sorts of gods Virgil devises in the lead-up to the seventh poem.

---

[3] Sullivan 2002.

I. THE GODS OF ROME IN *ECLOGUE* 1

It is the *Eclogues* themselves that introduce the reader to the rhetoric of divine models. Already in the book's first verses we have a man figured as a god by Tityrus: *o Meliboee, deus nobis haec otia fecit* (1.6). In this figure of a young *deus*, ancient readers rightly recognized the shadow of the young Octavian (the *diuinus adulescens* of Cic. *Phil.* 5.43).

The character (or *ethos*) of the ingenuous herdsman (*rusticus*) protects the text from the excesses of panegyric. And although they are undertaken by the private initiative of Tityrus, the rites performed for the *deus* in question are acts of worship that correspond to the model of Hellenistic sovereignty; later they will be introduced officially for the *princeps*.[4] We must point out here that the political use of gods is nothing new at Rome. At every social and cultural level, as Paul Zanker has shown, the Greek heroic models, divine and semi-divine, were able to provide the various political parties with precious principles of identification and, therefore, cohesion (also through the influence, of course, of the charismatic myth of Alexander).[5] At the close of the forties, and then for the whole of the thirties BC, as a further result of the divinity claimed for Julius Caesar, the confrontation between the various political leaders took shape in part as a confrontation between different models of divinity.

Hence, the paradoxical Mark Antony, warrior, but also pleasure-seeker, could be assimilated to the model of Hercules and, above all, of Dionysus: the first solid attestation we have of this is Antony's entrance into Ephesos in 41 BC, where he was worshiped as a new Dionysus.[6]

---

[4] Esp. 42–43 *quotannis | bis senos cui nostra dies altaria fumant*; monthly sacrifices are well attested, e.g. for Ptolemaic sovereigns: see Wissowa 1902, DuQuesnay 1981:40–44, Clausen 1994:48–49 ad loc.

[5] On Alexander himself as a "divine model," see Norden 1899:469–470, Kienast 1969:430n1; more recently Fredricksmeyer 1997 (with bibliography). On the various forms of charismatic sovereignty from the Hellenistic to the Roman age, see Musti 1986, Walbank 1987, La Penna 1988, Pollini 1990, Brenk 1992, La Rocca 1992, Koenen 1993, Virgilio 2003.

[6] Plut. *Ant.* 24.4, with Santi Amantini 1995:408 ad loc.; see Scott 1929 and 1933, Immisch 1931:13–21, Bruhl 1953:127–132, Mannsperger 1973 (and also Trillmich 1988:480–485, Zanker 1987:53–56, Brenk 1995). As a reply to Octavian's accusations, Antony wrote an *apologia*, *De sua ebrietate* (Plin. *HN* 14.148): Marasco 1992. In Egypt

For Sextus Pompeius, who placed all his hopes in his naval forces, the choice was Neptune: he could be found wrapped in a light blue cloak, the traditional attribute of his divine patron (Appian *Bell. Civ.* 5.100 [416–417]; cf. Hor. *Epod.* 9.7–8 *Neptunius | dux*). Another major divine figure, that of Apollo, was destined to become the Augustan god par excellence.[7] Consequently it becomes all too easy to jump ahead and fall prey to anachronism, by establishing an equivalence in the *Eclogues* between Apollo and Octavian, on the one hand, and Dionysus and Antony, on the other.

If, as I believe, we have no reason to imagine that the *Eclogues* were in wide circulation until after 38 BC,[8] it is possible that Virgil wrote them in an ideological context that already recognized an affinity between Apollo and Octavian.[9] But the point to be stressed is that Apollo and Dionysus were solidly established as players in a discourse possessing strong social and political implications for Virgil and his readers. Already among the Greeks the two gods had been construed as opposites, and that same opposition held true in Rome as well:[10] the cult of Apollo, the young god of light and rationality, had been long established in Rome, both in popular devotion and among aristocratic families,[11] while the Bacchic cults continued to be perceived as foreign and, above all, oriental. Admittedly, it is difficult to establish

---

Antony's divine assimilation comported well with the Pharaonic cult of the Ptolemies, as some iconographic evidence confirms: Brendel 1962.

[7] Zanker 1987:57–61; also Gagé 1955:479–637 and 1981:562–574, Kienast 1969:447 and n58, Weinstock 1971:12–15, Mannsperger 1973, Jucker 1982, Eder 1990:95, Strazzulla 1990, Hoff 1992, Gurval 1995:91–111 (rather skeptical about some interpretative excesses), Galinsky 1996:216, Miller 2009.

[8] From the ancient evidence it seems likely that Virgil worked on the *Eclogues* somewhere between 42–41 and 39 BC: for the publication of the poems in a single volume, directed towards a broad public, the date can be brought down to 38–37, but likely not farther. I do not think there are solid reasons for bringing the date down to 35 (following the well known thesis of Clausen). On this question (and for ample bibliography), see Perutelli 1995:28–31.

[9] On the famous "Banquet of the Gods," see the discussion in Miller 2009:15–19, 30–39.

[10] See Miller 2009:26–28.

[11] See again Gagé 1955:69–220; particularly devoted to the cult of Apollo was the *gens Iulia* (Gagé 1955:94–98, 445–478); for Apollo as an important god in the Late Republican political struggle, see Moles 1983, Gosling 1986.

what Antony's real political intentions were, and to what extent they were distorted by propaganda. It is significant that Antony himself was experimenting with solar (and maybe Apolline) symbolism in the early triumviral age.[12] But there is little doubt that for Octavian, who had concentrated his own political and military action in Rome and in Italy, it was easy to insist on the exotic deviancy of his great rival. It was Octavian, thereafter Augustus, who would make a strong, final claim on the model of Apollo.

The scenario I have tried to outline leads us to consider *Ecl.* 1 from a new perspective. The Virgil who writes the introductory composition of the collection, at the latest in 37 BC, has probably witnessed the destabilizing of the difficult equilibrium between the two greatest personalities of Rome: Antony had definitively settled in Egypt, while Octavian was organizing popular opinion against him in Rome. Two observations, therefore, should be made concerning a crucial assertion by Tityrus:

> quid facerem? neque seruitio me exire licebat
> nec tam praesentis alibi cognoscere diuos.
> hic illum uidi iuuenem, Meliboee

> 40–42

First, Rome is represented here as the dominion of gods who are actually 'present', *praesens* being the specific word for divine παρουσία.[13] Secondly, the terms of the assertion are contrastive: *nec ... alibi*—only in Rome does such divine intervention occur (*tam praesentis*). The words of Tityrus exclude from the horizon other, different divine possibilities. The Antony-Dionysus of Alexandria is an example of a god that is by now incomparably distant, unknown and perhaps hostile, in the eyes of the humble herdsman of Mantua. The primacy of Rome is won or lost in terms of divine availability: it is there, in Rome, and nowhere else, that

---

[12] Miller 2009:27 and n43; also Hardie 2006: 36–37; for the case of Hor. *Sat.* 1.9.78 *sic me seruauit Apollo* (possibly a refined allusion to Brutus), see Thomas 2009.

[13] The concept belongs to the lexicon of Hellenistic sovereignty: Clausen 1994:47 ad loc.; add, for example, Hor. *Carm.* 3.5.2–3 *praesens diuus habebitur | Augustus* (Nisbet and Rudd 2004:83 ad loc.).

the humblest inhabitants of the Italian peninsula can find their god of redemption.

II. APOLLO AND DIONYSOS
IN THE MIDDLE OF THE *ECLOGUES*

II.1 The *puer*

Let us now leave the *deus* of *Ecl.* 1 and make our way to the next "divine" protagonist of the book, the boy (*puer*) of *Ecl.* 4. If we are to imagine that *Ecl.* 1 was written shortly before the publication of the book itself, *Ecl.* 4 refers to a precise occasion, the consulate of Asinius Pollio, during which the birth, or the conception, of the boy is prophesied (11, *teque adeo decus hoc aeui, te consule, inibit*). This is the only reliable chronological detail provided by Virgil in a composition that is otherwise visionary and elusive. A dedication to Pollio in honor of his consulate must also refer to the brilliant diplomatic success that Pollio obtained in the year 40 BC. Together with Maecenas, who represented Octavian, he had in fact mediated, on behalf of Antony, the Pact of Brundisium, in September of the same year (Appian *Bell. Civ.* 5.64 [272–273]). In *Ecl.* 4, the dawn of the new age of universal happiness is bound—we would say necessarily bound—to the expectations aroused by the peace agreement between the two great antagonists. For this reason we have to exclude the hypothesis that Virgil had wanted to identify the *puer* with Pollio's son. We should rather consider the dynastic marriage between Antony and Octavian's sister, Octavia, that was a relevant part of the Brundisium concord. It seems quite reasonable that Virgil should imagine that, during the consulate of the man who had striven for peace and for that marriage, the hoped-for fruit would arrive: a common heir.[14]

What is relevant for us is that, in constructing his prophecy, Virgil uses images and symbols belonging to the rhetoric of divine models. Accordingly the sovereign god of the future age is named: *tuus iam*

---

[14] See Clausen 1994:121–122; for a review of the various identifications suggested, see *Enc. Virg.*, IV, 342b–343a, s.v. *puer* (F. Della Corte). For epigraphical evidence for Antony and Octavia honored in Athens as "divine benefactors," see Raubitschek 1946.

regnat Apollo (10). But the first words of the prophecy tell us that the Apollo referred to is clearly localized in Rome: the Sibylline verses, although of obvious foreign origin (4, *Cumaei ... carminis*), belong to the patrimony of Roman religion. The concept of *saeclorum ordo* (5) is Etruscan, while the *Saturnia regna* of line 6 refer specifically to Latium. Thus, we have a *Romanus Apollo* (a god who, in respect to the Roman goddess Lucina, is *tuus*): again a god localized in Rome.

After a rapid glance at the future heroizing of the *puer*, Virgil turns to the moment of the awaited birth:

> at tibi prima, puer, nullo munuscula cultu
> errantis hederas passim cum baccare tellus
> mixtaque ridenti colocasia fundet acantho.

18–20

According to a miracle stereotypical of divine births, the earth will spontaneously respond to the coming of the *puer*. But the first plant named by Virgil is the symbol of Dionysus, the "serpentine ivy", seen in its exuberant growth (*passim*). Already in Euripides *Phoen.* 649–654, it is precisely ivy that greets the birth of the god:

> Βρόμιον ἔνθα τέκετο μά-
> τηρ Διὸς γάμοισιν,
> κισσὸς ὃν περιστεφὴς
> ἑλικτὸς εὐθὺς ἔτι βρέφος
> χλοηφόροισιν ἔρνεσιν
> κατασκίοισιν ὀλβίσας ἐνώτισεν.[15]

It is as if Dionysus' power to quicken nature emerges precisely at the moment of his birth: Dionysus is born and the plant that symbolizes his power proliferates. All the other plants that frame the *puer* have, moreover, extra-Italian implications: *baccaris*, for which a certain specifically Bacchic phonic assonance cannot be excluded;[16] *colocasia*, exotic

---

[15] From births of other divine boys ivy is absent: see, e.g., Apollo in Callim. *Hymn* 4.255–263.

[16] Still together with ivy in the one other Virgilian occurrence: *Ecl.* 7.25–28 (see below, page 171). It is noteworthy that Servius' manuscripts include aspiration, *bacchar*

in tone, if its seeds are those of κύαμος Αἰγύπτιος, 'Egyptian bean' (*Nelumbium speciosum*; for the localization cf. Plin. *HN* 21.87, *in Aegypto nobilissima est colocasia quam cyamon aliqui uocant*; Athen. 3.72b, ῥίζας δὲ λέγει Νίκανδρος τὰ ὑπ᾽ Ἀλεξανδρέων κολοκάσια καλούμενα [= Nicand. fr. 81 Gow–Scholfield]); *acanthus*, with its well-known Greek cultural and artistic associations. It is in the kingdom of Apollo that the *puer* will come into being (10, *tuus iam regnat Apollo*), but the figuration of his birth suggests that he will emerge as a new Dionysus, surrounded by universal peace: the lions in harmony with the herds, the goats bringing milk to the stables, the disappearance of all poisons, the propagation of precious spices, such as the Assyrian cardamom (25). During his adolescence, once he learns what *uirtus* (27) is, the fruits of the earth will ripen: wheat, but also Dionysiac grapes and honey,[17] all produced automatically (28–30).

This deliberate syncretism between two divine models reflects, I think, the particular moment of political equilibrium that the diplomatic action of Pollio helped to bring about. Or, rather, Virgil, when he wants to prophesy a world of peace, founded on the agreement between the East of Antony and the West of Octavian, has recourse to images that could express such agreement in mythical terms. The different divine models are freely combined to formulate a well-articulated language. By allowing for the hypothesis that already in 40 BC Antony/Dionysus and Octavian/Apollo may have been defined as polar opposites, the conciliatory character of *Ecl.* 4 comes into clear view. But, even if Apollo was not yet directly linked to the figure of Octavian, the two models participate in the political and cultural language shared by Virgil and his audience: putting these models together, in any case, signifies a search for synthesis and equilibrium. To the oriental model of Dionysus is joined the contrasting image of a god perceived as rational and salutary, and with strong links to Roman cultural ideals. Thus we have no need of the crude allegory Apollo = Octavian in order

---

(attested also by the Greek counterpart βάκχαρις): on the other hand, the forms *Bacchus*, *baccha*, etc., introduced in Latin at an early date, had dropped the aspiration, which was subsequently restored; *TLL* 2.1660.3–5, 1664.73–77.

[17] Three fruits produced by the generating power of Bacchus and Ceres (*G.* 1.7–9). For Bacchus as inventor of honey, see Ov. *Fast.* 3.735–762.

to realize just how fertile a mix of this sort would have been, and how rich it was in potential for future development.

The Augustan cultural language would increasingly become composite and would include within it quite heterogeneous elements.[18] From this perspective, we would not wish to rule out that Virgil might consciously have taken up religious influences of eastern origin: an eastern religious sensibility would prove useful in solidifying a powerfully appealing ideology, for a political project that sought to be broadly based, and to attain a real capacity to govern over a social and cultural scene that was ever more complex.[19] It seems that Virgil is pointing the way to the future Augustus.

Therefore, in regard to *Ecl.* 4, I propose the following conclusion. When read in the context of 40–39 BC, shortly after stability had finally been achieved following Philippi, *Ecl.* 4 has the look of a project, and of a hope, that only the agreement between Antony and Octavian could fulfil. Read in the following years, when conflict appeared increasingly likely, it maintained all its meaning: Virgil's hope, like that of the entire generation of poets contemporary with him, was that, if it was impossible to fulfil that hope of peace, at least it could be remembered. It is also true that, for whoever remained in Rome on Octavian's side, it was all too easy to attribute the failure of that dream to "drunken" Antony, who had by now settled as a new Dionysus in the Alexandria of the Ptolemies. It would now rest with Octavian to take up that dream and make it his own.

II.2 Divinized Daphnis

In beginning his eclogues Virgil had avoided dealing directly with the subject of the first idyll of Theocritus. Instead he limited himself to an evocation of Daphnis' farewell through a subtle play of hints and implications. However, when one reaches the middle of the volume in *Ecl.* 5, the poet seems finally to allow himself a direct look at the great begin-

---

[18] See esp. Zanker 1987:73–79.

[19] With no specific regard to the Apolline/Dionysiac dyad (and its political relevance), the mixing of Eastern and Western elements in *Ecl.* 4 has been investigated by Nisbet 1978.

ning of Theocritus. At issue no longer is the languor of Daphnis, but the grief that follows his death and, then, the celebration for his divinization. It is almost as if Virgil were continuing where Theocritus had left off.

Yet, despite being recognized as Theocritean, *Ecl.* 5 continues the non-bucolic trend of the preceding poem. The information, passed on to us by Servius, according to which the deceased and divinized Julius Caesar is to be recognized in Daphnis, is surely quite old.[20] Although the discussion about the exact terms of the identification remains open, the substance meets with a certain consensus. Rightly, a comparison with *Ecl.* 9 appears decisive: there a character named Daphnis is exhorted to turn his head towards the *sidus Iulium*, which has shortly before appeared in the heavens (46–50). Here, therefore, after an atypical eclogue which treats the theme of divine birth, Virgil deals with another 'lexeme' of Hellenistic ideological language: the divinization of the dead hero.[21] This lexeme had been made considerably less abstract by the 'facts on the ground' in Rome, by the death and divination of Julius Caesar.

Here in dealing with a locus of such potential ideological weight, it might be appropriate to reflect further on the use of divine models. To begin with, Virgil seems to have intensified the Dionysiac connotations of Daphnis. It is, indeed, unlikely to be a matter of chance that in *Id.* 1 Daphnis' sufferings should be recounted by a character, Thyrsis, whose name evokes an icon of the Dionysiac cult (the thyrsos).[22] Yet, according to the Virgilian Mopsus, Daphnis actually had the role of a real Bacchic *archegetes* (Servius links this, without hesitation, to Julius Caesar):[23]

---

[20] See Serv. and Serv. Dan. *ad Ecl.* 5.20, 29, 56; Salvatore 1981:216–221.

[21] A fundamental element of Augustan iconography, the "star of Caesar" (*sidus Iulium*) is very frequent in figurative arts, coins, and literature: Weinstock 1971:370–384; Zanker 1987:43–44; Ramsey and Licht 1997.

[22] See Gow 1950: vol. 2, 5 *ad* 1.19. For Dionysiac connections of the figure of Daphnis (also in iconography), see *LIMC* III.1, 348–352, s.v. *Daphnis* (G. Berger-Doer), Merkelbach 1988:36–39.

[23] Serv. *ad Ecl.* 5.29: *hoc aperte ad Caesarem pertinet, quem constat primum sacra Liberi patris transtulisse Romam* (discussion in Pailler 1988:728–743).

Daphnis et Armenias curru subiungere tigris
instituit, Daphnis thiasos inducere Bacchi
et foliis lentas intexere mollibus hastas.

29–31

After the Bacchus of line 30, Mopsus proceeds to name other divinities, portraying them as sharing in sorrow for the death of Daphnis. Here Virgil follows his Theocritean model, in which Hermes, Priapus, and Aphrodite try to console the languishing lover: ἦνθ' Ἑρμᾶς πράτιστος ἀπ' ὤρεος ... ἦνθ' ὁ Πρίηπος ... ἦνθέ γε μὰν ἀδεῖα καὶ ἀ Κύπρις γελάοισα ..., "Hermes came first from the mountain ... Priapus came ... Also Cypris came laughing sweetly ..." (*Id.* 1.77, 81, 95). But Virgil introduces two substantial novelties. First, the gods of his eclogue are not linked personally to Daphnis, as is Hermes, or evoked precisely for their specific competences (*eros*). Second, they abandon the bucolic space, repeating the mythical paradigm of the "divine flight" from a decayed world. We read in lines 34–35:

postquam te fata tulerunt,
ipsa Pales agros atque ipse reliquit Apollo.

In Theocritus it was Priapus, Hermes, and Cypris who visited the dying Daphnis, and in an epigram of Meleager it was Pan who abandoned the woods following Daphnis' death (*AP* 7.535.5 = *HE* 4704 G.–P.). But here Virgil mentions alongside Apollo an exclusively Roman god: Pales, the old Italic deity whose name refers to a place destined to have a grand future, the Palatine Hill (the etymological connection is mentioned in Solinus 1.15; but we are still far from the monumental Palatine of Augustus, and from a text such as Tibullus 2.5, where Pales makes an appearance in verse 28). The Virgilian goatherd who sings first, Mopsus,[24] does not fail to recompose the Bacchus-Apollo dyad in his

---

[24] His name itself belongs to the Apolline world of prophecy: son of Manto and Teiresias' nephew, Mopsus was reputed to be the founder of Apollo Clarius' oracle (Paus. 7.3.1–2). And Mopsus was the protagonist, with Calchas, of a contest about "the art of prophesying" (*de peritia diuinandi*) in Euphorion's poem that Cornelius Gallus probably adapted in Latin: Serv. *ad Ecl.* 6.72 (= Euphorion fr. 97 Powell = 102 Lightfoot), *Enc. Virg.*, III, 584b, s.v. *Mopso* (F. Michelazzo).

verse: the two gods are juxtaposed here, with their names aptly located at the close of verses 30 and 35. And again, as in *Ecl.* 4, we have the two divine models together.

That this is not fortuitous is confirmed by Menalcas' song in reply to Mopsus. In the future rites for the divinized Daphnis, Menalcas imagines four altars, two as offerings dedicated to Daphnis, two to Phoebus (65–66, *en quattuor aras:* | *ecce duas tibi, Daphni, duas altaria Phoebo*).[25] But that Daphnis is also a Dionysiac figure for Menalcas is proved by his description of the god (69, *et multo in primis hilarans conuiuia Baccho*) and the subsequent description of his festival:

> cantabunt mihi Damoetas et Lyctius Aegon;
> saltantis Satyros imitabitur Alphesiboeus.

> 72–73

Among the expressions of convivial joy, the "satyric dance" of Alphesiboeus refers specifically to Dionysus.[26] Finally, if in line 66 the altars of Daphnis were associated with those of Phoebus, the conclusion associates the new god, once again, with the Bacchic cult:

> ut Baccho Cererique, tibi sic uota quotannis
> agricolae facient: damnabis tu quoque uotis

> 79–80

Following the Sibylline singer of *Ecl.* 4, we encounter two herdsmen, Mopsus and Menalcas, who again perceive the divine models of Dionysus and Apollo as strictly interrelated. Perhaps *Ecl.* 5 links such a unity to the authoritative figure of the "father" Julius Caesar: that is, to a time when Octavian and Antony had not yet begun to compete for the political and divine inheritance of *Diuus Iulius*.

---

[25] What Servius says ad loc. is interesting: *sed constat secundum Porphyrii librum, quem Solem appellauit, triplicem esse Apollinis potestatem et eundem esse Solem apud superos, Liberum patrem in terris, Apollinem apud inferos* (= Porphyr. fr. 477 Smith; cf. Arnobius *Ad nat.* 3.33, Macrobius *Sat.* 1.18.1).

[26] Alphesiboeus' etymology ("bringing in oxen", "earning many oxen": Hom. *Il.* 18.593) could be particularly apt for a dithyrambic poet, whose prize was the meat of a sacrificial ox: Pind. *Ol.* 13.19 (Ieranò 1997:26–28, TT 36–39).

II.3 Silenus between Dionysus and Apollo

Again in *Ecl.* 6 we find a balanced coupling of Dionysus with Apollo.[27] The Callimachean Apollo of the prologue (3–5) is neatly balanced against the song of Silenus, waking from a night of drunkenness: ... *inflatum hesterno uenas, ut semper, Iaccho* (15). The revelation of Silenus in turn culminates in the scene of Hesiodic initiation which, with Cornelius Gallus as protagonist, closes with the name of the god:

> ... his tibi Grynei nemoris dicatur origo,
> ne quis sit lucus quo se plus iactet Apollo.

72–73

Finally, at the conclusion of the eclogue, the reader will discover that all the songs of Silenus repeat songs sung by Apollo (82–83, *omnia, quae Phoebo quondam meditante beatus | audiit Eurotas*). Coming after the Apolline prologue, the song of Silenus establishes the second pole of the old Hellenistic antithesis between Apollo's water-drinkers and Dionysus' drinkers of wine. And thus the Dionysiac/Apolline dyad is found also at the level of poetic symbolism.

III. THE *AGON* TRIAL:
DIVINE MODELS IN *ECLOGUE* 7

With *Ecl.* 6 what has long been recognized as the central sequence of the Virgilian *liber* is completed. All three of the central eclogues (4–5–6), as we have seen, have in common that they avoid what is typically Theocritean. Once this sequence of "atypical" eclogues is concluded, the *liber* seems to return, with the *agon* of Corydon and Thyrsis, to a more Theocritean realm. The return is, however, only apparent.

It is true that borrowings and echoes from Theocritus are quite numerous at the beginning of the eclogue, but Servius' assertion that "this eclogue is almost entirely drawn from Theocritus" is certainly

---

[27] Cf. Segal 1969:420 and n40; Putnam 1970:218: "The poem as a whole is a fluctuation between—and ultimately a combination of—Dionysiac emotionality and Apolline order"; Boyle 1975:193.

excessive.[28] Such a judgement might rather fit the corresponding *Ecl.* 3. But, in the first place, competing with one another here there is no pair of singers bearing the names of Theocritean contestants, like Damoetas and Menalcas in *Ecl.* 3. Rather, *Ecl.* 7 opens with the meeting of two herders, who are said to have gathered their flocks by chance (*forte*) in the presence of Daphnis:

> forte sub arguta consederat ilice Daphnis,
> compulerantque greges Corydon et Thyrsis in unum,
> Thyrsis ouis, Corydon distentas lacte capellas,
> ambo florentes aetatibus, Arcades ambo

> 1–4

A remote time is hinted at (preceding that of *Ecl.* 5), in which Daphnis is still among the shepherds and can, moreover, also be a witness to their contests. Yet, if Thyrsis refers us to the Theocritean account of the death of Daphnis in *Id.* 1, the personality that is associated with the name of Corydon is more specifically Virgilian. Poetic genius was hardly pronounced in Theocritus' Corydon, a pleasant-mannered but rather anonymous cowherd in *Id.* 4, whose name recurs in *Id.* 5 in a context that is not exactly eulogistic: "And when have you, servant of Sibyrtas, ever possessed a pipe? Are you any longer content to toot, in the company of Corydon, with a piece of straw?" (*Id.* 5.5–7).

However, in the Virgilian bucolic world, Corydon's "Theocritean" handicap is not decisive. The reader of the *uolumen* surely remembers the performance of the shepherd who bore that name in *Ecl.* 2, a performance already deemed "classical" by Menalcas in *Ecl.* 5.86. And progressively in the course of the contest we understand that the two Corydons share much more than a name. The love of deer hunting (7.30 ≈ 2.29); the reference to Theocritus' Cyclops in lines 37–40, who is a fundamental model for *Ecl.* 2; finally, the name Alexis itself, with the ardor that his absence involves (7.55–56 ≈ 2, esp. 6–13)—these are all elements that link the two Corydons.

---

[28] Serv. *ad Ecl.* 7.1, *ecloga haec paene tota Theocriti est: nam et ipsam transtulit et multa ad eam de aliis congessit* (see Coleman 1977:225–226).

The very fact that Corydon shows such an evident Virgilian identity encourages the reader to look also at his adversary, Thyrsis, for a pastiche of texts and hints: in Thyrsis' case, as we have seen, we are referred to *Id.* 1 (Virgil does not use the name Thyrsis elsewhere). The *agon* fiction allows the Virgilian champion the anachronism of a contest and a demonstrative victory over the Theocritean Thyrsis. It is therefore a slight paradox that it is Thyrsis who is made to respond to the verses by Corydon (20, *hos* [scil. *uersus*] *Corydon, illos referebat in ordine Thyrsis*), almost as if the obvious relation of priority, between Virgil and Theocritus, were inverted: it is by no means easy to vary a theme treated by others (Servius, in the comment to 3.28, has already observed the difficulty of whoever, in a contest, is obligated to *respondere*).

The complex play of literary intelligence which we have tried to outline is indispensable for understanding the particular perspective of *Ecl.* 7. The poet Virgil, who by this point has deployed before the eyes of his reader nearly all of the bucolic forms he will use in the book, can now allow himself to set up an *agon* between two different poetic modes: his champion Corydon versus a Theocritean Thyrsis. And, unlike in *Ecl.* 3, he can now designate a winner.

The issue of why Corydon wins is currently among the most hotly debated issues in Virgilian studies: it corresponds to analogous issues in Theocritus (why in *Id.* 5 does Comatas defeat Lacon?). Formal criteria are not decisive: the numerous observations that have been advanced, for example, to discredit Thyrsis' verse-technique, as well as being debatable, stall before what seems a solid assumption: that it was impossible for Virgil to write deliberately badly (he himself will not fail to recall a verse of his Thyrsis: *G.* 2.325–326 ≈ *Ecl.* 7.60).[29]

More appropriate has been the attention centred on the thematic choice and, therefore, the characterization of the two contestants. As has long since been pointed out, what distinguishes Thyrsis from Corydon is an aggressive, almost polemical, spirit: he is touchy right from the first exchange of words.[30] Already in *Ecl.* 3, in close imitation of *Id.* 5, Virgil had shown that the poetics of the *Eclogues* is oriented

---

[29] But see Papanghelis 1997:144–145 (with extensive bibliography).
[30] See Coleman 1977:226, Clausen 1994:211–212.

towards stylization, a refinement that avoids the strong and at times vulgar aggressiveness of Theocritus' herdsmen. With his pungent expressions, like that of Codrus' "bursting loins" in line 26, Thyrsis avails himself of iambic-bucolic forms that Virgil has decided to restrict, if not entirely suppress.

Yet comparison with the other Virgilian *agon*, *Ecl.* 3, with respect to which *Ecl.* 7 places itself in a studied play of structural correspondences,[31] pushes us to a further set of considerations. The fact that the judgement of parity with which Palaemon concluded *Ecl.* 3 contrasts with the defeat of Thyrsis in *Ecl.* 7, against which there is no appeal, leads us to wonder what difference there is between the two *agones*. I think this difference lies somewhere in the nearby sequence of *Ecl.* 4–5–6. Namely, in the question of how the two contestants use the rhetoric of divine models.

In his first words Corydon does not fail to invoke the gods:

> Nymphae noster amor Libethrides, aut mihi carmen,
> quale meo Codro, concedite (proxima Phoebi
> uersibus ille facit) aut, si non possumus omnes,
> hic arguta sacra pendebit fistula pinu.

7.21–24

The mention of the nymphs as inspirers of song, a gesture typical of the bucolic tradition (e.g. Theocr. *Id.* 7.92), is enriched in line 21 by specific erudite resonances through the difficult epithet *Libethrides*, which is found in learned Hellenistic poetry, above all in Euphorion, and in Orphic literature.[32] Thus, the comparison between the *carmina* of Codrus and those of Apollo might not be a generic compliment, but refer precisely to those poetic values that the reader should by now

---

[31] That is, the relative position within the *liber* and the space dedicated to the true contest, which in both cases is 48 verses.

[32] Cf. 32.2 v. Groningen = fr. 34.2 Lightfoot (*SH* fr. 416.2), and also the *adespotus SH* fr. 993.7), where we have to recognize an initiation scene along the lines of Hesiod; Libethra was connected to the cult of Orpheus: Orph. Frag. TT 249, 250 Kern = 870I, VI; 507I–II Bernabé. What is clear is that Corydon agrees with the poetic values of *Ecl.* 6: Hellenistic *doctrina*, Euphorion (and Gallus?), Orphic and Hesiodic poetics.

know and appreciate, especially from *Ecl.* 6.64–73, 82–84 and from *Ecl.* 4.55–59 (but cf. also 5.9, *quid, si idem certet Phoebum superare canendo?*). In his reply Thyrsis names not a single divinity:

> pastores, hedera crescentem ornate poetam,
> Arcades, inuidia rumpantur ut ilia Codro;
> aut, si ultra placitum laudarit, baccare frontem
> cingite, ne uati noceat mala lingua futuro.

> 7.25–28

Even more than his Theocritean namesake, Thyrsis seems intent on reviving the Dionysiac implications of his own name. The ivy of Bacchus is all that he asks from his Arcadian companions (note, as in *Ecl.* 4.19, already discussed, the possible Dionysiac suggestion of *baccaris*, here once again conjoined with ivy).

In the subsequent exchange Corydon names the virgin Delia (29), thus recalling her hunting prerogatives, and finally Thyrsis finds a divinity to name: Priapus (33), a god decidedly not virginal, with obvious Dionysiac connections. After various exchanges, when Corydon outlines a pleasant landscape (Alexis, in fact, has still not gone away ...), Thyrsis responds with a desolate aridity, specifically naming Liber in his natural role of father of the grape and of wine: *Liber pampineas inuidit collibus umbras* (58). By contrast, Jupiter is evoked as a meteorological god, able to re-establish normalcy on the arrival of the beloved Phyllis: *Iuppiter et laeto descendet plurimus imbri* (60).

In passing to the last exchange, we see that the mention of Phyllis is taken up again by Corydon, who intensifies the divine references (he names four gods in two verses):

> populus Alcidae gratissima, uitis Iaccho,
> formosae myrtus Veneri, sua laurea Phoebo;
> Phyllis amat corylos: illas dum Phyllis amabit,
> nec myrtus uincet corylos, nec laurea Phoebi.

> 7.61–64

The natural connection established by Thyrsis between Liber and wine, between Jupiter and rain, is varied by Corydon in a botanical-divine sense. The poplar-tree is dear to Hercules,[33] the vine to Iacchus, the laurel to Phoebus (note, again, the juxtaposition at verse end of *Iaccho/ Phoebo*; cf. 5.30 and 35). Thus, Corydon shows that he is able to recognize in bucolic nature the aetiological links between the gods and their arboreal essences.

This is how Thyrsis responds to Corydon's challenge:

> Fraxinus in siluis pulcherrima, pinus in hortis,
> populus in fluuiis, abies in montibus altis:
> saepius at si me, Lycida formose, revisas,
> fraxinus in siluis cedat tibi, pinus in hortis

7.65–68

In his reply Thyrsis does not fail to reproduce the concept expressed by Corydon: most important is the beloved, and her/his predilections. But no divinity is mentioned in Thyrsis' reply, his judgement being a purely aesthetic one. The same tree, the *populus*, which for Corydon is linked to Hercules, now becomes "the most beautiful on the banks of the rivers."[34] The first impression one had of the contestants' initial exchange (where Thyrsis opposed only ivy to the nymphs and to Apollo) is now confirmed: Thyrsis does not respond to the divine solicitations of his adversary. In the previous exchange, Thyrsis mentioned one god alone, Jupiter: the supreme divinity appeared in line 60 as a

---

[33] By starting with Alcides, Corydon may be picking up Thyrsis' mention of Jupiter: also Hercules was the fruit of Jupiter's generating power, in one of his "descents" upon earth (also *G.* 2.325–326). Already in *Id.* 2.120–121 Dionysus' vine and Hercules' poplar are associated, whereas the Corydon of *Ecl.* 2 associates myrtle and laurel for their scent (54–55).

[34] Add that the *fraxinus* ('ash-tree') is not a common poetic tree and there is no mention in Virgil of its supposed primacy in the woods (*in siluis pulcherrima*). Notice also that in line 65 the specification *in hortis* must exclude every reference to the dimension of *siluae*, where the pine, at least in its sylvan variety, had experienced the unfortunate love of Pan: see instead 10.14–15 *pinifer … Maenalus*. Among those mentioned by Thyrsis, the one tree that has a real presence in Virgil's *Eclogues* is the poplar (9.40–42: again in a riverine landscape), but it has already been mentioned by Corydon, as we know. In this last exchange it appears that Thyrsis, for his preferences in the matter of trees, is the exponent of a poetic tradition that, at least in the *Eclogues*, has to remain peripheral, with no future development (differently from Thyrsis' wishes in 7.25–28).

figuration of natural power, and in an overtly sexual context.[35] But it is Corydon who mentions the gods who are fundamental in the bucolic world of Virgil, and exactly in that mixed way that, as we have seen, is characteristic of the *Eclogues*: Bacchus and his ivy, Apollo and his laurel together (but also Venus and Hercules).[36]

Corydon thus demostrates his mastery over the language of divine modeling, using the particular syncretistic and integrated formulation that is typical of Virgil's *Eclogues* and that, in turn, is not found in the corresponding verses of Thyrsis. From *Ecl.* 1 to 6 Virgil has striven to find a balance between divine models that are substantially different. One has to remember that in *Ecl.* 5 the two singers agreed in praising Daphnis as a god, and especially in locating in him the point of contact between Dionysus and Apollo: and here Daphnis is surely present, perhaps as the judge of the contest (it is not a surprise that many ancient readers identified him with Caesar again: Serv. *ad Ecl.* 7.21; see above, II.2, page 164).

According to the reading I offer above, the *Eclogues* appear to participate in a broader social and cultural discourse that is, at times, political, and within which the gods, through a whole host of complex associations, play an important role. I further conclude that it was precisely in his ability to invent a rhetoric of divine models that was complex and well-articulated, and that could put together forces that stood in striking contrast to one another, that the poet of the *Eclogues* was able to take up a dialogue with his own contemporary society, and to include in it some of Rome's most important figures: Antony, Octavian, and Pollio. It was along the path of this "articulated integration" that, over time, Augustan culture would follow. But here again I still need to insist that Virgil knew how to keep his distance from panegyrical excesses, whether from crude allegory or too-obvious

---

[35] As a consequence, it seems very difficult to interpret Thyrsis' Jupiter here as a divine figuration of Octavian (or of the political sovereignty in general): for Jupiter/Octavian, see Thomas 2001:42, Van Sickle 2004:xxvi–xxvii.

[36] A significant god in Augustan ideology, Hercules is already an important divine model in *Ecl.* 4 (esp. 63, with Clausen 1994:145 ad loc.): in the period of the *Eclogues* the figure of Hercules is easily linked to Antony (one readily thinks of, for example, Plut. *Ant.* 4.1). In this context, Venus, too, may remind the reader of Julius Caesar's ancestress and divine patron, on which see Weinstock 1971:80–90.

masquerade. Back in *Ecl.* 7, as a love poet, Corydon can take the liberty of preferring the nuts loved by Phyllis to other more reputable plants (and not without some "egocentric" assonance between *Corydon* and *corylos*). But a poet, like Thyrsis, who does not understand or respect that rhetoric of divine models, gifted as he may be, cannot be the winner of Virgil's contest. He cannot become a Corydon, perhaps not even a Virgil.[37]

UNIVERSITY OF ROME "LA SAPIENZA"

WORKS CITED

Athanassaki, L., R. P. Martin, and J. F. Miller, eds. 2009. *Apolline Politics and Poetics.* Athens.

Boyle, A. J. 1975. "A Reading of Virgil's *Eclogues.*" *Ramus* 4:187–203.

Brendel, O. J. 1962. "The Iconography of Marc Antony." In *Hommages à Albert Grenier,* ed. M. Renard, vol. 1, 359–367. Collection Latomus 58. Brussels.

Brenk, F. E. 1992. "Antony-Osiris, Cleopatra-Isis: The End of Plutarch's *Antony.*" In *Plutarch and the Historical Tradition,* ed. P. A. Stadter, 159–182. London.

———. 1995. "Heroic Anti-Heroes: Ruler Cult and Divine Assimilations in Plutarch's *Lives* of Demetrios and Antonius." In *Teoria e prassi politica nelle opere di Plutarco: Atti del V Convegno plutarcheo (Certosa di Pontignano, 7–9 giugno 1993),* ed. I. Gallo and B. Scardigli, 65–82. Naples.

Bruhl, A. 1953. *Liber Pater: Origine et expansion du culte dionysiaque à Rome et dans le monde romain.* Paris.

Clausen, W. 1994. *A Commentary on Virgil,* Eclogues. Oxford.

---

[37] There is another winner, who comes directly after Corydon in the sequence of the book, namely the addressee of *Ecl.* 8, who is regarded by the poet as a god in triumph. And around his head, in addition to the laurel leaves of victory, there is an intertwining of Dionysus' leaves of ivy. He is a soldier and a *triumphator,* but also a Dionysiac tragic poet: ivy and laurel, together again, in triumph. On the controversial question of the addressee (whether he is Octavian or, more likely, Asinius Pollio), see Tarrant 1978; further bibliography in Nauta 2006:312–313.

Coleman, R. 1977. *Vergil. Eclogues.* Cambridge.

DuQuesnay, I. M. Le M. 1981. "Vergil's First *Eclogue.*" *Papers of the Liverpool Latin Seminar* 3:29–182.

Eder, W. 1990. "Augustus and the Power of Tradition: The Augustan Principate as Binding Link between Republic and Empire." In Raaflaub and Toher 1990, 71–122.

Feeney, D. 1998. *Literature and Religion at Rome: Cultures, Contexts, and Beliefs.* Cambridge.

Fredricksmeyer, E. A. 1997. "The Origin of Alexander's Royal Insignia." *TAPA* 127:97–109.

Gagé, J. 1955. *Apollon romain: Essai sur le culte d'Apollon et le développement du "ritus Graecus" à Rome des origines à Auguste.* Paris.

———1981. "Apollon impérial, Garant des 'Fata Romana.'" *ANRW* II.17.2:561–630.

Galinsky, K. 1996. *Augustan Culture: An Interpretive Introduction.* Princeton.

Gosling, A. 1986. "Octavian, Brutus and Apollo: A Note on Opportunist Propaganda." *AJP* 107:586–589.

Gow, A. S. F. 1950. *Theocritus.* 2 vols. Cambridge.

Gurval, R. A. 1995. *Actium and Augustus: The Politics and Emotions of Civil War.* Ann Arbor, MI.

Hardie, P. 2006. "Virgil's Ptolemaic Relations." *JRS* 96:25–41.

Hoff, M. C. 1992. "Augustus, Apollo, and Athens." *Museum Helveticum* 49:223–232.

Ieranò, G. 1997. *Il ditirambo di Dioniso: Le testimonianze antiche.* Pisa.

Immisch, O. 1931. "Zum antike Herrscherkult." In *Aus Roms Zeitwende,* ed. O. Immisch, W. Kolbe, W. Schadewaldt, and H. Heiss, 1–36. Leipzig.

Jucker, H. 1982. "Apollo Palatinus und Apollo Actius auf augusteischen Münzen." *Museum Helveticum* 39:82–100.

Kienast, D. 1969. "Augustus und Alexander." *Gymnasium* 76:430–456.

Koenen, L. 1993. "The Ptolemaic King as a Religious Figure." In *Images and Ideologies: Self-Definition in the Hellenistic World,* ed. A. W. Bulloch, E. S. Gruen, A. A. Long, and A. Stewart, 25–115. Berkeley.

La Penna, A. 1988. "Brevi considerazioni sulla divinizzazione degli eroi e sul canone degli eroi divinizzati." In *Hommages à Henri Le Bonniec: Res sacrae*, ed. D. Porte and J.-P. Néraudau, 275–287. Collection Latomus 201. Brussels.

La Rocca, E. 1992. "*Theoi epiphaneis:* Linguaggio figurativo e culto dinastico da Antioco IV ad Augusto." *Studi italiani di filologia classica,* 3rd ser., 10:630–678.

Mannsperger, D. 1973. "Apollo gegen Dionysos: Numismatische Beiträge zu Octavians Rolle als *Vindex Libertatis.*" *Gymnasium* 80:381–404.

Marasco, G. 1992. "Marco Antonio 'Nuovo Dioniso' e il *De sua ebrietate.*" *Latomus* 51:538–548.

Merkelbach, R. 1988. *Die Hirten des Dionysos: Die Dionysos-Mysterien der römischen Kaiserzeit und der bukolische Roman des Longus.* Stuttgart.

Miller, J. F. 2009. *Apollo, Augustus, and the Poets.* Cambridge.

Moles, J. 1983. "Fate, Apollo, and M. Junius Brutus." *AJP* 104:249–256.

Musti, D. 1986. "Il dionisismo degli Attalidi: Antecedenti, modelli, sviluppi." In *L'Association dionysiaque dans les sociétés anciennes: Actes de la table ronde organisée par l'École française de Rome (Rome, 24–25 mai 1984),* 105–128. Rome.

Nauta, R. R. 2006. "Panegyric in Virgil's *Bucolics.*" In *Brill's Companion to Greek and Latin Pastoral,* ed. M. Fantuzzi and T. Papanghelis, 301–332. Leiden.

Nisbet, R. G. M. 1978. "Virgil's Fourth *Eclogue*: Easterners and Westerners." *Bulletin of the Institute of Classical Studies* 25:59–78 (= *Collected Papers on Latin Literature,* ed. S. J. Harrison, 47–75. Oxford, 1995).

Nisbet, R. G. M., and N. Rudd. 2004. *A Commentary on Horace,* Odes, Book *III.* Oxford.

Norden, E. 1899. "Ein Panegyricus auf Augustus in Vergils *Aeneis.*" *Rheinisches Museum* 54:466–482 (= *Kleine Schriften zum klassischen Altertum,* ed. B. Kytzler, 422–436. Berlin, 1966).

Pailler, J.-M. 1988. *Bacchanalia: La répression de 186 av. J.-C. à Rome et en Italie; Vestiges, images, traditions.* Rome.

Papanghelis, T. D. 1997. "Winning on Points: About the Singing-Match in Virgil's Seventh *Eclogue.*" In *Studies in Latin Literature and Roman History,* ed. C. Deroux, vol. 8, 144–157. Collection Latomus 239. Brussels.

Perutelli, A. 1995. "*Bucolics.*" Trans. N. Horsfall. In *A Companion to the Study of Virgil*, ed. N. Horsfall, 27–62. Mnemosyne Suppl. 151. Leiden.

Pollini, J. 1990. "Man or God: Divine Assimilation and Imitation in the Late Republic and Early Principate." In Raaflaub and Toher 1990, 334–363.

Putnam, M. C. J. 1970. *Virgil's Pastoral Art: Studies in the Eclogues.* Princeton.

Raaflaub, K. A., and M. Toher, eds. 1990. *Between Republic and Empire: Interpretations of Augustus and His Principate.* Berkeley.

Ramsey, J. T., and A. L. Licht. 1997. *The Comet of 44 B.C. and Caesar's Funeral Games.* Atlanta.

Raubitschek, A. E. 1946. "Octavia's Deification at Athens." *TAPA* 77:146–150.

Salvatore, A. 1981. *Lettura della quinta Bucolica.* In *Lecturae Vergilianae*, ed. M. Gigante, Vol. 1, *Le Bucoliche*, 199–223. Naples.

Santi Amantini, L., C. Carena, and M. Manfredini. 1995. *Plutarco. Le vite di Demetrio e Antonio.* Milan.

Scott, K. 1929. "Octavian's Propaganda and Antony's *De sua ebrietate.*" *CP* 24:133–141.

———. 1933. "The Political Propaganda of 44–30 B.C." *Memoirs of the American Academy in Rome* 11:7–49.

Segal, C. 1969. "Vergil's Sixth *Eclogue* and the Problem of Evil." *TAPA* 100:407–435.

Strazzulla, M. J. 1990. *Il principato di Apollo: Mito e propaganda nelle lastre "Campana" dal tempio di Apollo Palatino.* Rome.

Sullivan, M. B. 2002. "*Et eris mihi magnus Apollo*: Divine and Earthly Competition in Virgil's Seventh *Eclogue.*" *Vergilius* 48:40–54.

Tarrant, R. J. 1978. "The Addressee of Virgil's Eighth *Eclogue.*" *HSCP* 82:197–199.

Thomas, R. F. 2001. *Virgil and the Augustan Reception.* Cambridge.

———. 2009. "Homeric Masquerade: Politics and Poetics in Horace's Apollo." In Athanassaki, Martin, and Miller 2009, 329–352.

Trillmich, W. 1988. "Münzpropaganda." In *Kaiser Augustus und die verlorene Republik*, ed. M. Hofter et al., 474–528. Berlin.

Van Sickle, J. B. 2004. *The Design of Virgil's Bucolics.* 2nd ed. London.

Virgilio, B. 2003. *Lancia, diadema e porpora: Il re e la regalità ellenistica*. 2nd ed. Pisa.

Walbank, F. W. 1987. "Könige als Götter: Überlegungen zum Herrscherkult von Alexander bis Augustus." *Chiron* 17:365–382.

Weinstock, S. 1971. *Divus Julius*. Oxford.

Wissowa, G. 1902. "Monatliche Geburtstagsfeier." *Hermes* 37:157–159.

Zanker, P. 1987. *Augustus und die Macht der Bilder*. Munich. (Trans. by Alan Shapiro as *The Power of Images in the Age of Augustus* [Ann Arbor, 1988]).

NIGHTTIME *LABOR*

A METAPOETIC VIGNETTE ALLUDING TO ARATUS AT *GEORGICS* 1.291–296

John Henkel

et quidam seros hiberni ad luminis ignis
pervigilat ferroque faces inspicat acuto.
interea longum cantu solata laborem
arguto coniunx percurrit pectine telas,
aut dulcis musti Volcano decoquit umorem
et foliis undam trepidi despumat aëni.

Virg. *Geo.* 1.291–296

IN THE MIDST OF A NOTABLY HESIODIC DISCUSSION of nighttime and winter work (*Geo.* 1.287–310), Virgil inserts the brief episode above, describing the work done at night by a farmer and his wife. This rustic vignette has long charmed readers with its apparent simplicity, but, beneath its seeming humility, these lines effect a sophisticated metapoetic allusion to Aratus and his didactic poem, the *Phaenomena*. Other scholars have identified metapoetic passages in the *Georgics*,[1] but the present example is unique because the source text of the allusion is preserved in full and we have a substantial tradition of its Greek and Roman reception. The manner of Virgil's allusion is also unlike the metapoetic technique that scholars have seen elsewhere, since it is

---

Versions of this paper were presented at the 2008 meeting of the American Philological Association and at Grinnell College; thanks are due to both audiences for their feedback. In addition, I owe special thanks to Jim O'Hara, Stephen Harrison, Sharon James, and Bill Race.

[1] Notably in Virgil's description of the Corycian gardener (*Geo.* 4.125–148), on which see Thibodeau 2001 and Harrison 2004 for bibliography.

based for the most part on the critical reception of the *Phaenomena*, not on the poem itself: the chores that occupy the farmer and his wife in this passage are literalizations of the metaphorical terms in which Callimachus and Leonidas of Tarentum praise Aratus and his poem. Although *Georgics* 1.291–296 has no explicit reference to Latin terms relevant to Virgil's literary program, its dense and consistent metapoetic allusions forge a link between *labor*, the most important metaphysical theme of the *Georgics*, and λεπτότης ("refinement"), the stylistic virtue consistently associated with Aratus in Hellenistic epigram.

Both Callimachus *Epigram* 27 Pf. (= *AP* 9.507 = 56 Gow–Page) and, I believe, Leonidas *AP* 9.25 (= 101 Gow–Page) help shape the Roman reception of Aratus through their use of literary-critical metaphor. Both epigrams praise the refinement of the *Phaenomena* with the important stylistic term λεπτός, which Aratus himself had set as a programmatic acrostic in the poem (ΛΕΠΤΗ, *Phaen.* 783–787), and which becomes a key term for Augustan Callimacheanism.[2] Thomas and others, moreover, have shown that Roman poetry derives an important metaphor for poetic refinement from Callimachus' characterization of the *Phaenomena* as a "symbol of Aratus' *wakefulness*."

> Ἡσιόδου τό τ' ἄεισμα καὶ ὁ τρόπος· οὐ τὸν ἀοιδῶν
> ἔσχατον, ἀλλ' ὀκνέω μὴ τὸ μελιχρότατον
> τῶν ἐπέων ὁ Σολεὺς ἀπεμάξατο· χαίρετε λεπταί
> ῥήσιες, Ἀρήτου σύμβολον ἀγρυπνίης.

Callim. *Epigr.* 27 Pf.[3]

Because ἀγρυπνίη refers in Callimachus both to stargazing and to late-night toil over refined poetry, Roman poets starting with Cinna use the

---

[2] On the acrostic, its importance, and its contemporary recognition (λεπταὶ ῥήσιες, Callim. *Epig.* 27.3–4 Pf.; λεπτῇ φροντίδι … ἐφράσατο, Leonidas *AP* 9.25.1–2; cf. also λεπτολόγος, Ptolemy *SH* 712.4), see Jacques 1960, Vogt 1967, and Kidd 1997 *ad Phaen.* 783–787. Cameron 1995:321–328 suggests, perhaps rightly, that the Hellenistic stylistic program of λεπτότης originated not with Callimachus, but with Aratus.
[3] For the text of this problematic epigram I cautiously follow Pfeiffer. See now Obbink in Gonis et al. 2003:62 for new papyrus evidence and Stewart 2008 for an interesting new conjecture.

Latin calque *vigilare* to evoke laborious Callimachean refinement (*haec tibi Arateis multum vigilata lucernis | carmina*, Cinna fr. 11.1–2 Courtney).[4]

While Thomas discusses mainly elegy, others have shown that Lucretius alludes to Callimachus' ἀγρυπνίη in the proem to *De rerum natura* 1, where he explains his reasons for writing poetry:[5]

> sed tua me virtus tamen et sperata voluptas
> suavis amicitiae quemvis efferre laborem
> suadet et inducit *noctes vigilare serenas*
> quaerentem dictis quibus et quo carmine demum
> clara tuae possim praepandere lumina menti,
> res quibus occultas penitus convisere possis.

Lucr. 1.140–145

These lines, I believe, allude also to Leonidas, and thereby express Lucretius' motivation to write didactic in terms drawn not only from Callimachus, but more generally from the critical reception of Aratus, Lucretius' most eminent Hellenistic predecessor.[6] In light of the allusion to Callimachus in line 142 (as well as the importance of Leonidas to the Virgil passage discussed below), the phrase *quemvis efferre laborem* in line 141 can be seen as a specific allusion to Leonidas, who praised Aratus for "toiling at a great labor" in versifying a dry and abstruse subject like astronomy in a refined style.[7]

---

[4] See Thomas 1979:195–206 on the use of this metaphor as a "means of exclusive acknowledgment between contemporary writers of Alexandrian, neoteric, and Augustan verse" (205); cf. also Lyne 1978 *ad Ciris* 46 on the way that Roman elegists "humorously play between the ideas of lucubration the product of diligence and lucubration enforced by the cares of love." On the text of Cinna fr. 11.1–2, see Hollis 2007 ad loc. (*FRP* 13.1–2).

[5] See Brown 1982:83, Gale 1994:107n41. On Lucretius' Epicurean recontextualization of the metaphor (*noctes vigilare serenas*), cf. also Gale 2000:153n30, and compare Hardie 1986:178 and Gale 1994:185–189 on Lucretian "demythologization" of traditional mythological *topoi*.

[6] On Lucretius' knowledge of and engagement with Hellenistic epigram, see Kenney 1970:380–388, Brown 1987:132–135, and Edmunds 2002.

[7] Although Brown 1982:83n37 lists Leonidas' poem among Hellenistic comparanda for poetic *labor*, I know of no previous claim that Lucr. 1.141 alludes specifically to *AP* 9.25.5. Lucretius's metaphorical use of *labor* in this passage is somewhat surprising, since he generally deplores the vain *labores* that result from man's unenlightened condition;

Γράμμα τόδ' Ἀρήτοιο δαήμονος, ὅς ποτε λεπτῇ
φροντίδι δηναιοὺς ἀστέρας ἐφράσατο,
ἀπλανέας τ' ἄμφω καὶ ἀλήμονας, οἷσί γ' ἐναργής
ἰλλόμενος κύκλοις οὐρανὸς ἐνδέδεται·
αἰνείσθω δὲ <u>καμὼν ἔργον μέγα</u>, καὶ Διὸς εἶναι
δεύτερος, ὅστις ἔθηκ' ἄστρα φαεινότερα.

Leonidas AP 9.25

Such praise has clear relevance to the *De rerum natura*, a poem which Lucretius characterizes as the honeyed cup for the bitter wormwood of Epicurean philosophy (1.936–950). We will see below that Virgil too alludes to Callimachus and Leonidas in tandem, and that the metaphors drawn from their epigrams continue to shape the Roman reception of the *Phaenomena*.[8]

It is *prima facie* likely that Virgil knew the epigrams of Callimachus and Leonidas on Aratus, both because of Virgil's own extensive engagement with Aratus in *Georgics* 1 and because of the importance of Callimachean λεπτότης throughout his poetry. Not only does Virgil adapt Aratus' weather signs at length in the second half of the book, but he also emulates two remarkable features of the *Phaenomena*—its acrostic and a pun on Aratus' name—at points in *Georgics* 1 that correspond to their original placement in the *Phaenomena*.[9] Callimachus

---

Gale (2000:147–154), however, has shown that Lucretius consistently treats poetic *labor* as acceptable, even pleasant.

[8] Perhaps these two epigrams circulated together as a preface to a volume of the *Phaenomena*, as Cinna's poem seems to have done. Although Farrell (1991:47) points out that Callimachus, unlike Cinna, does not seem to have composed his epigram with this purpose in mind, the side-by-side allusions to these epigrams in Lucretius and Virgil suggest that this idea may have occurred to a later copyist or editor. It may even be that Cinna's reference to plural *carmina* (<u>haec</u> *tibi Arateis multum vigilata lucernis* | *carmina*, fr. 11.1–2) alludes to a volume with such a preface. On other prefatory epigrams (including Callim. *Epigr.* 6 Pf. on the ps.-Homeric *Capture of Oechalia*), see McKeown 1989 *ad* Ovid's preface to the *Amores*.

[9] On Aratus' pun at *Phaen.* 1–2 and its acknowledgment by Callimachus and Leonidas, see Bing 1993:105–107; on Virgil's imitation of it at *Geo.* 1.1–2 (*terram vertere* ≈ *arare*, *aratus*), see Katz 2008 and cf. Serv. *ad loc.*: TERRAM VERTERE περιφραστικῶς *arare*. A number of scholars have seen a pun on Aratus' name also at *Ecl.* 3.40–44: for references see O'Hara 1996:79–82, Lipka 2001:175, and Katz 2008:110n3. Already Jacques 1960 saw that Callimachus, Leonidas, and Ptolemy acknowledge Aratus' ΛΕΠΤΗ acrostic by praising

and Leonidas allude to both of these features in their epigrams, but there has been no firm evidence to connect either poem with Virgil's emulation of Aratus in this regard. Farrell has argued that Callimachus *Epigram* 27 Pf. is at least partly responsible for the imitative structure of *Georgics* 1, where Virgil treats Aratus as a latter-day Hesiod (Ἡσιόδου τό τ᾽ ἄεισμα καὶ ὁ τρόπος, *Epigr.* 27.1 Pf.),[10] but I know of no previously published suggestion that specific passages of *Georgics* 1—or of any other Virgilian poem—allude directly to the epigrams of either Callimachus or Leonidas. The vignette at *Georgics* 1.291–296, however, shows clearly that Virgil both knew the reception of Aratus in Hellenistic epigram and engaged deeply with it.

Like Cinna and Lucretius, Virgil alludes to the literary-critical metaphors that Callimachus and Leonidas use to praise Aratus for the refined style of his didactic verse. But while Cinna and Lucretius allude to these epigrams in contexts that explicitly concern either Aratus or didactic poetry, Virgil does so in a context that makes no explicit reference to poets or poetry. He instead literalizes the terms of their literary-critical metaphors—which either pertain to agriculture or can be so represented—and makes them part of the literal, agricultural reality of *Georgics* 1. The result is the vignette at *Georgics* 1.291–296, which describes the nighttime labor of a farmer and his wife in terms that refer metapoetically to Aratus and to the Hellenistic reception that praised him for "wakefulness" and "toil." Virgil's scene opens, following a brief introduction to the topic of nighttime work (287–290), at line 291, sixty lines before his large-scale adaptation of the *Phaenomena* in the weather signs of *Georgics* 1.351–463. In lines 291–292 Virgil introduces a certain anonymous farmer who stays up nights at his chores, carving torches by firelight.

Aratus as λεπτός. On Virgil's own (strange) acrostic at *Geo.* 1.429–433, see Brown 1963:96–104, Haslam 1992, and Feeney and Nelis 2005. Parallel Virgilian acrostics accumulate: see Horsfall 2000 *ad Aen.* 7.601–604 (add Feeney and Nelis 2005 and Brugnoli-Riccardo Scarcia 1987) and Grishin 2008; other possible Virgilian acrostics are noted by Clauss 1997 and Danielewicz 2005. Damschen 2004 sees 5-line programmatic acrostics in analogous passages of Ovid and other Latin poets. One wonders whether Cicero, whose knowledge of acrostics we know from *De Div.* 2.111–112, translated Aratus' ΛΕΠΤΗ acrostic in his *Aratea* with a 5-letter Latin equivalent like *TENVI* (the relevant section is lost).

[10] See Farrell 1991:157–168 (esp. 163–168).

> et quidam seros hiberni ad luminis ignis
> *pervigilat* ferroque faces inspicat acuto.

Geo. 1.291–292

The very first verb of this passage may be seen as a concrete manifestation of the metaphorical "wakefulness" that Callimachus used to praise
Aratus' careful style.[11] Virgil has followed Cinna and Lucretius in trans-
lating Callimachus' ἀγρυπνίη with a form of *vigilare*, but he has recast
the tireless effort of poetic composition in terms of the ceaseless toil
of farm work, demanded from farmers even at night. Thus we find "a
certain man" who "stays up nights" at his task (*quidam ... pervigilat*), just
as Callimachus implies of Aratus in *Epigram* 27 Pf. Callimachus' metaphor sits so easily in its new home, and resonates so deeply with the
fundamental conception of the *Georgics* and their theme of *labor*, that
its additional status as a metaphor has never been suspected.

The language that Virgil uses to describe this farmer's task,
however, alludes unmistakably not only to Callimachus' epigram (and
its Roman literary descendants), but also to the best-known passage of
Aratus' *Phaenomena*. Virgil's night-laboring farmer is said in line 292 to
spend his nights carving torches (*pervigilat ferroque faces inspicat acuto*),
a seemingly unremarkable task recommended also by Cato.[12] The verb
inspicat ("to make to resemble a *spica* [an ear of wheat]"), however, is
more remarkable than the activity it seems to describe: as commentators note, it is a *hapax legomenon* and appears nowhere independent of
this passage.[13] Virgil's "certain man" is said to use a sharp iron to make

---

[11] As an interesting, if indirect, measure of this metaphor's influence, compare
Horace's criticism of Homer for his occasional stylistic lapse: *indignor quandoque bonus
dormitat Homerus* (*Ars P.* 359). Brink 1963–1982 ad loc. points out similar language used
by Cicero about Demosthenes (*nonnumquam fatigantur, cum Ciceroni dormitare interim
Demosthenes, Horatio vero etiam Homerus ipse videatur*, Quint. *Inst.* 10.1.24; cf. 12.1.22) and
suggests that both Cicero and Horace reflect some Hellenistic criticism of Homer; it is
equally possible, however, that both reflect the language of Callimachus *Epigr.* 27, which
Cicero at least, as Aratus' first Latin translator, surely knew; Horace shows his familiarity
with Callimachus' metaphor also at *Ars P.* 269 (see Brink ad loc.).

[12] Cato *Agr.* 37.3: *faculas facito*; cf. also Col. 2.21.3, *faces incidere*, and Virgil *Ecl.* 8.29,
novas incide faces.

[13] For full citations, see *TLL* s.v. *inspicare*. Aside from glosses of this passage (including a
definition by Servius), a similar phrase appears only in the *Cynegetica* of Grattius (*spicatasque*

torches resemble ears of wheat. While much of the rest of this vignette alludes to the Hellenistic reception of the *Phaenomena*, a passage from the *Phaenomena* itself sheds light on this coinage. We find the target of this allusion in the opening lines of the poem's longest and most famous digression, the Departure of Δίκη (*Phaen.* 96–136), which contributes much to Virgil's treatment of the Golden Age theme in the *Georgics*:[14]

ἀμφοτέροισι δὲ ποσσὶν ὕπο σκέπτοιο Βοώτεω
Παρθένον, ἥ ῥ' ἐν χειρὶ φέρει Στάχυν αἰγλήεντα.

Arat. *Phaen.* 96–97

sub pedibus †profertur† finita Booti,
Spicum illustre tenens, splendenti corpore *Virgo*.

Cic. *Arat.* fr. 16.5–6 Soubiran

Aratus' well-known digression on Δίκη is introduced as a possible aetiology for the zodiacal constellation Maiden (*Virgo*, Παρθένος), whose essential attribute—the ear of wheat she holds in her left hand—is represented by the first-magnitude star that the ancients called *Spicum/ Spica* or Στάχυς.[15] Because Aratus uses both the beginning and end of his hexameters to emphasize important pairs of words (especially

---

faces, 484), which owes much of its diction to the *Georgics*. On the extent and degree of Grattius' debt to the *Georgics*, see Enk 1918:9–20.

[14] Virgil's debt to Aratus' myth of the Departure of Δίκη (narrated in a digression on the constellation Παρθένος/Virgo) is most vividly illustrated at the end of his praise of rustic life (*Geo.* 2.458–474): *extrema per illos | Iustitia excedens terris vestigia fecit* (473–474), on which see Barchiesi 1981, Thomas 1988 ad loc., Perkell 1989:113–115, and Farrell 1991:161–162. Regarding the fame of this passage cf. Kidd 1997:41–43, who notes that, although there are relatively few passages in Aratus with which the Roman poets show general familiarity, several of them belong to this digression.

[15] Cf. Bede *De orthographia* 1080: *Stachys graece, latine spica*. For the close association of Virgo with Spica, cf. Vitr. 9.4.1, Man. 5.271, Col. 11.2.65, Plin. *NH* 18.311, Nonn. *D.* 2.655. See Kidd 1997 *ad Phaen.* 96–136 for technical and historical information on Virgo and Spica, including evidence that the Babylonians also figured this star (also known as α [alpha] Virginis) as an ear of wheat, probably because its morning rising coincides with harvest-time. Regarding the star's Latin name, Ewbank 1933 *ad Cic.* fr. 16.6 notes that the word appears in all three genders. The Maiden's other important attribute, her wings, seems to have been a later development: see Kidd 1997 *ad Phaen.* 134 and 138.

proper names), the brightest star in the constellation, Στάχυς αἰγλήεις (Arat. *Phaen.* 97), seems to have emphasis comparable to the constellation's name, Παρθένος.[16] By apparently coining the word *inspicat* at *Georgics* 1.292, Virgil uses the Maiden's brightest star, Στάχυς/*Spica*, as a subtle and suitably agricultural metonym for alluding to Aratus' famous digression on the Maiden/Δίκη. He thereby makes direct reference to the *Phaenomena* in the course of his systematic allusion to its reception in Hellenistic epigram.[17]

Virgil's allusion continues in lines 293–296, where the wife of this unnamed farmer is described in terms no less metapoetic than those used of her anonymous husband. The husband and wife of this scene do not function as individual metapoetic figures, but rather as pieces of a single metapoetic tableau, the features of which are literal mani-

---

[16] Kidd 1997 notes enjambment at *Phaen.* 96–97, but the prevalence of this word pattern, which I would call "bookending" (cf. e.g. *Phaen.* 231–232, 445–446, 577–578, 607–609), argues that Παρθένον and Στάχυν αἰγλήεντα receive equal emphasis. Note that Cicero—who often respects Aratus' word patterns even while applying them to different words—has preserved Aratus' line-end emphasis on *Spicum illustre* and *Virgo*, but reversed their order (cf. Cic. *Arat.* fr. 33.183–134 Soubiran = Arat. *Phaen.* 402–403, where Cicero shows analogous enjambment, but of different words).

[17] The details of Virgil's vignette might also be seen to contribute to a metaphorical allusion to Aratus: (a) poets commonly use *ignis*, as in Virgil's *seros ignis* ("late-night fires"), as a metonym for "star" (so Cinna's *ignes aerios*, "heavenly stars," at 11.2 Courtney; cf. also *TLL* 7.1.290.45–62, which includes quotations from Catullus and Virgil); (b) stars are most visible in the winter (*seros hiberni ad luminis ignis*), when skies are clear (cf. Lucretius' *noctes serenas* above); (c) *fax*, "torch," is used sometimes for *sidus* (*TLL* 6.403.85–404.9) and might have been so used in now-lost portions of Cicero's *Aratea*; (d) "sharp iron" (*ferro acuto*) may suggest a stylus, especially since Isidore *Etymologiae* 6.9.1 reports that the Greeks and Etruscans used iron styli to write on wax until the Romans ordered a halt to the practice and bone styli came into prominence (cf. Plin. *NH* 34.139, where the development of bone styli is linked to Porsena's order that the Romans use no iron except in the cultivation of fields); a number of iron styli have been preserved in anaerobic conditions at Vindolanda: see Bowman and Thomas 1974:14 and plate 4. Thus the metaphor might be seen as thoroughgoing: there is a certain man (→ Aratus) who stays up nights in the wintertime (when skies are clear for stargazing) and uses a sharp iron instrument (→ stylus) to make torches (→ stars?) resemble an ear of wheat, i.e. he keeps late hours describing in verse how the stars of this constellation form [a maiden holding] an ear of wheat. The form of this cryptic reference might be compared to Menalcas' riddle at *Ecl.* 3.40–2, where at least two scholars have seen Aratus: see Ross 1975:23–24 and Fisher 1982; cf. Clausen 1994 ad loc.

festations of Hellenistic metaphors used to praise Aratus.[18] Skipping ahead for a moment to lines 295–296: Virgil has again precisely alluded to Callimachus *Epigram* 27 Pf., and seems even to have coined another new word to express its poetological metaphors. Here he describes the farmer's wife as cooking down and skimming grape must (the newly pressed, unfermented juice) to produce a sweet syrup fit for storage:

> aut *dulcis musti* Volcano *decoquit umorem*
> et foliis undam trepidi *despumat* aëni.

Geo. 1.295–296

Elsewhere in the poem, at the beginning of *Georgics* 2, unfermented grape juice (must) stands metaphorically for poetry, when Bacchus, as the patron god of a book dealing largely with vines and the vintage, is asked by the poet to remove his tragic buskins and stain his bare legs with the pressing of a new must.[19] We have evidence, too, from Cicero that Romans used "cooking down" as a stylistic metaphor for the production of a densely sweet quality (desirable in poetry, not in prose).[20] Here again, however, the precise language of these lines looks particularly to *Epigram* 27: ἀλλ' ὀκνέω μὴ <u>τὸ μελιχρότατον</u> | τῶν ἐπέων ὁ Σολεὺς <u>ἀπεμάξατο</u>. In discussing this epigram, Alan Cameron has emphasized that the metaphor that Callimachus uses for Aratus' imitation of Hesiod is one of wiping or skimming off the top of a liquid.[21] When the epigram is understood in this way, one can again see in

---

[18] This married couple is also noteworthy for being non-dysfunctional and apparently happy, a situation that is rare in Virgilian poetry, where couples more often resemble the highly dysfunctional models of Aeneas and Dido or Latinus and Amata.

[19] *huc, pater, o Lenaee, veni, nudataque* <u>musto</u> | *tinge* <u>novo</u> *mecum dereptis crura coturnis* (2.7–8); see Thomas 1988 ad loc.

[20] Cic. *De Orat.* 3.103, *suavitatem habeat [orator] austeram et solidam, non dulcem atque* <u>decoctam</u>. Bramble 1974:139n1 cites this and other stylistic uses of *decoctus* as a parallel to Persius 1.125 (*aspice et haec, si forte aliquid* <u>decoctius</u> *audis*). On the terminological overlap between rhetorical and poetic stylistic terminology, cf. Batstone 1998 and Keith 1999.

[21] See Cameron 1995:378, who points out that this root meaning of ἀπομάσσω (LSJ I, 'wipe off') is felt also in Callimachus' other metaphorical use of the word, of foam being "skimmed off" the sea (Ἰκαρίου πολλὴν <u>ἀπομάσσεται</u> ὕδατος ἄχνην, *Hymn* 4.14); although earlier translators of *Epigr.* 27 preferred renderings like "imitate," even in this sense the word retains much of its root force elsewhere (cf. LSJ s.v. III, 'imitate' < 'take an impression of').

Virgil's nighttime chores the literalization of Callimachean metaphor: in line 295, one sees the farmer's wife boiling down the sweet grape must (*dulcis musti umor*) to leave only the sweetest part (τὸ μελιχρότατον, Callim. *Epigr.* 27.2).[22] Moreover, just as Virgil coined the word *inspicat* to allude precisely to Aratus' Στάχυς, so in line 296 he has coined the word *despumat* to translate Callimachus' ἀπεμάξατο.[23] Thus, according to Callimachus, did Aratus boil down the poetry of Hesiod and skim off only the sweetest parts for his own didactic poem.

In the first two and last two lines of this passage, then, Virgil alludes precisely to literary-critical metaphors that neatly sum up Callimachus' views on (a) the stylistic refinement that Aratus demonstrates in putting didactic subject matter into verse, and (b) the admirable way that Aratus imitates his eminent generic predecessor, Hesiod. Together these metaphors constitute a manifesto with obvious implications for Virgil's own project of didactic imitation in the *Georgics*. Virgil effects these allusions, moreover, by literalizing the terms of stylistic metaphors. In the central two lines of this vignette, he literalizes two more such metaphors. The first of these he draws from Leonidas; the second involves the stylistic quality that Aratus claims for himself in his acrostic, and for which he is praised by Callimachus, Leonidas, and Ptolemy—λεπτότης.

In this central couplet, Virgil introduces the wife of his anonymous farmer, who sings and weaves cloth while he carves torches:

---

[22] It is worth noting that although both Virgil and Callimachus talk of reduction and skimming, the process that Virgil describes is not quite the same as the process that Callimachus' metaphor presupposes. While Virgil describes the reduction of wine must by boiling and skimming off the foam, Callimachus seems rather to refer to the skimming of cream off raw milk, since the sweetest part is what is skimmed off instead of what is left behind. Virgil may here be "correcting" Callimachus' metaphor, or he may simply be recontextualizing a literary-critical metaphor, as I believe he does elsewhere in his poetry.

[23] As Thomas 1988 notes ad loc., *despumare* appears first here, then not again until Silver Latin. Thomas also cites several epicisms in these lines (*Vulcano*, *undam*) and suggests that this passage, like Ovid's treatment of Baucis and Philemon in *Met.* 8, may owe something to Callimachus' *Hecale*. It is possible that Virgil here filters the language of Callimachus' epigram through an image drawn from Callimachus' epyllion.

interea longum cantu solata laborem
arguto coniunx percurrit pectine telas

Geo. 1.293–294

The poetological tenor of these lines is first suggested by Virgil's phrase *longum cantu solata laborem*, which links the Hellenistic notion that poetry is *labor* to the pastoral conceit that poetry/song is the most effective *solacium*.[24] This passage is no vague reference to a common conceit, however, since *labor* is distinct here from the wife's song of consolation and cannot therefore be simply a metonym for poetry. Like *quemvis efferre laborem* at Lucr. 1.141, Virgil's *longum ... laborem* at *Georgics* 1.293 is a metaphor for painstaking composition, because, like Lucretius' phrase, Virgil's alludes specifically to Leonidas *AP* 9.25, which characterizes Aratus as "toiling at a great labor" (καμὼν ἔργον μέγα, 5) in composing the *Phaenomena*.[25] Like Lucretius, Virgil alludes to Leonidas *AP* 9.25 in tandem with Callimachus *Epigram* 27, both Hellenistic epigrams on Aratus that themselves allude to stylistic features of the *Phaenomena* that Vergil replicates in analogous places in *Georgics* 1.

As she sings, the farmer's wife also weaves (*coniunx percurrit pectine telas*, 294), and through this activity too Virgil alludes to the metaphorical language used in Hellenistic epigrams on Aratus. The main feature shared by the epigrams of Callimachus and Leonidas—and which they share also with that of Ptolemy—is their praise of Aratus as λεπτός, a characterization that probably alludes to Aratus' ΛΕΠΤΗ acrostic. But although Virgil takes pains elsewhere in this passage to translate into Latin the Greek metaphors that he literalizes (even coining two new words), and although he uses two Latin equivalents of λεπτός programmatically in the *Eclogues* (*tenuis: Ecl.* 1.2, 6.8; *deductus: Ecl.* 6.5),

---

[24] On "toil" and poetry in Hellenistic and Roman poetry, see Brink 1963–1982 on Hor. *Epist.* 2.1.224–225 and Lyne 1978 on *Ciris* 99; particularly interesting in this context is *AP* 7.11 (= Asclepiades 28 G.-P.), where Asclepiades seems already to link poetry, weaving, and toil when he characterizes the *Distaff* of Erinna as a γλυκὺς πόνος. Regarding the consolatory power of song, pastoral song is specifically able to console the suffering of love. Theocritus thematizes this credo at *Id.* 11.1–3, and Virgil clearly intends this pastoral meaning when he uses the word *solari* at *Ecl.* 6.46 and *Geo.* 4.464.

[25] Horace too uses *labor* in this sense in connection with poetry; cf. *limae labor et mora, Ars P.* 291, with Brink 1963–1982 ad loc.

he uses no such equivalent term either in this passage or in his adaptation of Aratus' acrostic at *Georgics* 1.429–433. Remarking on Virgil's
acrostic—where the poet instead sets an odd form of authorial signature—Thomas has argued that Virgil's omission constitutes an intentional suppression, and that Aratus' λεπτός becomes conspicuous by
its absence.[26] Not all scholars have accepted Thomas's argument (not
to mention those who reject Virgil's acrostic altogether),[27] but the
suppression of λεπτός in Virgil's acrostic finds support in the present
metapoetic vignette, where again Virgil suppresses this term—here
in an allusion not only to Aratus but also to the Hellenistic epigrams
that specifically praised Aratus for his λεπτότης. Although we find no
translation of this important stylistic term, Virgil's method of literalizing metaphors remains unchanged: before λεπτός ('fine-spun') was
a Hellenistic program-word, it was in Homer a common attribute of
woven fabrics.[28] Virgil has literalized this Hellenistic metaphor in the
literal weaving of his farmer's wife, and by again suppressing the Latin
equivalents of λεπτός, he draws attention to his literal rendering of this
most important stylistic metaphor.[29]

---

[26] See Thomas 1988 *ad Geo.* 1.433, who suggests that either Virgil reserves such important literary terms for explicit discussions of poetics or "suppression of the expected
may serve as a means of emphasis." On suppression as a common feature of etymological wordplay (with which Virgil's metapoetic technique in this passage has much in
common), see O'Hara 1996:79–82, who notes both that Alexandrian and Augustan poets
use suppression broadly, and that the term itself comes from Servius (*ad Geo.* 2.126: *per
periphrasin ostendit, eius* <u>supprimens</u> *nomen*). On acrostics as a form of authorial signature
(their usual function), see Courtney 1990; on Virgil's acrostic, see references at n9 above.

[27] Haslam 1992:202, e.g., criticizes Thomas for resorting to the "deafening silence"
ploy.

[28] In ten of twenty instances of a form of λεπτός in Homer, the adjective is a direct
attribute of fabric: *Il.* 18.595, 22.511; *Od.* 2.95, 5.231, 7.97, 10.223, 10.544, 17.97, 19.140,
24.130. Cf. also Servius' note on *deductum* at *Ecl.* 6.5 (*translatio a lana, quae deducitur in tenui-
tatem*; cf. Clausen 1994 ad loc.). Already in Homer, however, the cognate term λεπταλέος,
in its single use, is an aesthetic term: in a pastoral scene on the shield of Achilles, a boy is
said to sing the Linus-song with a λεπταλέος voice to the accompaniment of a λιγύς lyre,
τοῖσιν δ' ἐν μέσσοισι πάϊς φόρμιγγι λιγείῃ | ἱμερόεν κιθάριζε, λίνον δ' ὑπὸ καλὸν ἄειδε |
λεπταλέῃ φωνῇ, *Il.* 18.569–571. On this acoustic aspect of λεπτός, see Asper 1997:177–179.

[29] Prominent passages in Catullus and Virgil show that Roman poets drew a persistent and important link between weaving and poetry: e.g. the Song of the Parcae in
Catullus 64.305–381; *Ecl.* 10.70-1, where Servius remarks that Virgil has used basket-
weaving as a metaphor for poetic style; and the spinning/singing scene from *Geo.* 4.345–

It is difficult to demonstrate suppression without arguing *ex silentio*. In the present case, however, we may look to Virgil's reuse of *Georgics* 1.294 in the opening of *Aeneid* 7, where he makes only a single change to the line. In this passage Aeneas and his crew sail past the palace of Circe, where the Homeric sorceress sits weaving and singing:

> proxima Circaeae raduntur litora terrae,
> dives inaccessos ubi Solis filia lucos
> adsiduo resonat cantu, tectisque superbis
> urit odoratam nocturna in lumina cedrum
> arguto <u>tenuis</u> percurrens pectine telas.

Aen. 7.10–14

These lines from *Aeneid* 7 have attracted considerable critical attention, not least because of Virgil's use of the term *tenuis*, an established equivalent of λεπτός (see above), in a passage with programmatic implications for the second half of the *Aeneid*. As Thomas has remarked, the substitution of *tenuis* for *coniunx* renders the *Aeneid* 7 line "oddly like a metaphor for Alexandrian or neoteric poetic composition."[30] Stratis Kyriakidis has argued more recently that the specific source of this programmatic language is Homer's description of Circe's weaving and singing in *Odyssey* 10: he proposes that *tenuis* alludes programmatically to the λεπτός quality of Circe's weaving in the passage, while *arguto pectine* alludes to the specification that her singing is λιγύς:[31]

> ἔσταν δ' ἐν προθύροισι θεᾶς καλλιπλοκάμοιο,
> Κίρκης δ' ἔνδον ἄκουον <u>ἀειδούσης</u> ὀπὶ καλῇ

351, in which the nymph Clymene recounts the Homeric story of the affair of Mars and Venus (known from Demodocus' song in *Od.* 8.266–366). These examples are discussed apropos of weaving in Ovid by Rosati 1999.

[30] Thomas 1985:66. Thomas 1988 discusses *Geo.* 1.293–294 at some length and finds "some tantalizing resonances" with other passages in Augustan poetry. Few readers, however, have been as captivated by the rustic housewife's song as they are by Circe's: Kyriakidis 1998:90–117, who is very sensitive to metapoetic significance in Circe's tuneful weaving, remarks insistently that the nearly identical weaving and singing of *Geo.* 1 "is to be taken literally and has no possibility of operating metaphorically" (100). Erren 2003, however, sees at *Geo.* 1.293 the traces of a neoteric adaptation of Homer.

[31] Kyriakidis 1998:96–102.

ἱστὸν ἐποιχομένης μέγαν ἄμβροτον, οἷα θεάων
<u>λεπτά τε καὶ χαρίεντα</u> καὶ ἀγλαὰ ἔργα πέλονται.

...

ἔνθα δέ τις μέγαν ἱστὸν ἐποιχομένη <u>λίγ' ἄειδεν</u>
ἢ θεὸς ἠὲ γυνή· τοὶ δ' ἐφθέγγοντο καλεῦντες.

Od. 10.220–223, 254–255

Kyriakidis's argument is attractive, but although Virgil's *tenuis* does seem to allude to Homer's use of λεπτός in this passage, his *arguto pectine* is not as close to λίγ' ἄειδεν as one might like. Instead, the clearest proof that *Aeneid* 7 relies specifically on *Odyssey* 10 comes from *Georgics* 1.293–294, where Homer's Circe serves as a model for Virgil's weaving *coniunx* before being a model for Virgil's Circe in *Aeneid* 7.[32] Not only does Circe's weaving in *Odyssey* 10 serve as a model for Virgil to literalize the weaving metaphor that underlies Callimachus' λεπταὶ ῥήσιες (*Epigr.* 27.3–4), Leonidas' λεπτῇ φροντίδι (AP 9.25.1–2), and Aratus' ΛΕΠΤΗ acrostic (*Phaen.* 783–787), but the program-word λεπτός, which Virgil suppresses in *Georgics* 1, is in *Odyssey* 10 a direct attribute of Circe's weaving (<u>λεπτά</u> τε καὶ χαρίεντα, 10.223). And it is at *Georgics* 1.293–294, not in *Aeneid* 7, that one finds intact the allusion to Homer's λίγ' ἄειδεν:

interea longum *cantu* solata laborem
arguto coniunx percurrit pectine telas

Geo. 1.293–294

Although most commentators have read *arguto* with *pectine*, as one must in *Aeneid* 7, the word's placement in *Georgics* 1 allows it to be read either with *pectine* in its own line or with *cantu* in the previous line.[33]

---

[32] The Circe scene at *Od.* 10:132–574 was familiar not only from Homer, but also from an allusion at Theocritus *Id.* 15.79: see Burton 1995:173–175.

[33] Adding to a clause that could be read as syntactically complete in itself constitutes "unperiodic" or "adding" enjambment, a type of enjambment especially common in oral poets like Homer and Hesiod (the latter is Virgil's primary model in this section); see conveniently Higbie 1990. This type of enjambment is less common in Virgil, but for the adding enjambment of an adjective cf. *Geo.* 1.145–6, *labor omnia vicit | improbus*, which similarly uses a runover adjective to cultivate ambiguity (here a temporary ambiguity

By reading it with *cantu* one finds an allusion to Homer's Circe and her melodious weaving in *Odyssey* 10.[34]

Virgil's reuse of this line in *Aeneid* 7 sounds (in Thomas's words, quoted in full above) "oddly like" a poetological metaphor because it alludes to his own literalization of a poetological metaphor in *Georgics* 1. In the *Georgics*, Virgil uses Homer's Circe to literalize the metaphorical λεπτότης that Hellenistic epigrams attributed to Aratus. In the *Aeneid*, he reuses his own allusion to Aratus through Circe instead of alluding directly to *Odyssey* 10; in this process he reveals the previously suppressed aesthetic term *tenuis* (= λεπτός), but he severs *cantu* from its complement *arguto*, obscuring the full allusion to Homer's Circe (λεπτὰ τε καὶ χαρίεντα, 10.223; λίγ᾽ ἄειδεν, 10.254) from any who did not recognize the allusion in *Georgics* 1. Why would Virgil so complicate an allusion to Homer's Circe in his own description of the Homeric sorceress? Thomas answers this question when he discusses the interaction of Callimacheanism and epic in the proem to *Aeneid* 7: "precisely because at the point where his epic will become particularly traditional or Homeric Virgil is concerned to avoid the taint deriving from mere Homeric imitation."[35] Certainly, Virgil cannot be accused of simplicity

---

between the conceivably positive phrase *labor omnia vicit* and the negative *labor improbus omnia vicit*). On the rhythm of enjambed *arguto*, cf. Eden 1975 *ad Aen.* 8.227, who notes that a line-initial molossus preceding a pause acts to support the meaning of the word.

[34] Page 1898, Thomas 1988, and Mynors 1990 all read *arguto* with *pectine*, following Heyne 1830 *ad loc.*, who argues the point based on "ratio poetica" and on the attribution of melodious sound to the shuttle by Greek poets. This reading, however, has sparked controversy over how the weaver's comb can be said to be *argutus*: see Mynors *ad* 1.293–294 and the reply of Horsfall 2000 *ad Aen.* 7.14; ingenious solutions are suggested by Henry 1889 *ad Aen.* 7.14 and by Yates 1842:943. More recently, Erren 2003 *ad Geo.* 1.287–96 and 1.293 has realized the degree to which *Aen.* 7.14 depends on *Geo.* 1.293–294 (although he sees a reference to Calypso, not Circe, in the *Georgics*) and has preferred *arguto cantu* to "dem unverständlichen Ausdruck" *arguto pectine*. While many factors urge one to read *arguto* with *pectine*—among them the symmetry of *Geo.* 1.294 and *Aen.* 7.14 (the latter, where *tenuis* is no longer suppressed, is a golden line)—there is much to gain from reading it with *cantu* and little to stop a Roman, reading or hearing lines 293–294 one word at a time, from connecting *arguto* with *cantu*.

[35] Thomas 1985:64. Here it is worth considering the implications of Cameron's argument (see above, n2) that the Hellenistic program of λεπτότης originated with Aratus rather than Callimachus. In that case, an allusion to Aratus could serve well as a modernist stylistic disclaimer in the most Homeric section of Virgil's epic.

or "mere" Homeric imitation in either *Aeneid* 7 or *Georgics* 1. In *Georgics* 1 he requires his reader to recognize an allusion to Homer's Circe and to read it against his systematic allusion to Hellenistic praise of Aratus, cross-referencing the two to arrive at the suppressed program-word λεπτός. In *Aeneid* 7 he makes a Homeric allusion less "merely" Homeric by requiring that it be read through his own earlier allusion to Aratus in *Georgics* 1.

Virgil's admiration for Aratus, evident in his large-scale adaptation of the *Phaenomena* in *Georgics* 1, has often puzzled modern critics, to whom technical verses on astronomy and meteorology seem dry and unengaging. I hope that, by demonstrating concerted intertextual engagement on Virgil's part with well-known Hellenistic praise of Aratus, I have shed some light not just on the nature of this admiration, but perhaps also on its origin. The fascinating complexity of Virgil's metaphorical allusion to Aratus suggests that the latter was no second-class model for *Georgics* 1. The association of *labor* with poetic refinement, moreover, may have implications not only for *Georgics* 1, with its heavy emphasis on this theme (especially in the "aetiology of *labor*," 1.118–159), but for other sections of the poem as well.

Virgil's method in these lines, furthermore, shows us much about the nature of this most complex poem. D. O. Ross remarked that Virgil wrote about agriculture partly because "the very subject allows metaphor to become reality."[36] We are familiar with this effect in Virgil's adaptation of Homeric similes—as in the allusion to Achilles and the Scamander in the passage on irrigation at *Georgics* 1.104–10—but Virgil's metapoetic vignette at *Georgics* 1.291–296 shows that we must also be alert to the adaptation of literary-critical metaphors in the *Georgics*, as we already are in the *Eclogues*. Indeed, the fact that such an important theme as *labor* is here revealed as a metaphor for poetry should put readers on their guard throughout this poem. It is characteristic of Virgil's technique in this difficult poem that passages of major significance, metapoetic or otherwise, are often not trumpeted with clearly programmatic language. Rather, every innovation or departure from a model may hide some important clue to Virgil's intentions in this chal-

---

[36] Ross 1987:26.

lenging and learned work. I do not suggest that we can find metapoetic meaning behind every passage of Virgil's poetry, but we should be willing to see metapoetic commentary in even the most unassuming line or passage. Although Virgil sometimes shouts his intentions to readers using clearly programmatic language (*Ascraeumque cano Romana per oppida carmen, Geo.* 2.176), he often whispers.

GEORGETOWN COLLEGE

WORKS CITED

Asper, M. 1997. *Onomata Allotria: Zur Genese, Struktur und Funktion poetologischer Metaphern bei Kallimachos.* Hermes Einzelschriften 75. Stuttgart.

Barchiesi, A. 1981. "Letture e trasformazioni di un mito arateo (Cic. *Arat.* XVII Tr.; Verg. *georg.* 2,473 sg.)." *MD* 6:181–187.

Batstone, W. W. 1998. "Dry Pumice and the Programmatic Language of Catullus 1." *CP* 93:125–135.

Bing, P. 1993. "Aratus and his Audiences." *MD* 31:99–109.

Bowman, A. K., and J. D. Thomas. 1974. *The Vindolanda Writing Tablets.* Newcastle upon Tyne.

Bramble, J. C. 1974. *Persius and the Programmatic Satire: A Study in Form and Imagery.* Cambridge.

Brink, C. O., ed. 1963–1982. *Horace on Poetry.* 3 vols. Cambridge.

Brown, E. L. 1963. *Numeri Vergiliani: Studies in "Eclogues" and "Georgics."* Collection Latomus 63. Brussels.

Brown, R. D. 1982. "Lucretius and Callimachus." *ICS* 7:77–97.

———. 1987. *Lucretius on Love and Sex: A Commentary on* De rerum natura *IV, 1030-1287.* Leiden.

Brugnoli-Riccardo Scarcia, S. 1987. "Numerologia." In *Enciclopedia Virgiliana,* ed. F. della Corte, vol. 3, 788–793. Florence.

Burton, J. B. 1995. *Theocritus's Urban Mimes: Mobility, Gender, and Patronage.* Berkeley.

Cameron, A. 1995. *Callimachus and His Critics.* Princeton.

Clausen, W. 1994. *A Commentary on Virgil,* Eclogues. Oxford.

Clauss, J. J. 1997. "An Acrostic in Vergil (*Eclogues* I 5–8): The Chance That Mimics Choice?" *Aevum Antiquum* 10:267–287.

Courtney, E. 1990. "Greek and Latin Acrostichs." *Philologus* 134:3–13.

Damschen, G. 2004. "Das lateinische Akrostichon: Neue Funde bei Ovid sowie Vergil, Grattius, Manilius und Silius Italicus." *Philologus* 148:88–115.

Danielewicz, J. 2005. "Further Hellenistic Acrostics: Aratus and Others." *Mnemosyne*, 4th ser., 58:321–334.

Eden, P. T. 1975. *A Commentary on Virgil:* Aeneid *VIII.* Mnemosyne Supplement 35. Leiden.

Edmunds, L. 2002. "Mars as Hellenistic Lover: Lucretius, *De rerum natura* 1.29-40 and Its Subtexts." *International Journal of the Classical Tradition* 8:343–358.

Enk, P. J. 1918. *Gratti Cynegeticon quae supersunt.* Zutphen.

Erren, M. 2003. *P. Vergilius Maro. Georgica.* Vol. 2. Heidelberg.

Ewbank, W. W. 1933. *The Poems of Cicero.* London.

Farrell, J. 1991. *Vergil's* Georgics *and the Traditions of Ancient Epic: The Art of Allusion in Literary History.* Oxford and New York.

Feeney, D., and D. Nelis. 2005. "Two Virgilian Acrostics: *Certissima signa?*" *CQ*, n.s., 55:644–646.

Fisher, R. S. 1982. "Conon and the Poet: A Solution to *Eclogue*, III, 40-2." *Latomus* 41:803–814.

Gale, M. R. 1994. *Myth and Poetry in Lucretius.* Cambridge.

———. 2000. *Virgil on the Nature of Things: The* Georgics, *Lucretius and the Didactic Tradition.* Cambridge.

Gonis, N., D. Obbink, and P. J. Parsons, eds. 2003. *The Oxyrhynchus Papyri.* Vol. 68. London.

Grishin, A. A. 2008. "*Ludus in undis*: An Acrostic in *Eclogue 9.*" *HSCP* 104:237–240.

Hardie, P. R. 1986. *Virgil's* Aeneid: *Cosmos and Imperium.* Oxford.

Harrison, S. 2004. "Virgil's *Corycius Senex* and Nicander's *Georgica: Georgics* 4.116–48." In *Latin Epic and Didactic Poetry: Genre, Tradition and Individuality*, ed. M. Gale, 109–123. Swansea, Wales.

Haslam, M. 1992. "Hidden Signs: Aratus *Diosemeiai* 46 ff., Vergil *Georgics* 1.424 ff." *HSCP* 94:199–204.

Henry, J. 1889. *Aeneidea, or Critical, Exegetical, and Aesthetical Remarks on the* Aeneis. Vol. 3. London.

Heyne, C. G. 1830. *Publius Vergilius Maro varietate lectionis et perpetua adnotatione illustratus.* 4th ed. Ed. G. P. E. Wagner. Vol. 1. London.

Higbie, C. 1990. *Measure and Music: Enjambment and Sentence Structure in the* Iliad. Oxford.

Hollis, A. S. 2007. *Fragments of Roman Poetry, c. 60 BC–AD 20.* Oxford.

Hopkinson, N., ed. 1988. *A Hellenistic Anthology.* Cambridge.

Horsfall, N., ed. 2000. *Virgil,* Aeneid *7: A Commentary.* Mnemosyne Suppl. 198. Leiden.

Hunter, R., ed. 1999. *Theocritus: A Selection.* Cambridge.

Jacques, J.-M. 1960. "Sur un acrostiche d'Aratos (*Phén.,* 783–787)." *Revue des études anciennes* 62:48–61.

Katz, J. T. 2008. "Vergil Translates Aratus: *Phaenomena* 1–2 and *Georgics* 1.1–2." *MD* 60:105–123.

Keith, A. M. 1999. "Slender Verse: Roman Elegy and Ancient Rhetorical Theory." *Mnemosyne,* 4th ser., 52:41–62.

Kenney, E. J. 1970. "*Doctus* Lucretius." *Mnemosyne,* 4th ser., 23:366–392.

Kidd, D. A. 1997. *Aratus. Phaenomena.* Cambridge Classical Texts and Commentaries 34. Cambridge.

Kyriakidis, S. 1998. *Narrative Structure and Poetics in the* Aeneid: *The Frame of Book 6.* Bari.

Lipka, M. 2001. *Language in Vergil's* Eclogues. Berlin and New York.

Lyne, R. O. A. M. 1978. Ciris: *A Poem Attributed to Vergil.* Cambridge.

McKeown, J. C., ed. 1989. *Ovid. Amores.* Vol. 2, *A Commentary on Book One.* Liverpool.

Mynors, R. A. B. 1990. *Virgil. Georgics.* Oxford.

O'Hara, J. 1996. *True Names: Vergil and the Alexandrian Tradition of Etymological Wordplay.* Ann Arbor, MI.

Page, T. E. 1898. *P. Vergili Maronis Bucolica et Georgica.* London.

Perkell, C. 1989. *The Poet's Truth: A Study of the Poet in Virgil's* Georgics. Berkeley.

Rosati, G. 1999. "Form in Motion: Weaving the Text in the *Metamorphoses.*" In *Ovidian Transformations: Essays on Ovid's* Metamorphoses *and Its Reception,* ed. P. Hardie, A. Barchiesi, and S. Hinds, Cambridge Philological Society Supplementary Volume 23, 240–253. Cambridge.

Ross, D. O. 1975. *Backgrounds to Augustan Poetry: Gallus, Elegy and Rome.* Cambridge.

———. 1987. *Virgil's Elements: Physics and Poetry in the* Georgics. Princeton.

Stewart, S. 2008. "Emending Aratus' Insomnia: Callimachus *Epigr.* 27." *Mnemosyne* 61:586–600.

Thibodeau, P. 2001. "The Old Man and His Garden (Verg. *Georg.* 4, 116-148)." *MD* 47:175–195.

Thomas, R. F. 1979. "New Comedy, Callimachus, and Roman Poetry." *HSCP* 83:179–206.

———. 1985. "From *recusatio* to Commitment: The Evolution of a Vergilian Programme." *Papers of the Liverpool Latin Seminar* 5:61–73.

———. 1988. *Virgil. Georgics.* 2 vols. Cambridge.

Vogt, E. 1967. "Das Akrostichon in der griechischen Literatur." *Antike und Abendland* 13:80–95.

Yates, J. 1842. "Tela." In *A Dictionary of Greek and Roman Antiquities*, ed. W. Smith, 940–944. London.

THE COROEBUS EPISODE IN VIRGIL'S *AENEID*

Salvatore Monda

I N DESCRIBING THE LAST NIGHT OF TROY Virgil remodels the previous tradition in many ways.[1] The Coroebus episode in the second book of the
Aeneid recounts the exploit which led to the death of this hero allied
with the Trojans. At 2.341 Virgil introduces Coroebus, son of Mygdon,
who *illis ad Troiam forte diebus | uenerat insano Cassandrae incensus
amore*.[2] He was in love with Priam's daughter,[3] who went unheeded
when she foretold his tragic fate (345–346). In Virgil's *Iliupersis* the

---

I am much indebted for advice and corrections to the anonymous referee.

[1] See Rossi 2002, with references.

[2] Coroebus' name appears among the traditional μωροί like Margites and Melitides:
see, among others, Call. fr. inc. 587 Pfeiffer: ἑπτὰ σοφοὶ χαίροιτε—τὸν ὄγδοον, ὥστε
Κόροιβον, οὐ συναριθμέομεν—; Serv. ad Aen. 2.341 (= Euphorion fr. 76 van Groningen):
hunc autem Coroebum stultum inducit Euphorion, quem et Vergilius sequitur, dans ei [*Aen.* 2.390]
"dolus an uirtus, quis in hoste requirat?" cum sit turpis dolo quaesita uictoria, on which Heinze
1915:37n1. Austin 1964:151 observes that "Virgil's Coroebus shows no trace of contamina-
tion from the 'silly' tradition, and Servius' ground for thinking so is absurd." Still, with
the words *insano ... incensus amore* Virgil probably meant to make an implicit reference to
the "silly tradition," but then he preferred to present his character in the heroic version
alone (see, too, Heinze 1915:36: "vielleicht gründete sie sich daneben auf den Leichtsinn,
mit dem er die Warnungen der Braut in den Wind schlug"; Mazzocchini 2000:318–319,
who also compares line 407, *furiata mente Coroebus*).

[3] In Hom. *Il.* 13.363–376 the suitor of Cassandra is Othryoneus, killed by Idomeneus.
But Coroebus appears already in pseudo-Euripides' *Rhesus* (539, Μυγδόνος υἱόν ...
Κόροιβον) and in the *Ilias parua* (on which see below). The hero is also mentioned in
P. Ryland 22 (1st cent. AD, see *FGrH* 18), killed by Diomedes during the theft of the
Palladion. Finally, Quintus Smyrnaeus in his *Posthomerica* (ca. 4th c. AD) describes him
as in love with Cassandra (13.168–176), and killed by Diomedes. He does not appear in
Tryphiodorus' *Capture of Troy* (3rd or 4th cent. AD). On Coroebus, see the commentaries by Heyne–Wagner 1832:403, esp. the "Excursus X. De Coroebo," 531–532; Forbiger
1873:233; Conington–Nettleship 1884:125 on line 341; Horsfall 2008:285–286. See also
Heinze 1915:36–39, and Gärtner 2005:233–235. The character should not be confused with
the hero mentioned by Stat. *Theb.* 1.605–616. and Paus. 1.43.7–8 (see Koroibos 1, in *RE* XI
[1922] 1418.49–1420.57).

aristeia of Coroebus develops through a double deception: first the
Greek Androgeus dies, deceived by the unexpected appearance of the
enemy (371–372, *socia agmina credens | inscius*), then Coroebus, spurred
on by this success, proposes that the Trojans strip the enemy dead and
disguise themselves as Greeks (386–395):

> atque hic successu exsultans animisque Coroebus
> "o socii, qua prima" inquit "Fortuna salutis
> monstrat iter, quaque ostendit se dextra, sequamur:
> mutemus clipeos Danaumque insignia nobis
> aptemus. dolus an uirtus, quis in hoste requirat?
> arma dabunt ipsi." sic fatus deinde comantem
> Androgei galeam clipeique insigne decorum
> induitur laterique Argiuum accommodat ensem.
> hoc Rhipeus, hoc ipse Dymas omnisque iuuentus
> laeta facit: spoliis se quisque recentibus armat.

But the first victories are gained through an *error* and a despoil-
ment, and as a result Coroebus and his comrades are fated to meet a
cruel end. After the first successes against the Greeks the episode
of Cassandra marks the reversal in the fortunes of Coroebus' band
(402–409): the Trojan defenders' error of judgment in attacking their
comrades, mistaking them for Greeks, arises just when Coroebus tries
to save his beloved as she is dragged from the temple of Minerva. Some
Trojans succumb to the arrows of other Trojans who take them for
enemies (410–412):

> hic primum ex alto delubri culmine telis
> nostrorum obruimur oriturque miserrima caedes
> armorum facie et Graiarum errore iubarum.

Then follows (413–430) the attack by the Greeks, who detect the deception because the Trojans speak a language different from their own
(422–423, *primi clipeos mentitaque tela | agnoscunt atque ora sono discordia
signant*).[4] Coroebus meets his death fighting to save Cassandra: he is

---

[4] Forbiger (1873:246–247) in his commentary on line 423 observes that Homer never
assumes that Greeks and Trojans spoke different languages, but the later Greek poets

killed by Peneleus (424–426),[5] whereas others die at the hands of their own comrades (428–429, *pereunt Hypanisque Dymasque | confixi a sociis*).

In this passage of the second book the episode of the massacre of Trojans through mistaken identity is entirely unnecessary in terms of narrative structure, since after this the slaughter described in detail is that by the Greeks,[6] and even the hero of the episode, Coroebus, dies at the hands of a Greek. But Virgil does not forego the opportunity to make this story more dramatic and exciting. The poet constructs two deceptions: after a fortuitous mistake that cuts short Androgeus' life, other Greeks are deceived by Coroebus, but then the Trojans are killed accidentally by other Trojans.

Scholars have always wondered about the literary antecedent of this episode. Virgil was probably looking back to earlier post-Homeric epic poetry, as the character of Coroebus is mentioned in the *Ilias parua*, a poem of the Homeric Cycle attributed to Lesches (*EGF* F 16 Davies, quoted by Paus. 10.27.1):[7]

> ἀφίκετο μὲν δὴ ἐπὶ τὸν Κασσάνδρας ὁ Κόροιβος γάμον,
> ἀπέθανε δέ, ὡς μὲν ὁ πλείων λόγος, ὑπὸ Νεοπτολέμου,
> Λέσχεως δὲ ὑπὸ Διομήδους ἐποίησεν.

But neither Pausanias nor Quintus Smyrnaeus[8] tell of the mistaken identity, and some scholars have suggested that Virgil has modeled this motif on historical events. For errors of this kind Heinze[9] quotes

---

make them differ. See also Conington–Nettleship 1884:133 on line 423, Ross 2005, and Horsfall 2008:333 on line 423.

[5] Heinze (1915:38 and n1) thinks that Coroebus' death in a desperate attempt to save Cassandra may be an invention of Virgil ("Coroebus im Kampf um die Braut fallend ist eine sehr glückliche, wie ich meine, Virgil gehörige Erfindung"). See, too, Heinze 1915:38n3 (in Paus. 10.27.1 Coroebus was killed by Neoptolemus, or, according to Lesches, by Diomedes).

[6] A reason that prompted Müller (1876) to transpose 420–423 to follow 412, and Baehrens (1876:152) to transpose 420–430 to follow 412; see also Heinze 1915:38n2. But, as Austin (1964:171 on line 414) stressed, "*primum* (410) and *tum* (413) introduce these disasters in general, and the details follow."

[7] There is nothing on this issue in Kopff 1981.

[8] See above, n3.

[9] Heinze 1915:36 (and n1).

Frontinus *Strat.* 3.2.4 and 11,[10] while Austin observes that "Virgil well knew that such things can happen in war, and our age knows it too."[11] On line 412 Austin refers to Livy 22.1.3[12] as well as Frontinus, and on line 389 he mentions Xen. *Hell.* 4.4.10[13] as "an interesting parallel to Virgil."[14] Yet, in addition to these suggestions that Virgil may be drawing on the reality of war and on historiography, we can also draw attention to a probable epic antecedent.

It seems likely that there is a parallel in the Cyzicus episode in Apollonius of Rhodes 1.936–1152.[15] Although the similarity is not complete, in Virgil's narrative there may be an echo of Apollonius' battle with the Doliones. The eponymous king Cyzicus and the Doliones are central figures in an episode of the Argonautic expedition,[16] the

---

[10] 3.2.4, *Arcades Messeniorum castellum obsidentes, factis quibusdam armis ad similitudinem hostilium, eo tempore quo successura alia praesidia his explorauerant, instructi eorum qui exspectabantur ornatu, admissique per hunc errorem ut socii, possessionem loci cum strage hostium adepti sunt.* 3.2.11, *Timarchus Aetolus, occiso Charmade Ptolomaei regis praefecto, clamide interempti et galeari ad Macedonici ornatus habitum <***>. per hunc errorem pro Charmade in Saniorum portum receptus <oppidum> occupauit.*

[11] Austin 1964:170 on 2.411.

[12] [Hannibal] *seruatus erat et mutando nunc uestem nunc tegumenta capitis errore etiam sese ab insidiis munierat.* Hannibal here defends himself from attacks by the Gauls who betrayed him, but in Livy's story the disguise is not followed by an accidental massacre.

[13] Πασίμαχος δὲ ὁ ἱππαρμοστής, ἔχων ἱππέας οὐ πολλούς, ὡς ἑώρα τοὺς Σικυωνίους πιεζομένους, καταδήσας ἀπὸ δένδρων τοὺς ἵππους, καὶ ἀφελόμενος τὰς ἀσπίδας αὐτῶν, μετὰ τῶν ἐθελόντων ᾔει ἐναντίον τοῖς Ἀργείοις. οἱ δὲ Ἀργεῖοι ὁρῶντες τὰ σίγμα τὰ ἐπὶ τῶν ἀσπίδων, ὡς Σικυωνίους οὐδὲν ἐφοβοῦντο. ἔνθα δὴ λέγεται εἰπὼν ὁ Πασίμαχος· Ναὶ τὼ σιώ, ὦ Ἀργεῖοι, ψευσεῖ ὑμὲ τὰ σίγμα ταῦτα, χωρεῖν ὁμόσε· καὶ οὕτω μαχόμενος μετ' ὀλίγων πρὸς πολλοὺς ἀποθνῄσκει καὶ ἄλλοι τῶν περὶ αὐτόν.

[14] Conington and Nettleship (1884:129–130 on *Aen.* 2.389) compare Tac. *Hist.* 1.38, *rapta statim arma, sine more at ordine militiae, ut praetorianus aut legionarius insignibus suis distingueretur: miscentur auxiliaribus galeis scutisque.* See also Horsfall 2008:303–304.

[15] On Apollonius' influence on Virgil, see La Ville de Mirmont 1894; Conrardy 1904; Rütten 1912; Leitich 1940; Mehmel 1940; Hügi 1952; Hunter 1993:170–189; Beye 1999; Nelis 2001; Nelis 2008. On the debts of the *Aeneid* to Hellenistic poetry, see Briggs 1981; Clausen 1987; Hollis 1992; La Penna 2005:173–181.

[16] On the Argonauts' meeting with the Doliones in Apollonius of Rhodes and the issue of the different versions of the myth, see Knaack 1887:33–41; Fitch 1912; Vian 1951; Hurst 1964; Vecchio 1998. On the history and antiquities of Cyzicus, see Hasluck 1910 (esp. 157–162 on the Argonautic legend). Ancient sources: Ephoros *FGrH* 70 F 61; Callisthenes *FGrH* 124 F 6; Deiochos *FGrH* 471 F 4–10. Ardizzoni (1967:234) observes that Apollonius combines the tradition represented by Ephorus and Callisthenes, according to which the Doliones were the Argonauts' enemies, with that of Deiochus of Proconnesus,

richest in *aetia* in the whole poem. After the Lemnian episode and the stop at the island of Samothrace, the Argo arrived at a small peninsula inside the Propontis, docking at the harbor of Cyzicus, a Phrygian town. King Cyzicus and the Doliones welcomed the Argonauts (961–971).[17] The next day the ship was brought from its first anchorage to the harbor Chytus, where Heracles and the Argonauts clashed with the Earthborn Giants (985–1011). They left at last, but, after one day at sea, the wind changed in the night and the Argonauts were unwittingly carried back to the same island (1015–1022). The Doliones mistook the Argonauts for their enemies, the Makries (a Pelasgian tribe), and engaged them in battle (1022–1028). The Argonauts, unaware of the mistake, killed many of the Doliones, and Cyzicus himself was slain by Jason's spear (1028–1039). At dawn they all realized the tragic error (ἀμπλακίην, 1053). They celebrated games in Cyzicus' honor and erected a monument (1057–1062) to him. Cleite, the young bride of Cyzicus, killed herself out of grief (1063–1069).[18]

---

according to which they welcomed the Argonauts in a friendly way. Apollonius—as Ardizzoni observes—combines and merges in his account a set of different and contradictory legends. After Apollonius of Rhodes, Cyzicus is mentioned by: Conon *FGrH* 26 F 1 (Cyzicus, attempting to stop the battle between his people and the Argonauts, mistaken for Thessalian enemies, was killed by Jason; see Hasluck 1910:160); Val. Flacc. 2.627–3.458 and *Orphic Argonautica* 484–600 (on both, see below n18). Finally, we must remember P. *Köln* 8, 332 (ed. Gronewald 1997), which contains a commentary on a (Callimachean?) poetical text mentioning the Doliones.

[17] This episode can be examined in the light of the Hellenistic hospitality theme, on which see Hollis 1990, Appendix III: "The Hospitality Theme."

[18] Valerius Flaccus 2.627–3.458 greatly amplifies Apollonius' narrative and introduces some variations, among which the most remarkable are: Jason's speech to the host (2.659–662) that seems to presage the events which follow; the absence of the battle of Heracles and the Argonauts against the Earthborn Giants; the sacrilege of Cyzicus in killing a lion sacred to the Magna Mater, which gives rise to the *infanda proelia* (3.20–31); the sleep of the helmsman Tiphys brings the ship back again (3.39–42); the battle is recounted in detail (3.95–256); Castor and Pollux by mistake (*tenebris fallacibus*) almost fight against each other (3.186–189); Cleite, the bride of Cyzicus, does not kill herself (3.314–331). See Hasluck 1910:160–161; Burck 1969; Manuwald 1999. Valerius' reworking of Apollonius' Cyzicus episode does not show any evidence of imitation of *Aeneid* 2. In the *Orphic Argonautica* (522–525) Cyzicus was killed by Heracles by mistake during the battle against the Giants; see Vian 1987:111 on lines 512–525: "Le poète combine le combat diurne contre les fils de la Terre (AR, 1, 989–1011; cf. 941–946) et la bataille nocturne où périt Kyzicos (AR, 1, 1026–1052)"; see, too, Hasluck 1910:161.

During the second visit to Cyzicus, in the darkness the Argonauts were mistaken for the Pelasgians, just as Coroebus and his *socii* were taken for Greeks. These two episodes have never been compared by scholars, perhaps because the imitation of *Arg.* 1.936–1077 in *Aen.* 2.386–430 does not involve verbal allusions but only similarity of action, and there is no connection in the broader narrative pattern; indeed, throughout the second book Apollonian material is very slight. In spite of this, I think that a connection between the scene involving Coroebus and the Cyzicus episode can be proposed.

There are other elements from Apollonius' episode in Virgil's. First, the most obvious feature common to both stories is that the mistake was committed in the confusion of night: the night setting makes the error more realistic. Apollonius of Rhodes insists on this aspect in several verses: 1015–1016, ἰούσης | νυκτός; 1019, αὐτονυχί; 1022, ὑπὸ νυκτί, as does Virgil: 360, *nox atra*; 397, *per caecam ... noctem*; and 420–422, *illi etiam, si quos obscura nocte per umbram* | *fudimus insidiis totaque agitauimus urbe,* | *apparent.* Moreover, the name of the Thracian people, the Doliones, is associated with δόλιος and δόλος. Note that Coroebus' ruse is described in his own words as a trick (390, *dolus an uirtus, quis in hoste requirat?*).[19] By introducing a word like *dolus* in Coroebus' speech, Virgil is probably signaling his imitation.[20] Comparable too is the way in which Virgil describes the heroes' deaths. With the exception of Cyzicus' and Coroebus' deaths, treated with a few more details, the deaths of Doliones (*Arg.* 1.1040–1047) and Trojans (*Aen.* 2.426–430) are told quickly, like simple catalogues that, unusually in the *Aeneid*, omit the names of the killers.[21] And then it should be recalled that Coroebus is not Trojan, but a Phrygian *socius* of the Trojans, like Cyzicus in the *Argonautica*. The Doliones were Phrygians who occupied Cyzicus after the Trojan War. As Carrington notes: "In Thrace, the Mygdones would

---

[19] In Virgil's narrative Coroebus' *dolus* is opposed to the Greeks' deception with the wooden horse.

[20] On the etymological wordplay between the name of Dolopes and *dolus* with regard to the theme of deceptive gifts in *Aeneid* 2 (2.7, MyrmiDONVM DOLOpumue; 2.252, MyrmiDONVMque DOLOS), see Moskalew 1990:275–279.

[21] For Apollonius, see Hunter 1993:43: "The basic technique is Iliadic: many brief deaths set off a more elaborate treatment of one death." On Virgil, see Mazzocchini 2000:330.

have been the southern neighbors of the 'Paeonian' Phrygians. The appearance of Mygdon, presumably the eponymous leader of this tribe, as a Phrygian leader in the *Iliad* may suggest that the Mygdones were thought of as a sub-group of Phrygians, as were the Doliones, neighbors of the Mygdones, in Homeric times, according to Apollodorus."[22] We must remember that the Phrygian king Mygdon is Coroebus' father.

But, quite apart from these clues that may support Virgil's borrowing, the main connection between the two episodes is the heroes' death at the hands of friends. Virgil could not ignore what seems to be the only example of its kind in Greek epic poetry. Lines 936–1011 of the first book of the *Argonautica* are compared by Rütten[23] with *Aen.* 1.157–197 "als der Handlungsgrundlage": Virgil, in Rütten's opinion, here follows Apollonius in the organization of the material, while he derives the rest from Homer.[24] But this comparison may be inappropriate. According to Nelis[25] there is no connection with *Arg.* 1.936–1011 to be found in *Aen.* 1.157–197. He argues,[26] on the contrary, that the landing of the Trojans in Libya (*Aen.* 1.159–169) "recalls Apollonius' description of the Argonauts sailing into the Phasis" (2.1266–1285). In Nelis' view,[27] however, Virgil uses part of the Cyzicus episode in the third book, when the Trojans land on the island of Delos:[28] "In both this friendly reception is followed by a near disastrous reversal in fortunes. The Trojans misread the oracle of Apollo on Delos

---

[22] Carrington 1977: 119. The reports of the Phrygians' migration from Europe to Asia Minor are from Herodotus and Xanthus of Lydia (quoted by Strabo 14.5.29 C 680).

[23] Rütten 1912:59–62.

[24] Both the Aeneadae and the Argonauts arrive at a harbor (*Aen.* 1.157–169 and Ap. Rhod. 1.936–941) and dock (*Aen.* 1.170–173 and Ap. Rhod. 1.953–954); they climb a rock from where they can observe the sea (*Aen.* 1.180–181 and Ap. Rhod. 1.985–986); the Aeneadae hunt deer and the Argonauts fight against the Earthborn Giants (*Aen.* 1.184–193 and Ap. Rhod. 1.989–1011); wine is offered to comrades (*Aen.* 1.195–197) or to guests (Ap. Rhod. 1.968).

[25] Nelis 2001:455 "Tables of Correspondences."

[26] Nelis 2001:71.

[27] Nelis 2001:27.

[28] It is generally agreed that the third book of the *Aeneid* is largely "Apollonian": see Nelis 2001:59–66 and 406 (with Diagram 3). With regard to the third book, let me recall the words of Richard Hunter 1993:172: "Apollonius' use of Homer, Virgil's use of Apollonius, and Virgil's use of Homer are inter-related studies. While the *Argonautica* is a voyage through the Homeric texts, Virgil voyages past and beyond both Greek epics."

as an instruction to sail to Crete; when they try to settle there a plague hits them (3.85–142); then they consider returning to Delos (3.143–146). When the Argonauts sail away from the land of the Doliones adverse winds blow them back and in the darkness of night Doliones and Greeks inadvertently engage in a violent battle in which Jason tragically kills Cyzicus."

As is typical of Virgil, he rearranges what he borrows. He has the Cyzicus episode in mind,[29] but chooses to break up this intertextual link and in the third book of the *Aeneid* he uses only part of Apollonius' passage.[30] The "friendly-fire" massacre, in contrast, appears at lines 386–430 of the second book, in remembering the last night of Troy.

Università del Molise, Isernia (Italy)

WORKS CITED

Ardizzoni, A. 1967. *Apollonio Rodio. Le Argonautiche, Libro I.* Rome.

Austin, R. G. 1964. *P. Vergili Maronis Aeneidos liber secundus.* Oxford.

Baehrens, E. 1876. "Jahresbericht über die römischen Epiker für 1875-1876." *Jahresbericht über die Fortschritte der classischen Alterthumswissenschaft* 6:149–158.

Beye, C. R. 1999. "Vergil and Apollonius." In *Reading Vergil's* Aeneid: *An Interpretive Guide*, ed. C. Perkell, 271–284. Norman, OK.

Briggs, W. W., Jr. 1981. "Virgil and the Hellenistic Epic." *ANRW* II 31.2:948–984. Berlin.

Burck, E. 1969. "Kampf und Tod des Cyzicus bei Valerius Flaccus." *Revue des études latines* 47bis:173–198 (*Mélanges offerts á Marcel Durry*).

Carrington, P. 1977. "The Heroic Age of Phrygia in Ancient Literature and Art." *Anatolian Studies* 27:117–126.

Clausen, W. 1987. *Virgil's* Aeneid *and the Tradition of Hellenistic Poetry.* Berkeley, CA.

---

[29] It should be noted that, in addition to Apollonius' account, the episode also appeared in the lost poem commented on in *P. Köln* 8, 332 (as noted above, n16).

[30] Virgil's use of Cyzicus episode in both *Aeneid* 2 and 3 is an example of his so-called 'distribution' technique, on which see Hardie 1984.

Conington, J., and H. Nettleship. 1884. *P. Vergili Maronis Opera* (= *The Works of Virgil*). Vol. 2. 4th ed. London.

Conrardy, C. 1904. *De Vergilio Apollonii Rhodii imitatore.* PhD diss., University of Fribourg.

Fitch, E. 1912. "Apollonius Rhodius and Cyzicus." *AJP* 33:43–56.

Forbiger, A. 1873. *P. Vergili Maronis Opera.* Vol. 2. 4th ed. Leipzig.

Gärtner, U. 2005. *Quintus Smyrnaeus und die* Aeneis*: Zur Nachwirkung Vergils in der griechischen Literatur der Kaiserzeit.* Zetemata 123. Munich.

Gronewald, M., K. Maresch, and C. Römer. 1997. *Kölner Papyri (P. Köln)* (= Vol. 7 of *Papyrologica Coloniensia*). Vol. 8. Opladen.

Hardie, P. R. 1984. "The Sacrifice of Iphigeneia: An Example of 'Distribution' of a Lucretian Theme in Virgil." *CQ*, n.s., 34:406–412.

Hasluck, F. W. 1910. *Cyzicus.* Cambridge.

Heinze, R. 1915. *Virgils epische Technik.* 3rd ed. Leipzig.

Heyne, C. G., and G. P. E. Wagner. 1832. *Publius Virgilius Maro varietate lectionis et perpetua adnotatione illustratus.* 5 vols. 4th ed. Leipzig.

Hollis, A. S. 1990. *Callimachus. Hecale.* Oxford.

———. 1992. "Hellenistic Colouring in Virgil's *Aeneid.*" *HSCP* 94:269–285.

Horsfall, N. 2008. *Virgil. Aeneid 2: A Commentary.* Mnemosyne Supplement 299. Leiden.

Hügi, M. 1952. *Vergils Aeneis und die hellenistische Dichtung.* Bern.

Hunter, R. L. 1993. *The* Argonautica *of Apollonius: Literary Studies.* Cambridge.

Hurst, A. 1964. "Le retour nocturne des Argonautes." *Museum Helveticum* 21:232–237.

Knaack, G. 1887. "De fabulis nonnullis Cyzicenis." In *Commentationes philologae in honorem sodalitii philologorum Gryphiswaldensis,* 33–41. Berlin.

Kopff, E. C. 1981. "Vergil and the Cyclic Epics." *ANRW* II 31.2:919–947. Berlin.

La Penna, A. 2005. *L'impossibile giustificazione della storia: Un'interpretazione di Virgilio.* Bari.

La Ville de Mirmont, L. de. 1894. *Apollonios de Rhodes et Virgile: La mythologie et les dieux dans les Argonautiques et dans l'Enéide.* Paris.

Leitich, R. 1940. *Der Einfluss der* Argonautika *des Apollonios von Rhodos auf Vergil und Ovid.* PhD diss., University of Vienna.

Manuwald, G. 1999. *Die Cyzicus-Episode und ihre Funktion in den* Argonautica *des Valerius Flaccus.* Hypomnemata 127. Göttingen.

Mazzocchini, P. 2000. *Forme e significati della narrazione bellica nell'epos virgiliano: I cataloghi degli uccisi e le morti minori dell'*Eneide. Fasano.

Mehmel, F. 1940. *Virgil und Apollonius Rhodius: Untersuchungen über die Zeitvorstellung in der antiken epischen Erzählung.* Hamburg.

Moskalew, W. 1990. "Myrmidons, Dolopes, and Danaans: Wordplays in *Aeneid* 2." *CQ*, n.s, 40:275–279.

Müller, L. 1876. "Zu Virgil." *Rheinisches Museum*, n.F., 31:305–307.

Nelis, D. 2001. *Vergil's* Aeneid *and the* Argonautica *of Apollonius Rhodius.* Leeds.

———. 2008. "Apollonius and Virgil." In *Brill's Companion to Apollonius Rhodius*, ed. T. D. Papanghelis and A. Rengakos, 341–362. 2nd ed. Leiden.

Ross, S. A. 2005. "Barbarophonos: Language and Panhellenism in the *Iliad*." *CP* 100:299–316.

Rossi, A. 2002. "The Fall of Troy: Between Tradition and Genre." In *Clio and the Poets: Augustan Poetry and the Traditions of Ancient Historiography*, ed. D. S. Levene and D. P. Nelis, 231–251. Mnemosyne Supplement 224. Leiden.

Rütten, F. 1912. *De Vergilii studiis Apollonianis: Commentatio philologica.* Münster.

Vecchio, L. 1998. *Deioco di Proconneso. Gli Argonauti a Cizico.* Naples.

Vian, F. 1951. "Les Γηγενεῖς de Cyzique et la Grande Mère des Dieux." *Revue archéologique*, 6th ser., 37:14–25.

———. 1987. *Les Argonautiques Orphiques.* Paris.

HEROD'S LAST DAYS

Mark Toher

JOSEPHUS' ACCOUNT OF THE CAREER OF HEROD in the *Antiquitates Judaicae* is notable in that work for its length and narrative quality. A career of forty-three years (*AJ* 14.158–17.190) occupies almost twenty percent of a work that covered thousands of years of Jewish history from the Creation to AD 66 (*AJ* 20.259). The historian apparently found a congenial topic in Herod and his career, or a very good source. Josephus' Herodian books present a moral saga of Herod's struggle to attain power in Judaea that then evolves into an artful characterization of the king's steady descent into paranoia, cruelty, and murder due to domestic intrigue. Probably the most striking part of Herod's story is Josephus' account of the king's last days, which interweaves the gruesome nature of Herod's illness, his paranoid plotting, and dramatic turns to conclude appropriately the life of the most (in)famous character in the *Antiquitates*. It is also an account that presents enigmatic episodes in the last week of Herod's life that require explanation.

Energetic leadership, risk-taking, and a canny ability to ally himself with the dominant Romans in the region (the assassin Cassius, Mark Antony, and Octavian, in succession) secured Herod the kingship of Judaea, which he held against the will of a significant portion of its population for more than thirty-five years. That Herod's external success then engendered domestic discord and intrigue is the main theme of Josephus' account.[1] Herod would end up executing his grandfather-in-law, a mother-in-law, two brothers-in-law, an uncle, a wife, and three sons in the course of thirty years. Such a dramatic and sordid career called for an appropriately theatrical conclusion, and Josephus provides it.

---

[1] Cf. *AJ* 15.218, 16.62–66 and 76–77; also *BJ* 1.431.

First there is the repulsive nature of Herod's final illness, described in graphic detail and attributed to divine wrath (*AJ* 17.168–170):

Ἡρώδῃ δὲ μειζόνως ἡ νόσος ἐνεπικραίνετο, δίκην ὧν παρανομήσειεν ἐκπρασσομένου τοῦ θεοῦ· πῦρ μὲν γὰρ μαλακὸν ἦν, οὐχ ὧδε πολλὴν ἀποσημαῖνον τοῖς ἐπαφωμένοις τὴν φλόγωσιν ὁπόσην τοῖς ἐντὸς προσετίθει τὴν κάκωσιν. ἐπιθυμία δὲ δεινὴ τοῦ ὀδάξασθαί τι ἀπ' αὐτοῦ, οὐ γὰρ ἦν μὴ οὐχ ὑπουργεῖν, καὶ ἕλκωσις τῶν τε ἐντέρων καὶ μάλιστα τοῦ κόλου δειναὶ ἀλγηδόνες, καὶ φλέγμα ὑγρὸν περὶ τοὺς πόδας καὶ διαυγές· παραπλησία δὲ καὶ περὶ τὸ ἦτρον κάκωσις ἦν, ναὶ μὴν καὶ τοῦ αἰδοίου σῆψις σκώληκας ἐμποιοῦσα, πνεύματός τε ὀρθία ἔντασις καὶ αὐτὴ λίαν ἀηδὴς ἀχθηδόνι τε τῆς ἀποφορᾶς καὶ τῷ πυκνῷ τοῦ ἄσθματος, σπασμός τε περὶ πᾶν ἦν μέλος, ἰσχὺν οὐχ ὑπομενητὴν προστιθέμενος. ἐλέγετο οὖν ὑπὸ τῶν θειαζόντων καὶ οἷς ταῦτα προαποφθέγγεσθαι σοφία πρόκειται, ποινὴν τοῦ πολλοῦ δυσσεβοῦς ταύτην ὁ θεὸς εἰσπράσσεσθαι παρὰ τοῦ βασιλέως.

But Herod's illness became more and more acute, for God was inflicting just punishment upon him for his lawless deeds. The fever that he had was a light one and did not so much indicate symptoms of inflammation to the touch as it produced internal damage. He also had a terrible desire to scratch himself because of this, for it was impossible not to seek relief. There was also an ulceration of the bowels and intestinal pains that were particularly terrible, and a moist, transparent suppuration of the feet. And he suffered similarly from an abdominal ailment, as well as from a gangrene of his privy parts that produced worms. His breathing was marked by extreme tension, and it was very unpleasant because of the disagreeable exhalation of his breath and his constant gasping. He also had convulsions in every limb that took on unendurable severity. Accordingly it was said by the men of God and those whose special wisdom led them to proclaim their opinions on such matters that all this was the penalty that God was exacting of the king for his great impiety.

Text and trans. Marcus and Wilkgren 1963

The precise nature of Herod's illness cannot be deduced from Josephus' description, nor is it relevant to this discussion,[2] but its repulsive character and the theme of moral retribution are the context for Josephus' account of the end of Herod.

At the onset of his illness in 4 BC Herod revised his will: he named as his successor Antipas, his younger son by his wife Malthace and then about 21 years old, and he bequeathed to Augustus and his household 1,500 talents (*AJ* 17.146). But it was not due solely to his illness that Herod rewrote his will, since he had recently imprisoned his heir Antipater for conspiracy. His downfall was the culmination of more than a decade of competition and plotting among three of Herod's sons for his succession. Antipater was Herod's eldest son by his first wife Doris, but Herod's marriage to the Hasmonaean Mariamme in 37 BC and the birth of two sons, Alexander and Aristoboulos, resulted in the dismissal of Antipater and his commoner mother from Herod's court in favor of these sons of Hasmonaean blood. Passion and jealousy led Herod to the fateful act of executing Mariamme in 29 BC, and so began many years of tension and suspected conspiracy between Herod and her sons. In 14 BC Antipater was brought back to the court at Jerusalem to curb the audacity of Alexander and Aristoboulos, but with this move Herod only exacerbated his domestic troubles. Antipater skillfully manipulated the increasingly paranoid king into believing that the sons of Mariamme were plotting against him, and they were executed in 7 BC. Antipater rose to be a co-equal in power with his father and was named his heir in 5 BC.[3] Nevertheless, he still aspired to Herod's crown, and in that same year the king prosecuted this son before a

---

[2] Prause 1977:328–329 and Ladouceur 1981:25–34, who detects the terminology of Thucydides' description of the plague (2.47.3–53.4) in Josephus.

[3] *AJ* 17.3: συνῆρχέν γε τῷ πατρὶ οὐδὲν ἄλλο ἢ ὡς βασιλεὺς ὤν (also *BJ* 1.632); Antipater named Herod's successor: *AJ* 17.53 and 96.

Roman council convened by the legate of Syria, Quinctilius Varus, and Antipater was convicted of conspiring to poison Herod.

During his illness, the paranoia that increasingly characterizes Herod in the *Antiquitates* reaches a climax. The king's conviction that he was despised by his people and that they now rejoiced at his misfortune (*AJ* 17.148) was confirmed when a group of religious radicals acted on the rumor that Herod was already dead and tore down the image of a golden eagle that he had erected over a gate to the Temple in Jerusalem (*AJ* 17.149–160). After punishing the perpetrators, Herod devised a nefarious plan to have the "notable Jews" (ἀξιολόγων, 17.174) gathered under guard in the hippodrome at Jericho, where, upon his death, they were all to be slaughtered to ensure that the country would be filled with lament rather than joy at his demise (*AJ* 17.173–179). In the end, Herod's plan was not carried out, and there is good reason to doubt there ever was such a plan.[4] But the story of Herod's order to murder innocent citizens at his death does nicely complement that other slander in the Herodian tradition, his slaughter of the innocent children in Bethlehem at the birth of Jesus (Matthew 2:16).[5]

Herod's last days have their dramatic moments. At one point the king is thought to be dead, but he is roused by the cries of lamentation around him (*AJ* 17.172). Eventually the pain of his illness becomes too much and Herod attempts suicide with a paring knife, but his hand is stayed by his cousin Achiab (*AJ* 17.183–184). However, news of Herod's suicide attempt emboldens Antipater, now held under guard after his conviction for conspiracy, and he attempts to bribe his jailor to release him so that he can claim the throne. When Herod learns of this, although he is at the point of death himself (καίπερ ἐν τῷ ὑστάτῳ ὤν), he literally raises himself up in his deathbed and decisively orders the execution of his eldest son, just five days before his own death

[4]   Otto 1913:144, Willrich 1929:183–184, Sandmel 1967:261, Schalit 2001:640–641, Vogel 2002:271–272 and Günther 2005:179–182. Otto believes that the Jewish leaders were gathered in the hippodrome at Jericho, but only to forestall an uprising on Herod's death; it was Herod's sister Salome who, on releasing the men, claimed that her brother had intended to kill them.

[5]   Smallwood 2001:103–104. It is surprising that Schalit 2001:648n11 deems the story of Herod's order for the massacre of Bethlehem's infants and children credible.

(*AJ* 17.187). Finally, in his remaining three or four days of life Herod radically revises his will. In place of Antipas Herod named his older brother Archelaus as his successor, even though Josephus says that the king had previously refused to do so because of his hatred of that son (*AJ* 17.146). In addition, he increases his bequests to Augustus and his wife to fifteen million pieces of silver, along with valuable golden and silver vessels and garments (*AJ* 17.188–190). Finally, Herod now adds a codicil stating that the arrangements of his will would only be valid on the confirmation of Augustus himself.[6] Having made these important decisions, Herod died.

Josephus is not generally esteemed for his narrative talent, but his account of the last days of Herod is equal to his characterization of Herod's rule as tyranny and impiety receiving its just reward (*AJ* 17.168 and 170). However, this same narrative strategy presents historical problems and raises questions.

Scholars have long been suspicious of Josephus' description of Herod's illness and death. It contains many of the characteristics of the "death of a tyrant" found throughout Greco-Roman histories and biographies. Among these characteristics are unendurable pain, infestation by worms, bad breath, and skin eruptions.[7] It was a theme that appealed to Josephus. The *Bellum Judaicum* closes with a description of the foul death of Catullus, the Roman governor of the Libyan Pentapolis, after he had conspired against the most reputable Jews of Alexandria and Rome through charges of sedition and had even incriminated Josephus himself (*BJ* 7.437–450). Although Catullus avoided punishment by Vespasian, not long afterwards he became deranged, was haunted by the ghosts of his victims, and was attacked by an incurable disease that culminated in his ulcerated bowels falling out (*BJ* 7.451–453).

But, even beyond the generic character of Josephus' description of Herod's end, there are other significant problems with his account. From the time Herod falls ill until his death there is no mention of the king's φίλοι ("friends") and even his family members are virtually

---

[6]   A point stressed by Josephus: *AJ* 17.195, 202, 209 and 222–223.

[7]   Cf. Prause 1977:328–329, Ladouceur 1981:25–34, Africa 1982:1–17, and Gauger 2002:52–56.

absent. This has the effect of focusing the reader's attention on Herod alone and so enhances the drama of Josephus' account. But in reality such φίλοι as Nicolaus, Herod's closest advisor and envoy to high Roman officials; Nicolaus' brother Ptolemaeus, said to have been among the closest of Herod's "friends" (*AJ* 17.225 and *BJ* 2.21); and Ptolemaeus, the king's minister of finance and the executor of his will (*AJ* 16.191 and 17.195), must have been deeply involved in advising, protecting, and administering for Herod as he lay dying. These figures are prominent before and after Herod's death in Josephus, but they are entirely absent from his account of the end of the king's reign.

That Herod could have acted solely on his own counsel, as in Josephus' account, becomes more improbable when the events of his narrative are considered in their chronological context. It cannot be determined precisely how long an interval there was between the time Herod fell ill and when the image of the golden eagle was torn down from the Temple gate, but it could not have been all that long, possibly only weeks. Josephus says that the perpetrators were punished on the day of a lunar eclipse (*AJ* 17.167), which can be dated to the night of 12/13 March of 4 BC. He then says that disturbances broke out after the death of Herod during the celebration of Passover (*AJ* 17.213), which commenced on 11 April (15 Nisan) of that year.[8] Furthermore, he says

---

[8]   For this generally accepted chronology of events, cf. Schürer 1973:326–327. Some have questioned (not unreasonably) whether the events that Josephus presents could fit into the four weeks or so between the lunar eclipse and the disturbances at Passover, as his narrative seems to present them, and have suggested that the lunar eclipse that he mentions was not that of March 4 BC but that of 15/16 September 5 BC; cf. Barnes 1968:204–209 and Schwartz 1992:157–166 (with citation of previous scholarship). But this dating leaves eight months from the lunar eclipse to the demonstrations at Passover, probably too long a time for the events as narrated by Josephus; cf. Smallwood 2001:104n158. The problem is vexing, not least because Josephus' account may not be chronologically accurate, but there is no way of knowing how he may have distorted the arrangement of events. Nevertheless, the circumstances suggest that there would have been rapid obsequies for the king that would accommodate the chronology in Josephus. There was ample warning that Herod's death was imminent and therefore much of the organization and preparation for his funeral would have taken place before he died. Furthermore, Jewish tradition called for burial within twenty-four hours of death. Whether or not this rule was applied (or could have been applied) in the case of Herod, it seems reasonable that his obsequies would have been completed soon after his death. In light of the ambiguous status of Archelaus as Herod's declared but unconfirmed

that his son Archelaus mourned for seven days and the sequence of his narrative indicates this week of mourning occurred after the completion of the funeral rites for Herod (*AJ* 17.200). The disturbances of Passover seem to occur just days after the end of Archelaus' mourning. If it is the case that Archelaus' seven days of mourning were subsequent to rather than coincident with Herod's funeral rites and if one allows four or five days for the organization and execution of those rites,[9] then it would seem that Herod could not have died later than 28 March, and it could well have been earlier. When Herod arrived at Jericho, Josephus says that he was dying (τελευτῶν, *AJ* 17.173). Therefore, Herod's punishment of those who tore down the eagle, his plot to ensure universal mourning at his death through mass murder, his attempted suicide, his decision to execute Antipater, and his revisions of his will all occur in the last two weeks of his life, and the most crucial actions, the execution of his son and the revision of his will, in the last five days. It seems hardly likely that a man on his deathbed could have done all of this on his own initiative, as Josephus' account would have us believe.[10]

In addition to this improbable aspect of Josephus' account, two questions arise: why is Antipater only executed just days before the death of Herod and why does Herod suddenly change his will after the execution?

After Antipater was convicted by Varus and the Roman council, it was revealed that a servant of Augustus' wife Livia had been involved in Antipater's plot (*AJ* 17.134–141). Based on this revelation, Herod was ready to execute Antipater immediately, but because his plot now involved the household of Augustus, it was decided to stay any execution until the *princeps* had been consulted on the matter. In Josephus'

---

successor, it would have been in his interest to take a prominent role as soon as possible as Herod's chief mourner in executing the king's final rites.

[9] A reasonable estimate for royal funerals in ancient and traditional cultures. In general on royal funeral rites, cf. Metcalf and Huntington 1991:133–188.

[10] The "death of a tyrant" scene is improbable in a similar way in Plutarch's description of the last days of Sulla. Even as the retired dictator was being consumed by worms, ten days before his death he arbitrated a dispute at Dicaearchia (Puteoli) and wrote out regulations for the city's government, two days before he expired he finished his autobiography, and one day before he summoned a defaulting magistrate and upbraided him strenuously (Plut. *Sulla* 37.1–3).

account in the *Antiquitates*, these events take place immediately before Herod falls ill, and it is just after Herod has developed his plan for universal mourning through mass murder that the message comes from Augustus saying that Herod can punish Antipater as he sees fit. Josephus says that Herod, though now very ill, was temporarily elated by the news that he could execute Antipater, but then he fails to do so. Instead, the king attempts suicide (*AJ* 17.182–184 and *BJ* 1.662). Josephus' description of Herod's eagerness to execute Antipater and his elation when the permission comes, followed immediately not by Antipater's execution but by Herod's own attempt at suicide, is odd and suspect. It is now just five days before Herod will die, and his attempt at suicide in the circumstances seems plausible. What does not is the king's immediate order to execute Antipater when he is stayed from his suicide attempt. A more likely explanation is that by the time the permission for Antipater's execution came, Herod was simply too ill to act on it, just as Josephus says at *BJ* 1.645 and 647.[11]

According to Josephus, almost immediately after Antipater's conviction before Varus and while he is still under guard, Herod revised his will and named Antipas as his heir (*AJ* 17.146). Josephus seems to imply that he made this will due to his illness, but it is clear on the historian's own evidence (*AJ* 17.53; cf. *BJ* 1.646, where the new arrangements are described as corrections: ταῦτα διωρθώσατο) that this was a revision of an earlier will in which Antipater had been named his heir. Therefore, the new will was due not to Herod's illness but to the fact that his designated heir had just been convicted of trying to murder him. Then, just three or four days before he dies, Herod seems well enough to revise this will in significant ways. He names as his heir Archelaus, the older brother of Antipas, he increases his bequests to Augustus and Livia, and he predicates the validity of the will on Augustus' confirmation of it. There is no explanation in the tradition for why Herod revised his will in this way at this point.[12] More star-

---

[11] It has been suggested that Josephus in the *Antiquitates* has given a depiction just the opposite of Herod's attitude at the time. Rather than being elated by Augustus' permission, Herod was so dispirited by the news that he attempted suicide; cf. Sandmel 1967:256 and Prause 1977:330.

[12] Otto 1913:145 suggests that Herod revised his will in accordance with instructions

tling is the fact that, as he lay dying, Herod now picked as his heir a son whom Josephus says he deliberately passed over in his earlier will due to his hatred of him (*AJ* 17.146). He says that this hatred arose from Antipater's calumnies (διαβολαί), but when he made out the will that named Antipas as heir rather then Archelaus, Antipater had already been convicted and his true nature revealed. Hence, one cannot explain the change in heirs on the grounds that Antipater's slander of Archelaus had been revealed as baseless after Antipater's plot to poison Herod had been exposed.[13]

For all of its drama and detail, Josephus' account of Herod's last days has improbable aspects and generates questions. One might suppose that Antipater was executed at the point when Herod, in the throes of his illness, was able to give the order. But one cannot so easily explain the sudden, enigmatic revision of Herod's will that also occurs at this point. Josephus' account has the mortally ill king incapacitated and suicidal at some points and then at others rising from his deathbed to make significant decisions and issue crucial orders, all seemingly on his own initiative.

Just how strange this account is for an alert reader can be judged by its treatment in Günther's recent book on Herod.[14] In effect, she rewrites Josephus and explains what happened in the final week of

---

given by Augustus, presumably in the same message that gave permission to the king to punish Antipater. But if Herod revised his will on the explicit instructions of Augustus at this point, why did all parties involved have to travel to Rome for the long process of adjudication of Herod's will before Augustus (cf. *AJ* 17. 219–249 and 299–320)? This would hardly have been necessary if Augustus had already instructed Herod about who his successor was to be. Furthermore, Augustus had explicitly granted Herod the right to name his successor (*AJ* 15.343; also 16.92, 129 and *BJ* 1.454) and it seems unlikely that Augustus would have intervened so directly in the affairs of the house of Herod; cf. Schuol 2007:151–152. Even when Herod's designated heir Archelaus proved incapable in his role as ethnarch, it was a decade before Augustus removed him. "Wir haben keinen Grund, in dieser Regelung die Folge einer Einmischung des Augustus in die Verfügungen des Herodes zu sehen" (Schalit 2001:642).

[13] As supposed by Vogel 2002:272. Günther 2005:176 thinks that Herod made Archelaus his successor in place of Antipas when he came to realize just days before his death that his succession was likely to be turbulent. Richardson 1996:36, suggests that the effects of Antipater's campaign against Archelaus "had worn off." Both explanations seem improbable.

[14] Günther 2005:185–187.

Herod's life as the product of court intrigue. In her hypothesis, Herod did not revise his will after the conviction of Antipater in 5 BC, since Antipas had been already named a tetrarch in the revision of the will after the executions of the sons of Mariamme in 7 BC and the naming then of Antipater as Herod's successor. Herod then died before the execution of Antipater and before the king had removed Antipater from his will. There was no suicide attempt by Herod, but the rumor of such was concocted to explain the commotion and alarm in the palace after Herod's death, which did in fact embolden Antipater to bribe his guards to release him. With that as a pretext, the order was given for the execution of Antipater, who was now better positioned to claim the throne due to the confusion surrounding the death of Herod. The final revision of Herod's will that named Archelaus his successor was counterfeited only after Herod's death and the execution of Antipater, and Herod's death itself was only made public almost a week after the event.

Once we reject the account of Josephus, who is our sole source for these crucial events, any other account can only originate in conjecture inspired by imagination. But Günther's radical revision of Josephus is unnecessary. Sense can be made of what Josephus tells us through reasonable conjecture that supplements and accommodates his account of the facts. Günther's hypothesis, however, is predicated—correctly—on the fact that Herod's final illness leading to his death was not a one-man drama. There were other interested parties.

Just how interested is clear from the number of family members and "friends" of Herod who made the long trip to Rome to participate in the contest for the succession. Of Herod's φίλοι, Nicolaus was the chief (and successful) advocate for Archelaus. He was joined in this by Ptolemaeus, Herod's minister of finance (*AJ* 17.219). Ptolemaeus, the brother of Nicolaus, supported the claim of Archelaus' brother and rival for the succession, Antipas, as did another "friend" Ireneus, and Antipater, Herod's nephew and the son of Salome. The details of the adjudication of Herod's will at Rome are not relevant to the issue here, but the wide and intense involvement of those closest to Herod in it supports what is obvious even without this indirect evidence: as Herod lay dying there were those close to him who would have had a keen interest in "advising" the king and influencing the arrangements for a future without him.[15]

And none had a greater interest than Herod's son Archelaus and Herod's "friend" and closest advisor Nicolaus. Both had a deadly enemy in Antipater, now under guard but still alive and dangerous.[16] Antipater's persistent slander of Archelaus engendered such hatred in Herod that he refused to name Archelaus as an heir even after the conviction of Antipater. But the situation for Nicolaus was even more dangerous.

Utterly Greek by education and culture, if not by ethnicity, and originally from Damascus, Nicolaus first appears in Herod's retinue as his advisor when the king accompanied Marcus Agrippa during his sojourn in Asia Minor in 14 BC.[17] In 10 or 9 BC Augustus broke off *amicitia* with Herod because of the king's invasion of Arabia, and in his anger and intransigence the *princeps* refused to receive embassies from Herod or countenance a defense of him.[18] Finally, Herod sent Nicolaus to Rome in 8 BC, where he was able to demonstrate through skillful argument that Herod was not at fault and so save the *princeps* from inflicting unjust treatment upon this most faithful *socius et amicus populi Romani*. Augustus' regret about the misunderstanding (and so presumably his debt to Nicolaus for having set him right on the issue) can be estimated by his plan to compensate Herod by significant expansion of the areas that he controlled—until the king's age and increasingly fractious domestic situation made Augustus think better of such a move (*AJ* 16.353–355). Nicolaus seems to have spent extensive

---

[15] Günther 2005:182.

[16] Still in Jericho with Herod, it seems reasonable that the former co-regent would yet have had informers and supporters acting in his interest; cf. Günther 2005:175–176. From the time he returned to Herod's court in 14 BC, Antipater had shown himself skillful in organizing a network of allies; cf. *AJ* 16.83. Herod had decided against sending Antipater to Rome after his conviction, since he feared that with the help of his friends there he might be able to evade punishment by Augustus (*AJ* 17.144–145).

[17] *AJ* 16.27–58 and *FGrH* 90 F 134.

[18] γράφει πρὸς τὸν Ἡρώδην τά τε ἄλλα χαλεπῶς καὶ τοῦτο τῆς ἐπιστολῆς τὸ κεφάλαιον, ὅτι πάλαι χρώμενος αὐτῷ φίλῳ νῦν ὑπηκόῳ χρήσεται (*AJ* 16.290); cf. *AJ* 16.289–290 and 293 and *FGrH* 90 F 136.1. On the gravity of Herod's transgression as a "client-king," cf. Bowersock 1965:56 and Weber 2003:82–83.

time in Rome in 8/7 BC, since he returned from there only after Herod's sons by Mariamme had already been convicted of treason before a Roman tribunal at Berytus in 7 BC. Herod consulted with Nicolaus on his arrival in Tyre about what punishment would be appropriate for his seditious sons. Nicolaus offered Delphic counsel: the king should not be seen to give way to anger if he should punish them nor ignore his own misfortune should he decide to pardon them—for that was the opinion of Herod's friends in Rome (*AJ* 16.372). In the end, Herod did execute his sons, an act which was the beginning of all his troubles, according to Nicolaus in his autobiography (καὶ οἱ μὲν ἀπέθανον, Ἡρώδῃ δὲ τῶν συμπάντων ἤδη γίνεται κακῶν ἀρχή, *FGrH* 90, F 136.4). In two years, Herod would be before another Roman tribunal, this time to accuse Antipater of plotting against him, and Nicolaus was deeply involved in the proceedings.

Herod himself opened the prosecution, but he was overcome and unable to continue (ταῦθ' ἅμα λέγων εἰς δάκρυα τρέπεται λέγειν τε ἄπορος ἦν, *AJ* 17.99); the prosecution of Antipater was placed in the hands of Nicolaus, the king's closest advisor and confidant (φίλος τε ὢν τοῦ βασιλέως καὶ τὰ πάντα συνδιαιτώμενος ἐκείνῳ, *AJ* 17.99; also *BJ* 1.629). Nicolaus already had an enemy in Antipater due to his advice to Herod to exercise prudence in his punishment of the sons of Mariamme (*FGrH* 90, F 136.4–5). After Nicolaus' presentation of the evidence, the accused son responded with an emotional appeal that moved the council and possibly even Herod himself.[19] Josephus depicts Nicolaus' involvement in the prosecution of Antipater as happenstance, but once he had made his initial statement against Antipater it became critical for Nicolaus that Antipater not be acquitted. His acquittal and restoration as Herod's partner in power would likely put Nicolaus in mortal danger. Antipater's conspiring had brought down "friends" at Herod's court in the past.[20] Therefore, through a rebuttal in which he repeated and exaggerated the charges against Antipater (*AJ* 17.106–121 and *BJ* 1.637–638), Nicolaus left Antipater with only an appeal to God as his

---

[19] *AJ* 17.106, but cf. *BJ* 1.636, where Josephus says Herod was unmoved by Antipater's defense.

[20] E.g. Antipater had manipulated Herod into executing many of the φίλοι of his rival Alexander, son of Mariamme; cf. *AJ* 16.235–253, esp. 244–253.

defense. Nicolaus' prosecution and the lethal evidence of the poison that Antipater was alleged to have sent from Rome secured his conviction by the presiding magistrate Quinctilius Varus (*AJ* 17.127–133).

The evidence is that, by the end of his reign, no one among his "friends" had more influence with Herod than Nicolaus, and it is reasonable to suppose that, as his health and strength deserted him, Herod became ever more dependent on Nicolaus for advice and support. It is this close relationship with Nicolaus and the influence that he exercised over the king that can explain Herod's actions in the days before he died.

The critical episode was Herod's attempted suicide. While the king had been ill for some time before, it was this event that demonstrated that all could change in a moment for the man responsible for bringing down Antipater and now dependent on the protection of Herod against his revenge. Josephus depicts Antipater as emboldened by Herod's attempt at suicide to think that in increasingly uncertain circumstances, with some money and influence, he could go from being a prisoner to a player in contention for the throne, and this is certainly what Nicolaus and Archelaus must have feared. Immediately after his attempt at suicide and just five days before his own death, Herod gave the order and Antipater was executed. As set out above, the sequence of Herod's actions seems odd, especially when Josephus himself says that the king was too ill to act on the permission to execute Antipater. All becomes obvious when the interests of those around Herod are taken into account. In the aftermath of his suicide attempt, the king acted on the advice and urging of his trusted φίλος, who had a great deal at stake in ensuring that Antipater did not survive Herod. Nicolaus would not have found it difficult to persuade his moribund patron of the sense and necessity of acting on the permission of Augustus to ensure the continuity of the kingdom that Herod had worked so hard to build and maintain.

Nicolaus' influence can also explain Herod's puzzling and radical revision of his will just three or four days before he died. The change in heir, the increased bequests to Augustus and Livia, and the condition that the will be validated by Augustus at Rome all become explicable when the interests of Nicolaus are considered.

The crucial change was the introduction of the provision that the will would only be valid on confirmation by Augustus,[21] and this involves two important points. The first is that such a provision was clearly not part of the earlier will that named Antipas Herod's heir. In fact, possibly as early as 22 BC Herod had been given explicit permission by Augustus to bequeath his kingdom to whomever of his children he wished (*AJ* 15.343). That this provision of its confirmation by Augustus was only introduced in Herod's final will is clear from the arguments presented by the contending parties before Augustus at Rome after Herod's death. Antipater, the son of Salome and an advocate of Antipas, reasonably argued that the earlier will of Herod (made soon after the conviction of Herod's son Antipater) should be accepted as valid because Herod had made it while he was of sound mind and in reasonable health, while the later will was composed when the king was in the depths of his illness and just days before he died (*AJ* 17.238). Nicolaus refuted this point by arguing that the provision in the later will for the confirmation of all its arrangements by Augustus was proof in itself that Herod was of sound judgment when he made it.[22] If there had been such a provision in the earlier will, Nicolaus' argument here would have been nonsensical.[23] This fact leads to the second important point about this provision: it ensured that not Herod's will but a process of argument and adjudication at Rome would determine the final settlement of Herod's succession.

With these two points established, the two other provisions in Herod's final will also become explicable. Josephus says that Herod in his earlier will had excluded Archelaus in favor of his younger brother

---

[21] See above, n6.

[22] *AJ* 17.244. Cf. *BJ* 2.35–36: τήν γε μὴν ἐπιδιαθήκην ἠξίου διὰ τοῦτο μάλιστα εἶναι κυρίαν, ὅτι βεβαιωτὴν ἐν αὐτῇ Καίσαρα καθίστατο τοῦ διαδόχου· ὁ γὰρ σωφρονῶν ὥστε τῷ δεσπότῃ τῶν ὅλων παραχωρεῖν τῆς ἐξουσίας οὐ δήπου περὶ κληρονόμου κρίσιν ἐσφάλλετο, σωφρονῶν δ' ᾑρεῖτο καὶ τὸν καθιστάμενον ὁ γινώσκων τὸν καθιστάντα.

[23] This is not to suggest that Augustus would not have been consulted for his approval of the terms of Herod's earlier wills, despite the privilege granted to Herod of naming his successor(s); cf. Schalit 2001:595, Braund 1984:26 and 139–143, and Schuol 2007:128–129. The circumstances of Herod's last will did not leave time for consultation with Augustus, and so the explicit codicil about the *princeps'* approval was necessary, and, as will be seen, advantageous to one party.

Antipas due to his hatred of him (*AJ* 17.146), but then, without explanation, he says that Herod, just days before his death, made this hated son his successor. Then Nicolaus appears, again without explanation, as the advocate of Archelaus before Augustus at Rome. The obvious explanation is that it was Nicolaus who urged the weak and dying king to make this paradoxical change (it is hardly likely that the hated Archelaus could have persuaded Herod to do it), which had its origin in an alliance between Nicolaus and Archelaus. They had a mutual interest in making sure that Antipater did not survive Herod.[24] With Archelaus named as Herod's successor and the provision that the will had to be validated by Augustus, Archelaus was put in a position of great dependency on Nicolaus as the agent of his confirmation at Rome against the universal opposition to his succession by all of his family and relations, the Roman procurator of Syria, and a significant portion of the Jewish population.[25]

The increase in the bequests by Herod to Augustus and his wife Livia would seem to have no connection with these issues until one considers what actually happened to the money that Herod willed to the *princeps* (*AJ* 17.322–323 and *BJ* 2.99–100): Augustus gave 500,000 pieces of silver to Herod's two unmarried daughters and another 1,500 talents (1,000 talents in the *BJ*) to his other children. According to Josephus, all that Augustus kept from Herod's bequests were some vessels of sentimental value. Herod's bequests, then, were not gifts to Augustus and his family but a legacy entrusted to Augustus for redistribution to Herod's heirs at the *princeps*' discretion. In fact, according to Suetonius (*Aug.* 66.4), it was Augustus' practice to pass on any bequests to the surviving children of the men who made them, and Herod must have known this. The increase in his bequests amounted to an extension of Augustus' influence over the succession, and as such makes sense as part of a larger plan that put the arrangement of Herod's succession in the hands of Augustus.

---

[24] Antipater's intrigue and slander had turned Herod against Archelaus; cf. *AJ* 17.80 and 146.

[25] That all his relatives opposed his claim: *AJ* 17.220, 224–227 and 302; Sabinus, procurator of Syria, had filed charges against Archelaus by a letter to Augustus: *AJ* 17.227; and the Jews rebelled in the period after the death of Herod and sent an embassy to petition Augustus not to give Archelaus any office: *AJ* 17.304–314.

The situation for a close "friend" of Herod was privileged and always precarious,[26] and never more so than for Nicolaus in early 4 BC. His archenemy Antipater remained alive and a threat, and Herod's final illness introduced a crisis, but also an opportunity. In his last five days his closest advisor persuaded the moribund king to make decisions that worked to the benefit of two individuals and put Nicolaus in a position to influence significantly the final disposition of Herod's will. By now Nicolaus' relationship with Augustus must have been more than casual. The tradition makes it clear that they were friends: Athenaeus calls Nicolaus a ἑταῖρος of Augustus, and in the Suda (s.v. Νικόλαος Δαμασκηνός) Nicolaus is called γνώριμος Ἡρώδου ... καὶ Αὐγούστου Καίσαρος, while in Photius (*Bibl.* 189, 146a) he is described as Νικόλαος ὁ ἐπὶ τῶν Αὐγούστου χρόνων ἀκμάσας καὶ φίλος αὐτῷ χρηματίσας; Nicolaus had written (or would write) an encomiastic biographical work on Augustus (*FGrH* 90, FF 125–130); and, according to tradition, the *princeps* named a certain type of date after him, supposedly because the color and taste of the fruit reminded him of the complexion and sweet temperament of his friend at Herod's court.[27] It is reasonable to suppose that by 4 BC Nicolaus would have been very confident that if the succession of Herod were to be negotiated at Rome before Augustus he would be at a considerable advantage in determining the outcome of that negotiation. Nicolaus had had success in pleading before Augustus

[26] In his grief and depression after his execution of Mariamme in 29 BC, Herod executed four of his closest friends (ἀναγκαιότατοι αὐτῷ φίλοι); cf. *AJ* 15.252–266. In general, due to his character, Herod punished his "friends" as readily as his enemies (*AJ* 16.156). The list of Herod's φίλοι who suffered banishment or worse is extensive: Andromachos and Gemellus, tutors of the sons of Herod (*AJ* 16.241–243); Antipatros Gadia, one of Herod's closest φίλοι, Lysimachos and Dositheos for complicity in the revolt of Herod's brother-in-law Kostobaros (*AJ* 15.252–266); Diophantis, described as a scribe but not explicitly as a φίλος of Herod, was executed for forgery (*AJ* 16.319 and *BJ* 1.529); Ptolemaios and Sappinios, two of Herod's closest φίλοι, were accused but survived (*AJ* 16.257). Philostratus, who enjoyed royal favor in Egypt and probably Judaea but was condemned to exile in Ostrakina east of Pelusium (Crinagoras *AP* 7.645 = 20 Gow–Page), might plausibly be included among the φίλοι who fell out of favor at the court of Herod.

[27] Ath. 14.652a and Plut. *Mor.* 723d; also Pliny *HN* 13.45 and Isid. *Etym.* 17.7.1. Plutarch says that it was "the king" (ὁ βασιλεύς) who named the dates after Nicolaus, possibly referring to Herod rather than Augustus. On the other hand, Athenaeus says that Nicolaus regularly sent the eponymous dates to Augustus from the East.

in much more difficult circumstances a few years before, and any man who could explain and help resolve the fractious and murderous domestic situation at the court in Jerusalem would have the *princeps* in his debt.[28] Nicolaus' claim that Augustus honored him (ἐτίμησεν) for his work in the adjudication of Herod's succession is obviously a boast, but not an improbable one (*FGrH* 90, F 136.11).[29]

An obvious question arises: if Nicolaus played the crucial role in the acts of Herod's final days, why is there no mention of him in Josephus? But the fact that there is no evidence of Nicolaus in Josephus' account actually lends plausibility to the hypothesis presented here, once the historiographical background is understood.

Nicolaus was not only Herod's agent, he was also his author. It is generally agreed that Josephus' account of the career of Herod goes back to an account he found in the work of Nicolaus.[30] It is also generally thought that he found this account in the universal history of Nicolaus. This is a misapprehension. Nicolaus makes it clear that he had finished that work (ἐξετέλεσεν) by 12 BC, just before he and Herod traveled to Rome (*FGrH* 90 F 135). The obvious source for Josephus' detailed account of Herod's career would have been Nicolaus' autobiography, which must have been written and circulated only after the death of Herod.[31] What evidence there is indicates this: the three extensive fragments of the autobiography that deal with the events in the reign of Herod differ in no substantial way from the parallel accounts in Josephus' *Antiquitates*. Both Josephus and Nicolaus emphasize that Antipater's conspiracy against his brothers earned him the hatred of

---

[28] The exasperation of Augustus is reflected in his famous quip about Herod and his sons, whose pun only works if it was originally made in Greek (ὗς/υἱός), possibly to Nicolaus himself: *melius est Herodis porcum esse quam filium* (Macrob. *Sat.* 2.4.11).

[29] Nicolaus may have done Augustus the service of reconciling Archelaus to the office of ethnarch, as opposed to the full kingship he aspired to (*AJ* 17.317). Nicolaus did persuade Archelaus to renounce any claim to authority over the Greek cities in the area (*FGrH* 90 F136.10).

[30] Cf. Toher 2003:428–431.

[31] Josephus says that an account of the Ionian Jews' appeal to Agrippa in 14 BC could be found in books 123 and 124 of Nicolaus' universal history (*AJ* 12.127). This would indicate that in later times Nicolaus' account of the reign of Herod in his autobiography was appended to his universal history, just as Josephus' own autobiography was appended to his great historical work; cf. Misch 1950:1.316.

the people and the armed forces.[32] All the fragments of Nicolaus that deal with the reign of Herod (*FGrH* 90 FF 134–136) are from his autobiography, and the purpose of that work, like all ancient autobiography, would have been to present an *apologia pro vita sua*. In the case of Nicolaus, that would have meant a defense of his career at the court of Herod.[33] In Josephus, Nicolaus the agent of Herod disappears from his account right after the prosecution of Antipater and does not reappear until after the king's death, and then as the advisor and advocate of Archelaus. As argued above, it seems highly unlikely that Nicolaus would not have been deeply involved in affairs during Herod's last days, affairs that developed in accord with his own interests. On the other hand, for Nicolaus the author, shaping history in his autobiography after he had made it, it would have been advantageous to have the reader's attention drawn exclusively to Herod's grim drama, just as happens in Josephus.[34] In the final scene of the dramatic career of Herod, the king has the stage to himself, alternately suffering and administering for a future in which he would have no part. Very theatrical, and very convenient for a friend of that king.

UNION COLLEGE

WORKS CITED

Africa, T. 1982. "Worms and the Death of Kings: A Cautionary Note on Disease and History." *Classical Antiquity* 1:1–17.

Barnes, T. D. 1968. "The Date of Herod's Death." *Journal of Theological Studies* 19:204–209.

---

[32] Cf. *FGrH* 90 F 136.1 with *AJ* 16.271–299 and 335–355; F 136.3–4 with *AJ* 16.370–372; F 136.5–7 with *AJ* 17.93–133; and F 136.8–11 with *AJ* 17.219–249 and 299–320. On the hatred of Antipater, cf. F 136.5 with *AJ* 17.1–2 and 17.

[33] On the purpose, audience, and place of composition of Nicolaus' autobiography, cf. Toher 2009:65–81.

[34] While it seems likely that Josephus would have derived his outline of the events of Herod's final days from the account in Nicolaus, this is not to suggest that Josephus has simply transcribed that account. Josephus likely embellished the factual narrative that he found in Nicolaus' work by adding the gruesome description and the theme of moral retribution.

Bowersock, G. 1965. *Augustus and the Greek World*. Oxford.

Braund, D. 1984. *Rome and the Friendly King: The Character of Client Kingship*. London.

Gauger, J.-D. 2002. "Der 'Tod des Verfolgers': Überlegungen zur Historizität eines Topos." *Journal for the Study of Judaism in the Persian, Hellenistic, and Roman Period* 33:42–64.

Gow, A. S. F., and D. L. Page. 1968. *The Greek Anthology: The Garland of Philip and Some Contemporary Epigrams*. 2 vols. Cambridge.

Günther, L.-M. 2005. *Herodes der Große*. Darmstadt.

Ladouceur, D. J. 1981. "The Death of Herod the Great." *CP* 76:25–34.

Marcus, R., and A. Wikgren. 1963. *Josephus*. Vol. 8, *Jewish Antiquities, Books XV to XVII*. Cambridge, MA.

Metcalf, P., and R. Huntington. 1991. *Celebrations of Death: The Anthropology of Mortuary Ritual*. 2nd ed. Cambridge.

Misch, G. 1950. *A History of Autobiography in Antiquity*. Vol. 1. Trans. E. Dickes. London.

Otto, W. 1913. "Herodes (nr.14)". *RE* Suppl. Bd. 2:1–158.

Prause, G. 1977. *Herodes der Grosse: König der Juden*. Hamburg.

Richardson, P. 1996. *Herod: King of the Jews and Friend of the Romans*. Columbia, SC.

Sandmel, S. 1967. *Herod: Profile of a Tyrant*. Philadelphia.

Schalit, A. 2001. *König Herodes: Der Mann und sein Werk*. 2nd ed. Berlin.

Schuol, M. 2007. *Augustus und die Juden: Rechtsstellung und Interessenpolitik der kleinasiatischen Diaspora*. Frankfurt am Main.

Schürer, E. 1973. *The History of the Jewish People in the Age of Jesus Christ*. Rev. ed. G. Vermes, F. Millar, and M. Black. Vol. 1. Edinburgh.

Schwartz, D. R. 1992. *Studies in the Jewish Background of Christianity*. Tübingen.

Smallwood, E. M. 2001. *The Jews under Roman Rule: From Pompey to Diocletian; A Study in Political Relations*. 2nd ed. Boston.

Toher, M. 2003. "Nicolaus and Herod in the *Antiquitates Judaicae*." *HSCP* 101:427–447.

———. 2009. "Herod, Augustus, and Nicolaus of Damascus." In *Herod and Augustus: Papers Presented at the IJS conference, 21st-23rd June 2005*, ed. D. M. Jacobson and N. Kokkinos, 65–81. Leiden.

Vogel, M. 2002. *Herodes: König der Juden, Freund der Römer*. Leipzig.

Weber, F. 2003. *Herodes—König von Roms Gnaden?: Herodes als Modell eines römischen Klientelkönigs in spätrepublikanischer und augusteischer Zeit.* Berlin.

Willrich, H. 1929. *Das Haus des Herodes: Zwischen Jerusalem und Rom.* Heidelberg.

THE RHETORICAL COLLECTION
OF THE ELDER SENECA

TEXTUAL TRADITION AND TRADITIONAL TEXT

Bart Huelsenbeck

*Should not the authority of a text be considered to extend equally
to the texture of the text, to the relationship of its elements to
one another and to the whole, and therefore to what constitutes a text as a text, to what makes it into a particular version?*

Hans Zeller[1]

THIS ARTICLE TAKES AS ITS IMMEDIATE SUBJECT the three primary manuscript witnesses (**VBA**) to the rhetorical collection of the elder
Seneca. My research into the manuscripts was initiated by questions
about the striking way in which one of the witnesses (**B**, Brussels, B.R.
9594, Figure 1) arranges its text into long, well-defined word-groups.
What was the reason for it? It quickly became evident that an answer to
this original question about textual presentation was deeply implicated
in the transmission history of the elder Seneca's work—the stemmatic

I want to express thanks to: Francis Newton, for his continuous support and feedback; Baudouin Van den Abeele, for his assistance during an extended stay in Belgium;
Jacqueline Hamesse, Lucien Reynhout, Hendrik D. L. Vervliet, Frank T. Coulson, and the
participants in the Texts & Contexts conference (Ohio State University, October 2008),
where a portion of this article was first attempted; and Harald Anderson, David Ganz,
William A. Johnson, Jerome McGann, and Larry Richardson Jr. For financial assistance in
obtaining copies of MSS, I am grateful to the Classical Studies Department and the librarians (especially Joline Ezzell) of Duke University. The final stages of this article were
completed with support from an ACLS New Faculty Fellows award and the Andrew W.
Mellon Foundation.

[1] Zeller 1975:237, quoted by McKenzie 1981:85–86. The quotation evokes for
McKenzie the possibility of greater historical sensitivity to textual editing, the possibility
of treating the physical organization of a text—composed not just of lections but of a
complex of organizational elements—as embodied meaning.

relationships of **VBA** to one another, of **VBA** to potential hyparchetypes, and to a shared lost ancestor manuscript **α**. Further research
also made it clear that more was involved in understanding what
produced each of the texts of **V**, **B**, and **A** than their respective positions in a stemma. More specifically, the culturally informed attitudes
and procedures that produced one of the three manuscripts, a ninth-
century manuscript (**V**) copied at Corbie, were significantly different
from those that produced the other two. The different procedures and
attitudes are made manifest not solely in the individual variant readings contained in the manuscripts, but also in the physical organization of text. A text, both in its history and in how it creates meaning,
consists not just of isolated, abstracted readings but of a full textual
fabric. This perspective on the nature of texts has served as the premise
of my investigations and underlies the entire article.

The article is organized into three sections. We begin in Section I
with a summary of what is known about the manuscript tradition of
the elder Seneca's work.

Section II reexamines the relationships among the manuscripts
at the top of the stemma: **VBA**, potential hyparchetypes of **VBA**, and
the shared ancestor **α**. The examination draws on methods not yet
applied to the tradition of the elder Seneca's work, and seldom applied
to other textual traditions. Not just the individual variant readings are
taken into account, but also textual layout, verse lengths, groupings of
letters and word-strings, and script-types. This recognition of the full
texture of the Seneca text leads to new conclusions about its history. A
synthesis of methods, besides supplying a firmer basis for the conclusions reached, is itself one of the main objectives of this section. The
arguments about Seneca's textual tradition are meant to address how
we should reconstruct textual histories: implicit in the demonstration
is an argument for a more holistic view of the features that count when
studying textual histories.

In Section III, drawing on evidence in our extant Seneca manuscripts and on external evidence, I explore the possibility that a late-
antique reader, conversant in the practice of declamation and in
declamatory collections, gave our Seneca text its definitive form—by
preserving the *Suasoriae* and *Controuersiae* together, by graphically

articulating the larger component pieces of the collected declamatory material, and by punctuating and giving shape to the text. This readerly engagement, instantiated in graphic signs and textual organization, offers us a reading of Seneca's work that is at once knowledgeable, valid, and situated in an historical context.

For these reasons, I propose that traditional graphic signs and textual organization should be more fully and explicitly admitted into modern editions and interpretations of the elder Seneca's collection. In an age when we are experiencing firsthand how digital media change the way we interact with and understand texts, when we are undergoing a revolution in the history of reading and book publishing comparable to the introduction of the printing press, it is becoming increasingly relevant and necessary to adopt a philosophy about our ancient texts that responds fully to what they are and to their places in history. The philosophy that underlies this proposal about taking the physical shapes of texts seriously can be summed up as follows: the textual medium matters and participates in meaning.

I. BACKGROUND: THE MANUSCRIPT TRADITION

The rhetorical anthology of the elder Seneca has come down to us in two traditions:[2] The first is a "full" tradition, which endeavors to preserve the integrity of Seneca's work, but descends from a mutilated ancestor manuscript (α). Of an original ten books of *Controuersiae*, only Books 1, 2, 7, 9, and 10 survive more or less complete. Of Seneca's wonderfully engaging epistolary prefaces, only those to Books 7, 9, and

---

[2] On the textual tradition of the elder Seneca: see Håkanson 1989:v–xvii (with reviews by Watt 1991; Winterbottom 1991); Winterbottom 1974a:xxvi–xxviii, 1974b:21–24, and 1983; H. J. Müller 1887:viiii–xxxxi. For the tradition in the later middle ages, see Vervliet 1964. For print editions, Vervliet 1957. Håkanson (1989:xiii, xxii) was working on a commentary on the tradition, but was prevented from completing and publishing the work by his death. Our understanding of the manuscript tradition is poorer for the loss. I hope that his notes, which I have not seen, will yet be published. (Since completing this article, I have learned that Håkanson's unpublished notes are almost entirely text-critical in nature and that the notes on Book 1 are being prepared by Francesco Citti, Antonio Stramaglia, and Michael Winterbottom.) The contributions of Winterbottom and Håkanson to Seneca's text, and to other rhetorical texts, are immense. My discussion, which challenges some of their conclusions, would not be possible without their work.

10 survive. The full tradition also transmits a book-length collection of *Suasoriae*. It is unknown how many *Suasoriae*, or books of *Suasoriae*, Seneca actually compiled.

The second stream of the tradition is a collection of excerpts taken from Seneca's work, perhaps representing the efforts of a late-antique rhetor.[3] It appears that the complete collection of *Controuersiae* was available to the excerptor, who was able consistently to draw from all ten books. Prefaces from Books 1, 2, 3, 4, 7, and 10 are preserved by the excerpted tradition. However, there is no excerpted tradition of the *Suasoriae*—a fact best explained if we assume that in antiquity *Controuersiae* and *Suasoriae* circulated separately.[4] This possibility is supported by internal evidence that Seneca composed them separately: at *Contr.* 2 pr.5, Seneca comments that he has collected into the current book (Book 2) all his quotations of the declaimer/philosopher Papirius Fabianus. But, as it turns out, additional quotations of Fabianus appear in the *Suasoriae*. Either it slipped Seneca's mind that additional quotations of Fabianus would in fact be included later in the same collection, or, more likely, he regarded the *Suasoriae* as a separate collection from that of the *Controuersiae*.

Modern editions of the full tradition depend on three closely related but independent manuscripts. None of the three is a *descriptus* ('copy') of another. The manuscripts are Vaticanus latinus 3872 (**V**, Figure 2), a Corbeiensis, copied in the middle to third quarter of the ninth century at Corbie; Brussels, Bibl. Royale, 9581–9595 (**B**, Figure 1), copied in the latter half of the ninth century, perhaps in NE France; and Antwerp, Erfgoedbibliotheek Hendrik Conscience (formerly Stadsbibliotheek), 411 (**A**, Figure 3), copied in the tenth century, also

---

[3]   Bursian 1857:vii plausibly conjectures that the excerpted collection was made in the fourth or fifth century. See also Müller 1887:xxii; Hagendahl 1936:300n1, 308. The best MS of the excerpted tradition is Montpellier, Faculté de médecine, H 126; see Chatelain 1884–1900: pl. 166.2 The earliest (ca. 800) surviving manuscript witness to the excerpted tradition, a remarkable fragment consisting of just four leaves, has yet to be accounted for in a critical edition: Bamberg, Staatsbibliothek, Msc.Class 45m; cf. Figure 4. See Winterbottom 1983:357n6; Bischoff 1966–1981:3.14, 3.158n43.

[4]   Fairweather 1981:35–36 speculates on other possibilities for the arrangement of *Suasoriae*.

perhaps in NE France.[5] An unpublished thesis by H. D. L. Vervliet informs us that later manuscripts of the full tradition derive from the Corbeiensis.[6]

The 1887 edition of H. J. Müller (xii–xiii) established a basic fact about the relationship between **VBA**: variant readings and errors show a closer link between **B** and **A** than between **V** and **A**, or between **V** and **B**. Despite agreement on this point, precisely how the three manuscripts stand in relation to the archetype (α)[7] of the full tradition has been left open to debate: Were **BA** copied directly from α, whereas **V** was copied from an apograph of α, as Håkanson (1989:v–xii) believed? Or, were **BA** copied from one hyparchetype and **V** from a second hyparchetype, as was the view of H. J. Müller?[8] Does textual and manuscript evidence suggest other stemmatic possibilities?

How and why the text of **V** is at times strikingly different from **BA** remains something of an unsolved puzzle.[9] The consensus view is that the Corbeiensis is different because it was copied from a corrected and interpolated exemplar: **V** must be read with "distrust"; **BA**, while often presenting a more difficult and more corrupt text, are more "faithful"

---

[5] For **V**, see Chatelain 1884–1900: pl.166.1 (fol.23v, not 21v), and especially Bischoff 1961 (= Bischoff 1966–1981:1.49–63, in German), a ground-breaking and inspiring study that places **V** in the context of other MSS copied at Corbie in the middle to the third quarter of the ninth century. For the date and origin of **B**, see Bischoff 1998–2004:1.158. Bischoff, in a quotation by Vervliet 1955 from a private correspondence (found in part also at Håkanson 1989:vi n1), appears at one time to have held slightly different opinions about the three manuscripts: he once estimated that **V** was copied *in the first half* of the ninth century, **B** copied around the *middle* of the ninth century and "probably not in France" ("Frankreich ist nicht sehr wahrscheinlich"), and **A**, he writes, may have been copied as late as the eleventh century.

[6] Vervliet 1955. I wish to thank Hendrik D. L. Vervliet for meeting with me and very graciously lending me a personal copy of his thesis.

[7] In this study the 'archetype' (α) refers to the lost manuscript that is the ultimate ancestor of **VBA**. It does not refer to a common ancestor shared by the full tradition *and* the excerpted tradition; see the stemma of Håkanson 1989:v.

[8] H. J. Müller 1887:xii–xiii. Winterbottom 1991:338 is skeptical of Håkanson's argument that **BA** are direct copies of α and thus are not more closely linked by a hyparchetype.

[9] The question remains open because: 1) it is difficult, and 2) it is thought to make little difference when it comes to constituting the text. See Håkanson 1989:vii; Winterbottom 1991:339.

textual witnesses of α.[10] Even if these descriptors are just metaphorical, this view, which imputes to **V** a desire to deceive while seeing
fidelity in **BA**, mischaracterizes the cultural and intellectual motives
that produced the three manuscripts. The mischaracterization is in
part responsible for a misapprehension of the relationships of **VBA** to
one another and to α. The evidence of our three principal surviving
manuscripts is not well understood; as a consequence, the stemma for
Seneca's text remains vague and unsettled.

II. STEMMATIC RELATIONSHIPS, VISIBLE TEXT

In this section the following conclusions are drawn with regard to the
relationships of the principal manuscripts **VBA** to one another, to
potential hyparchetypes, and to their common ancestor α:

1) **BA** were not copied directly from α, but were copied from an
intermediate manuscript, what I call **(y)**. This is what H. J. Müller 1887
believed, but has been cast in doubt by the most recent critical edition,
Håkanson 1989.

2) The readers and scribes of Corbie had access to a manuscript
unavailable to the scribes of **BA**. Most importantly, this manuscript was
not a *twin* of **(y)**, but was an *ancestor* of **(y)**: it was α itself.[11]

3) In producing **V**, the Corbie scribes followed a complex copying
procedure that employed two manuscripts: an older manuscript,
namely the archetype α, and a more recent manuscript, a descendant
of α. This conclusion rests on the examination of multiple kinds of
evidence: variant readings, textual organization (punctuation, verse-
lengths, letter-groupings), types of textual corruption, and the script-
types of exemplars. Using this evidence we detect in **V** the lectional
and text-organizational patterns of two different exemplars: an exem-

---

[10] In those passages where **BA** suggest that α is corrupt, Håkanson (1989:xi) warns
about **V** that "*non nisi summa cum cautione ille incertae fidei liber adhibendus est.*" See also
Winterbottom 1974a:xxviii ("the prudent editor will always weigh its [i.e. **V**'s] readings
with suspicion"); Winterbottom 1974b:21 says that the ancestor of **BA** was "infinitely
more like the archetype than **V**."

[11] The idea that **V**'s scribes had access to genuinely transmitted readings unavailable
to **BA** has been suspected by H. J. Müller 1887:xii–xiii; Winterbottom 1974b:21; Håkanson
1989:x–xi.

plar that is behind **(y)** and an exemplar very much like **(y)**. Although absolute certainty is impossible, I strongly suspect that the exemplar very much like **(y)** was in fact **(y)**.

4) The copying procedure followed by the scribes of **V** involved corrections, drawn from **α**, and also conjectures by a corrector working *suo Marte*. These alterations were not applied consistently to the same manuscript, but were inserted in different manuscripts—most frequently in **α**, often in **V** itself, and occasionally in its younger exemplar, which I think was **(y)**.

If we take together these conclusions about how the Corbie scribes worked—they compared manuscripts, they added corrections and conjectures both to **α** and to what was likely **(y)**—we reach an important possibility that cannot be ignored: corrections to the exemplar of **BA**, which Håkanson (1989:xii–xiii) at times thought he could detect, may have been put there by the scribes and readers responsible for **V**.

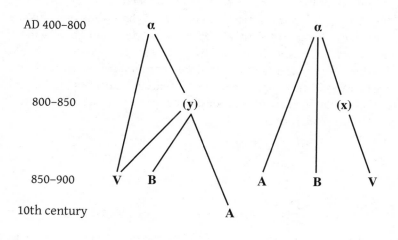

Proposed stemma

Stemma according to Håkanson 1989:v

This idea that behind **V** are two exemplars has, to a degree, been antic-ipated.[12] Its implications have not. Recognition of a complex copying procedure, and a complex engagement with the text (collating manu-scripts, reading and correcting), brings into relief the fact that textual reproduction at Corbie was qualitatively different from that of the unidentified scriptoria of **B** and **A**.[13] Many classical Latin texts were copied at Corbie.[14] Several of these, like **V**, betray indications of the collation of manuscripts and the application of conjectures. There are also hints that the activities of Corbie scribes/readers extended into manuscripts not copied in the Corbie variety of caroline minuscule. These complications show (if it needed showing) that the sigla of stem-mata can be misleading, since they are meant to represent manuscripts and not the patterns of human activities, perceptions, and interpreta-tions that produced manuscripts.

The Corbeiensis is different, we know. How do we understand and respond to this difference? The critical role played by our responses emerges from the fact that we can come to two different, almost diametrically opposite conclusions about how we regard **V**. The current view, it seems, is that **V** cannot be trusted; it is a distortion and a degeneration of the textual tradition when compared with **BA**. The view argued in this article, by contrast, is that, while one must be aware of conjectures in **V**, the Corbeiensis is a more traditional, a more ancient and classical, representative of the Seneca text than are **BA**. This difference in attitudes about **V** stems from whether we take into consideration the visual dimension of textual transmission. Regard for the visible text is not gratuitous, but a question of whether we will consider a broader spectrum of evidence.

---

[12] H. J. Müller 1887:xii–xiii.

[13] For studies of Corbie and its MSS, see Jones 1947, Bischoff 1961, Bishop 1972, Ganz 1990.

[14] Classical Latin authors copied at Corbie in the second half of the ninth century include Livy, Cicero, Columella, Vegetius, Germanicus, Marius Victorinus, Terence, Statius, Martial, Ovid, Martianus Capella, Vitruvius, the younger Pliny, and Sallust. See Bischoff 1961:52–54, Ganz 1990:151–155.

II.1 Punctuation and Textual Arrangement in α

Some visual features of **VBA**—specifically, details of textual layout and spatial organization, punctuation, and script—were inherited and represent visual features of α. Among these inherited features is punctuation: the signaling of the boundaries between sentences and sense-units[15] through spacing and punctuation marks.

The first, and most immediately striking, clue that the punctuation in our three principal manuscripts represents something earlier than the ninth century is provided by **B**, which divides its text into long, cramped word-strings separated by generous spacing.[16] This spatial arrangement, to greater and lesser degrees, can be observed throughout **B**. However, it is most clearly seen in the first two-thirds of Seneca's anthology (fols.88r–140v), which was copied by a different scribe from the remainder (fols.141r–167v). A dramatic example appears on fol.107r (Figure 1), where word-groups are especially well-defined. Furthermore, when we read the text of **B** we quickly discover that its sentences have not been divided arbitrarily. Isolated word-groups correspond to sense-units. For example, fol.107r (*Contr.* 1.2.11–12), beginning at the end of the first line:[17]

---

[15] The term 'sense-unit' is meant as a neutral term. Carter, Day, and Meggs 2007:83–84, in a study of modern typography, speak of textual organization according to such units as "thought-unit typography." I do not use the term '*colon*' (pl. *cola*), only because the latter term can lead one to think of the system of punctuation, found especially in medieval MSS containing biblical texts, that is called *per cola et commata* (see Jerome, prol. Isaiah). Texts laid out *per cola et commata* assign sense-units to their own verses. When we see manuscript text divided into sense-units, as in **B**, we must not assume that these sense-units were formerly assigned their own verses in an ancestor MS.

[16] This peculiarity of **B** is singled out by Bischoff (1998–2004: vol. 1, 158), who describes the script as "schmal, gedrängt, aber mit sehr weiten Zwischenräumen zwischen den Wortgruppen."

[17] Punctuation marks in transcriptions visually mimic punctuation marks in **B**; see Parkes 1993:301. I have resolved some abbreviations in the transcription. In the following translation major space divisions found in **B** are marked with vertical lines (all translations are my own): "The pirates preserved that girl | just as those do who are about to sell to a pimp. | [lacuna] ... stand in that rank | eat from the same table, live in the same space | in which even if you do not experience sex you see it. | Someone perhaps was found | whom the very act of your begging aroused. | But the pimp himself spared you? | Are we unaware of those men | for whom this is a peculiar attraction of that line of work |

Sic |
istam seruaueruntpiratae   quemadmodum quilenoni
    essentuendituri;   Stare inillo |
ordine   exeademues<c>imensaineolocouiuere   inquo&-
    iamsinonpatiaris stuprumuideas· Aliquis |
fortasseinuentusest   quemhocipsuminritar&quod-
    rogabas·ʾ   Ipseautemlenopepercit   ignoramus |
istos   quibusuelhocineismodiquestupraecipue-
    plac&   quodinlibata<m>uirginitatem decerpunt· |

All three manuscripts, here and generally throughout the text, agree in demarcations of sense-units (cf. Figure 2, V, fol.32v, starting at the end of tenth line). This agreement is compelling evidence that the divisions were present already in **α**.

Nonetheless, reconstruction of the punctuation in **α**, through study of the punctuation in **VBA**, is not without complication. As can be seen even on fol.107r, where sense-unit divisions are very well-defined, the application of spacing in **B** is not entirely uniform or singular in purpose. In addition to the large spaces dividing sense-units, also within sense-units smaller spaces, corresponding to word boundaries, occasionally appear. This hierarchy of major and minor spaces in fact is not uncommon in Carolingian manuscripts, as the instructive and fascinating studies by Paul Saenger have demonstrated.[18] Saenger insists that the insertion of additional spacing in medieval manuscripts was done to good purpose, even when it resulted in inaccurate word divisions, since it rendered texts that had been in *scriptura continua* ("continuous script") more legible:[19] space makes texts easier to read.

Saenger's point, which effectively challenges the perception, widely held (particularly by classicists), that spacing added by medieval scribes often betrays scribal stupidity, is well taken and impor-

---

the fact that they deflower untouched virginity?" The passage is in **V** on fol.32v, in **A** on fol.26v.

[18] Saenger 1982, 1990a, 1990b, 1997:32–44.

[19] In addition to the studies of Saenger, see Parkes 1987, who uses (16) what has become a key phrase of studies about textual organization in medieval MSS: "grammar of legibility."

tant. Spacing has a practical value. It makes a reader's interaction with a text quicker and more efficient. However, this insight about improved "legibility" should not mislead us into thinking that there was a lack of *organization* in ancient and late-antique texts.[20] A broad, evolutionary movement towards greater ease in reading, through the middle ages and into the modern era, does not amount to a progressive advancement away from textual disorganization and shapelessness in antiquity.[21]

It would be more accurate to speak of different "legibilities"—different grammars of reading, each with its own textual organization. Among the key factors in the complex historical process towards more textual spacing is not just the value of efficiency, but cultural practices and values:[22] the roles played by texts in social contexts, who uses them, and the particular reading/interpretive experiences created by the system of textual organization in which a literary work is presented. Of particular interest to the present investigation, and to classicists more generally, are those textual traditions—of which I suspect there are many[23]—where spacing by medieval scribes was inserted into, or

[20] R. W. Müller 1964:8–9 addresses the widespread misperception that ancient Latin texts (on papyrus, parchment, wax, stone) lack punctuation. The misperception is in part due to what moderns regard as punctuation: spacing and textual shape also count as punctuation. And punctuation is sometimes undervalued, since it is not always accurately recorded in transcriptions: Habinek 1985:42, 62n31; R. W. Müller 1964:22–23. For ancient Latin punctuation see also Moreau-Maréchal 1968; Wingo 1972; Rafti 1988.

[21] An impulse to see disorder in ancient Latin texts can be further detected in Saenger's comments about ancient Latin word order, characterized as lacking conventions (71–72) and very rarely influencing the meaning of a sentence (14). For the opposite view, that ancient Latin word order is fundamental to meaning, see e.g. Devine and Stephens 2006:5.

[22] This point made by Petrucci 1995:134–135, in response to Saenger 1982. Saenger 1997:11 describes cultural differences between ancient and modern readers. On the sociology of reading in classical antiquity, see Johnson 2000; Johnson and Parker 2009, with bibliographical survey (333–382) by Shirley Werner.

[23] Examples of MSS of classical Latin texts exhibiting textual organization, especially sense-unit strings, that is inherited from late antiquity: Paris, B.N. Nouv. Acq. lat. 454, a Corbie product (Chatelain 1884–1900: pl.40b.1; Ganz 1990:153); Bamberg, Staatsbibl., Ms.Class. 46 (Chatelain 1884–1900: pl.173.1; Bischoff 1966–1981: vol.3., pl.XI; Reynolds 1965:54–65, 149); Florence, Bibl. Med. Laur. 76.40 (Chatelain 1884–1900: pl.170.3; Reynolds 1965: pl.III); London, British Library, Harley 2736 (Beeson 1930); London, British Library, Add. 47678 (Chatelain 1884–1900: pl.27a; Parkes 1993: pl.58); Paris, B.N. 6332 (Chatelain

blended with, an already existing *orderly* system of punctuation found in late-antique exemplars.[24] It is this multi-layered textual organization that is reflected in the striking punctuation of **B**.

B's complex use of major and minor spaces simultaneously can result in inconsistencies, ambiguities, and obvious errors. Minor spatial divisions at times interfere with the boundaries of major sense-unit divisions. For example, the lengths of space separating minor and major textual units become roughly equal. Or, a word that should clearly belong to a preceding sense-unit is set nearer to the following word-string. Spaces can even occur mid-word, such that a single word is split between two major sense-unit strings. Thus, in examining the punctuation of **B**, we encounter something of a contradiction. On the one hand, the text was clearly shaped by a reading sensitive to the larger component, textual pieces (*cola*, or phrases) that build sentence architecture. On the other hand, there appear intrusions of spacing violating the boundaries of both major and minor sense-units.[25] The contradiction is explained, however, if we suppose that the spatial arrangement in **B** is a fusion of two separate layers in the tradition: an older layer, represented by the major sense-divisions, and a contemporary (i.e. Carolingian) layer responsible for most of the arbitrary or faulty divisions.[26]

1884–1900: pl.44.1; Parkes 1993: pl.14); Vat. lat. 3246 (cover of Giusta 1991); Vatican, Arch. S. Petri H. 25 (Chatelain 1884–1900: pl.26; Bischoff 1966–1981: vol. 3, 30n124; Clark 1918:162–201), copied in three columns; and Bamberg, Staatsbibl., Msc.Class 45m (see Figure 4), a fragment containing the excerpted tradition of the elder Seneca.

[24] On *codices distincti*, MSS that received graded pointing in late antiquity, see Parkes 1993:11–13, 67–68, 119. The phrase *codex distinctus* is found in Sergius, *De distinctione*; see Keil 1857–1880:4.484: *nam cum sit codex emendatus distinctione, media distinctione, subdistinctione, dicitur tamen codex esse distinctus.* Markus and Schwendner 1997:75–76 describe punctuation in a fragment from a fourth-century vellum codex, found in Egypt, that contains the "Medea" of Seneca *Tragicus*.

[25] For example, *Suas.* 2.1, **B**, fol.90r. Note faulty word-divisions (*Lacedaemonios* and *excidia*) disturbing good sense-unit divisions (|): *quiddicam potissimosgraecae an<u>lace</u>* [verse-end] <u>daemonio</u> | <u>s</u>aneleo sanereptum totaciespatrum | totque<u>excidi</u> <u>a</u>urbium | totuictarum gentiumspolia?*

[26] Cf. Vanderhoven and Masai 1953:107, for scribal copying rhythms at variance with sense-unit divisions in an exemplar.

That this is the correct explanation is supported by a comparison of **B** with **A**, and especially with **V**. The Corbeiensis (**V**, Figure 2) observes the same major sense-unit divisions as **B**, insofar as they are maintained in **B**, while it generally lacks its erratic and arbitrary minor divisions. **A** too (Figure 3), although it has far more inter-word spacing than either **B** or **V**, highlights where **B**'s spacing is idiosyncratic: **B** stands alone in its abundant spacing between major sense-units, in its exaggerated hierarchy of spacing, and in many of its confusions of this hierarchy. The Corbeiensis, it appears, better preserves a textual organization established earlier in the tradition.

Other pieces of evidence confirm the impression that **V**, when compared with **BA**, maintains an older visual organization of the text. The system of punctuation and textual shaping in **V** is older: its script is closest to *scriptura continua*. The Corbeiensis, strictly speaking, was not copied in continuous script—but the shape given to the text is something near to continuous script. The organization of **V**'s text is hierarchical:[27] major sense-units are demarcated by spacing and graphic signs, and within these major sense-units there is often very slight word spacing, though this is sometimes absent.

As for the method of punctuation in **V**, major sense-units are defined by moderate spacing and by single 'points' placed at low, medium, and high positions in the line, corresponding to increasingly greater pauses or sense-breaks. High and medial points are followed by *litterae notabiliores* (prominent, majuscule letters).[28] This system of

---

[27] Saenger 1997:18–51, with a summary on p45, offers a much needed typology of spacing, providing graded categories of spacing between continuous script, on one end of the spectrum, and separated script, on the other. His discussions (ibid. and in Saenger 1982, 1990a, 1990b) have greatly helped my thinking about the spacing in **VBA**. However, lacking in Saenger's typology is appreciation of (ninth-century) MSS that organize their text into large, non-arbitrary (rhetorically or grammatically informed) sense-units. Saenger (1997:32–44) defines textual blocks according to letter, syllable, and word, but mentions only in passing (33) larger grammatical blocks.

[28] In his study of Vat. Reg. Lat. 1762, a mid-ninth-century classical florilegium compiled by the librarian Hadoard ("*bibliothecae custos*," he calls himself), Schwenke 1889:414 notes that higher points are followed by majuscules. He identifies two kinds of points in the Hadoard classical florilegium. Parkes 1993:31 observes a tendency in the middle ages for the three-level point system of antiquity to become simplified to a two-level system. There appear to be three levels of points in Vat. lat. 3872.

punctuation by points, called *distinctiones*, has a long history stretching back into antiquity. It is explained by late-antique grammarians,[29] most notably by Donatus and later by Isidore, and it is seen in practice in some of our earliest surviving Latin manuscripts.[30] But the idea that the scribes of **V** are simply mirroring what they found in an exemplar must be tempered by the observation that the system of punctuation in **V** is found also in other Corbie manuscripts of the same period as **V**:[31] at least for some texts, punctuation by points appears to have been standard practice at mid-ninth-century Corbie. Still, this caution does not prevent us from reaching an important conclusion about textual arrangement in **V**: it is traditional and harks back to older, late-antique models.[32] Recognizing that surely both these forces— textual arrangement found in an exemplar and standard Corbie proce- dure—ultimately played a part in the look of **V**, we can discern in the scribes of **V** an attitude towards the text they were copying: a "classi- cizing" impulse, whether the impulse be characterized as conservative or reactionary.

There are in fact good indications, provided by **BA**, that *distinctiones* were used to define major sense-units in **α**. Points appear in both

---

[29] R. W. Müller 1964:73–85; Hubert 1970:20–76; Habinek 1985:52–57; Parkes 1993:13– 14. For Donatus, see Holtz 1981. On the grammarians and ancient punctuation, see also Blank 1983.

[30] R. W. Müller 1964:41–45. Examples: 1) The Medicean Vergil, Florence, Biblioteca Medicea Laurenziana 39.1 (Parkes 1993: pl.2). 2) Vatican Vergil, Vat. lat. 3225. 3) A fifth- century fragment of Sallust: Oxoniensis Bodl. Lat. class. e. 20 – *P.Oxy.* 884 (*CLA* [= Lowe 1934–1971] 2.246). 4) A fourth-century fragment of Livy: *P.Oxy.* 1379 (*CLA* 2.247). 5) A fifth- / sixth-century fragment of Juvenal (*CLA* Suppl. 1710; Roberts 1935). For punctua- tion in Homeric papyri, see Lameere 1960:74–92.

[31] Punctuation by points can be seen in the two Hadoard florilegia: Paris, B.N. lat. 13381 (Ganz 1990:191, pl.15) and Vat. Reg. Lat. 1762 (Schmidt 1974: Taf. III). And it can be seen in: Paris, B.N. lat. 2863; Ghent, Bibl. univ. 909; and Paris, B.N. lat. 18296 (Ganz 1990:190, pl.14). For these last three MSS, see Bakhuizen van den Brink 1974:9–10, figures 1–3, 5–7, 10, 15, 18.

[32] For features of Corbie book production reflecting practices seen in late-antique codices, see Bishop 1972:14–15; Ganz 1990:56–67. Cf. Ganz 1990:56, speaking of the caro- line script used at Corbie during the time of Radbert and Hadoard: "The quality of the parchment, its codicology, and the layout of the page, all reveal a distinctive and elegant scriptorium at the height of its powers. *One spur to such restrained expertise was the use of Late Antique exemplars, especially of classical texts* [my emphasis]; another was the general evolution of caroline minuscule throughout the empire."

manuscripts, though infrequently. This inconsistency likely reflects haphazard copying of points present in the exemplar of **B** and **A**. Contemporary, ninth- and tenth-century punctuation in **BA**, especially spacing, superseded the older system of *distinctiones* appearing in the tradition; nonetheless, the scribes of **B** and **A** casually adopted points found in their exemplar. The passage below (*Contr.* 1.2.1) is an example of pointing in **B** and **A**. We see that spaces in **B** or **A** can correspond to points in **V** (so after *uiuer&*). Arbitrary minor spacing in this passage (e.g. the various groupings of *sacerdos uestra adhuc in lupanari uiueret*),[33] which I have attempted to reproduce along with verse lengths, suggests that α was in continuous script, or something close to it. It will be noticed, again, how **B** exaggerates major sense-unit divisions through the use of large spaces. This exaggeration, in part, is certainly a function of the much larger page dimensions that the scribes of **B** (315 × 234 [247 × 170] mm) had to work with relative to the page dimensions of **V** (230 × 185 [165 × 140] mm) and **A** (215 × 135 [152 × 90] mm).[34] All pointing was original to the copying of the text.[35]

[33] Another example: **A**, fol.1v (*Suas.* 1.3): *Terre quo quesuum finem habent· & ipsiusmundi aliquisoccasusest· Nihil* ... Points in the same positions appear in **V**, fol.2r.

[34] Van den Gheyn 1902:305; Dermul 1939:23; Vervliet 1955:68, 74, 117, 119; Bischoff 1998–2004:1.23, 158.

[35] Pointing in **B** and **A** was verified by firsthand study of the MSS in Brussels and Antwerp. The Corbeiensis at the Vatican Library, which was closed for renovations during the period of my investigations (2007–2010), I know from microfilm and photographs. Lowe (*CLA* I.x) admonishes that punctuation can be studied "only by inspecting the original." Nonetheless, the consistency with which the pointing is applied in **V** and the fact that the pointing is in lockstep agreement with textual arrangement (the spacing between sense-units) leaves little doubt that the points were original to the copying of the text. Black-ink commas and colons in **A**, which I have taken care to ignore, are the work of the humanist scholar Andreas Schott. Schott's punctuation in **A** often corresponds to the points in **V**, which he consulted in Rome. He can be seen at work in Figure 3, adding punctuation and, in the margins, puzzling out the Greek. For Schott, see Fabri 1953; Vervliet 1964:431–432. For Greek declaimers in Seneca's work, see Citti 2007.

Sen. *Contr.* 1.2.1[36]

Vat. lat. 3872, fol.29v–30r

> Sacerdos uestraadhucinlupanari uiuer& nisihominem occidiss& |
> Interbarbarosquidpassasitnescio·quidpatipotueritscio˙ Sacer |
> dotinepurusquidem contigitdominus˙ Absint

Brussels 9594, fol.105r

> Sacerdos uestra adhuc inlupanariuiuer& nisihominem
>   occidiss&·₇   Interbarbaros quidpassasit |
> nescio quidpati potuerit scio·   Sacerdoti nepurus-
>   quidem   contigit dominus· Absint

Antwerp 411, fol.24v

> Sacerdosuestra adhuc inlupanari uiuer& nisihominem occidiss&· |
> Interbarbaros quidpassasit nescio quidpati potuerit scio·
>   Sacerdoti ne |
> purus quidem contigit dominus· Absint

Agreement among **VBA** in the placement of *distinctiones* demonstrates that pointing seen in the three manuscripts is inherited, that it is as old as **α**, perhaps older. Further support of this interpretation, that punctuation in **VBA** belongs to an earlier stage of the tradition, comes from the fact that **VBA** agree in punctuation even in corrupt passages. The ninth- and tenth-century scribes simply reproduce passages, including punctuation, that at this stage in the transmission of the text have become nonsensical.[37]

---

[36] Håkanson 1989: *Sacerdos uestra adhuc in lupanari uiueret, nisi hominem occidisset. Inter barbaros quid passa sit, nescio: quid pati potuerit, scio. Sacerdoti ne purus quidem contigit dominus. Absint ...*, "Your priestess would still be living in a whorehouse, if she had not killed a man. What she suffered among barbarians, I don't know; but I know what she *could* have suffered. She had a master—and an impure one at that. Keep away ..."

[37] E.g., *Contr.* 7.7.3, Håkanson 1989 reads: *si silentium eius intellexissemus et tunc nobis uerecunde indicauerat* ("If we had understood his silence, even then he had discreetly given us a sign"). **VB** have a point before *et tunc* (**A** adds space). Preceding this punctuational division the text of all three MSS is unintelligible: *intellexissemus*] Håkanson *intellegeres scisses* **V** *intellegerescissem s* **B** *intelligerescissent s* **A**. At times, I suspect, punctuational

II.2 A Complex Copying Process
Produced the Corbeiensis

Of the three principal Seneca manuscripts, **V** in many respects most closely reflects an older visual organization of Seneca's text: in its unambiguous punctuation of major sense-units, in the use of near-continuous script, and in the consistent application of *distinctiones*. To this list of traditional visual features can be added the approximately square text-block of **V**'s page.[38] In its restraint and uniformity, **V** possesses the same elegant simplicity of some of our late-antique manuscripts.

Furthermore, it has not been noticed hitherto that **V** further manifests a conservative, historicist nature by replicating the verse lengths of an ancestor of **BA**, whether this ancestor was the exemplar of **BA** or a parent of **BA**'s exemplar (= α).[39] Proof of this procedure appears in several places. An instance has been included in the text quoted just above (*Contr.* 1.2.1), where the first verses (*Sacerdos ... occidiss&*) of **V** and **A** match. A similar example occurs at *Contr.* 1.4.1 (**V**, fol.37v; **B**, fol.110r; **A**, fol.31r).[40] A third example appears at *Contr.* 2.2.1, where a single

---

division appearing in a corrupt passage did not originate as punctuation but rather was inserted to signal corruption. E.g. at *Contr.* 1.3.3, **VB** show a division (by a point in **V**) in the middle of a phrase (*electus · potissimum locus*). A comparable marking of corruption (with spacing and/or the cryphia) can be seen in Harley 2736, Lupus of Ferrières' copy of Cicero's *De oratore*; Beeson 1930:21–29.

[38] Lowe 1925:207, 1928:59; Bishop 1972:14. See also Bishop's comments (13, 14–15n5) on St. Petersburg (Leningrad), F.v.Lat. Class. 8 (*Rhet. Her.*, Cic. *Inv. rhet.*) and on Florence, Laur. S. Marco 257 (Cicero).

[39] Winterbottom 1974b:40n6 is presumably being critical of the results of particular studies when he disparages efforts to discover the verse lengths of an archetype. The present investigation, I hope, will show the relevance of verse lengths in studying textual transmission. The estimates of α's verse lengths by Håkanson 1989:xiii are not supported by the results of my investigations.

[40] **V**, fol.37v: Adulterosmeos tantumexcitauime miserum quamdiu iacuer̄

A, fol.31r: Adulteros meos tantum excitaui memiserum qucon di   acuer̄

Here the Antwerp scribe, misunderstanding the script of his exemplar at verse-end (*quamdiu iacuerunt* **VB**), produces nonsense. In an effort to get as close as possible to what he cannot understand, the scribe adheres to the verse length of his exemplar. The **A** scribe writes *qucon di* for *quamdiu*, misreading *co* for an open *a* in the exemplar. Evidence for an open *a* in the exemplar appears elsewhere (see Section III).

verse in **B**, fol.121v, is identical to two verses in **V**, fol.59v.[41] (The verses of neither **V** nor **B** match verses in **A**, fol.49r.)

These three examples occur at the beginning of quotations, immediately following the name of the speaker quoted. Coincidence of verse length is more likely to occur here because, as consensus of **VBA** reveals, new quotations in α often began with a new verse. However, it is significant that, when there is agreement in verse length at these points in the text, it is with **V** that either **B** or **A** agrees: **V** is consistently concerned to follow the verses of the shared ancestor of **VBA**, whereas **B** and **A** do so only occasionally and rather indifferently.

The indifference of **BA** to preserving verse lengths makes it a challenge to discover corroborating evidence of transmitted verse lengths appearing in text that is not at the beginning of a quotation. Nonetheless, there is such supporting evidence at hand, and it is compelling. At *Contr.* 9.2.4, in the middle of a quotation, **B** (fol.149r) omits text (*meretrice ... uoluisses*) identical to a verse in **V**, fol.110r (this is not a verse in **A**).

> euerritur· Gratulor sortituaeprouintia quoddesiderante tale-
> spectaculū |
> meretrice˙ Plenū carcerē dāpnatis habuisti· seruū siuerberari
> uoluisses |
> extraconuiuium abduxisses   ROMANI HISPONIS · Quisferr&tequi |

V, then, has the verse lengths of an ancestor manuscript of **BA**.[42] Is the lost manuscript containing these traditional verse lengths α itself? Is it another manuscript, a hyparchetype shared between **VBA**? What, in short, is the exemplar or exemplars of **V**?

To attempt to answer these questions, *Contr.* 9.2.4 and passages immediately surrounding it repay scrutiny. In this portion of Seneca's text (9.2.2–9.2.7), **V** offers a series of variant readings (seen in the list below) against the shared testimony of **BA**. Lemmata are the readings

---

[41] The second verse ends mid-word (*sed ex* | *perimentum*). Vat. lat. 3872, fol.59v, reads:
   DII INMORTALES· QUADE BETIS PROUIDENTIA HUMANŪ |
   genus regitis·effecistis·utillud nonpericulum ess&amantis sedex |
[42] Further evidence that **V** contains an older pattern of verse lengths can be found in Section II.3.

accepted by Håkanson. Numbers, separated by commas, refer to page and line in Håkanson.[43]

> 242,16 reliquiae] *V* relique *BA* || 242,30 populus Romanus dederat] PR dederit (diderit *A*) *BA* perdiderat *V* || 243,1 quoi esset] quot esset *A²* [= *A. Schott*] quod (quot *A*) esset *BA* cui te est *V* || 243,3 istud mulierum] *V* istum mulierum *BA* || 243,6 cibos] *V* ciuos *BA* || 243,6 humanum caput] *BA*   caput humanum *V* [*unreported by editors*][44] || 243,11 si] *BA*   qui *V* || 243,16 quis] *BA* quid *V* || 243,18 cogitat] *V* concitat *BA* || 243,18 alioqui] alio quid (*ex* quod *B*) *BA*   alio quem *V* || 243,21 clementem] *V* clementer *BA*

Since the idea that **BA** are copies of **V** is out of the question, the most probable explanation of the verse lengths in **V** would be that **V** is copying the same exemplar as **BA**. However, this probability is not borne out by a study of the readings in this passage. **V**, we know, contains conjectures, and undoubtedly several of **V**'s variants above are unconvincing corrections or copying mistakes peculiar to **V**: 243,1 243,11 243,16 243,18 (*alio quem*). Still, other superior variants are not easily attributed to conjecture: 242,16; 243,3; 243,18 (*cogitat*); 243,21. The very quality of these readings, particularly 243,3 and 18 (*cogitat*), makes it at least as likely that they were *found* by Corbie scribes in a manuscript as felicitously conjectured by them.

But the difficult question of the authenticity of **V**'s variants does not obscure a crucial fact: the variant readings of **V** listed above do not manifest themselves as corrections made to the manuscript page. The variants were not generated in **V**, but rather the Corbie scribe of fol.110r copied them from an exemplar. This situation differs notably from other portions of **V**, where its variants (against the shared testimony of **BA**) appear as corrections made by a contemporary scribe applied directly to the page. A lengthy stretch of such 'variants as

---

[43] The following reading, which I do not list above, involves a correction (unreported by editors as a correction) made to the page of **V**: 243,28 distinguuntur] *V¹* [main scribe of this portion of *V*, not *V²*]   distinguitur *VBA*.

[44] There seem to be dots signaling a transposition.

corrections to the page' occurs on fols. 63r–68r (*Contr.* 2.3.4– 2.4.9). Results from an analysis of this portion of text are given below. What emerges from comparison of the two passages is that **V**'s variant readings appear in different places: sometimes they have been added to the page of **V**, sometimes they simply appear for us in the text of **V** without scribal alteration. At *Contr.* 9.2.4, where we know that **V** is copying the verse lengths of its exemplar, corrections have already been assimilated into the text. The process of correcting this portion of text was completed prior to its being copied into **V**. Here **V** is a fair copy. Therefore, the variants in the shorter list above (*Contr.* 9.2.2–9.2.7) may have been transmitted, unchanged, in the text of an exemplar, or a contemporary collaborating scribe (**V²**) may have added them to the exemplar. In either case, the main scribe responsible for copying fol.110r found the readings in his exemplar. This exemplar was different from that of the later Brussels and Antwerp manuscripts, otherwise **BA** would also contain some of these readings.

The steps, then, in our thinking about *Contr.* 9.2.2–9.2.7, which takes advantage of the simultaneous availability of two different kinds of evidence—significant lectional variants and patterns of verse length[45]— can be outlined as follows: 1) Verse-length patterns reveal that **V**, for this section of text, copies an exemplar that lies behind **BA**. 2) Lectional variants, taken together with patterns of copying and correction, reveal that the manuscript that **V** is copying here and that lies behind **BA** is different from the exemplar of **BA**. It is older than the exemplar of **BA**.

The section of text at *Contr.* 2.3.4–2.4.9 (**V** fols. 63r–68r), an analysis of which appears below, poses a revealing contrast with *Contr.* 9.2.2–9.2.7. As pieces of evidence the two sections of text are complementary, each exposing to view a different facet of the copying process that produced **V**. In the list given below, note in particular: a consistent qualitative distinction between the readings of **V²** and the group **VBA**. The scribe **V²** alone in this section of text is responsible for those significant variant readings whose speciousness or authenticity has puzzled

---

[45] Because **BA** do not attempt to copy the verse lengths of their exemplar, this double analysis cannot be performed in Seneca's text wherever we choose.

editors. Throughout the Corbeiensis, variants, whether copied by the original scribe or added by a corrector, often enter a critical gray area where it is impossible to differentiate between what has been conjectured and what most plausibly was transmitted and found. The variants listed below fall in this gray area. And, as can be seen, there are many of them.[46] But it is not just the fact that **V²** gets it right (or seems to) that is notable. Also significant is the fact that **VBA** are so precisely close in getting it wrong. As a group **BA** and the main scribe of **V** show exact agreement in idiosyncratic textual corruptions, including agreement in arbitrary, faulty letter-groupings.

An asterisk (*) is set next to those readings whose quality is such that the idea that they would or could be conjectured by a medieval reader strains credibility. Omitted from the list below are lections by **V²** that seem clearly to be inauthentic corrections or inventions. Comments have been set in brackets [ ] where **BA** and the main hand of **V** witness precisely the same idiosyncratic corrupt readings: the same misunderstandings of scribal abbreviations, the same faulty letter-groupings, and the same textual corruptions originating in well-known kinds of copying errors (e.g. dittography).[47] These identical copying patterns of **VBA** contribute to the evidence suggesting that the main scribe of **V** here is copying an exemplar different from that copied into **V** elsewhere (e.g. *Contr.* 9.2.2–9.2.7, and see Section II.3). The valuable testimony of the excerpted tradition (**E**), when available, has been included. Finally, I note where readings have been imprecisely or erroneously reported by editors.[48]

---

[46] It is remarkable just how indebted our modern editions of the elder Seneca are to the readings in **V**, a debt easily overlooked (in my experience) in a negative textual apparatus such as that of Håkanson.

[47] These errors, I believe, were in the exemplar of **BA** and in the exemplar of **V** for this section. The closeness of **V** and **BA** in these errors means that their exemplars are very similar. 'Very similar' of course need not mean 'identical,' but precise similarities do suggest that **V** is here using the same exemplar as **BA**: (y).

[48] Were it not for these errors and imprecisions, it would be easier to discern simply from an apparatus criticus the sharp divide I am pointing out between **VBA** and **V²**: **VBA** are a closely related group, they are in effect—and I suspect were in material fact—direct witnesses to the same hyparchetype. By contrast, **V²** alone here witnesses readings from a second MS, a MS older than the hyparchetype witnessed by **VBA**.

Significant Variants in **V**, fols.63r–68r (*Contr.* 2.3.4–2.4.9)

A is absent until Contr. *2.3.9 (H 90,20)*: *88,24 facile
puellam] *V²* facilem puellam **VB** ‖ *89,11
propinquis] *V²E* propriasquis **VB** ‖ 89,18
consenuit] *V²* ē senuit (est senuit *V*)**VB** [est senuit
is a misreading of c̄senuit] ‖ 89,19 uult temere]
V² uultemere **VB** [*haplography*] ‖ 89,27 tu scis]
Bursian autem scis *V* hiscis *B* [hi *is a misreading
of the insular abbreviation* autem[49] ‖ 90,6 propius]
V² proprius **VB** ‖ 90,7 pars] *V²* par **VB** ‖ 90,18
qua mihi] *V²* quam mihi **VB** [*dittography*] ‖
   A rejoins (Contr. *2.3.9, H 90,20*): 91,8 agere] *V²* egere
VBA ‖ 91,10 possit] *V²* posset **VBA** ‖ 91,13
ratione] *V²* [*misreported*] rationem **VBA** ‖ 91,14
causas] *Bursian* causam *V²* causa **VBA** ‖ *91,17–18
paternos adfectus] *V²* pater non adfectos
VBA ‖ 91,25 res iudicatas] *V²* resi iudicatas **VBA**
[*dittography stemming from a break in the verse: after* resi *there
is a verse-end in* V]*[50] ‖ 92,1 sicut] *V²* situt **VBA** *92,3
accusari] *V²* accusante **VBA** ‖ 92,8 uideri tamquam]
V² uiderit tamquam **VBA** [*dittography*] ‖ 92,9–10 illum
re scholasticum deprendi] *V²* illū rescolasti cumdeprendi
VBA [*shared false word-divisions*] ‖ *92,11 ualentis-
sima] *V²* alentissima **VBA** ‖ 92,18–19 exorauisti sed]
excrasti sed *V²* excratistis & *VA* [*A misreported*] exora-
tistis & *B* [*VBA share idiosyncratic error*] ‖ 93,1 exorari]
VBA exorare *V²* [*misreported by Håkanson*] ‖ 93,5
habeat] *del. Håkanson V²A²* (*A²* = *Andreas Schott*) [*A²
unreported by Håkanson*] habeat **VBA** ‖ 93,5 uiam]
V² uiuam **VBA** ‖ 93,6 patrem] *V²A²* (*A²* = *Schott*)
[*A² unreported*] patre **VBA** ‖ *93,13 quam miles]
V² quam ille **VBA** [*haplography of* m] ‖ *93,14

---

[49] See Havet 1967:183 (§778), and especially Lindsay 1915:13–25. The passage needs
re-examining.
[50] The verse lengths are ultimately those of α. Dittography originated in (y).

morieris] *V²*   moreris *VBA*   ‖   *93,17 exigere legem
ab eo ut] *V²*   exiere legem habeo *VBA* [*idiosyncratic error,
shared letter-groupings*]   ‖   *93,17 habet] *V²*   habeo
VBA   ‖   93,18 esse tam] esse an *V²*   esset an *VBA*
[*shared false word division*]   ‖   *93,18 furiosum] *V²*   furi-
orem *VBA* [s/r *confusion*]   ‖   *94,4 reum] *V²E*   rerum
VBA   ‖   94,8 haberet] *V²* haberes *VBA*   ‖   *94,16
tum hercules fateberis] tum aercule f. *V²*   tum aergules
f. *VBA* [*V²* *corrects, but his correction does not produce a
Latin word.*]⁵¹   ‖   *95,8 ex] *V²* *om.* *VBA*   ‖   *95,18
tardius meum exorari] *Gertz* quod tarde exorari *V²*   trade
sum exori *VBA*   ‖   *95,20 hoc curemus] *V²*   occur-
remus *VBA* [*false word-grouping*]   ‖   *95,22–23 etiam<si>
exoratus est (*Håkanson, ad loc., thinks* est *should perhaps
be omitted*)] &iam exoratus *V²*   &iam exoratus est
VBA   ‖   95,24 mutari semel] mutarei semel *V²A²* [*A²* =
Schott]   mutareis semel *VBA* [*dittography*]   ‖   *95,26
legis] *V²*   tegis *VBA*   [L *confused with* T]   ‖   96,1
argueret dum] *Haase* arguendum *VBA*   arguendum
putaret *V²*   ‖   96,1 uult uideri] *V²*   uultu uideri
VBA [*dittography*]   ‖   *96,6 raptae] *V²*   raste (rastę
V) *VBA*   [PT *confused with* ST]⁵²   ‖   *96,12 Lepidus]
V² lepibus *VBA*   ‖   *96,17–18 ex illa sustulit] *V²* ex
ea sustulit *E*   exillas tulit *VB*   &illas tulit *A*   [*VBA
share false letter-grouping*]   ‖   97,6 uenias] *V²*   ueniat
VBA   ‖   97,7 permitteret amens cucurri] permitteret
tamen scucurri *V²*   permittere tamen scucurri *VBA¹* (*A¹*
= *correction by main scribe*) [*identical false word-groupings;
misreported*]   permittere tamen succurri *A*   ‖   97,8
steterim] si steterim *V²*   iste terim *VBA* [*A* *misreported;*⁵³
false word-groupings]   ‖   97,8–9 hoc unum [huius unum]]
A²(= Schott) [*misreported*]   hoc unum huius unum

<hr/>

⁵¹ Perhaps read: *tum mehercule fateberis.*
⁵² Cf. 99,4 mimicae nuptiae] *Madvig* mimice nustis (nustus *V*) *VBA*   mimice nostis *V²*.
⁵³ In **A** a mark by A. Schott has obscured the first *i*: Schott has either deleted the first
i or set an *s* next to it. The original reading (*iste terim*) is the same as that of **VB**.

A hoc unum h' unum [= hoc unum hoc unum] *VB* [*misreported by Håkanson*][54] || *97,15 agnoscerem meos] *V²E* agnosceres meos *VBA* [*haplography*] || *97,19 insanum] infanem *V²* infanum *VB* nifanum *A* [*BA misreported*][55] || *97,21 uidi] *V²* uidit *VBA* || *97,24 domum] *V²* demum *VBA* || 98,1 durus] *V²* dusus *VBA* || 98,4 adulescentis spiritus] *V²* adulescenti spiritus *VBA* [*haplography*] || *98,4 aduentum] *V²E* aduertum *VBA* || *98,9 uixisset] *V²* dixisset *VBA* || *98,11 securior eram quoniam] *V²* securiorem quam *VBA* || *98,18–19 Catone moderatio] *V²* catone deratio *V* catonem deratio *BA*[56] || *98,24 quis] *V²* quid *VBA* || 99,1 adsueui coheredem] adsuaeuico heredem (asuaeuico haeredem *V*) *VBA* [*identical false wordgroupings*] || *99,11 puerum][57] *V²* epuernam (epuernā *BA*) *VBA* || *99,15 iudicum recuso] *V²* recuso iudicem *V* iudicem recuso *BA* || *99,26 unum] *V²* uni *VBA* || 100,13 declamauit] *V²* declamant *VBA* || 100,15 quidam] *V²* quodam *VBA*[58]

[54] The repetition (*hoc unum hoc unum*) should be admitted into the text. The same abbreviation (*h'* = *hoc*; Lindsay 1915:97–102) appears frequently in **B**, for example, at fol.95r (*Suas.* 5.7), where the reading, hitherto misreported, is *prius hoc atos*. Other select instances in **B**: fol.121r (H 80,21), twice on fol.121v (H 82,7 and 82,24), 122r (H 84,11), 123v (H 89,1), 125r (H 95,12). Håkanson 1989 seems unaware of the meaning of the abbreviation.

[55] The reading *insanum* has no manuscript support. Should we assume a confusion of *s/f*?

[56] I suspect an abbreviation (*modo*) has been misunderstood, or partially lost, in the exemplar(s) copied by **VBA**; Lindsay 1915:129–131.

[57] Kiessling 1872 conjectured *uernam*, which may be preferable: was *EP* written in anticipation of *ER* (*epuernam*)? In that case, the reading of **V²** would be an inauthentic correction.

[58] At H 100,17–19 **A** omits text (*efficiendum ... circumferebat*) found in **BV**. The reason for the omission can be seen in **V**, which preserves the verse lengths of its exemplar: *aiebat* is the penultimate word of a verse, and two verses down, immediately below *aiebat*, is *circumferebat*. The exemplar of **V** has the same verse lengths as the exemplar of **A** because, I believe, for the section of text just analyzed they are the same MS.

The above analysis of *Contr.* 2.3.4–2.4.9 exposes a pattern of lectional variation between **V²** and **VBA** similar to that noted between **V** and **BA** at *Contr.* 9.2.2–9.2.7. In both sections the Corbeiensis (**V** or **V²**) contains significant variants against the shared readings of **BA**. However, there is an important difference. In 9.2.2–9.2.7, the variants are woven into the fabric of the text (**V**), whereas in the longer section immediately above the variants are in the corrections (**V²**).[59] *The mixed quality of the variants is the same in both*: some are clearly fabrications, while others possess at least the appearance of transmitted authenticity.

Two different textual qualities make up **V**. We register the two textual qualities not solely in the split between **V/V²** and **BA** in lectional variants: two textual qualities are detected also in verse-length patterns, letter-groupings, and types of corruption. Taking this diversity of evidence together, we are approaching two conclusions: 1) A complex copying process produced the Corbeiensis. The Corbie scribes had two exemplars—a possibility suspected already by H. J. Müller (1887:xii–xiii).[60] 2) Of the two exemplars available to the Corbie scribes, one manuscript was older and the second more recent. These

---

[59] There is no want of evidence to show that the Corbie scribes have access to a second MS (i.e. a MS different from the exemplar copied by a main hand of **V**), and that one method for drawing on this second MS is through 'V² applying corrections to the page of **V**.' See, e.g., the apparatus criticus of Håkanson 1989:27–37 (**V**, fols.35r–40v). Selections from this section: 27,3 circumlatis] *V²*   circumlapis *VBA* [*misreading of majuscule* T/P]   ‖   28,19 coepi] *V²* [*wavy line in mg.*]   que pii *VBA*   ‖   29,2 superos inferosque] *V²* [*inferos in mg.*]   superosque *VBA*   ‖   29,32 an huius] *V²*   tanius *VBA*   ‖   30,4 uoluntate deorum] *V²* [*wavy line in mg.*]   uoluntates seruorum *VBA*   ‖   30,6 praeposui] *V²*   praepotui *VBA*   ‖   32,20 manus] *V²E om. VBA*   ‖   32,21 et has aliquis] *V²*   etasali quis (etasaliquis *A*) *VB*   ‖   33,17 licuerit] *V²* uouerit *VB*   uotierit *A*   ‖   34,24 fatebor] fateor *V²*   patebor *VBA*   ‖   34,28 pater] *V²* [*in mg.*]   om. *VBA*   ‖   35,29 exeuntes] *V²*   exeuntibus *VBA*   ‖   36,16 fortior] *V²E*   portior *VBA* [*misreading of majuscule* F/P]   ‖   37,9 retro amnes fluant et] *V²*   regno amnes fruaret *VBA*. The quire containing this section of text is begun (fol.33r) by a hand with script characteristics similar to the **V²** appearing on fols.63r–68r (*Contr.* 2.3.4–2.4.9) and elsewhere. And, as noted, some corrections coincide with a wavy line in the margin (33r, 34v, 36r, 36v), meaning in effect, I take it: 'check the other MS.' The wavy line appears to be a Tironian Note; see Chatelain 1964:27 and Kopp 1965:312. The meaning of the sign is made explicit on fol.7r, where it is accompanied by the abbreviation *R̄q̄* (= *require*).

[60] Håkanson 1989:xi, 60 ("*sequitur, ut hic illic librum manuscriptum adhibuerit* **V²**").

conclusions are somewhat anticipatory, since there is further corroborating evidence not yet discussed—some of which I shall now introduce, some of which appears in Sections II.3 and III.

As additional supports to the first conclusion—a complex copying process, involving two exemplars, produced the Corbeiensis—I draw attention to the following: a) a confusion of the order of quires in **V**, b) a correlation between the work of a certain scribe (**V²**) and the kind of variants offered by this scribe, and c) Corbie precedents for collating manuscripts.

a) There is a confusion of the order of quires in **V**.[61] The confusion confirms that the text was copied into quires before these were bound into a codex. Piecemeal copying would be well suited to the availability of two exemplars.[62] We can imagine that each of the two available models served in turn as the main exemplar for different portions of text copied into **V**. This process is suggested by the evidence of *Contr.* 2.3.4–2.4.9, where for eleven manuscript pages we observe a sharp, clean divide between **VBA** and **V²**.[63] Different scribes—and there are several scribal hands in **V**—could copy different parts of the text simultaneously: with different scribes, different responsibilities and exemplars. A delegation of responsibilities can be plausibly reconstructed, whereby it was the task of more expert readers to employ a second

---

[61] H. J. Müller 1887:xi n2.

[62] Clemens and Graham 2007:22. It may be relevant, with respect to the copying procedures followed and the scribes/readers involved, that at least one other MS, copied within the same period (850–900) and connected with the scriptorium at Corbie, has a confused order of quires: St. Petersburg, F.v.Lat. Class. 8, also containing works of classical rhetoric (*Rhet. Her.*, Cic. *Inv. rhet.*). For the confused quires, see Marx 1894:15–16; Hafner 1989:50–51; Taylor 1993:198. For the date and a description of the St. Petersburg MS, see Bishop 1972:13. For distribution of copying assignments involving several scribes: Rand and Howe 1915–1916:24; Ganz 1987:35–36.

[63] Ideally we could identify throughout **V** where now one MS was the main exemplar, now the other. Unfortunately, this is impossible: we should have to know for certain the origin of **V**'s significant variants (ninth-century conjecture? transmitted?) from moment to moment. And, I believe, the copying process was not so uniform as we should like (see n71 on the use of the Leiden corpus at Corbie). Corrections/authentic variants were inserted in multiple places (**α**, **V**, and the younger exemplar of **V**) and correcting hands visible to us in **V** may at times represent corrections performed *secundis curis*, i.e. after corrections/additions have already been made to one of the two exemplars.

available manuscript—a manuscript that was older, perhaps damaged, and at any rate more difficult to read because of its continuous script and script-type.

b) Nearly all the corrections made in the list above (*Contr.* 2.3.4–2.4.9) are by the same contemporary scribe (**V²**). In this portion of text, in other words, the significant difference in the readings found in **V** versus the text of **BA** almost perfectly correlates with the work of a particular corrector. He corrects the text, both by conjecture and by comparing readings found in another manuscript. Corrections are sometimes accompanied by a short, wavy horizontal line in the margin (~ or :~) (Figure 2),[64] whereby **V²** signals that he should check another manuscript.[65] If **V²** worked directly with the team of scribes who copied **V**, it is clear that he was given some greater authority in the project. In addition to applying corrections to the text, such as those seen in the list above, he corrects the confused order of quires, with directions at the bottom of fols.72v and 96v, and he gives textual corrections in the margins (8r, 9r, 36r, 81r).[66] And, it seems to me,[67] the same hand may have copied the last page of a quire (16v) and the first page of a quire (33r).

---

[64] The line can be seen also in the plate (166.1) of **V** in Chatelain 1884–1900. The same wavy line appears in the margins of other classical MSS copied or used at Corbie: Paris, B.N. lat. 7714 (*Rhet. Her.*) (fols.13r, 16v, 36r); Leiden, Voss. Lat. F. 84 (Cicero) (fols.92r, 107v, 111v; see Plasberg 1915); Flor., Laur. S. Marco 257 (Cicero) (fols.68v, 73v, 77r, 77v, 84v).

[65] The sign, I believe, is a Tironian Note: see n59. The appearance of the wavy line is not always accompanied by a correction and was perhaps used also to signal passages of interest.

[66] On fol.8r (*Suas.* 2.14) the reading *honores* is witnessed by **V²** alone. On fol.9r (*Suas.* 2.20), where Vergil is quoted (*Aen.* 11.288), **V²** gives a correction in the margin (*apud durae*) for an unorthodox but authentic reading (*ad aduersae*). For the correction by **V²** at the bottom of fol.81r see Håkanson:187,19–20. Also, a heading on fol.35r (*Latronis*) was filled in by **V²**.

[67] It is less certain whether **V²** is identical to a main hand of these early folios: complicating the matter is the fact that marginal and interlinear corrections require less formality than copying the main text. But it is significant that we get a different kind of main scribal hand in the early folios (1–27r) and at the beginning of a quire (33r), where we know leading scribes often worked, and that this scribal hand shares characteristics with **V²** (see below).

Who was this reader and scribe? Intriguing possibilities arise from comments by T. A. M. Bishop concerning a certain master scribe who, in a group of Corbie manuscripts copied in the middle to third quarter of the ninth century, performed "the unmistakable role of the scribe who gives a lead"—that is, who copied the beginning of a quire or quires.[68] Is the scribe identified by Bishop our V^2?[69] In the work of V^2 we can trace how a ninth-century reader's understanding of a text shaped the transmission of Seneca's anthology: has he played a role in shaping the traditions of other classical texts?

c) Even if the hand of V^2 does not appear in the extant manuscripts of other classical works, similar processes and interventions appear operative in traditions involving other Corbie manuscripts, e.g.: Livy's third decade,[70] the so-called Leiden corpus containing philosophical and rhetorical works of Cicero,[71] Cicero's *De inuentione* and the *Rhetorica*

---

[68] Bishop 1972:11; Ganz 1990:57–58. The MSS are St. Petersburg, F.v. Class 1 (Columella); Laon 330 (Basilius, *Regula*; Orosius, *Commonitorium*); and several MSS at Paris, B.N.: 7886 (Germanicus, *Aratea*), 8051 (Statius), 12125 (Origen, *De principiis*), 12272 (Bede, *In Samuelem*), 13020 (Boethius, *De musica*, Ps. Boethius, *Geometria*), 13956 (Ps. Apuleius, Boethius, *Peri Hermeneias*).

[69] At the present time I can neither confirm nor refute this possibility. The question requires thorough study of the MSS listed by Bishop. Bischoff 1994:120–132 discusses prominent personalities of the ninth century (e.g. Walahfrid Strabo, Lupus of Ferrières, and Heiric of Auxerre) and our ability to identify their individual scripts in MSS of classical texts.

[70] Flor., Laur. 63.20 (**M**) was copied at Corbie, a manuscript whose script characteristics link it closely with Flor., Laur. S. Marco 257 (see following note), and Paris, B.N. 454 (Cic. *Sen.*). On the Corbie Livy, which was copied from both the Puteanus (Paris, B.N. 5730, **P**) and the famous Carolingian Tours *descriptus* (Vat. Reg. lat. 762, **R**) of the Puteanus, see Walters and Conway 1967:xiv–xviii; Bischoff 1961:47, 52; Dorey 1971:ix; Reeve 1987:135. An important and, so far as I know, unexplored question: to what extent can Corbie hands be seen at work correcting the Puteanus and/or the Vatican Livy?

[71] For the complex copying process, involving two exemplars (Leiden, Voss. Lat. F. 84 and 86) with corrections by ninth-century Corbie hands appearing in both exemplars, that produced Flor., Laur. S. Marco 257 (**F**) and, from **F**, the classical florilegium (Vat. Reg. lat. 1762) of the Corbie librarian Hadoard, see Schmidt 1974:121–152; Rouse 1983:125; Ganz 1990:61–62 (there is some confusion of the two Leiden MSS) ; Bischoff 1998–2004:2.54–55; Reinhardt 2003:79–80; Powell 2006:xxxii–l. See also Clark 1918:324–363. For dissenting opinions: Pascucci 1973; Zelzer and Zelzer 2001.

ad Herennium,[72] and Germanicus' *Aratea.*[73] The complexities of copying that we are detecting in the ninth-century transmission of the elder Seneca's work are too suspiciously reminiscent of the copying complexities described by P. L. Schmidt, which involve Hadoard's classical florilegium (Vat. Reg. Lat. 1762) and other manuscripts of the Leiden corpus, and too suspiciously similar to what seems to be happening in Corbie's participation in the transmission of the *Rhetorica ad Herennium,* to be dismissed as chance. What is needed is broader investigation, with close attention to scribal hands, into the role of Corbie in the transmission of classical Latin texts and other non-classical texts. Such an investigation would look not only at Corbie manuscripts, but also at manuscripts copied elsewhere that could reveal interlinear and marginal Corbie interventions. The present article is meant to initiate such a project.

As to the second conclusion—of the two exemplars available to the Corbie scribes, one manuscript was older, the second more recent—I offer an overview of the kinds of evidence under examination (some already presented, some appearing below) and how this evidence is being interpreted. Within **V** can be discerned two major, discrete stages in the transmission of the elder Seneca's work. I have spoken of two different "textual qualities" constituting **V**. "Textual quality" refers not only to lections, but also to verse-length patterns, letter-groupings, punctuation, types of lectional corruption, and script-types.[74]

---

[72] Paris, B.N. lat. 7714 (**P**)(*Rhet. Her.*) was copied at Corbie. There is disagreement about whether St. Petersburg, F.v.Lat. Class. 8 (**C**)(*Rhet. Her.,* Cic. *Inv. rhet.*) was in fact copied at Corbie: see Taylor 1993:197–201; Bischoff 1998–2004:2.77. However, **C** came into the possession of Corbie, and Corbie hands seem responsible for some corrections and notes. According to Taylor (1993:211, 212, 217), **C** combines two traditions of *Rhet. Her.,* the **M**- and **I**-recensions, and she (200) speculates that **C** was collated against **P**. Given the fact that the **C** scribes collated MSS, the fact that Corbie hands likely appear in **C**, and the fact that a correcting hand in Corbie-produced **P** (**P²**) is collating manuscripts, the all-important, lingering question is: what, if any, is the relationship between **P²** and the hands of **C**? This mingling of textual streams can be detected even in the (now outdated) apparatus criticus of Marx 1894, where so often is seen the cluster **P²CE**.

[73] Bischoff 1961:53 identified Paris, B.N. 7886 as a Corbie product. Gain 1976:8 remarks that Paris 7886 "contains many conjectures."

[74] For an examination of the different script-types that lie behind **V** and **BA**, see Section III.

Generally speaking, differences between manuscripts with respect to these several elements of textual quality correlate with different chronological stages of textual transmission. These elements are properties of organic historical evolution and reflect the text in movement.

As regards our Seneca manuscripts **VBA**, the elements of textual quality in **V** sometimes reflect precisely the same stage of transmission witnessed by **BA**, sometimes an older stage of transmission. Where, as at *Contr.* 2.3.4–2.4.9, **V** joins **BA** to form a closely related group, **VBA** witness the same stage of transmission. **V** is so close to **BA** that—though it cannot be proven definitively—we should suspect that Corbie has access to the same hyparchetype (**y**).[75] In other sections of **V**, when we examine the several elements of textual quality together, we see that the Corbie scribes have access to a manuscript that is at an earlier stage of transmission and that lies behind (**y**): the Corbie scribes have access to α.[76] A split in textual qualities where **BA** represent the younger stage, i.e. (**y**), and **V** the older stage (α) of the tradition is the focus of Section II.3.

II.3 **BA** Share a Hyparchetype;
The Scribes of **V** Had Access to α

We now consider additional passages where **V**'s exemplar is seen to be α. Sample passages are adduced from the *Suasoriae*, which occur before

---

[75] For the near impossibility of proving definitively that one MS derives from another, see Reeve 1989:1; Reynolds 1965:55; Pasquali 1962:30–40. The fact that Corbie is involved may be further suggestive of the identity of **V**'s younger exemplar with (**y**). As is well known, it is rare for a MS to survive with its exemplar. Is it purely accidental that in two notable cases of such survivals—the third Decade of Livy, the Leiden corpus of Cicero—Corbie is involved? Could frequent sharing of MSS, such as seems to have happened with Corbie, and the employment of multiple exemplars when copying texts instill in Corbie readers and scribes the importance of careful preservation of more than one copy of the same text? Further, we know that (**y**) circulated: it was used by the two different scriptoria that produced **B** and **A**—and it is (**y**) that is used by **A**, even though the latter was copied roughly a half-century later than **B**. All three scriptoria responsible for **VBA** were geographically close (NE France).

[76] The possibility cannot be totally ruled out that the scribes of **V** used not α, but a second apograph of α ((**x**)), to which **BA** did not have access. At any rate, the traditional features discovered in **V** (verse lengths, textual shape and punctuation, superior variants) would still derive from α. And we should have to imagine that both (**x**) and **V** stuck very close to their respective exemplars in preserving the verse lengths of α.

the *Controuersiae* in our manuscripts. It is noteworthy that in these early folios of **V** (fols.1–27r, 33r; *Suas.* 1–*Contr.* 1.1.15, 1.2.13–15), where α seems to be the main exemplar, a different, older kind of scribal hand is at work than the hands that follow (Figure 2).[77] The early script is squat, laterally taut, and broader—characteristics that are shared with the corrector **V²** and that pertain to an older variety of Corbie minuscule. The two different kinds of exemplars that make up **V** correlate to a significant degree with different kinds of scripts, with the different copying roles and abilities of ninth-century scribes. The script appearing on subsequent folios is typically taller, upright, and with gentler, rounded angles.

The sample passages that follow are meant to demonstrate, first, that **BA** are copies of the same hyparchetype, and, secondly, that the scribes of **V** see what the scribes of **BA** cannot. The **V** scribes can look behind **BA**, seeing a manuscript that contains older features of the tradition. They see a Seneca text with an older texture—not just lections, but the textual organization and shape into which these lections are woven.

---

[77] It is very interesting that this phenomenon is paralleled in another Corbie MS, Leiden, Universiteitsbibliotheek, B.P.L. 52, containing Servius' commentary on Vergil: see Lieftinck 1960, who offers a complete facsimile. The Leiden codex is a composite: most of the quires were copied in the early ninth century, but the second and twelfth quires were copied circa mid-ninth century. In the second quire (copied mid-ninth century), there are two kinds of script. A more rugged, broader, angular, and older-looking script (very similar to **V**, fols.1–27r, 33r) begins the quire and is succeeded by a script of smoother, rounded, more recent appearance (similar to other folios of **V**). The contrast of script in the Leiden MS can be seen by comparing fols.12v and 13r. Lieftinck (xvi), who evinces surprise at the contrast ("le style d'écriture va changer brusquement"), entertains, and then rejects, the possibility that the early scribe of the second quire might be imitating the older script of the first quire. The difference of scripts should be seen as a difference in the ages of the scribes. Bischoff 1998–2004:2.40, in a description of the Leiden codex, calls the script in the second and twelfth quires (i.e. the mid-ninth century script) a "Vorstufe" ("preliminary stage") to the kind of script written in the period of Hadoard (middle to third quarter of the ninth century). Although Bischoff (1961:51) recognized varieties of script—namely, "severe" and "softer" styles—written at Corbie in the time of Hadoard, he does not seem to have taken full account of this broader, more rugged and older-looking script appearing alongside a more familiar, rounded Corbie script. An instinct to assign MSS containing the rugged script to the first half of the ninth century could explain why Bischoff, in his correspondence with Vervliet (cited above, n5), initially believed **V** was copied before 850: Bischoff refers to the plate of **V** in Chatelain 1884–1900 (166.1), which shows an early folio (23v) containing the rugged variety of script.

We have already observed that sometimes **VBA** share letter-arrangements, particularly when **V** is using a younger exemplar very similar, likely identical, to **(y)**. It often happens, however, that **BA** share peculiar letter-arrangements not seen in **V**. Sometimes the peculiar arrangements in **BA** are "harmlessly" incorrect: all letters are preserved in the correct sequence, even if spacing is faulty. At other times, these shared arrangements are involved in textual corruptions: repetitions (dittography), omissions (haplography), and scrambling of letters. At *Suas.* 2.17[78] there is an apparently minor, "harmless" misgrouping of letters in **BA**.

Vat. lat. 3872, fol.8v

> <u>morbo</u>huiusrei &tener&ur&rideretur · Nam&seruos |
> nolebathaberenisigrandes · &<u>argenteauasa</u>nonnisigrandia˙ |
> Credatismihiuelimnoniocanti · eoperuenitinsaniaeius·<u>utcal</u> |
> ceos

Brussels 9594, fol.92r

> <u>Morbo</u>huius regi &teneretur & rideretur   Nam-
>   &seruos   nolebat habere   nisigrandes |
> & <u>argente auasa</u> nonnisigrandiagredatismihiuelim   nonio-
>   ganti   eoperuenit   insaniaeius<u>utcal</u> |
> ceos

Antwerp 411, fol.9v

> re adeo ut nouissime <u>morbo</u> huius rei &teneret² &rideret² |
> nā   &seruos nolebat habere nisi grandes   &<u>argente</u> |
> <u>auasa</u> ñ nisi grandia   gredatis mihi uelī   ñ ioganti eo |
> peruenit   insania e'i <u>ut ca ceos</u> quoq; maiores sumer &ficus |

[78] Håkanson 1989: *morbo huius rei et teneretur et rideretur. nam et seruos nolebat habere nisi grandes et argentea uasa non nisi grandia. credatis mihi uelim non iocanti: eo peruenit insania eius, ut calceos quoque maiores sumeret, ficus ...*, "He was both captivated and made ridiculous by his obsession for this [i.e. largeness]. For, he was only willing to have slaves that were large and only silver vessels that were large. Believe me, I'm not joking. His obsession even reached a point where he wore oversize shoes, figs ..."

For the adjective-noun pair *argentea uasa* ("silver vessels") **BA** agree in the nonsensical grouping *argente auasa*. At the same time, the passage is important in that it again shows how **V** maintains a master pattern, a kind of "blueprint," of textual arrangement that chronologically precedes and has shaped the texts of **BA**: the precise text that **V** sets in three verses (*morbo huius … ut cal-*) is contained in two verses of **B**. This arrangement, which splits *cal - ceos* between the end of one line and the beginning of the next, caused the Antwerp scribe to write *ca ceos*, omitting the *l* and adding extra space mid-word because he did not know whether *ca ceos* was one word or two. **V** closely reproduces the textual arrangement of **α**. The misgrouping *argente auasa*, seen in **BA**, witnesses how the textual arrangement of **α** has been altered by an intermediate manuscript (**y**).[79]

A similar example appears at *Suas.* 3.1.[80] Here, however, the letter-groupings in **BA** are tending toward corruption.

Vat. lat. 3872, fol.10r

Aliaserena |

clauduntur . &omnisdiescaelumnubilograuasubsidissolum |
&creditumsibiterranonr&in&

Brussels 9594, fol.93r

serena claudunt   ur&omnisdies caelumnubilo   graua subsidis
    solum &creditum sibiter ra |

---

[79] There are indications found in **B** of the length of verses in (**y**). At *Contr.* 7.8.6, **B** (fols.144v–145r) momentarily ceases to copy out text in its customary long lines, instead producing seven lines in a narrower text-block. Something similar also appears in **B**, fol.116v. If this interpretation of the anomalous short verses in **B** is correct, it is telling that these verses are *close* to the length of **V**'s verses but are slightly different: (**y**) had verse lengths similar but not identical to those of **α**.

[80] Håkanson 1989: *alias serena clauduntur, et omnis dies caelum nubilo grauat; subsidit solum, et creditum sibi terra non retinet*, "At another time, clear skies are pent up, and every day weighs down the sky with cloud; the ground sinks, and the earth does not retain what has been entrusted to it."

Antwerp 411, fols.10v–11r

> lexes alia serena claudunt ur&omnis [*a short line due to a hole in
> the parchment*] |
> dies celum nubilo graua subsidis solum &creditum sibi t'ra
> n̄r&in& alias incer |

Instead of *clauduntur et omnis*, **BA** produce the faulty *claudunt uretomnis*.
It is uncertain whether the scribe of **V** found the passage less corrupt
in α or if he adeptly corrected what was in α. The passage at any rate
is difficult to understand, not least because in several spots it remains
corrupt in **VBA**.[81] The punctuation in **V** is correct, despite the corruption. Another, if less harmful, instance of **BA**'s false letter-groupings
occurs above in the word *ter ra*.

A few sentences later in *Suas.* 3.1,[82] we find:

V, fol.10r

> Quicquid asperatū estu est .quicq̇d |
> nimio defluxit imbre . inuicem tēperatur altero · Siue |
> ita natura disposuit . siue ut ferunt luna cur sugerit · Que |

B, fol.93r

> quidquid asperatum   estus est quid |
> quid nimio   difluxit imbre   inuicem temper-
> atum   alteros iuit anatura disposuit siue |

A, fol.11r

> quid quid asperatū estus ē quid quid nimo difluxit |
> inbre inuicē tēperatū alterosiuit natura disposuit siue ut ferunt
> luna cur |
> sugerit q;

[81] See preceding footnote for an emended text.
[82] Håkanson 1989: *quidquid asperatum aestu est, quidquid nimio diffluxit imbre, inuicem
temperatur altero. siue ita natura disposuit, siue, ut ferunt, luna cursu gerit ...*, "Whatever is
made harsh from heat, whatever has dissolved from excessive rain, is offset in turn by
its opposite. Whether nature has disposed it thus or, as they say, the moon in its course
arranges it ..."

This passage too is remarkable for its difficulty. The text of **V** is in the "gray area" mentioned above, where there can be no certain differentiation between felicitous, plausible conjecture and transmitted, authentic reading. But could the scribes of **V** have corrected the passage from the confusion seen in **BA**? **V** again maintains a correct division between sense-units: *temperatur altero · Siue...* And, perhaps as a function of this successful retention of punctuation, **V** was able to preserve a lection (*ita*) corrupted by **BA**, or rather by their parent (**y**). The reading *ita* has all but disappeared from **BA**.

At *Suas.* 2.2, **V** (fol.5v) reads:[83] Sed&sicadendūest . erratis sim&uendācreditis mortem · By contrast, both **B** (fol.90v) and **A** (fol.5v) produce a muddle with very similar groupings of letters:

> **B**: sedet sicandi   dumest   terratis sime   tuendamcreditis |
> mortem

> **A**: sed &sic candi dū ē t' ratissime tuendam creditis mor | tē

The difference between **V** and **BA**, as regards the intelligibility of the text, is profound. On closer inspection, however, one sees that the reading of **BA** is indeed corrupt but not so very different from that of **V**. The corruptions consist of dittography (*est t*), anticipation (*candi*),[84] and the misgrouping of letters (*me tuendam*). These are copying errors. They are the sort of errors to which a scribe is especially susceptible when copying from a manuscript in continuous script, where it is more difficult to maintain one's place in the source text.

Håkanson (1989:x–xi) concedes that **V** sometimes possesses genuine readings against the corruptions of **BA**, readings either conjectured or possibly found in another manuscript outside the family of **α** and imported into **V**'s parent.[85] He provides a list of select

---

[83] Håkanson 1989: *sed et si cadendum est, erratis, si metuendam creditis mortem*, "But even if we must fall, you are mistaken if you think death ought to be feared."

[84] As I interpret it, *candi* represents a miscopying of *cadendum*, where *i* is a vertical stroke of the *u* in *du*. Next, the scribe writes *dum est*, repeating part of what he had already copied. For a similar error (anticipation + repetition), cf. Verg. *Ecl.* 10.56, where the Codex Palatinus (**P**) has *ullantetabunt* for *ulla uetabunt*; Havet 1967:175 (§711).

[85] Håkanson does not explicitly assert that genuine variants in **V** came from outside the family of **α**, but it follows from his other statements: he thought that **BA** descended directly from **α**. Hence, where **BA** agree in their corruption, except for the occasional

passages—similar to the passage from *Suas.* 2.2 immediately above—where in his opinion this is the case. However, Håkanson appears unaware that in the majority of these passages, and in very many others like them, **V** and **BA** do not offer two altogether dissimilar lections. The two sets of variants are related to each other mechanically, the difference between them the result of successful versus unsuccessful readings of script.[86] According to Håkanson, **V** is further removed from α than **BA**, which he thought were direct copies of α. But many passages in **BA** are corrupt because the passages were copied inexpertly by (y). **V** is sometimes more successful because its scribes could look directly at α, and they were better than the scribes of (y) at reading the continuous script of α and better at reading Latin. Such readerly skill is hardly surprising at Corbie, given the work there of such readers and writers as Hadoard, Ratramnus, and Paschasius Radbertus.[87]

Contr. 1.1.7 contains a telling passage from Håkanson's list of **V**'s genuine, superior variants. The passage is instructive since it witnesses two different outcomes from scribal attempts to copy the same

---

coincidental error this corruption must have been in α: any genuine readings found by the scribes of the Corbeiensis would have been taken from a MS that does not descend from α. Cf. Winterbottom 1991:338–339: "when...H[åkanson] has to admit the possibility that **V** contains readings from outside the tradition altogether, he is bowing to facts that have led others to see **V** as independent from, though even more corrupt than, the common parent of **A** and **B**. H[åkanson] does, however, seem to be right (xi) that **V**'s corrector, at least at *Contr.* 1.5.2, gives us something not found in the archetype of the manuscripts we possess and not easily won by conjecture."

[86] The following passages in Håkanson's list can be explained in this way. In some of these **E** is available and supports **V**: *Contr.* 1.1.4, naturam mutare] *V* natura militare *BA* [*by haplography an* m *is omitted and a misreading of* UT *produces* ILI]; 1.1.7 [*see below*]; 1.1.10, ii] *V* u *BA* [*confusion of vertical strokes*]; 1.1.23, (*mistakenly cited 1.1.22*) arbitrum odia] *VE* arbitriudi odia *BA* [-udi *is an anticipating miscopy of part of* odia]; 1.2.7, emit] *VE* enim *BA* [*confusion of vertical strokes*]; 1.5.5, raptori praestare] raptori prestare *V²* [*misreported by* Håkanson] *E* raptor ipse stare *BA* [*misgrouping of letters, and perhaps confusion of* s/r]; 9.4 argum., pulsauerit manus ei] *VE* plus haberit manus si *BA* [*transposition of* l/u, *mispronunciation of* u/b, *and dittography of* s]; *Suas.* 1.15, hesperii metas] *V* asperum metas *BA* [*misreading of* II/U *and repetition of* m]. In this last instance, Winterbottom 1974b:40n4 calls **V**'s reading a flagrant interpolation.

[87] See Ganz 1990:68–120.

sequence of letters in **α**. The passages in **BA** are corrupt because the passages were copied inexpertly by **(y)**.[88]

V, fol.25r: Non fefellit . &qualisessem sciuisti cūadoptares |

B, fol.102v: Nonfefellit& qualis esse miscuistieum adoptares·7

A, fol.20v: N̄ fefellit& qualis esse · miscuisti eū adoptares ·

As in the previous example, the crucial difference between the authentic lection offered by **V** and the corrupt lection offered by **BA** is rooted in the material conditions of copying texts. It is not the case that **V** offers something very different from **BA**, something that must have been imported from elsewhere. Nor would it have been easy for a scribe to conjecture the correct reading from the sort of corruption seen in **BA**. The errors of **BA**, while resulting in serious confusion, are copying/reading mistakes: a misgrouping of letters (*esse m*), which then leads to the misreading *miscuisti* for *sciuisti*,[89] and a misapprehension of letter-shape (*eum* instead of *cum*). In **V**, direct access to the source and better ability to read the source result in an essentially successful transmission of a genuine reading.[90]

To corroborate these statements, I draw attention to two passages where omissions by **BA** witness how the Corbie scribes can see into the

---

[88] Beginning with Bursian 1857, and followed by H. J. Müller, Winterbottom, and Håkanson, editors have altered the reading of **V** slightly: *Non fefelli te, qualis essem: sciuisti, cum adoptares*, "I did not deceive you about what I'm like: you knew it when you adopted me."

[89] Another example of a letter scramble in **BA** is *Contr.* 7.1.24 (Håkanson 179,12): color] *VE* locor *BA*.

[90] Other examples where textual corruptions in **BA** have their basis in misreading by **(y)** while the variants in **V** result from good copying/reading (lemmata are the readings of **V** and have been accepted by Håkanson 1989): 20,12 custodita] *VE* custodia *BA* ‖ 20,17 uiolauerit] *V* uia lauerit *BA* ‖ 21,7 inimiciis] *V* inmiticus *B* inimiticus *A* inimiticiis *A²* (= *Schott*) ‖ 39,2 impunitatis] *V* imputatis *BA* ‖ 56,28 ut pluribus] *V* ut (aut *B*) tribus *BA* [(y) omitted PLU and added T to form a word] ‖ 108,6 nisi] *V* nise *B* inse *A* ‖ 110,6 fuisse quaerendum] *V* tuis sequerendum *BA* [*misreading of majuscules* F/T] ‖ 110,16 peperissent] *V* reperiss& *BA* [*misreading of majuscules* P/R] ‖ 121,9 notata] *V* nofata *BA* [*misreading of majuscules* T/F] ‖ 332,2 iuga uictor] *V* pugali ictor *BA* [*misreading of majuscules* I/P, and of majuscules* U/ LI] ‖ 332,25 saeuiat] sẹuiat *V* sibi ad *BA*.

manuscript ancestry of **BA**. In these passages the readings of **V** are not conjectures by the scribes of **V**; they are transmitted readings found in α.[91]

In the *thema* for *Contr.* 7.7, **V** has the accepted reading (*ad crucifixum*) where **BA** (*fixum*) share a partial omission. Håkanson (1989:ix), remarking that the reading *ad crucifixum* could easily be divined from the context, believed the Corbie scribes conjectured it. But the Corbie scribe did not supply the reading: he read it in his exemplar, as inspection of textual layout in **VBA** reveals. All three manuscripts are close in verse lengths here, as they often are in the presentation of *themata*.[92] The reading *adcrucifixum* is split mid-word in **V** (fol.100r), so that *adcruci*—precisely the text omitted by **BA**—appears at the end of one verse and *fixum* begins the next verse. **B** (fol.142r), which also begins the following verse with *fixum* (*fixum* is at verse-end in **A**, fol.82r), would have had this exact arrangement, were it not for the omission.

---

[91] Relevant here is a passage cited by Winterbottom 1974b:21 and Håkanson 1989:ix as exemplary of the kind of interpolations occurring in **V** and absent from α. Their explanation, in my view, is not compelling. At *Contr.* 1.6.2, the words *nisi corpus oม̃a* (= *omnia*) *uinculis* (**VBA**) derive from text appearing about a verse later: *pan̲n̲i̲s̲ ̲c̲o̲r̲p̲u̲s̲ ̲o̲m̲̃a̲ membra u̲i̲n̲c̲u̲l̲i̲s̲*. The word *membra*, present in both **V** and **E**, was omitted by **BA**. There is no doubt about its authenticity. The fact that *membra* is absent from **BA** in both instances led Winterbottom to conclude that it was absent also from α (Håkanson is somehow confident that it was absent even from the parent of α). But with good evidence of a complex copying process employed by **V** that involved two MSS, we are not reduced to attributing **V**'s impressive variants to uncanny conjecture. Either of the following explanations I believe more plausible: 1) (**y**) omitted *membra*, 2) **BA** omitted *membra* independently. *membra* would be omitted for the same reason that the two words together (*omnia membra*) cause problems elsewhere for **BA**. When juxtaposed, especially if abbreviated as they were in (**y**) (*om̃a m̃bra*, with abbreviations, can be seen in **BA** at *Contr.* 2.3.15), they look alike, and omission is easy (Havet 1967:183–184 [§781, 782]). So, at *Contr.* 2.5.5 (Håkanson 105,13), **B** alone omits *membra* in the same phrase *omnia membra*. Absence of *membra* from the intrusion *nisi corpus omnia uinculis* (so **VBA**) does not mean that α omitted *membra* from *pannis corpus omnia membra uinculis*. The intrusion, besides being in the wrong place, is internally corrupt (*nisi* for *pannis*): in the corruption we cannot assume accurate transmission of readings elsewhere. It is telling that in the surrounding text, **V** again exhibits superior traditional variants against corruptions in **BA**: 41,4 patres timuerunt] *V*   patri inuerunt *BA*   ‖   41,6 introrsus] *V*   inrursus *BA*   ‖   41,6 obtritas] *V*   obrias *BA*   ‖   41,18 maioribus] *V²*   moribus *VBA*   ‖   41,19 clarius] *V*   carius *BA*.

[92] The *thema* of *Contr.* 1.2 in **VB** is laid out in a narrow column and the verse lengths are nearly identical.

The omission originated in (**y**), whose scribe was confused by two verse-endings in its exemplar (**α**) that were very similar: immediately above *adcruci* in **α** was written *crucifixum* at verse-end, where it occurs in both **V** and **A**. The juxtaposition of very similar text caused the scribe to omit *adcruci* at verse-end and proceed to the next verse beginning with *fixum*.[93]

At *Contr.* 1.2.19, **BA** omit text found in **VE**. Winterbottom and Håkanson print: *inter tot pericula non seruassent illam dii nisi sibi* ("among so many perils the gods would not have saved that girl except for themselves"). After *sibi*, **E** reads: *seruaturi fuissent* ("... unless they were going to save her for themselves").[94] After *sibi* in **V**: *seruata fuissent*, which was corrected, by a deletion dot, to *seruata fuisset* ("... unless it was for them she had been saved"). **VE** testify that *something* followed *sibi*, even if it is not precisely what is offered by either **V** or **E**.[95] The reading of **E** is better than that of **V**, but perhaps we should read: *nisi sibi seruitura fuisset* ("unless for their own service").

III. SENECA'S COLLECTION
IN LATE ANTIQUITY, AD 400–600

There is a palpable human presence, a readerly, culturally informed engagement with the text of Seneca in the pieces of evidence that we have been tracking. This engagement has been emphasized especially for that moment in the transmission history of the elder Seneca's work when it was at ninth-century Corbie: in the use of more than one exemplar and the comparison of the exemplars' readings, in the addition of corrections where sense is lacking, in the interest in preserving and

---

[93] In the theme of *Contr.* 7.6, discussed by Hagendahl 1936:312–313 and Winterbottom 1974b:21–22, **BA** omit text that the scribes of **V** read from **α**: *dominabus suis nubant.* Winterbottom's arguments for finding **V**'s reading corrupt may be correct, but they do not prove that the Corbie scribes did not *find* the reading in **α**, i.e. that the reading was not transmitted from late antiquity.

[94] The reading accepted by H. J. Müller 1887.

[95] Winterbottom 1974b:22 argues that since both **V** and **E** have different texts following *sibi*, both offer interpolations. But the texts are close. The reading of **V** seems to be corrupt, that of **E** a correction or deliberate alteration of something found in its model.

imitating a "classical look" to the page by copying in an approximately square textual block, and in the preservation of a system of points for punctuation.

But a stage of the text's history at least as crucial was earlier, as a comparison of **VBA** also shows. Consider in particular: 1) the fact that someone brought together the *Suasoriae* and *Controuersiae*—portions of Seneca's work that in antiquity had been composed and circulated separately—into one codex. 2) The good, rhetorical punctuation dividing the text into sense-units through a system of points and spacing shows that a reader cared for this severely damaged, lacunose work and invested energy in preserving it as best he could. 3) Further indication of the same effort, perhaps by the same reader, appears in the many critical signs found throughout the text. They are attested by all three principal manuscripts. *Paragraphoi* (paragraph signs) and *hederae* (punctuational ivy leaves)[96] are consistently set next to names of speakers, and they are applied to mark out the larger component parts of Seneca's collection: *themata, sententiae, diuisiones, colores.* Somebody—a late-antique reader, I suspect—had a good, valid understanding of this declamatory text. 4) Besides the punctuation and critical signs, this reader may have left further traces of his involvement in an admonition found within the colophon at the end of *Contr.* 1.[97] There, again in all three manuscripts, we read: Lege et Stude, "Read and Study."[98]

Was this preservation and critical organization of Seneca's work carried out in the production of α, or did it happen in an earlier manuscript? This question, touching on the chronology of manuscripts now lost, is undeniably difficult. But light in the darkness can still be found in the form of letter-reading errors appearing in **VBA**. Study of copying

---

[96] For *hederae*, see Wingo 1972:122–127; Parkes 1993: pl.6, line 2. For other examples of signs similar to those in Seneca's text: *CLA* 3.280 (fols.241r, 158v), 3.296 (Medicean Vergil, fol.8r), 6.774a (fol.142v), 6.830.

[97] On colophons, see the important work of Lucien Reynhout 2006. Dr. Reynhout graciously provided detailed responses to my questions about the colophon in the tradition of Seneca's text.

[98] The exact phrase Lege et Stude, Dr. Reynhout informs me, does not seem attested in the colophon of another MS. Other similar phrases appear, for example, in sixth-century (*Lege feliciter*) and fifteenth-century (*legens et studens*) MSS. Cf. the phrase *Feliciter legas* in the colophon of a sixth-century MS, Orléans, Bibl. Municip. 192 (169); *CLA* 6.806 (fol.4r).

confusions brought about by script-types has two positive results. First, it confirms, by means of a different kind of evidence (script-type), that **V** had access to an older part of the tradition not available to **BA**—a manuscript copied in a different script from the script of **(y)**. Second, the errors give information about when approximately **(y)** was copied and when approximately **α** was copied.

There is no question that **(y)** was written in a minuscule script. The Corbie scribes, as has been demonstrated, used a manuscript that was very much like **(y)** and that, like **(y)**, was copied in minuscule. But they could draw also on an exemplar written in majuscules—in uncial, I believe. Letter-reading errors, some of which have already been included in the course of the discussion,[99] point out this division between **V** (or **V²**) and **BA**. Now for a synthesis, with additional evidence. I am aware of the hazards that can attend attempts to deduce script-types based on copying errors.[100] Investigations of this type are complicated by the number of potential variables involved in producing any given error. Among the most important of these variables are the variety of scripts, since different scripts can produce similar errors, and a phonetic component of copying texts: pronunciation by scribes varies and influences what a scribe copies.[101] However, we have already seen ample evidence of a significant visual/material factor in how **VBA** copy their text. So, **BA** often agree in definitions of nonsensical letter-groups: the scribes are here reproducing not abstract speech patterns, but the *material shapes* of the language of their exemplar. I have exercised great caution in drawing conclusions about script-types from reading confusions. Despite difficulties, there are nonetheless conclusions to be drawn. Among the most compelling evidence that **(y)** was in minuscules are:

Confusion of *a* with *u*. There are many instances of this error, provided especially by **A**. We can conclude that the scribe of the hyparchetype **(y)** often wrote an open *a*. Examples: 57,5 iuuentuti iam] *VA*   iuuenitatuam *B*   ‖   73,2 abolita] *VB*   abolitu *A*   ‖   77,25

---

[99] Section II.2, in the analysis of *Contr.* 2.3.4–2.4.9.

[100] Timpanaro 2005:145–156.

[101] Gribomont and Mallet 1979 study confusions of letters resulting from scribal pronunciation; Ganz 1987:28–29, 37–38.

frugalissimus] *VB*   fragalissimus *A*   ‖   199,27 parcam] pargam
V   purgam *BA*   ‖   209,23 hunc] *V*   hanc *BA*   ‖   220,1 quam]
VB quum *A*   ‖   342,1 fugacissimi] *V*   fagacissimi *BA*   ‖   345,19
litteras] *V*   literas *B*   literus *A*   ‖   350,1 hanc] *VB*   nunc
A   ‖   351,11 Gallione] *VB*   gullione *A*.

Confusion of *s* with *f* or *t* or *r*. Except perhaps for the confusion
of *s* and *t*, these errors must be visual errors. The scribe of (**y**) wrote
a straight, minuscule *s*.   13,27 adfectu] *VB*   adsectu *A*   ‖   20,28
potuisti] *VB*   posuisti *A*   ‖   31,25 adulter effugit] *VB*   adul-
teres fugit *A*   ‖   38,11 seruatus] *VB*   fruatur *A*   ‖   68,4 soli]
sili *VB*   fili *A*   ‖   99,3 fecundam] *VB*   secundam *A*   ‖   105,1 si
de] *VB*   fide *A*   ‖   124,12 aduersus] *VA*   aduerrus *B*   ‖   187,28
Cestius] *VA*   certius *B* [*same error at* 208,17]   ‖   192,25 filium meum]
VB   silium in eum *A*   ‖   193,28 certe eruam] *V*   ceste erbam
BA   ‖   197,4 anticum rhetorem] *B*   (antiquum r.) *V*   anticums
hetorem *A*   ‖   209,27 pestiferam] *V*   rertiferam *BA*   ‖   273,8
absurdum] *VB*   adfurdum *A*   ‖   342,28 Fuscus] fuscus *VB*   suscus
A   ‖   368,26–7 si suum] *V*   fisum *A*   sisum *B*.

Confusion of *g* with *t* or *i*. In majuscule scripts *G* is arc-shaped and
easily distinguishable from characteristically vertical *t* or *i*. In most
minuscule scripts, the confusion is much easier. And the mistake
would be particularly easy in those minuscule scripts where the belly
of the *g* is small or absent, e.g. semi-uncial, insular, some pre-caroline scripts. However, these confusions cannot be due exclusively
to visual misreading, but scribal pronunciation too is a factor. 13,29
aiebat] *Bursian* aiebant *VB*   agebant *A* [*confusion of these two words
is very common*] [102]   ‖   19,13 maiestatisque] [103] *VB*   magestatisque
A   ‖   34,13 maius] *VA*   magis *B*   ‖   79,22 egregie] *VA*   egretiae
B   ‖   174,7 nauigio] *V A²* [= *Schott*]   nauitio *BA*   ‖   215,17 ageretur]
VA   aieretur *B*   ‖   237,23 maiorum] *VA*   magorum *B*   ‖   257,9
coniuges] *VB*   coniuies *A*   ‖   268,21 adiecit] *VA*   adgecit *B*

[102] Also found in **B**, Håkanson 39,28. The fact that the two words sound alike is
certainly a contributing factor. But the error is so common in **A** that I cannot believe
homophony alone is responsible.

[103] Substitution of *g* for *i* in the word *maiestas* occurs also in Würzburg, Universitäts-
bibliothek, M.p.misc.f.2, at *Rhet. Her.* 2.17.

Misreading of *cl* as *d*. These errors can only be explained as visual errors: 177,11 hoc loco] *VB*   hodoco *A* || 248,5 clementia] *VB*   dementia *A* || 274,2 declamavit] *VB* dedamavit *A* || 345,8 Lesbocles] *VB*   lesbodes *A* || 361,6 declamasse] *VB*   dedamasset *A*.

The above letter-confusions, particularly in those cases where the confusions are obviously visual misreadings, would not have occurred if **BA**'s exemplar had been written in majuscules. Apparent peculiarities of the minuscule script of **(y)**, such as an open *a* and a *g* perhaps lacking a lobe, suggest a manuscript in pre- or early caroline.[104] Based on these considerations, I tentatively estimate that **(y)** was copied in the early ninth century.

α, the older exemplar of **V**, was written in majuscules. Good evidence of this is the frequent shared confusion by **BA** of the letters *C/G*.[105] The confusion originated in **(y)** when its scribe or scribes were copying from **α**; the idea that **V** had direct access to **α** is suggested by its scribes' ability to offer these readings free of the errors in **(y)**. A selection: 70,19 negetur] *V*   necetur *BA* || 71,8 secatur] *V*   segatur *BA* || 104,4 garrulitate] *VE*   carrulitatem *BA* || 108,21 garrulitati quae] *VE*   cartulitati qui *BA* || 172,3 fragmentum] *V*   fracmentum *BA* || 184,17 incendium] *V*   ingendium *BA* || 208,11 suffigi] *V*   sufficit *BA* || 334,1 iocatur] *V*   iogatur *BA* || 343,6 descriptiunculas subtexam] *V*   descriptiungula subtexam *BA* descriptiunculam s. *B²* [modern-era hand]

This error is so persistent in **BA** that I cannot believe that the correct orthography in **V** is due (solely) to vigilant correction by its scribes. And, although there can be a close phonetic relationship between *g* and *c* (the former voiced, the latter unvoiced), **BA** could not so often agree in making this mistake unless the mistake was already in a shared exemplar. The split between **V** and **BA** follows too distinct a pattern not to reflect a difference in exemplars. This evidence alone should raise suspicion that the scribes of **V** are at times looking at an older exemplar in majuscules, while the scribes of **BA** copy a younger

---

[104] For a study of pre-caroline, with plates, see Collura 1943.
[105] From *Suas.* 2.17 Håkanson 346,9: credatis] *V B²* [*modern-era hand*] gredatis *BA* || iocanti] *VB²* [*modern-era hand*]   ioganti *BA*.

hyparchetype. But there is additional, more specific, confirmation in other letter-confusions.

Another revealing kind of error, pointing to **V**'s exemplar being in majuscules, is confusion of *P* with *R*, *F*, and *S*.[106] *P* can only be confused with these letters if it is at the same height and occupies roughly the same spatial dimensions as they do. *P* is similar to these three letters, particularly *F* and *S*, only in majuscules.

P/R confusions: 104,22 artus] *V*   aptus *BA*   ‖   110,16 peperissent] *V*   reperiss& *BA*   ‖   209,27 pestiferam] *V*   rertiferam *BA*. In the case of 104,22, the lection *aptus* is already a Latin word, although it does not fit with the rest of the sentence: would a ninth-century scribe have corrected it, exchanging *aptus* for *artus*? In the case of 209,27, the idea that a medieval scribe/reader could have conjectured *pestiferam* from the nonsensical *rertiferam* seems unlikely. The split between kinds of variants offered by **V** and those offered by **BA** has a more plausible explanation in the reading by **V** and misreading by **(y)** of letter-forms.

P/F confusions: 34,24 fatebor] fateor *V²* patebor *VBA*   ‖   206,8 fatebor] *V*   patebor *BA*   ‖   351,21 fabula] *V² B²* [*modern-era hand*] pabula *VBA*.   ‖   357,11 in pectus sacerrimum] *Bursian*   infectas acerrime *V* [*misreported by Håkanson*] insectus acerrimem *BA*.[107]

P/S confusions: 96,6 raptae] *V²*   raste (rastę *V*) *VBA*   ‖   99,4 mimicae nuptiae] mimice nustis (nustus *V*) *VBA*   mimice nostis *V²*.[108]

The above confusions are of particular interest, since they generally do not occur in minuscule scripts—unlike, for example, the confusion *m/in*, which can occur when copying either majuscule or minuscule exemplars. Another kind of error, even more specific, is the confusion *G/S*. This error, which is not common, is significant because it is peculiar to the copying of an exemplar in uncial.[109] In some vari-

---

[106] For these confusions when copying from an uncial model, see Shipley 1904:42–43.

[107] Possible sequence of miscopying in this last instance (357,11): **V** and **(y)** misread *inpect-* as *infect-* in majuscule **α** (**V**'s substitution of -*as* for -*us* is an independent error due to the anticipation of the *a* in -*acer*-). Then **BA** misread *infectus* as *insectus* (confusion of minuscule *s/f*).

[108] These examples appear in that section of text, analyzed in Section II.2, where **V²** adds corrections directly to the page of **V**. In the former instance (Håkanson 96,6), **V²** corrects from **α**. In the latter instance, (Håkanson 99,4) **V²** offers a false correction.

[109] Shipley 1904:43 cites from the Vatican Livy (Livy 29.19.12): *Syracugarum*.

eties of uncial the *cauda* ("tail") of *G* is extended,[110] so that the letter form as a whole takes on a sinuous appearance similar to *S*. So we find *G* read as *S*: Håkanson 118,4 patri gregem] patris regem *VBA* ‖ 334,10 castigatae] *B²* [*modern-era hand*] cassatae *V* castis ate *BA*.[111] In the former instance (Håkanson 118,4), *V*'s exemplar is seen again to have a corruption identical to that in the model of *BA*. And we find *S* read as *G*: Håkanson 9,25 aperis mihi] aperigmi *V B*[*corrected, it seems, from* aperiomi *by main scribe*] aperigini *A* ‖ 344,4 stratique] *B²* [*modern-era hand*] gratique *VBA* ‖ 346,6 confusi ac] *V²* confugi ac *V* confugiae *BA* confusi et *B²* [*modern-era hand*].[112]

There are additional, miscellaneous clues that α was in uncial. At the end of *Controuersiae* Book 1, after the admonition ʟᴇɢᴇ ᴇᴛ Sᴛᴜᴅᴇ, a note follows in **VBA**: *omissa prefatione et epistula controuersia haec est* ("The epistolary preface has been omitted; this is the *controuersia*"). In the Corbeiensis this note is in uncial, while the texts that precede (the *explicit* to Book 1) and follow (the *thema* of *Contr.* 2.1) are in capitalis.[113] There are three different kinds of text in this transition from Book 1 to Book 2: the *explicit*, the *thema*, and this notice that the book is missing its preface. Effective visual communication of the types of text could be achieved by using different types of script: in what type of script should this kind of marginal notice about the omitted preface be copied? Rather than reinterpreting the notice, by setting it in a different script from that seen in their model, the Corbie scribes simply adopted the uncial script of the exemplar.

At *Suas.* 2.1 (Håkanson 339,3), the **B** scribe betrays an intriguing misunderstanding of what is in his exemplar. Håkanson 1989: *At, puto, rudis lecta aetas, animus qui frangeretur metu* ("But I suppose you're young, raw recruits, your courage easily shattered by fear ..."). The **B**

---

[110] See Petrucci 1969:193–195; Bischoff 1990:71.

[111] **V** here may more accurately reflect what was in α. The letters *is* in the reading of **BA** may be a further corruption of an already corrupt reading in α.

[112] In this last instance (Håkanson 346,6), the sharing of two corruptions by **BA** (confusion of *S/G*, in majuscules, and confusion of *e* for *c*, in majuscules or minuscules) is illustrative of how they are linked together and at one remove from the archetype.

[113] I strongly suspect that in α also ʟᴇɢᴇ ᴇᴛ Sᴛᴜᴅᴇ was in uncial rather than in capitalis, as it is in **V**. The *G* of ʟᴇɢᴇ has the swinging *cauda* of an uncial *G*: this is not the *G* that the Corbie scribes write elsewhere when writing capitalis.

scribe writes *adputorudis lectaaetas* and then continues, but now inexplicably in uncial: ЄTASCT. This reading, *aetas <e>t*, was written in α as a correction for *aetas*. It was copied in uncial in (**y**) because it was not understood:[114] it was thought to be a name or a heading, or it was thought to be Greek. Names and headings are often written in majuscule in **VBA** (most frequently and consistently in **V**), and Greek is always written so.[115] The scribe or scribes of (**y**), as has by now become clear from the evidence surveyed, could not read Latin well. The **A** scribe ignored the correction, whereas in **V** a contemporary corrector, perhaps the original scribe for this page, when he saw the correction in α, comprehended it and simply added & after *aetas*.

When was α copied? Some basic facts, and firm conclusions, about α are consistent with its being produced in late antiquity, that is between AD 400 and 600. These are: 1) It stands at the head of our surviving Carolingian manuscript witnesses. 2) It is the parent of a lost hyparchetype (**y**) that was copied, I think, at the earliest circa 800. 3) α was copied in majuscules, probably in uncial. The date range 400–600 for α is hardly surprising, given that many of the reconstructed archetypes for classical works are thought to belong to this period.[116] As is well known, a robust copying of texts in late antiquity, together with the Carolingian renaissance in the ninth century, proved to be most critical for the survival of the Latin classics.

However, a further important consideration for estimating the date of α is the length of its verses, as reflected in **V**. α was written out in

---

[114] In the word *et* (**y**) again misreads *c* for *e*; cf. Håkanson 346,6 where (**y**) misread *confugiae* (**BA**) for *confusi ac* (**V²**).

[115] The Greek, since it was not understood in the ninth century, was copied simply as patterns of lines, not letters. Since the scribes were unable to translate the Greek writing into a different kind of script from that seen in an exemplar, it is graphically one of the most conservative elements in the tradition: the Greek remains in majuscules in **VBA**, which further confirms that at some point the Latin too was in majuscules. Evidence for former homogeneity of scripts between Greek and Latin texts is seen in a revealing error at *Contr.* 9.1.13 (Håkanson 241,7), where Greek words are interspersed with Latin. There the scribes of **VBA** copy Latin *deme* in uncials—not recognizing the word as Latin and thus revealing the script-type of an older layer in the tradition (α). For Greek in Carolingian monasteries, see Berschin 1988:126–156.

[116] Bloch 1963; Markus 1974; Cameron 1977; Reynolds 1983:xiii–xxx; Pecere 1986 and 1990:342–366; Reynolds and Wilson 1991:36–43; Zetzel 1993:100–101, 105–106.

long verses containing as many as fifty letters per verse, a high number for a majuscule manuscript. The high number does not contradict the evidence presented above suggesting that α was in uncial. Yet, it could mean that α was copied at the latter end of the time frame 400–600,[117] and could have been copied as late as the seventh or eighth centuries. If it is accepted that the scribe(s) of α wrote an uncial G with a long *cauda*, so that G could be confused with S, this would corroborate a later date, since this particular feature has been identified as distinguishing so-called "new" uncial (after c. 600) from "old" uncial (400–600).[118]

III.1 Editorial Shaping in Late Antiquity

Above was posed the question when certain organizational and interpretive features of Seneca's text entered the tradition: 1) rhetorical punctuation, particularly by points, and 2) critical signs that differentiate and articulate the work's component pieces, thereby giving the text meaningful shape. To be sure, the precise shape and look of the text in the ninth and tenth centuries are an amalgam of interventions and adaptations over several stages of transmission. The scribes of **VBA** occasionally modified the punctuation that was in α—but only slightly, for example by substituting different, contemporary punctuation signs for signs found in an exemplar.[119] The system of punctuation and critical signs found in **VBA**—a system that *fundamentally* determined how Seneca's work was organized and how it could be read—originated earlier in the tradition than these manuscripts. There is no

---

[117] For uncial MSS with long verses, see Chatelain 1901–1902: pl.19 (Paris 2235), 27, 33, 38, 48. Of especial interest, since it was copied in uncial in long verses and contains several rhetorical texts (Fortunatianus, Marius Victorinus, Augustine), is Cologne, Dombibliothek 166, which can be seen online in its entirety in high quality digital images: http://www.ceec.uni-koeln.de. Cologne 166 (seventh/eighth century or second half of eighth century) is not a late antique MS and, although in uncial, its textual organization is relatively "modernized"—through a good amount of punctuation signs, spacing, and abbreviations. The Cologne MS is an interesting comparandum for reconstructing α also in another regard: in the former we see (misunderstood) Greek script homogenized with Latin script, since both are in majuscule.

[118] Petrucci 1969:193–195; Petrucci 1971; Bischoff 1990:67, 71; and, for dating of uncial MSS, Lowe and Rand 1922:13–20.

[119] For sample outcomes of this process, see Parkes 1993:242–261.

question about this. The basic graphic organization of the collection, through punctuation and critical signs, is as least as old as **α**, as agreement between **V** and **(y)** overwhelmingly attests.

The consistent nature of the punctuation and critical signs, with regard both to the particular graphic signs used and to how they divide the text, argues that these were applied to the text as a unified, systematic effort. A reader, or group of readers working together, was critically engaged with the text, adding signs according to their understanding and interpretations, and in the process giving the text the definitive shape in which it has been transmitted. This organization is of good quality. The understanding that the organization betrays deserves to be taken seriously. The quality of the organizing graphic features is such that they are most likely to have originated in late antiquity—perhaps in **α**, if **α** was copied in late antiquity, or at any rate before AD 600.[120]

The chronology has significant implications for how we regard the graphic signs in the tradition; for as late as the sixth century, at least in certain social circles in areas of western Europe, rhetorical education still retained continuity with the classical past.[121] Declamation was a living, actively practiced tradition. Indeed, it seems to have enjoyed a reflorescence beginning in the fourth century, if we judge from events in literary history and in the manuscript histories of declamatory texts:[122] some of the declamations in the *Major Declamations*, falsely attributed to Quintilian, were composed in the fourth century, which is also when the collection assumed a definitive shape and

---

[120] Given the fact that **α** contained 1) verses of considerable length for the main body of the text, and 2) narrow columns for many of the declamatory *themata*, we might posit that **α**'s exemplar was laid out in columns. The copying of **α** from this exemplar would have involved an innovative *mise en page*: a greater textual density brought about through the introduction of long lines and a reduction of script module. See Vanderhoven and Masai 1953:107 for this kind of difference between two late-antique Paris MSS.

[121] Luiselli 1982:62–75; Pecere 1993; Kennedy 1994:273–280, 282–284; Riché 1995:9–41.

[122] Literary aesthetics support the same conclusion. Auerbach 2003:63–66 points out that the pagan Ammianus Marcellinus and the church father Jerome resemble each other in their literary sensibilities. A formative influence shared between these two writers is declamation: their aesthetic has much in common with the *Major Declamations*, from which Jerome borrowed (Schneider 2000:616–617n10). Stramaglia 1999:27 suggests that Jerome read the *Major Declamations* while under the tutelage of Donatus.

was circulated.[123] A famous subscription in the manuscript tradition may reveal the names of those readers involved in the "editing" process:[124] Domitius Dracontius and Hierius, a renowned rhetor to whom Augustine dedicated his *De pulchro et apto*.[125] A late-antique manuscript is thought to be the basis of a ninth-century Montpellier manuscript (Faculté de médecine, H 126) that shows several declamatory texts programmatically brought together in the same volume: the *Minor Declamations*, the excerpts from the elder Seneca's work, and the declamatory excerpts of Calpurnius Flaccus. Further, there are the several fourth- and fifth-century rhetorical works, relevant to declamation, that are collected in Halm's *Rhetores Latini minores*: Marius Victorinus, Fortunatianus, Julius and Sulpicius Victor, Grillius, and Julius Severianus. In the sixth century, Ennodius—who, like his contemporaries Boethius and Cassiodorus, represents a stunning unification of Christian culture and deeply imbued pagan learning—composed a declamation (*Dictio XXI*) in direct reaction and opposition to *Major Declamation V*.[126]

It is from the perspective just sketched—the graphic signs as originating in the context of a living ancient cultural practice—that I wish briefly to reflect on potential interpretive ramifications that the signs have for our understanding of Seneca's text and on the justifications for including them in the process of interpretation.

If, as I am proposing, the fundamental graphic organization of Seneca's work was made by a late-antique reader, by someone who understood declamation as a living practice and knew in a way we no longer can the conventional organizational logic of declamatory collections, then we are not only justified in taking account of this graphic organization but are obligated to do so. In the first place, the transmitted signs and organization are part of the history of the reception

---

[123] Schneider 2000. The date and number of authors for the works in the *Major Declamations* remain debatable: Håkanson 1986:2284–2285; Schneider 2004:34–37.

[124] For subscriptions in classical Latin MSS: Jahn 1851; Zetzel 1973, 1980, and 1984; Pecere 1982, 1984, and 1986.

[125] Sussman 1987:ix–x.

[126] On Ennodius: Håkanson 1986:2285–2290; Winterbottom 2003; Schröder 2003; Schröder 2007.

of Seneca's collection. They concern not solely the copying and preservation of the work, but also how it was read and understood. Secondly,
the organization reflects an interpretation of the work at least as old
as late antiquity: herein is the possibility of learning something about
Seneca's text that we did not know.

Two visual features in particular are of interest: the editorial signs,
and the punctuation (points and spacing) that divide continuous script
into rhetorical sense-units. First, the editorial signs and the structure
of Seneca's work. The organization of Seneca's collection is perplex-
ing.[127] It is unique among surviving ancient literature, idiosyncratic
even among other declamatory collections. The consensus view, it
seems, is that the material—quotations of speakers, anecdotes, critical judgments—collected under each declamatory theme in Seneca's
work falls into three roughly symmetrical parts, each part defined by
a rhetorical-technical function: 1) the *sententiae* or 'epigrams', 2) the
'divisions' (*diuisiones*), and 3) the 'colors' (*colores*).

A known problem with this interpretation is that whereas the
material appearing under the 'divisions' and the 'colors' sections has
clearly recognizable rhetorical-technical applications, the *sententiae*
often cannot accurately be called epigrams. These *sententiae* are so
heterogeneous, so unpredictable in their effects and interests, that no
single term from ancient rhetorical theory suffices. All that can be said
for certain of the *sententiae* is that they are short, typically no more
than four or five continuous sentences.[128] They are presented one after
another without interruption or comment from Seneca. It is only when

---

[127] Sussman 1978:34–75; Fairweather 1981:29–30; Fairweather 1984:538–539; Berti
2007:25–26; Huelsenbeck 2009:11–72.

[128] Since the beginning of the twentieth century, editors of the elder Seneca's work
(Bornecque 1902, Winterbottom 1974a, Håkanson 1989) have used punctuation to delimit
what they perceive as boundaries between *sententiae*—that is, breaks within a quotation
attributed to a given speaker. A question I had in studying the MSS of the elder Seneca
was whether they exhibited systematic punctuation, of any variety, to mark divisions
between *sententiae*. In the medieval MSS there is no systematic, consistent marking of
these kinds of boundaries. And in late antiquity and earlier, I have no doubt, the material
organization of Seneca's text (and of other declamatory texts) would not signal, in any
systematic way, the boundaries of *sententiae*. This means that late antique (and ancient)
readers were comfortable with ambiguity, and they were sensitive to other cues, internal
to the language and content of the quotations themselves, that signaled divisions.

the section of *sententiae* has concluded that Seneca *qua* author speaks, providing anecdotes about the declaimers and comments of technical interest. The so-called *sententiae*, in other words, stand as raw quotations, faithfully recorded, fixed and unalterable. This observation warrants speculation whether we should regard the declamatory material following the *themata* as apportioned not into three symmetrical parts, but into two asymmetrical parts: on the one hand, the *sententiae*, which are in effect a collection of *lemmata*, i.e. quotations of passages of interest, as in an ancient commentary or specialized monograph;[129] on the other hand, supporting commentary that is designed to elucidate and elaborate on the quoted passages (*lemmata*) and that happens to include discussions of *diuisiones* and *colores*.

It is significant that the hypothesis of a bipartite organization, split between *lemmata* and commentary, finds *visual* corroboration in **α**. Methods of textual display, particularly in **V** and **B**, appear sensitive to two different qualities of text. In the section comprising *sententiae*, devices of textual display—kinds of script, spacing, and critical signs— serve to isolate the name of the declaimer together with his quotation. One declaimer and his quotation form a unit distinctly marked from that of another declaimer and *his* quotation: this section, so the visual communication signals, belongs to the individual speakers, to authors and authorities. In order to achieve this graphically, the names of speakers have been made prominent through the use of majuscule script, namely capitalis. Generous spacing works in conjunction with capitalis script: names are afforded often an entire line to themselves, so that they serve as headings. The feature is constant among **VBA**. Even though names are usually in minuscule in **BA**, all three manuscripts, in the section of *sententiae*, witness how names create space. Furthermore, names are marked with signs that can take on slightly different forms. Sometimes they are simple medial points. Often they are *paragraphoi* and *hederae*. In introducing a quotation, typically three signs appear: one marking the conclusion of the preceding quota-

---

[129] For ancient Greek commentaries, which can contain *lemmata* of significant length, see Del Fabbro 1979; for specialized monographs (*hypomnemata*), see Turner 1988:112–124.

tion, one between the speaker's *nomen* and *cognomen*, and one just before the beginning of the quotation. Editors cannot afford to ignore such signs.[130] The isolating effect produced by the devices of textual display just described—majuscule script, critical signs, and patterns of spacing—can be quite profound, resulting in individual quotations appearing as stand-alone blocks.

It is noteworthy that this system of signs and textual arrangement in α shows continuity with practices in antiquity. The use of signs and spacing to communicate different types of texts (*quotations* and *commentary*) also appears in surviving ancient copies of commentaries—for example, in a Berlin papyrus (*P.Berol.* 9780) that contains Didymos' *On Demosthenes* and dates from the second century AD.[131] There, and also in other papyri,[132] *lemmata* are marked off from commentary typically through *ekthesis*—that is, by projecting the beginning of a *lemma* into the left-hand margin—and through critical signs, such as the *paragraphos* and *diple*.

This isolation of quotations and the prominent display of declaimers' names in the section of *sententiae* stand in significant contrast to the manner of textual display for the subsequent commentary section devoted to technical discussions and anecdotes—the section containing the divisions and colors. Typically in this commentary section the names of declaimers, though sometimes still accompanied by critical signs, are of a greatly diminished visual importance. The use of majuscules is inconsistent and scarce. Names are not afforded the same spacing as in the section of quotations. In short, they do not function as headings. The text in this section is homogenized and smoother, and gives the impression of a single textual body.

---

[130] At *Contr.* 2.1.17, in **B**, fol.119r, three such signs appear in a row (between *meus non timet* and *Fabriciorum imagines*) followed by generous spacing, thus marking a significant break in the text. The break, which has gone unobserved by editors, seems to indicate that a speaker's name has fallen out. The same break is also marked in **A** (fol.45v) and **V** (fol.55v) through a large space followed by a very large initial (*Fabriciorum*).

[131] Cancik 1979:90–91. For detailed studies of Didymos' work, see Harding 2006; Gibson 2002. Harding 2006:13–20 ("Commentary or Monograph?") reviews the debate about the genre of Didymos' work. For continuity in textual presentation, from antiquity to the middle ages, see Holtz 1981:342 and 1984:152.

[132] Del Fabbro 1979:87–90; Turner 1988:114–118; Harding 2006:6.

All this, I must point out, is not to deny a tripartite structure of *sententiae, diuisiones, colores.*[133] But, if we are reading the visual communication of the text accurately, the recognized threefold division seems to be operating in counterpoint with a hierarchical division between the authoritative *sententiae*, on the one hand, and the supporting *diuisiones* and *colores*, on the other. This interpretation, which is recommended by virtue of the fact that it takes account of history and historical processes, has a further advantage in that it now reveals greater organizational consistency between Seneca's collection and the *Declamationes minores* (second century AD).[134] In the latter collection, too, we find a (more obvious) bipartite organization: parts of fair copies of speeches, introduced by the heading *Declamatio*, and commentary, introduced by the heading *Sermo.*

Now some remarks on the punctuation in α, specifically the division and grouping (*Gliederung*) of continuous text into sense-units. The manner in which, as early as α, Seneca's text was divided into sense-units has already been demonstrated in passages cited above. When considering the relevance of the transmitted punctuation, it is crucial to observe, as others have done already,[135] that *ancient punctuation is qualitatively different from modern punctuation.* This is the conclusion of the seminal, and still unsurpassed, survey of ancient Latin punctuation by R. W. Müller (1964). What is the essence of this difference? Ancient punctuation has been broadly characterized as 'rhetorical.' It is concerned with marking pauses that occur in oral delivery, in marking rhythms. By comparison, modern Western punctuation is concerned to mark logical-syntactical breaks—breaks that are more frequent and

---

[133] This hypothesis of a twofold structure makes no claim about the authenticity (i.e. Senecan origin) or inauthenticity (non-Senecan origin) of the labels in the imperfectly transmitted title to Seneca's work: *sententiae diuisiones colores.* The three labels do, to some extent, correctly describe the content of the collection; however, they certainly do not reflect all that is in the collection, nor do the labels constrain us to find a tripartite arrangement whereby each part carries equal weight and performs a similar function to each of the other two parts.

[134] For comparisons of the organization of Seneca's collection, the *Minor Declamations*, and the collection of Calpurnius Flaccus, see Dingel 1988:11–32.

[135] Kauer 1900:64–72; Norden 1958: vol. 2, 952–953; R. W. Müller 1964:105–145; Powell 1988:51.

only sometimes coincide with rhetorical pauses. As a consequence, modern punctuation is too often an imposition on ancient Latin texts, frequently disguising and even distorting the rhythms and architecture inherent in the language.

This is important: rhetorical punctuation was an ancient practice of punctuation, a practice that continued into late antiquity and even beyond. Furthermore, rhetorical punctuation more accurately represents the internal organizing structures of Latin. That there is consonance, or at least a nearer proximity, between rhetorical punctuation and the inherent structure of Latin was confirmed by R. W. Müller,[136] who compared punctuation in late-antique manuscripts with the results from the ground-breaking investigations into language structures by Eduard Norden and by Eduard Fraenkel in his studies on colometry.[137] A correlation between ancient punctuation and colometry has been further supported by the investigations of Thomas Habinek.[138]

In practical terms, modern punctuation differs most obviously from rhetorical punctuation, and can be most damaging to Latin, in the way in which it obscures the visual markers of higher-order sentence structures.[139] Modern punctuation divides text into tiny pieces, each piece seemingly of equal value. By contrast, rhetorical punctuation is concerned with the demarcation of the super-structures of a sentence.[140] The two methods are juxtaposed in the following passage (*Contr.* 2.6.4, Håkanson 115,18–21):

---

[136] R. W. Müller 1964:121–143.

[137] Norden 1903:369–381; Fraenkel 1964, 1965, and 1968.

[138] Habinek 1985:42–88. See also two dissertations on punctuation in late antique MSS of Vergil: Meny 1994; Pontes 1995.

[139] Rhetorical punctuation also draws divisions between units where we sometimes do not expect them: cf. Habinek 1985:128; Fraenkel 1964:83.

[140] Simply to gain a rough sense of what an eclectic method of punctuation, with obvious visual signaling of larger and smaller sentence structures, might look like in a modern edition, see Seyfarth 1978 (Ammianus Marcellinus). Use of hierarchical punctuation in editing Ammianus goes back to C. U. Clark (2 vols., 1910 and 1915), who punctuated his edition according to rhythm. Seyfarth (1978: vol. 1, xv, xxi) insists that he, unlike Clark, punctuates by the modern laws of grammar and logic.

Rhetorical punctuation

> Nemo puto uitia quia odit imitatur.   quis imperator
> ob hoc ipse de proelio fugit   ut bene pugnaret exer-
> citus?   quis ut ambitum comprimeret   ipse
> honores mercatus est?   quis ut seditionem
> leniret   turbauit rem <publicam>?   non
> coercet uitia qui prouocat.

> "Nobody I suppose imitates vices because he hates
> them.   What general has himself fled from
> battle   so that his army will fight well?   Who
> in order to suppress bribery   has himself purchased
> political offices?   Who in order to calm civil discord
> has stirred up the state?   He does not restrain vices
> who conjures them."

Modern punctuation

> "Nobody, I suppose, imitates vices because he hates them.
> What general has himself fled from battle, so that his army
> will fight well? Who, in order to suppress bribery, has
> himself purchased political offices? Who, in order to calm
> civil discord, has stirred up the state? He does not restrain
> vices who conjures them."

The quality of punctuation in α is rhetorical; it follows an ancient tradition. R. W. Müller, it is true, casts doubt on the possibility of discovering or reconstructing ancient punctuation from medieval manuscripts.[141] But, even if one takes a hard-line view that punctuation cannot be traced across stages of transmission, a fact remains that should not be ignored: the punctuation in α is generally preferable because it is rhetorical, and is thus consistent in *kind* with ancient

---

[141] Consequently, R. W. Müller 1964:21 is sometimes cited as support for *ignoring* punctuation in the tradition, e.g. Håkanson 1986:2293–2294, 2294n65. However, a logical *non sequitur* is often involved in the neglect of textual arrangement/punctuation in manuscripts: if it is difficult to recover traditional elements of textual organization, do we then have license to impose on a literary work an organization of our own choosing?

punctuation. This is not to say that the punctuation in **α** is always good. Like the readings in **α**, it is at times corrupt. It is legitimate and necessary, therefore, to disagree in specific instances with the transmitted punctuation. However, it is difficult to justify ignoring the *principles* of the transmitted punctuation. Simply on the basis of *kind* of punctuation we should feel very reluctant to scrap the transmitted rhetorical punctuation altogether and replace it with a modern system.

As it turns out, justification for paying attention to the transmitted graphic organization goes deeper than this. It is in fact possible, within limits, to trace punctuation diachronically. This possibility is the acknowledged position of Malcolm Parkes in his fascinating overview of punctuation in the West.[142] And this position is confirmed by the results of the present investigation. Punctuation in **VBA** is not just of the same *kind* found in ancient manuscripts and inscriptions: it is demonstrably *old*. In the case of the tradition of the elder Seneca's work, the basic punctuation and graphic organization found in ninth- and tenth-century manuscripts can be shown to originate in late antiquity. Of course there is no denying that the punctuation of **α** is not directly from the pen of the elder Seneca (how could it be?), but neither is it negligible.

The issue raised here—the relevance that transmitted punctuation has for the reading of ancient texts by us moderns—has been broached by scholars in the past, with mixed results and reactions.[143] A synthesis of past work and a new inquiry into this question is needed, particularly in light of studies over the last three decades (especially in disciplines such as bibliography, History of the Book, and English) that have in various ways argued—convincingly, in my opinion—for the integral, collaborative role of the material book in creating meaning.[144] These

---

[142] Parkes 1993:31. And see Parkes' comments (1993:185, 187, 265) on British Library, Harley 2736; Paris, B.N. 6332; and the codex Holkhamicus of Cicero, London, B.L., Add. 47678.

[143] Tarrant 1995:97: "In matters of 'accidentals'—punctuation, capitalization, and paragraphing and other divisions—manuscript testimony carries virtually no weight." This statement, by one of today's most eminent critics of classical Latin texts, attempts to summarize current practices. I take it as representative of scholarly consensus.

[144] An unsystematic, very partial selection of works that I have found fruitful: McGann 1983 and 1991; Gumbert 1993; Drucker 1994; McKenzie 1999 and 2002; Lanham 2003:79–

studies, while generally not investigating ancient texts, have nonetheless brought forward justifications for studying the material text as a site of meaning that are relevant to ancient literature. Once we are prepared to recognize that texts acquire meanings in historical and social contexts,[145] and not solely by virtue of the fact that they have authors, the familiar objection that we cannot definitively attribute graphic signs and textual organization to an author cannot invalidate the textual organization transmitted in the manuscripts. Text is not abstract: it has a material history,[146] it has an historically and socially informed texture.

How do the material instantiations of an ancient text, at different points in the text's history, determine and express its meanings? The question is of the greatest importance, and at least when it comes to ancient texts it has seldom been addressed directly. A survey considering to what extent and in what particulars the physical embodiments of ancient texts can shape their meanings cannot be attempted here. Different texts have different traditions, and each tradition will present its own possibilities and limitations with regard to what we can reconstruct of its graphic history (although, of course, many traditions share some basic transmission patterns). Among the objectives of the present study has been to establish what the possibilities and limitations of the historical record are for including the visual, physical communication of the text in interpretations of the work of the elder Seneca. The visible, physical text in our analysis—verse lengths, letter-groupings, kinds of script, abbreviations—has proven integrally important for working out stemmatic relationships. What is valuable for tracing

---

101 ("Styles Seen"); McKitterick 2003. For *History of the Book*, Febvre and Martin 1958 is seminal.

[145] For texts as socially collaborative products, see McGann 1983; also, McGann 1991, e.g. (58): "As the process of textual transmission expands, whether vertically (i.e., over time), or horizontally (in institutional space), the signifying processes of the work become increasingly collaborative and socialized."

[146] Clark 1918 attempts to deduce verse lengths over several stages of copying. Clark's methods do not always inspire confidence. But, at the very least, his investigation with its long list of numbers for reconstructed verse lengths is impressive for what is implicit in it: throughout its history an ancient text has physical shape—always.

a text's material history cannot be irrelevant for considering how an historical text produces meaning.[147]

CORNELL UNIVERSITY

WORKS CITED

Auerbach, E. 2003. *Mimesis: The Representation of Reality in Western Literature*. Trans. W. R. Trask. Princeton.

Bakhuizen van den Brink, J. N. 1974. *Ratramnus. De corpore et sanguine domini*. Amsterdam.

Beeson, C. H. 1930. *Lupus of Ferrières as Scribe and Text Critic: A Study of his Autograph Copy of Cicero's* De oratore. Cambridge, MA.

Berschin, W. 1988. *Greek Letters and the Latin Middle Ages: From Jerome to Nicholas of Cusa*. Trans. J. C. Frakes. Washington, D.C.

Berti, E. 2007. *Scholasticorum studia: Seneca il Vecchio e la cultura retorica e letteraria della prima età imperiale*. Pisa.

Bischoff, B. 1961. "Hadoardus and the Manuscripts of Classical Authors from Corbie." In *Didascaliae: Studies in Honor of Anselm M. Albareda, Prefect of the Vatican Library, Presented by a Group of American Scholars*, ed. S. Prete, 39–57. New York.

———. 1966–1981. *Mittelalterliche Studien*. 3 vols. Stuttgart.

———. 1990. *Latin Palaeography: Antiquity and the Middle Ages*. Trans. D. Ó Cróinín and D. Ganz. Cambridge.

———. 1994. *Manuscripts and Libraries in the Age of Charlemagne*. Ed. and trans. M. M. Gorman. Cambridge.

———. 1998–2004. *Katalog der festländischen Handschriften des neunten Jahrhunderts (mit Ausnahme der wisigotischen)*. 2 vols. Wiesbaden.

Bishop, T. A. M. 1972. "The Script of Corbie: A Criterion." In *Varia codicologica* (= Litterae textuales 1), vol. 1 of *Essays Presented to G. I. Lieftinck*, 9–16. Amsterdam.

Blank, D. L. 1983. "Remarks on Nicanor, the Stoics and the Ancient Theory of Punctuation." *Glotta* 61:48–67.

Bloch, H. 1963. "The Pagan Revival in the West at the End of the Fourth

---

[147] Chartier 1997:83 on the legacy of D. F. McKenzie: "By assigning to bibliography the fundamental task of comprehending the relations between form and meaning, McKenzie obliterated the old divisions between sciences of description and sciences of interpretation."

Century." In *The Conflict between Paganism and Christianity in the Fourth Century*, ed. A. Momigliano, 193–218. Oxford.

Bornecque, H. 1902. *Sénèque le rhéteur. Controverses et Suasoires.* 2 vols. Paris.

Bursian, C. 1857. *Annaei Senecae Oratorum et rhetorum sententiae divisiones colores.* Leipzig.

Cameron, A. 1977. "Paganism and Literature in Late Fourth-Century Rome." In *Christianisme et formes littéraires de l'antiquité tardive en occident* (= Entretiens sur l'antiquité classique 23), ed. A. Cameron and M. Fuhrmann, 1–40. Vandoeuvres.

Cancik, H. 1979. "Der Text als Bild: Über optische Zeichen zur Konstitution von Satzgruppen in antiken Texten." In *Wort und Bild: Symposion des Fachbereichs Altertums- und Kulturwissenschaften zum 500jährigen Jubiläum der Eberhard-Karls-Universität Tübingen 1977*, ed. H. Brunner, R. Kannicht, and K. Schwager, 81–100. Munich.

Carter, R., B. Day, and P. Meggs. 2007. *Typographic Design: Form and Communication.* 4th ed. Hoboken, NJ.

Chartier, R. 1997. *On the Edge of the Cliff: History, Language, and Practices.* Trans. L. G. Cochrane. Baltimore.

Chatelain, É. 1884–1900. *Paléographie des classiques latins.* 2 vols. Paris.

———. 1901–1902. *Uncialis scriptura codicum Latinorum novis exemplis illustrata.* 2 vols. Paris.

———. 1964. *Introduction à la lecture des notes tironiennes.* New York (orig. pub. Paris, 1900).

Citti, F. 2007. "La declamazione greca in Seneca il vecchio." In *Declamation: Proceedings of the Seminars Held at the Scuola Superiore di Studi Umanistici, Bologna (February–March 2006)* (= Papers on Rhetoric 8), ed. L. Calboli Montefusco, 57–102. Rome.

Clark, A. C. 1918. *The Descent of Manuscripts.* Oxford.

Clemens, R., and T. Graham. 2007. *Introduction to Manuscript Studies.* Ithaca, NY.

Collura, P. 1943. *La precarolina e la carolina a Bobbio.* Milan.

Del Fabbro, M. 1979. "Il commentario nella tradizione papiracea." *Studia Papyrologica* 18:69–132.

Dermul, A. 1939. *Catalogue des manuscrits de la bibliothèque de la ville d'Anvers.* Vol. 5. Gembloux.

Devine, A. M., and L. D. Stephens. 2006. *Latin Word Order: Structured Meaning and Information.* Oxford.

Dingel, J. 1988. *Scholastica materia: Untersuchungen zu den* Declamationes minores *und der* Institutio oratoria *Quintilians.* Berlin.

Dorey, T. A. 1971. *Titi Liui Ab urbe condita libri xxi–xxv.* Vol. 1: *Libri xxi–xxii.* Leipzig.

Drucker, J. 1994. *The Visible Word: Experimental Typography and Modern Art, 1909–1923.* Chicago.

Fabri, J. 1953. "Un ami de Juste Lipse: L'humaniste André Schott (1552–1629)." *Les Études classiques* 21:188–208.

Fairweather, J. 1981. *Seneca the Elder.* Cambridge.

———. 1984. "The Elder Seneca and Declamation." *ANRW* II 32.1:514–556.

Febvre, L., and H.-J. Martin. 1958. *L'apparition du livre.* Paris.

Fraenkel, E. 1964. "Kolon und Satz: Beobachtungen zur Gliederung des antiken Satzes" (I and II). In *Kleine Beiträge zur klassischen Philologie,* vol. 1, 73–92 and 93–139. Rome.

———. 1965. "Noch einmal Kolon und Satz." *Sitzungsberichte der Bayerischen Akademie der Wissenschaften, Philosophisch-Historische Klasse* 2:3–73.

———. 1968. *Leseproben aus Reden Ciceros und Catos.* Rome.

Gain, D. B. 1976. *The Aratus Ascribed to Germanicus Caesar.* London.

Ganz, D. 1987. "The Preconditions for Caroline Minuscule." *Viator* 18:23–44.

———. 1990. *Corbie in the Carolingian Renaissance.* Sigmaringen.

Gibson, C. A. 2002. *Interpreting a Classic: Demosthenes and His Ancient Commentators.* Berkeley, CA.

Giusta, M. 1991. *Il testo delle "Tusculane."* Turin.

Gribomont, J., and J. Mallet. 1979. "Le latin biblique aux mains des barbares, les manuscrits VEST des Prophètes." *Romanobarbarica* 4:31–105.

Gumbert, J. P. 1993. "'Typography' in the Manuscript Book." *Journal of the Printing Historical Society* 22:5–28.

Habinek, T. N. 1985. *The Colometry of Latin Prose.* Berkeley, CA.

Hafner, A. 1989. *Untersuchungen zur Überlieferungsgeschichte der Rhetorik ad Herennium.* Bern.

Hagendahl, H. 1936. "Rhetorica." In *Apophoreta Gotoburgensia Vilelmo Lundström oblata,* 282–338. Göteborg.

Håkanson, L. 1986. "Die quintilianischen Deklamationen in der neueren Forschung." *ANRW* II 32.4:2272–2306.

———. 1989. *L. Annaeus Seneca Maior. Oratorum et rhetorum sententiae, divisiones, colores.* Leipzig.

Halm, K. 1863. *Rhetores Latini minores.* Leipzig.

Harding, P. 2006. *Didymos. On Demosthenes.* Oxford.

Havet, L. 1967. *Manuel de critique verbale appliquée aux textes latins.* Rome (orig. pub. Paris, 1911).

Holtz, L. 1981. *Donat et la tradition de l'enseignement grammatical.* Paris.

———. 1984. "Les manuscrits latins à gloses et à commentaires: De l'antiquité à l'époque carolingienne." In Questa and Raffaelli 1984, 139–167.

Hubert, M. 1970. "Corpus stigmatologicum minus." *Archivum Latinitatis Medii Aevi* 37:5–171.

Huelsenbeck, B. 2009. *Figures in the Shadows: Identities in Artistic Prose from the Anthology of the Elder Seneca.* Ph.D. diss., Duke University.

Jahn, O. 1851. "Über die Subscriptionen in den Hss römischer Classiker." *Berichte über die Verhandlungen der Königlich-Sächsischen Gesellschaft der Wissenschaften zu Leipzig* 3:327–372.

Johnson, W. A. 2000. "Toward a Sociology of Reading in Classical Antiquity." *AJP* 121:593–627.

Johnson, W. A., and H. Parker, eds. 2009. *Ancient Literacies: The Culture of Reading in Greece and Rome.* Oxford.

Jones, L. W. 1947. "The Scriptorium at Corbie" (I and II). *Speculum* 22:191–204 and 375–394.

Kauer, R. 1900. "Zu Terenz." *Wiener Studien* 22:56–114.

Keil, H. 1857–1880. *Grammatici Latini.* 7 vols. Leipzig.

Kennedy, G. A. 1994. *A New History of Classical Rhetoric.* Princeton.

Kiessling, A. 1872. *Annaei Senecae Oratorum et rhetorum sententiae divisiones colores.* Leipzig.

Kopp, U. F. 1965. *Lexicon Tironianum.* Osnabrück.

Lameere, W. 1960. *Aperçus de paléographie homérique.* Paris.

Lanham, R. 2003. *Analyzing Prose.* 2nd ed. London.

Lieftinck, G. I. 1960. *Servii Grammatici. In Vergilii carmina commentarii: Codex Leidensis B.P.L. 52.* Amsterdam.

Lindsay, W. M. 1915. *Notae Latinae: An Account of Abbreviation in Latin Mss. of the Early Minuscule Period (c. 700–850).* Cambridge.

Lowe, E. A. 1925. "Some Facts about Our Oldest Latin Manuscripts." *CQ* 19:197–208.

———. 1928. "More Facts about Our Oldest Latin Manuscripts." *CQ* 22:43–62.

———. 1934–1971. *Codices Latini antiquiores: A Palaeographical Guide to Latin Manuscripts Prior to the Ninth Century.* 11 vols., suppl. Oxford.

Lowe, E. A., and E. K. Rand. 1922. *A Sixth-Century Fragment of the Letters of Pliny the Younger: A Study of Six Leaves of an Uncial Manuscript Preserved in the Pierpont Morgan Library, New York.* Washington, D.C.

Luiselli, B. 1982. "La società dell'Italia romano-gotica." In *Atti del 7° congresso internazionale di studi sull'alto medioevo,* 49–116. Spoleto.

Markus, D., and G. W. Schwendner. 1997. "Seneca's *Medea* in Egypt (663–704)." *Zeitschrift für Papyrologie und Epigraphik* 117:73–80.

Markus, R. A. 1974. "Paganism, Christianity and the Latin Classics in the Fourth Century." In *Latin Literature of the Fourth Century,* ed. J. W. Binns, 1–21. London.

Martin, H.-J., and J. Vezin, eds. 1990. *Mise en page et mise en texte du livre manuscrit.* Paris.

Marx, F. 1894. *Incerti auctoris de ratione dicendi ad C. Herennium libri IV.* Leipzig.

McGann, J. J. 1983. *A Critique of Modern Textual Criticism.* Chicago.

———. 1991. *The Textual Condition.* Princeton.

McKenzie, D. F. 1981. "Typography and Meaning: The Case of William Congreve." In *Buch und Buchhandel in Europa im achtzehnten Jahrhundert: Fünftes Wolfenbütteler Symposium vom 1. bis 3. November 1977,* ed. G. Barber and B. Fabian, 81–126. Hamburg.

———. 1999. *Bibliography and the Sociology of Texts.* Cambridge.

———. 2002. *Making Meaning: "Printers of the Mind" and Other Essays.* Ed. P. D. McDonald and M. F. Suarez. Amherst, MA.

McKitterick, D. 2003. *Print, Manuscript and the Search for Order, 1450–1830.* Cambridge.

Meny, J. S. 1994. *On Reciting the Aeneid: The Testimony of Ancient Punctuation.* Ph.D. dissertation, University of Texas at Austin.

Moreau-Maréchal, J. 1968. "Recherches sur la ponctuation." *Scriptorium* 22:56–66.

Müller, H. J. 1887. *L. Annaei Senecae Oratorum et rhetorum sententiae divisiones colores.* Vienna (repr. Hildesheim, 1963).

Müller, R. W. 1964. *Rhetorische und syntaktische Interpunktion: Untersuchungen zur Pausenbezeichnung im antiken Latein.* Tübingen.

Norden, E. 1903. *P. Vergilius Maro. Aeneis, Buch VI.* Leipzig.

————. 1958. *Die antike Kunstprosa vom VI. Jahrhundert v. Chr. bis in die Zeit der Renaissance.* 5th ed. 2 vols. Leipzig.

Parkes, M. B. 1987. "The Contribution of Insular Scribes of the Seventh and Eighth Centuries to the 'Grammar of Legibility.'" In *Grafia e interpunzione del latino nel medioevo: Seminario internazionale, Roma, 27–29 settembre, 1984,* ed. A. Maierù, 15–30. Rome.

————. 1993. *Pause and Effect: An Introduction to the History of Punctuation in the West.* Berkeley, CA.

Pascucci, G. 1973. "La tradizione medievale del *De legibus* e la posizione del codice S. Marco 257 ai fini della *recensio.*" *Ciceroniana,* n.s., 1:33–46.

Pasquali, G. 1962. *Storia della tradizione e critica del testo.* 2nd ed. Florence.

Pecere, O. 1982. "La 'subscriptio' di Statilio Massimo e la tradizione delle 'Agrarie' di Cicerone." *Italia medioevale e umanistica* 25:73–123.

————. 1984. "Esemplari con *subscriptiones* e tradizione dei testi latini: L'Apuleio Laur. 68,2." In Questa and Raffaelli 1984, 111–137.

————. 1986. "La tradizione dei testi latini tra IV e V secolo attraverso i libri sottoscritti." In *Società romana e impero tardoantico. IV. Tradizione dei classici, trasformazioni della cultura,* ed. A. Giardina, 19–81. Bari.

————. 1990. "I meccanismi della tradizione testuale." In *Lo spazio letterario di Roma antica,* ed. G. Cavallo, P. Fedeli, and A. Giardina, vol. 3, 297–386. Rome.

————. 1993. "La cultura greco-romana in età gota tra adattamento e trasformazione." In *Teoderico il Grande e i Goti d'Italia: Atti del XIII congresso internazionale di studi sull'alto medioevo, Milano, 2–6 novembre 1992,* vol. 1, 355–394. Spoleto.

Petrucci, A. 1969. "Scrittura e libro nell'Italia altomedievale: Il sesto secolo." *Studi medievali,* 3rd series, 10.2:157–213.

————. 1971. "L'onciale Romana: Origini, sviluppo e diffusione di una stilizzazione grafica altomedievale (sec. VI–IX)." *Studi medievali,* 3rd series, 12.1:75–134.

————. 1995. "Reading in the Middle Ages." In *Writers and Readers in Medieval Italy,* ed. and trans. C. M. Radding, 132–144. New Haven.

Plasberg, O. 1915. *Cicero. Operum philosophicorum codex Leidensis Vossianus Lat. fol. 84.* Leiden.

Pontes, H. R. 1995. *Callida iunctura: The Divided Heroic Clausula in Virgil.* Ph.D. diss., University of Cincinnati.

Powell, J. G. F. 1988. *Cicero. Cato maior de senectute.* Cambridge.

———. 2006. *M. Tulli Ciceronis De re publica, De legibus, Cato maior de senectute, Laelius de amicitia.* Oxford.

Questa, C., and R. Raffaelli, eds. 1984. *Il libro e il testo: Atti del convegno internazionale, Urbino 20–23 settembre 1982.* Urbino.

Rafti, P. 1988. "L'interpunzione nel libro manoscritto: mezzo secolo di studi." *Scrittura e civiltà* 12:239–298.

Rand, E. K., and G. Howe. 1915–1916. "The Vatican Livy and the Script of Tours." *Memoirs of the American Academy in Rome* 1:19–57.

Reeve, M. D. 1987. "The Third Decade of Livy in Italy: The Family of the Puteanus." *Rivista di filologia e di istruzione classica* 115:129–164.

———. 1989. "*Eliminatio codicum descriptorum*: A Methodological Problem." In *Editing Greek and Latin Texts: Papers Given at the Twenty-Third Annual Conference on Editorial Problems, University of Toronto, 6–7 November 1987*, ed. J. N. Grant, 1–35. New York.

Reinhardt, T. 2003. *Marcus Tullius Cicero. Topica.* Oxford.

Reynhout, L. 2006. *Formules latines de colophons.* 2 vols. Turnhout.

Reynolds, L. D. 1965. *The Medieval Tradition of Seneca's Letters.* Oxford.

———, ed. 1983. *Texts and Transmission: A Survey of the Latin Classics.* Oxford.

Reynolds, L. D., and N. G. Wilson 1991. *Scribes and Scholars: A Guide to the Transmission of Greek and Latin Literature.* 3rd ed. Oxford.

Riché, P. 1995. *Éducation et culture dans l'Occident barbare, VIe–VIIIe siècle.* 4th ed. Paris.

Roberts, C. H. 1935. "The Antinoë Fragment of Juvenal." *Journal of Egyptian Archaeology* 21:199–209.

Rouse, R. H. 1983. "*De natura deorum, De divinatione, Timaeus, De fato, Topica, Paradoxa Stoicorum, Academica priora, De legibus.*" In Reynolds 1983, 124–128.

Saenger, P. 1982. "Silent Reading: Its Impact on Late Medieval Script and Society." *Viator* 13:367–414.

———. 1990a. "La naissance de la coupure et de la séparation des mots." In Martin and Vezin 1990, 447–449.

———. 1990b. "Coupure et séparation des mots sur le Continent au Moyen Âge." In Martin and Vezin 1990, 451–455.

———. 1997. *Space Between Words: The Origins of Silent Reading*. Stanford, CA.

Schmidt, P. L. 1974. *Die Überlieferung von Ciceros Schrift "De legibus" im Mittelalter und Renaissance*. Munich.

Schneider, C. 2000. "Quelques réflexions sur la date de publication des *Grandes déclamations* pseudo-quintiliennes." *Latomus* 59:614–632.

———. 2004. *[Quintilien]. Le soldat de Marius: Grandes déclamations, 3.* Cassino.

Schröder, B.-J. 2003. "Charakteristika der 'Dictiones Ethicae' und der 'Controversiae' des Ennodius." In Schröder and Schröder 2003, 251–274.

———. 2007. *Bildung und Briefe im 6. Jahrhundert: Studien zum Mailänder Diakon Magnus Felix Ennodius*. Berlin.

Schröder, B.-J., and J.-P. Schröder, eds. 2003. *Studium declamatorium: Untersuchungen zu Schulübungen und Prunkreden von der Antike bis zur Neuzeit*. Munich.

Schwenke, P. 1889. "Des Presbyter Hadoardus Cicero-Excerpte." *Philologus Supplementband* 5:397–588.

Seyfarth, W. 1978. *Ammiani Marcellini Rerum gestarum libri qui supersunt.* 2 vols. Leipzig.

Shipley, F. W. 1904. *Certain Sources of Corruption in Latin Manuscripts*. New York (repr. from *American Journal of Archaeology* [1903] 1:1–25 and 157–197).

Stramaglia, A. 1999. *[Quintiliano]. I gemelli malati: un caso di vivisezione (Declamazioni maggiori, 8)*. Cassino.

Sussman, L. A. 1978. *The Elder Seneca*. Mnemosyne Suppl. 51. Leiden.

———. 1987. *The Major Declamations Ascribed to Quintilian: A Translation.* Frankfurt.

Tarrant, R. J. 1995. "Classical Latin Literature." In *Scholarly Editing: A Guide to Research*, ed. D. C. Greetham, 95–148. New York.

Taylor, P. R. 1993. "'Pre-History' in the Ninth-Century Manuscripts of the Ad Herennium." *Classica et Mediaevalia* 44:181–254.

Timpanaro, S. 2005. *The Genesis of Lachmann's Method*. Ed. and trans. G. W. Most. Chicago.

Turner, E. G. 1988. *Greek Papyri: An Introduction*. Oxford (orig. pub. 1968).

Van den Gheyn, J. 1902. *Catalogue des manuscrits*. Vol. 2. Brussels.

Vanderhoven, H., and F. Masai. 1953. *La Règle du Maître. Édition diplomatique des manuscrits latins 12205 et 12634 de Paris*. Brussels.

Vervliet, H. D. L. 1955. *L. Annaeus Seneca Pater: Een Onderzoek naar de Tekstcritische Traditie der Suasoriae van Seneca Pater*. Ph.D. dissertation, Katholieke Universiteit Leuven.

———. 1957. "De Gedrukte Overlevering van Seneca Pater." *De Gulden Passer* 35:179–222.

———. 1964. "Les manuscrits médiévaux de Sénèque le Rhéteur." *L'antiquité classique* 33:431–441.

Walters, C. F., and R. S. Conway 1967. *Titi Liui Ab urbe condita*. Vol. 3, *Libri XXI–XXV*. Oxford (orig. pub. 1929).

Watt, W. S. 1991. Review of Håkanson 1989. *Gnomon* 63:314–317.

Wingo, E. O. 1972. *Latin Punctuation in the Classical Age*. The Hague.

Winterbottom, M. 1974a. *The Elder Seneca. Declamations*. 2 vols. Cambridge, MA.

———. 1974b. "Problems in the Elder Seneca." *Bulletin of the Institute of Classical Studies* 21:20–42.

———. 1983. "The Elder Seneca." In Reynolds 1983, 356–357.

———. 1991. "The Elder Seneca." *CR*, n.s., 41:338–340.

———. 2003. "Ennodius, Dictio 21." In Schröder and Schröder 2003, 275–287.

Zeller, H. 1975. "A New Approach to the Critical Constitution of Literary Texts." *Studies in Bibliography* 28:231–264.

Zelzer, M., and K. Zelzer. 2001. "Zur Frage der Überlieferung des Leidener Corpus philosophischer Schriften des Cicero, mit einer Kritischen Bewertung karolingischer Textemendation." *Wiener Studien* 114:183–214.

Zetzel, J. E. G. 1973. "*Emendavi ad Tironem*: Some Notes on Scholarship in the Second Century A.D." *HSCP* 77:225–243.

———. 1980. "The Subscriptions in the Manuscripts of Livy and Fronto and the Meaning of *Emendatio*." *CP* 75:38–59.

———. 1984. *Latin Textual Criticism in Antiquity*. Salem, NH.

———. 1993. "Religion, Rhetoric, and Editorial Technique: Reconstructing the Classics." In *Palimpsest: Editorial Theory in the Humanities*, ed. G. Bornstein and R. G. Williams, 99–120. Ann Arbor, MI.

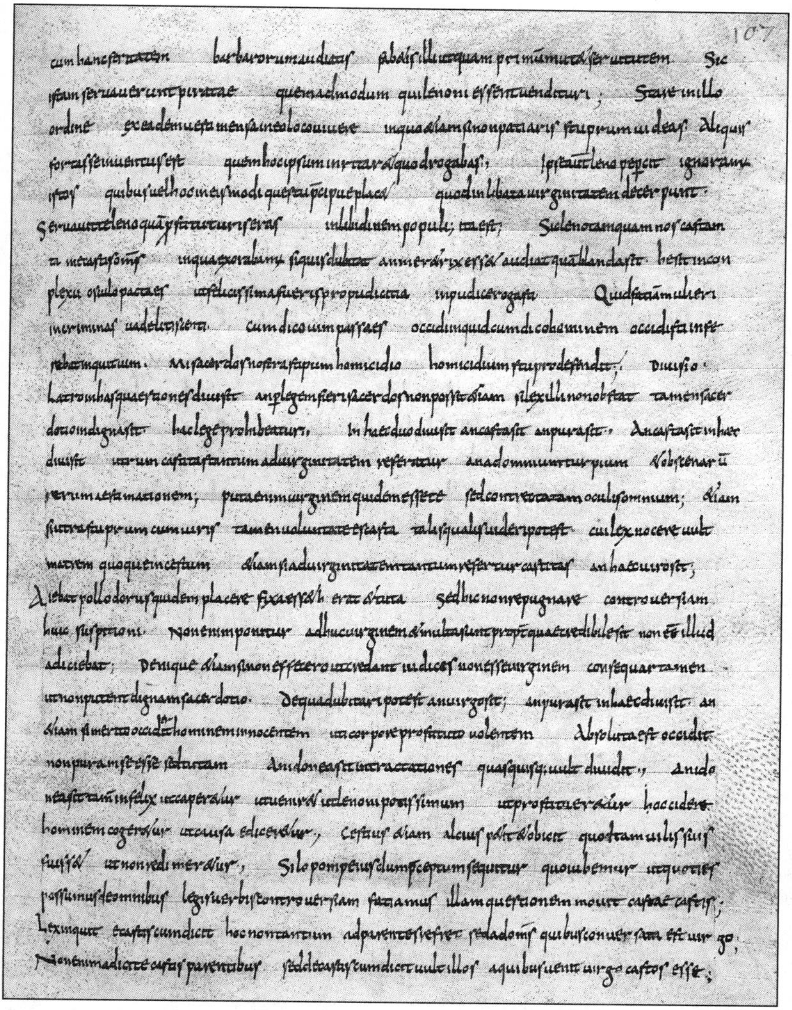

Figure 1. Brussels, Bibliothèque Royale, 9581–9595, fol.107r (Sen. *Contr.* 1.2.11–12). Copied 850–900, probably in NE France. The text is divided into continuous word-strings that correspond to sense-units. The word-strings, which were inherited from an exemplar, have been exaggerated by a ninth-century scribe who inserted extra space between sense-units.

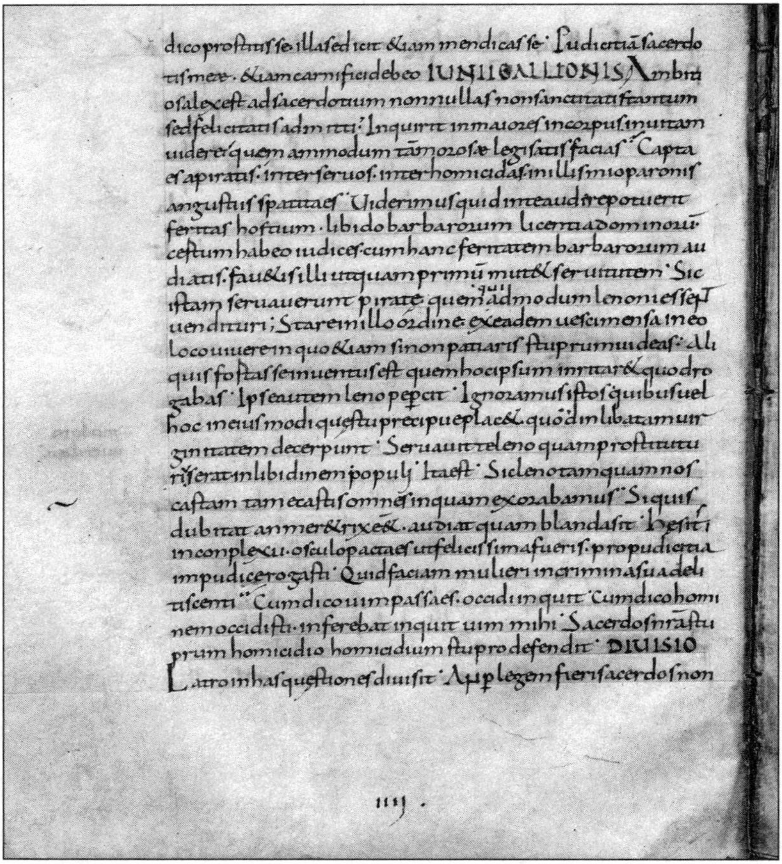

Figures 2a and 2b. ©2011 Biblioteca Apostolica Vaticana. Vatican Lat. 3872, fols.32v–33r (*Contr.* 1.2.10–15). Copied at Corbie, 850–880. A good example of two sub-varieties of ninth-century Corbie script, written side-by-side and used in collaboration. The script of fol.32v (Figure 2a) is taller, more rounded,

> possit. &iam si lex illi non obstat. tamen sacerdotio indignasit.
> Apu lege prohibeatur. ipsa haec duo diuisit. an castasit. an purasit.
> Apu castasit in haec diuisit. utrum castitas tantum ad uirginitatem
> referatur. an ad omnium purum &cob scenarum rerum estimatione;
> putauerunt uirginem quidem deesse se. sed contrectatio oculis omnium
> iuiuam si uitiatas stupru cum uiris. tam uoluntate esca sta talis
> qualis uideri potest. cui lex nocere uult; Matre quoq. ipi
> castam. &iam si ad uirginitatem tantum refertur castitas. an haec
> uiro sit. / Aiebat apollodorus quide placere fixa esse &c herat
> accutata. Sed hic non repugnare controuersia huic suspicioni.
> Non enim potitur ad huc uirgine. Et multas sunt p prter que cred i
> bile sit non eo illud adiciebat. Deniq. &iam si non effecero ut
> credant iudices non esse uirginem. consequar tamen ut non
> putent dignam sacerdotio. De qua dubitari potest an uirgo
> sit. an purasit. ipsa haec diuisit. an &iam si merito occidit
> hominem. puta tamen si non si homicidio coinquinatec.
> Deinde an merito occiderit hominem innocentem. ut corpore
> p stituto uolentem. Absoluta est. occidit. non puram se
> esse sed tutam. Apu idonea sit. in tractatione si quis quisq.
> uult diuidit. An idonea sit tam infelix ut capertur utuem
> r sit non potissimu ut p statuetur occidere homine coge
> retur ut causa a diceret ur = Cestut &iam altius p sit. &
> obiciet qd tam uiri si si fuit &c ut non redimeret ur = Silo
> pompeius dum p ceptu sequitur quo iubemur ut quotiens
> possumus de omnib. legi fuerit bis controuersia faciamus.
> illa questione mouit. Caste castas. Lex in quit de castis

and a more recent development in the history of Corbie script. The script of 33r (Figure 2b) is more rugged, laterally taut, and older: it belongs to an older, more senior scribe, who begins a quire.

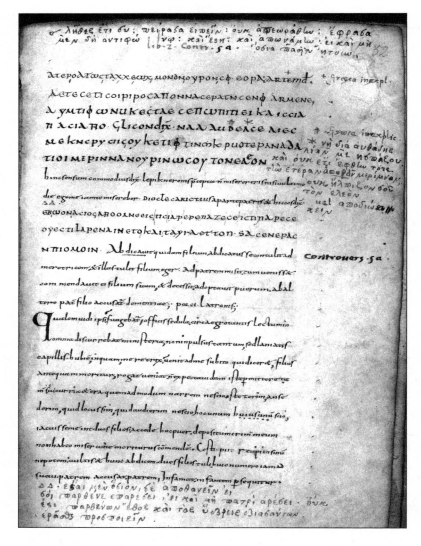

Figure 3. Source: Collection of the Erfgoedbibliotheek Hendrik Conscience, Antwerpen (Belgium), manuscript B 411, fol.52r (*Contr.* 2.3.22–2.4.2). Copied 10th cent., perhaps NE France. In the margins can be seen the writing of Andreas Schott, appearing on other folios with signatures ("Schottus" or "Schot"), as he attempts to recover sense from the garbled Greek text.

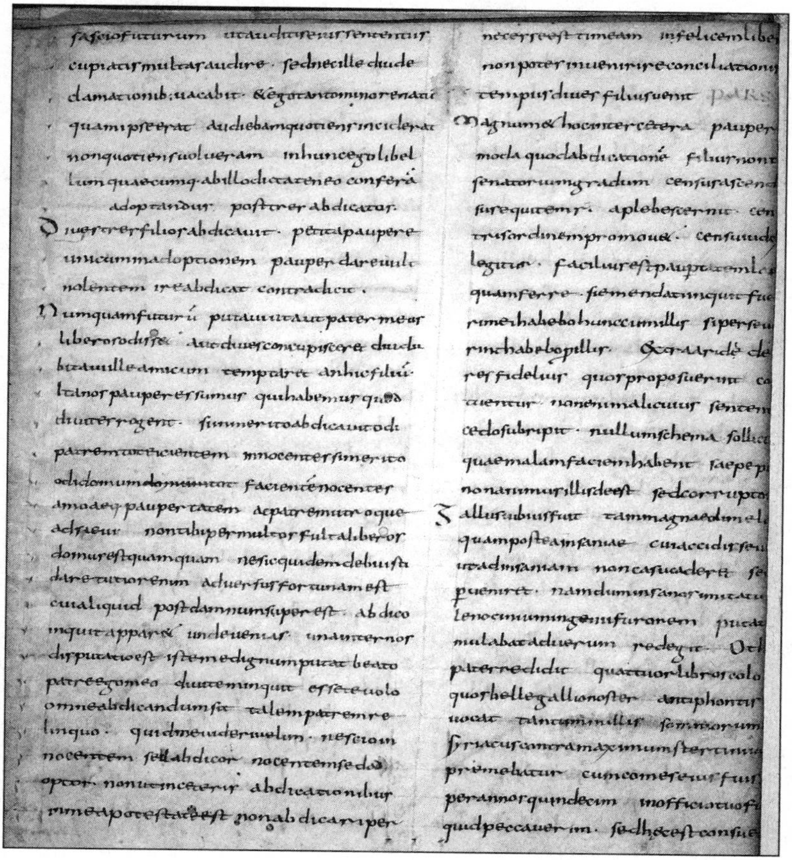

Figure 4. Bamberg, Staatsbibliothek, Msc.Class.45m, fol.1r (originally a verso side) (Sen. *Contr.* 2 pr.5–2.1). The earliest extant MS witness (ca. 800) to the excerpted tradition. Copied in two columns with pronounced sense-units divisions comparable, though less exaggerated, to those seen in **B**. The surviving MSS of the full and excerpted traditions descend from different archetypes; therefore, punctuation in the Bamberg MS is probably independent of that in **VBA**. Photo by Gerald Raab.

LUCAN'S THUNDER-BOX

SCATOLOGY, EPIC, AND SATIRE
IN SUETONIUS' *VITA LUCANI*

ROBERT COWAN

*"Apthorpe removed his steel helmet, recovered his cap, straight-
ened his uniform, put up a hand to assure himself that his new
stars were still in place. He looked once more on all that remained
of the thunder-box; the mot juste, thought Guy."*

Waugh 1952:157

THE *LIFE OF LUCAN* ATTRIBUTED TO SUETONIUS marks the breakdown in
relations between the poet and Nero with a low but amusing anecdote in which the former quotes a half-line by the latter while noisily
emptying his bowels:[1]

> siquidem aegre ferens, <quod Nero se> recitante subito ac
> nulla nisi refrigerandi sui causa indicto senatu recessisset,
> neque uerbis aduersus principem neque factis exstantibus
> post haec temperauit, adeo ut quondam in latrinis publicis

This article developed from a section of a paper delivered at a conference on
Suetonius at Manchester University in June 2008. I am very grateful to the organizers,
Roy Gibson and Ruth Morello, and to the other participants for their helpful comments. I
am also grateful to *HSCP*'s editor and anonymous reader for their suggestions and corrections.

[1] On this passage, see Plinval 1956, Morford 1985:2017, Hunink 1993:139, Gowers
1995:29–30, Narducci 2002:10, Baldwin 2005:317–318. It is beyond the scope of this article
to revisit the extensive debate on Lucan's attitudes to Nero and their chronology as
reflected in his "historical" actions and in the *Bellum ciuile*. On this issue, see, *inter multos
alios*, Hunink 1993, Dewar 1994, Weston 1994:280–316, Rudich 1997:107–185, and Narducci
2002:5–41.

clariore cum crepitu[2] uentris hemistichium Neronis magna consessorum fuga pronuntiarit:

> sub terris tonuisse putes.

sed et famoso carmine cum ipsum tum potentissimos amicorum grauissime proscidit.

For piqued because Nero had suddenly called a meeting of the senate and gone out when he was giving a reading, with no other motive than to throw cold water on the performance, he afterwards did not refrain from words and acts of hostility to the prince, which are still notorious. Once for example in a public privy, when he relieved his bowels with an uncommonly loud noise, he shouted out this halfline of the emperor's, while those who were there for the same purpose took to their heels:

> you might suppose it thundered 'neath the earth.

He also tongue-lashed not only the emperor but also his most powerful friends in a scurrilous poem.

Suet. *Vita Luc.* p. 51 Reifferscheid. Trans. Rolfe–Goold.

The joke works, of course, on a simple and even obvious level, albeit one with a clear literary heritage.[3] As Jeffrey Henderson notes, "the noise and odor of gas being expelled from the bowels is considered to be universally and unconditionally humorous," but context adds to the inherent comedy.[4] The aural similarity between thunder and farting permits an incongruous parallelism between a low, socially-deprecated bodily function and what is at least an awesome and sublime act of nature, if not a divine signal from the supreme deity. This comic poten-

---

[2] Of the MS readings, P's *crepitu*, printed by Reifferscheid, is marginally preferable to B's *strepitu* (Rolfe–Goold). Both provide one half of the *double entendre*, since they can be used of thunder, but only the former regularly applies to farting (*OLD* s.v. *crepitus* c., citing Suet. *Claud.* 32.1, *inter alia*).

[3] On the humor of crepitation and defecation in the Classical world, see Hošek 1962:160–174, Henderson 1991:195–199, Watson and Watson 2003 *ad* Mart. 4.87. In later cultures, see Greenblatt 1982, Anspaugh 1994, Dawson 1999, Bowen 2004.

[4] Henderson 1991:195.

tial was harnessed long before Waugh's Apthorpe and the thunderous explosion of his portable chemical latrine, or "bush thunder-box," in a running gag in Aristophanes' *Clouds*, where Socrates etymologizes βροντή from πορδή and Strepsiades vows to fart in response to the clouds' thundering.[5] Moreover, Baldwin has traced further parallels in an epigram of Martial and a Sotadean quoted by Athenaeus.[6]

However, the joke is *about* poetry as well as being featured in it, since thunder and farting are not merely high and low; they are emblematic of high and low literature. Of course, "thundering," at least since Callimachus' *Aetia* prologue, has been a metaphor for the composition of epic poetry, especially epic polemically constructed as overblown and excessive; it is Zeus' to thunder, not the Callimachean poet's. In contrast, defecation and breaking wind serve as tropes for the production of unambiguously bad poetry and bad oratory. Catullus claims that the execrable *Annales* of Volusius cover papyrus rolls with excrement; indeed Lindsay Watson convincingly argues that Catullus here provides "a wickedly scatological recasting of the image of the turbid, mud-polluted Euphrates which Callimachus famously employed in the *envoi* to *Hymn 2*," so that both strands of imagery in the Suetonian passage could have Callimachean implications.[7] Aristophanes' Karion asks the rhetorical question that surely Agyrrhios farts for the sake of wealth; Major, citing Eubulus fr. 106.1–6 among other parallels, convincingly argues that this is an instance of farting as a dysphemism for bad oratory.[8] Suetonius' Lucan thus derides Nero's hemistich on

---

[5] Waugh 1952; Ar. *Clouds* 394, 293–294. As the anonymous reader observes, it should, of course, be noted that, although Waugh's "thunder-box" parallels the meteorological and scatological imagery of the Suetonian anecdote, its evocation of a small, private, enclosed "water closet" is quite alien to the large, communal, open *latrinae* of the Roman world, on which see Neudecker 1994, esp. 62–71, Hodge 2002:270–272, Hobson 2009.

[6] Baldwin 2005:317, citing Mart. 12.77 and Ath. 14.621b.

[7] Catullus 36, with e.g. Farrell 2009:172. Watson 2005, quoting from 270. He also cites an epigram in which Erycius upbraids Parthenius for the madness of calling the *Odyssey* mud and the *Iliad* dung (*AP* 7.377.5–6, ἤλασε καὶ μανίης ἐπὶ δὴ τόσον, ὥστ᾽ ἀγορεῦσαι | πηλὸν Ὀδυσσείην καὶ πάτον Ἰλιάδα); the imagery here is focused on the end product rather than the process of defecation, but the implications are surely the same.

[8] Ar. *Plut.* 176, Ἀγύρριος δ᾽ οὐχὶ διὰ τοῦτον [i.e. τὸν πλοῦτον] πέρδεται;. Major 2002. Cf. O'Regan 1992:57–60. The poetic connotations of urination seem to be more varied, encompassing Dionysos' accusation that the successors of Euripides piss on (personi-

two levels.[9] Its emblematic description of thunder (or rather a simile comparing something *to* thunder) renders it in itself an act of thundering, and hence of overblown, un-Callimachean epic composition. Lucan, by recontextualizing the phrase, then equates that thundering with farting, so that Nero's epicizing is of as little merit as Volusius' crap poetry or Agyrrhios talking out of his arse. The joke can thus be understood on the levels of basic toilet humor and of broadly Callimachean poetics, but I would like to argue that it functions most elaborately as an enactment of the composition of satire.

Bodily functions—sexual, alimentary, and excretory—are the very stuff of satire, not least because they are alien to the higher genres of epic and tragedy which are its antitheses.[10] This apparently Rabelaisian engagement with the low and the grotesque has encouraged Bakhtinian analyses of satire as a carnivalesque genre, but, as Miller in particular has demonstrated, the bodily functions of satire emphasize sterility and decay rather than fertility and vitality.[11] However, these bodily functions are not merely the decayed subject-matter of satire; they are embodiments of satire itself, and their enactment serves as a trope for its performance.[12] In particular, crepitation, micturition, and defecation (to use very unsatiric euphemisms) are regular tropes for satiric utterance.[13]

---

fied) tragedy, impotently defiling rather than creatively inseminating her (*Frogs* 95, with Dover ad loc. and Henderson 1991:194), and Trugaios' claim that the boys will "piss" the rehearsal of their dithyrambic performance (*Peace* 1265–1269, with Egan 2005).

[9]   On Nero's poetry and its early reception, see esp. Griffin 1984:150–152, Morford 1985, Rudich 1997:227–228, Baldwin 2005, Cowan 2009. Merivale 1858:190 intriguingly suggests another level, comparing the description of Nero's voice as κοῖλον μὲν φύσει καὶ βαρύ (Philostr. *Nero* 6, which he attributes to Lucian). Cf. Narducci 2002:10 on the audacity of Lucan's evoking in a degrading manner the line's "studiata sonorità."

[10]   "[M]an is caught in his animal functions of eating, drinking, lusting, displaying his body, copulating, evacuating, scratching": Kernan 1959:11. Satiric sex: Richlin 1992, Gunderson 2005. Food: Hudson 1989, Gowers 1993:109–219. Excretion: Gowers 1995:30–32 and, in later satire, Clark 1974. Two fragments of Lucilius (frr. 253 and 400 Marx) tantalizingly refer to *latrinae*.

[11]   Miller 1998. Cf. Gowers 1993:30–31.

[12]   Cf. the use of food and especially an excess thereof as a symbol, etymologically justified, of *satura*, with Gowers 1993:109–126.

[13]   For later instances of these tropes, see Persels 1996 and 2006. Persels 1996:104 quotes Thomas More's *Responsio ad Lutherum* 1.14 (p. 244 Headley), which includes an appropriation (not explicitly noted by Persels) of Juv. 1.131.

In Horace *Satire* 1.8, Priapus, in keeping with the moderation of Horatian satire, dispels the malign presence of the witches Canidia and Sagana, not by his traditional violent act of rape (which is implicitly aligned with the violence of Lucilian satire), but with the humorous and low action of an enormous fart, analogous to the comic, but non-aggressive, satire which is the hallmark of the collection.[14] Persius figures his constructed interlocutor's warning against the dangers of writing satire as the painting of an apotropaic sign of two snakes with the epigram "piss outside."[15] Juvenal, perhaps in an act of *aemulatio* competing with this very passage of Persius, adds defecation to the list when he describes the statue set up in the forum by an Egyptian Arabarch, at which it would be permissible to do more than piss.[16] Lucan's act of combined defecation and crepitation is thus in itself a satiric act, or rather a trope for satiric utterance.[17]

This metaphorical satirical utterance is, of course, paralleled by Lucan's verbal act of satire, transforming and debasing to the lowest level a lofty epic phrase about a sublime phenomenon originally composed by the *princeps*. The parallelism between fart and speech is reflected in Suetonius' remark that Lucan was moderate in neither his words nor his actions. For the combination of three parallel transformations, or more precisely debasements, from elevated to low language, from lofty to scatological subject matter, and from the politically eminent to the humble object of abuse, we might compare the

[14] Hor. *Sat.* 1.8.46, 50: *nam, displosa sonat quantum uesica, pepedi ...* [the witches' flight] *cum magno risuque iocoque uideres.* Gowers 2005:52: "When Horace speaks as a statue of Priapus ... [he] frightens away trespassing witches with a comic fart rather than sexual aggression." Cf. Anderson 1982:80–83, Sharland 2003:106, and Plaza 2006:70–71. The efficacy of both the fart and the satire has been questioned (Gowers 2003:83), but this reinforces rather than undermines their parallelism.

[15] Pers. 1.113–114: *pinge duos anguis: "pueri, sacer est locus, extra | meiite."* Also Bramble 1974:134 on the "uncompromising implication that satire is equivalent to excretion." Cf. Richlin 1992:187, 206, Freudenburg 2001:177–178, and Plaza 2006:152–153.

[16] Juv. 1.129–131: *inter quas ausus habere | nescio quis titulos Aegyptius atque Arabarches, | cuius ad effigiem non tantum meiiere fas est.*

[17] See Weston 1994 and Coffey 1996:86–92 for explicit discussion of satiric elements in the *Bellum ciuile*, though many discussions stress its deformation of epic propriety (notably Henderson 1987) in a manner which implicitly likens it to satire.

conversion in Juvenal 10 of Sejanus' statue into piss-pots, and Morgan's elegant analysis thereof:

> iam strident ignes, iam follibus atque caminis
> ardet adoratum populo caput et crepat ingens
> Seianus, deinde ex facie toto orbe secunda
> fiunt urceoli, pelues, sartago, matellae.

> Now the flames are hissing, now that head idolised by the people is glowing from the bellows and furnace: huge Sejanus is crackling. Then the face that was number two in the whole world is turned into little jugs, basins, frying pans, and chamber pots.

Juv. 10.61–64. Trans. Braund.

> The violence done to elevated modes of speech precisely reflects the violence being done to a former symbol of authority. Sejanus *was* great, and the epic language of *toto orbe secunda* expresses this at a stylistic as well as semantic level. What he, or rather his statue, becomes, on the other hand, is both base—kitchenware and toiletries—and basely expressed in a plain, unembellished list of words which themselves have no possible place in respectable literature.[18]

The parallel is close, except that Lucan's deformation is not of epic language but of a specific epic phrase. Rather than marking the deformation of epic propriety by a jarring drop in linguistic register, Lucan retains meter, diction, and phrasing, transmuting epic into satire only by the incongruous recontextualization and hence reinterpretation of the phrase. On one level, this is what all Roman verse satire had done since Lucilius moved from composing *satura* in the traditional mixture of meters to epic hexameters: an elevated form debased by incon-

---

[18] Morgan 2005:185. It is interesting to compare Nero's *damnatio memoriae* of rival athletic victors at Suet. *Ner.* 24.1: *ac ne cuius alterius hieronicarum memoria aut uestigium extaret usquam, subuerti et unco trahi abicique in latrinas omnium statuas et imagines imperauit.*

gruous context.[19] This is especially so when satire debases epic motifs and scenes, once more beginning with Lucilius book 1 and its parody of Ennius' *consilium deorum*, and extending through Horace's sub-Homeric *nekyia* (2.5) to Juvenal's anti-Statian epic *consilium* about Domitian's turbot (4). A degree closer still is the alteration of an epic phrase, especially with the introduction of an incongruously low word, in register and/or meaning, such as Juvenal's replacement of σίδηρος in *Od*. 16.294 = 19.13 to produce the satiric advice to the sexually-obliging *cliens* Naevolus that αὐτὸς γὰρ ἐφέλκεται ἄνδρα κίναιδος (9.37).

However, the precise parallel for Lucan's action here is the scenario where satirists recontextualize, reinterpret, and debase actual epic lines and hemistichs. Thus the Iliadic Apollo's rescue of Hector is incongruously recontextualized to refer to (perhaps) Lucilius' or Scipio's deliverance from an ancestor of the Horatian "pest."[20] Persius, in his typically boiled-down manner, creates a pseudo-Virgilian phrase from three more widely distributed words, and then debases it to refer to the addressee's sexual organs: *ilia subter | caecum uulnus habes, sed lato balteus auro | praetegit.* (Pers. 4.43–45) ~ *[pharetram] lato quam circum amplectitur auro | balteus* (Virg. *Aen*. 5.312–313). Juvenal reduces the strong spear which Turnus snatches up for the duel to the effeminate Otho's mirror, in which he only plays soldier; both objects are described as *Actoris Aurunci spolium.*[21] The practice has a parallel in the composition of centos, where epic lines and hemistichs were given a totally new meaning by their recontextualization; the parallel is closest in Ausonius' famous *Cento Nuptialis*, where Virgilian hexameters and hemistichs referring to battle and other epic subject-matter are

---

[19] "Couching the anti-literature of satire in the metre of heroes clarified the status of Lucilius' genre as the 'evil twin' of respectable poetry, epic above all": Morgan 2004:8. On epic and satire, see, *inter multos alios*, Winkler 1989, Schmitz 2000, esp. 208–221, and Connors 2005.

[20] <nil> *ut discrepet ac* τὸν δ' ἐξήρπαξεν Ἀπόλλων | *fiat*: Lucil. 231–232 Marx, quoting Hom. *Il*. 20.443b. Cf. Horace's rendering of the phrase into Latin at *Sat*. 1.9.78, in accordance with the practice advocated in *Sat*. 1.10.20–35.

[21] Virg. *Aen*. 12.94a = Juv. 2.100a, with Lelièvre 1958, Braund 1996 ad loc. and Schmitz 2000:189–190, *inter alios*. This verbatim quotation is combined with an alteration of the kind just discussed, since the previous line turns *magni gestamen Abantis* (Virg. *Aen*. 3.286) into *pathici gestamen Othonis* (Juv. 2.99).

recontextualized to refer to sexual intercourse. Just as, for example, *itque reditque uiam totiens* is debased from Pollux's repeated visits to the Underworld to refer to the repeated insertion and withdrawal of the penis, so Nero's simile is debased to refer to Lucan's bowel movements.[22] The satiric treatment of Nero's hemistich is also connected with the aesthetic judgment upon it noted above, since satire's preoccupation with literary criticism goes back to Lucilius and is most prominent in the first Satire of Persius, whose quotations of "bad poetry" the scholiast (perhaps improbably) attributes to Nero.[23]

If, then, the character Lucan acts as a satirist in this anecdote, it only remains to consider how this action functions within the Suetonian *Vita*. It could be argued that the satiric mode is a pervasive presence in Suetonius' biographies and especially the *Caesars*. Anecdotal structure, an untempered emphasis on vice and folly (often in flat contradiction of the corresponding virtues catalogued earlier), illusion and theatricality, and especially the subject-matter—material and corporeal excess and perversion in all their forms—are all common to the two genres.[24] Moreover, both satire and Suetonian biography combine mimetic looseness and bloatedness of form, a complex mixture of condemnation and collusion, and a self-conscious opposition to the higher forms (epic and historiography respectively) whose artistic sublimity matches that of their subject-matter.[25] Indeed it is this episode as a whole which has a satiric flavor and not only the action of Lucan. Rose draws a tentative parallel with the slave Corax's crepitation at *Satyrica* 117, which might be seen as a commentary on Eumolpus' literary diatribe in 118 and even a response to this action by Lucan, though an indeterminate lacuna after 117 makes this very speculative indeed.[26]

---

[22] Virg. *Aen.* 6.122a = Auson. 18.126a Green.

[23] Lucilius: Koster 2001. Persius: Schol. *ad* 1.93, dismissed by Courtney 1993:358.

[24] Anecdotal structure: Pausch 2004:274. Sex in Suetonius: Gugel 1977:73–95, Baldwin 1983:501–507.

[25] Incoherence: Ramondetti 2000:19. Bloatedness: Gowers 1993:36 on satire and Vitellius' "Shield of Minerva" in Suetonius. Genre: Wallace-Hadrill 1983:8–22 on Suetonian biography as self-consciously "not-history."

[26] Rose 1971:62.

If Rose is right, the episode as a whole would have a parallel in a satiric text. For it is notable that the humor of our episode does not only derive from Lucan's own joke, but also from the reaction of the others in the latrine. The motivation for their flight—hyperbolically cast as a *magna consessorum fuga*—is most obviously to be interpreted as fear at being in any way associated with this dangerously seditious action. However, this reasonable concern is humorously blurred with their implicit desire to escape the terrifying noise and smell of Lucan's defecation, and—if Morford is correct that Nero's simile originally referred to an earthquake[27]—their anxiety at being caught up in the tremor which the very quotation of the hemistich might summon. There may be further humor in crepitation's potential to be ill-omened or even sacrilegious when performed during a religious ritual, as attested by Cato's reference to slaves farting under their rags and Martial's to the repeated offence taken by Jupiter at Aethon's behavior.[28] If the thundering princeps is equated to Jupiter and his presence conjured by quoting this hemistich, then farting in that presence could be taken as sacrilege as well as satire. Since the character's joke is paralleled by that of the narrator, the narrator cannot but be paralleled by the character.[29] On one level, then, the anecdote of Lucan's thunder-box could be seen as a sort of *mise-en-abîme*, embedding Suetonius' own satiric project as an episode in his narrative.

The other possibility (though the two are not mutually exclusive) is that the anecdote in some way derives from Lucan himself. It may be significant that Suetonius immediately proceeds to describe the *famosum carmen* which Lucan composed against Nero and the most powerful of his friends.[30] This allusion to Horace's description of Archilochus' fatal invective against Neobule (*Epist.* 1.19.31) marks the poem as akin to *iambos* rather than *satura*, but the two genres are

---

[27] Morford 1985:2017, citing Sen. *Q Nat.* 6.12–26 and 6.13.5 quoting Virg. *Aen.* 6.256. Cf. Gowers 1995:31n92, Baldwin 2005:317.

[28] Cato *Orat.* 60 Sblendorio Cigusi = Fest. 234.14–20 Marx.; Mart. 12.77, with Jahn 1855:48–50. I am indebted to the anonymous reader for this suggestion.

[29] Humor in Suetonius: Baldwin 1983:511–513.

[30] On the identification of the *famosum carmen*, and the possibility that it is the same as the *De incendio urbis* mentioned by Vacca, see Ahl 1976:333–353 and Champlin 2003:320. Griffin 1984:278n103 and Rudich 1993:277 are skeptical.

closely related, as shown by Persius' use of Hipponactean choliambics for his prologue. It is certainly tempting to see Lucan's composition of a *famosum carmen* as structurally parallel to his satiric act of defecation and crepitation. Though it can never be more than speculation, one wonders whether that libellous poem might also be Suetonius' source for Lucan's thunderous fart.

UNIVERSITY OF SYDNEY

WORKS CITED

Ahl, F. M. 1976. *Lucan: An Introduction.* Ithaca, NY.

Anderson, W. S. 1982. *Essays on Roman Satire.* Princeton.

Anspaugh, K. 1994. "Powers of Ordure: James Joyce and the Excremental Vision(s)." *Mosaic* 27:73–100.

Baldwin, B. 1983. *Suetonius.* Amsterdam.

———. 2005. "Nero the Poet." In *Studies in Latin Literature and Roman History*, ed. C. Deroux, vol. 12 (Collection Latomus 287), 307–318. Brussels.

Bowen, B. C. 2004. "The 'Honorable Art of Farting' in Continental Renaissance Literature." In *Fecal Matters in Early Modern Literature and Art: Studies in Scatology*, ed. J. Persels and R. Ganim, 1–13. Aldershot.

Bramble, J. C. 1974. *Persius and the Programmatic Satire: A Study in Form and Imagery.* Cambridge.

Braund, S. M. 1996. *Juvenal. Satires: Book 1.* Cambridge.

———. 2004. *Juvenal and Persius.* Cambridge, MA.

Champlin, E. 2003. *Nero.* Cambridge, MA.

Clark, J. R. 1974. "Bowl Games: Satire in the Toilet." *Modern Language Studies* 4.2:43–58.

Coffey, M. 1996. "Generic Impropriety in the High Style: Satirical Themes in Seneca and Lucan." In *Satura lanx: Festschrift für Werner A. Krenkel zum 70. Geburtstag*, ed. C. Klodt, 81–93. Hildesheim.

Connors, C. 2005. "Epic Allusion in Roman Satire." In Freudenburg 2005, 123–145.

Courtney, E. 1993. *The Fragmentary Latin Poets.* Oxford.

Cowan, R. 2009. "Starring Nero as Nero: Poetry, Role-Playing and Identity in Juvenal 8.215–21." *Mnemosyne*, 4th ser., 62:76–89.

Dawson, J. 1999. *Who Cut the Cheese?: A Cultural History of the Fart*. Berkeley.

Dewar, M. 1994. "Laying it on with a Trowel: The Proem to Lucan and Related Texts." *Classical Quarterly*, n.s., 44:199–211.

Egan, R. B. 2005. "Making Water Music: A *Double-Entendre* in Aristophanes *Pax* 1265–9." *Classical Quarterly*, n.s., 55:607–609.

Farrell, J. 2009. "The Impermanent Text in Catullus and Other Roman Poets." In *Ancient Literacies: The Culture of Reading in Greece and Rome*, ed. W. A. Johnson and H. N. Parker, 164–185. Oxford.

Freudenburg, K. 2001. *Satires of Rome: Threatening Poses from Lucilius to Juvenal*. Cambridge.

———, ed. 2005. *The Cambridge Companion to Roman Satire*. Cambridge.

Gowers, E. 1993. *The Loaded Table: Representations of Food in Roman Literature*. Oxford.

———. 1995. "The Anatomy of Rome from Capitol to Cloaca." *Journal of Roman Studies* 85:23–32.

———. 2003. "Fragments of Autobiography in Horace *Satires* 1." *Classical Antiquity* 22:55–91.

———. 2005. "The Restless Companion: Horace, *Satires* 1 and 2." In Freudenburg 2005, 48–61.

Greenblatt. S. 1982. "Filthy Rites." *Daedalus* 111.3:1–16.

Griffin, M. T. 1984. *Nero: The End of a Dynasty*. London.

Gugel, H. 1977. *Studien zur biographischen Technik Suetons*. Wiener Studien Beiheft 7. Vienna.

Gunderson, E. 2005. "The Libidinal Rhetoric of Satire." In Freudenburg 2005, 224–240.

Headley, J. M. 1969. *The Complete Works of St. Thomas More*. Vol. 5, Part 1. New Haven, CT.

Henderson, Jeffrey 1991. *The Maculate Muse: Obscene Language in Attic Comedy*. 2nd ed. Oxford (orig. pub. New Haven, CT, 1975).

Henderson, John 1987. "Lucan/The Word at War." *Ramus* 16:122–164.

Hobson, B. 2009. *Latrinae et foricae: Toilets in the Roman World*. London.

Hodge, A. T. 2002. *Roman Aqueducts and Water Supply*. 2nd ed. London (orig. pub. 1992).

Hošek, R. 1962. *Lidovost a lidové motivy u Aristofana*. Prague.

Hudson, N. A. 1989. "Food in Roman Satire." In *Satire and Society in Ancient Rome*, ed. S. Braund, 69–87. Exeter.

Hunink, V. 1993. "Lucan's Praise of Nero." *Papers of the Leeds International Latin Seminar* 7:135–140.

Jahn, O. 1855. "Über den Aberglauben des bösen Blicks bei den Alten." *Berichte über die Verhandlungen der Königlich Sächsischen Gesellschaft der Wissenschaften zu Leipzig, Philologisch-historische Classe* 7:28–110.

Kernan, A. 1959. *The Cankered Muse: Satire of the English Renaissance.* New Haven, CT.

Koster, S. 2001. "Lucilius und die Literarkritik." In *Der Satiriker Lucilius und seine Zeit,* ed. G. Manuwald, 121–131. Munich.

Lelièvre, F. J. 1958. "Juvenal: Two Possible Examples of Wordplay." *Classical Philology* 53:241–242.

Major, W. E. 2002. "Farting for Dollars: A Note on Agyrrhios in Aristophanes *Wealth* 176." *American Journal of Philology* 123:549–557.

Merivale, C. A. 1858. *A History of the Romans under the Empire.* Vol. 6. London.

Miller, P. A. 1998. "The Bodily Grotesque in Roman Satire: Images of Sterility." *Arethusa* 31:257–283.

Morford, M. 1985. "Nero's Patronage and Participation in Literature and the Arts." *Aufstieg und Niedergang der römischen Welt* II.32.3:2003–2031.

Morgan, L. 2004. "Getting the Measure of Heroes: The Dactylic Hexameter and Its Detractors." In *Latin Epic and Didactic Poetry: Genre, Tradition and Individuality,* ed. M. Gale, 1–26. Swansea.

———. 2005. "Satire." In *A Companion to Latin Literature,* ed. S. Harrison, 174–188. Oxford.

Narducci, E. 2002. *Lucano: Un'epica contro l'impero; Interpretazione della Pharsalia.* Rome.

Neudecker, R. 1994. *Die Pracht der Latrine: Zum Wandel öffentlicher Bedürfnisanstalten in der kaiserzeitlichen Stadt.* Munich.

O'Regan, D. 1992. *Rhetoric, Comedy, and the Violence of Language in Aristophanes'* Clouds. Oxford.

Pausch, D. 2004. *Biographie und Bildungskultur: Personendarstellungen bei Plinius dem Jüngeren, Gellius und Sueton.* Berlin.

Persels, J. 1996. "'Straitened in the Bowels,' or Concerning the Rabelaisian Trope of Defecation." *Études Rabelaisiennes* 31:101–112.

———. 2006. "Taking the Piss out of Pantagruel: Urine and Micturition in Rabelais." *Yale French Studies* 110:137–151.

Plaza, M. 2006. *The Function of Humour in Roman Verse Satire: Laughing and Lying*. Oxford.

Plinval, G. de. 1956. "Une insolence de Lucain." *Latomus* 15:512–520.

Ramondetti, P. 2000. *Tiberio nella biografia di Svetonio*. Naples.

Richlin, A. 1992. *The Garden of Priapus: Sexuality and Aggression in Roman Humor*. Rev. ed. Oxford (orig. pub. New Haven, CT, 1983).

Rolfe, J. C. 1998. *Suetonius*. Vol. 2. Rev. ed. G. P. Goold. Cambridge, MA (orig. pub. 1914).

Rose, K. F. C. 1971. *The Date and Author of the Satyricon*. Mnemosyne Suppl. 16. Leiden.

Rudich, V. 1993. *Political Dissidence under Nero: The Price of Dissimulation*. London.

———. 1997. *Dissidence and Literature under Nero: The Price of Rhetoricization*. London.

Schmitz, C. 2000. *Das Satirische in Juvenals Satiren*. Berlin.

Sharland, S. 2003. "Priapus' Magic Marker: Literary Aspects of Horace, Satire 1.8." *Acta Classica* 46:97–109.

Wallace-Hadrill, A. 1983. *Suetonius: The Scholar and His Caesars*. London.

Watson, L. 2005. "Catullan Recycling? *Cacata carta*." *Mnemosyne*, 4th ser., 58:270–277.

Watson, L., and P. Watson. 2003. *Martial. Select Epigrams*. Cambridge.

Waugh, E. 1952. *Men at Arms*. London.

Weston, E. T. 1994. *Lucan the Satirist*. PhD diss. Bryn Mawr College.

Winkler, M. M. 1989. "The Function of Epic in Juvenal's *Satires*." In *Studies in Latin Literature and Roman History*, ed. C. Deroux, vol. 5 (Collection Latomus 206), 414–443. Brussels.

SYMPHOSIUS 93.2

A NEW INTERPRETATION

ERIN SEBO

EACH OF THE ONE HUNDRED DACTYLIC HEXAMETER RIDDLES in the early fifth-century CE *Symphosii Scholastici Aenigmata* by the otherwise unknown Symphosius comes down to us neatly solved by its title. Yet, though the riddles are answered, some of the clues remain enigmatic. In relation to *Miles podagricus* (93) there is considerable debate over the meaning of the soldier's insistence that he once had *quinque pedes*. In the following, I will review this debate and propose my own solution. Here is the riddle:

> Bellipotens olim, saevis metuendus in armis;
> quinque pedes habui, quod numquam nemo negavit.
> Nunc mihi vix duo sunt; inopem me copia fecit.[1]

> Once valiant in war, to be feared amongst savage weapons,
> I had five feet, which none ever denied.
> Now I have barely two; plenty has made me poor.

On the crucial point of how many feet are indicated at line 2, the manuscript tradition is split between the D recension, which reads *quinque*, and the B recension, which reads *sex*. The latter is unmetrical. However, because it is found in the earliest extant manuscript, Paris BN lat. 10318,[2] it was preferred by early editors, including Glorie, who

---

I am indebted to Gavin Betts and Shona Nolan for their comments on an earlier version of this note.

[1] I am using Bergamin's edition of the *Aenigmata* (Bergamin 2005). All translations are my own.

[2] Also known as the Codex Salmasianus. It probably dates from the late eighth or early ninth century and so post-dates Symphosius by four centuries. See Spallone 1982.

emended it to *sex qui*, and Perionius and Pithou, who emended it to *sexque* to correct the scansion. There is now a consensus, supported by Shackleton Bailey and Bergamin, that the reading of the more reliable D recension, *quinque*, is correct.[3]

Still, it is not clear to what the line refers. The most popular of the various solutions—the one first proposed by Castalio—is that the "five feet" refers to the height requirement for soldiers in the Roman army.[4] However, this suggestion is problematic, because the minimum height for soldiers in the Roman army was always greater than five feet. According to the fifth-century military writer Vegetius,[5] during the Republic and early Empire it was *VI pedum vel certe V et X unciarum* (*Mil.* 1.5.1, "six feet or at least five feet and ten inches").[6] Even after the reduction of the height requirements recorded in 367 CE, it was greater than five feet: *in quinque pedibus et septem unciis usualibus delectus habeatur* (*Codex Theodosianus* 7.13.3, "a chosen man shall be five feet seven inches in the common measure"). This problem cannot be addressed by reading "six feet" rather than "five feet," since Symphosius was almost certainly writing after 367 CE, when the height requirement was considerably less than six feet.[7]

Shackleton Bailey proposes a different solution. He emends the line to *quinque pedes habui bis, numquam nemo negavit*[8] ("no one ever denied I had twice five feet") and takes the "twice five feet" to refer to the *decempeda*, a ten-foot measuring pole used by surveyors, both civil and military. This solution is unsatisfactory because, even in the military context, surveying is an unbellicose activity. In claiming that he was *saevis metuendus in armis* (93.1, "to be feared amongst savage weapons"), the old soldier is boasting of his erstwhile military prowess, and it is unlikely that he would cap this boast by stating that he once

---

[3]   Shackleton Bailey 1979:41 and Bergamin 2005:194.

[4]   Bergamin 2005:194.

[5]   Vegetius' *Epitoma rei militaris* was written between 387 and 450 CE; see Barnes 1979.

[6]   Phang (2007:288) suggests that Vegetius—our only source on this and many other aspects of the Roman military—may well be idealizing here. Idealized or not, Vegetius' comment suggests that height was a prized attribute for a soldier in late antiquity.

[7]   There is a growing scholarly consensus that the *Aenigmata* belongs to the fifth century: Bergamin 2005:xiv and Ohl 1928:15.

[8]   Shackleton Bailey 1979:41.

held the *decempeda*. On the contrary: amongst Augustus' punishments for soldiers, Suetonius lists the humiliation of being made to stand all day in front of the general's tent, holding a *decempeda* instead of the soldier's customary weapons (Suet. *Aug.* 24. 2).[9] Shackleton Bailey's emendation therefore does not solve the riddle.

I would like to propose a new solution: that the "five feet" refers to the soldier's own two feet in addition to the three feet of battle line occupied by each man. Vegetius, Symphosius' contemporary, who gives a detailed account of the spacing of infantrymen, tells us that each was allowed three feet of frontage ("Singuli autem armati in directum ternos pedes inter se occupare consuerunt," Veg. *Mil.* 3.14.6). There is some debate as to whether this spacing reflects the preference of the later Empire,[10] since our only other source, the Hellenistic historian Polybius, claims that while each Roman infantryman occupied a space of three feet, a looser formation in which each man had six feet of frontage had to be adopted in order for them to fight effectively.

> ἵστανται μὲν οὖν ἐν τρισὶ ποσὶ μετὰ τῶν ὅπλων καὶ
> Ῥωμαῖοι· τῆς μάχης δ᾽ αὐτοῖς κατ᾽ ἄνδρα τὴν κίνησιν
> λαμβανούσης διὰ τὸ τῷ μὲν θυρεῷ σκέπειν τὸ σῶμα,
> συμμετατιθεμένους αἰεὶ πρὸς τὸν τῆς πληγῆς καιρόν, τῇ
> μαχαίρᾳ δ᾽ ἐκ καταφορᾶς καὶ διαιρέσεως ποιεῖσθαι τὴν
> μάχην, προφανὲς ὅτι χάλασμα καὶ διάστασιν ἀλλήλων
> ἔχειν δεήσει τοὺς ἄνδρας ἐλάχιστον τρεῖς πόδας κατ᾽
> ἐπιστάτην καὶ κατὰ παραστάτην, εἰ μέλλουσιν εὐχρηστεῖν
> πρὸς τὸ δέον.

Polyb. 18.30.6–8.[11]

---

[9] Suetonius, commending Augustus for the ruthless discipline that he imposed on the army, places this punishment after decimation and execution, which, being capital, are clearly more severe penalties. Nevertheless, to appear in Suetonius' list at all, the humiliation that it entailed must have been significant.

[10] Phang (2008:55) suggests that this close order "was a preference of Vegetius' later Empire, displaying archaizing Greek influences."

[11] For the larger context, a comparison between the Greek phalanx and the Roman legion (Polyb. 18.29–32), see the translation and explanatory note at Campbell 2004:28–31.

This apparent discrepancy raises a number of interesting questions for military historians,[12] but in terms of Symphosius' riddle Polybius' comments only confirm the strength of what was, by Symphosius' time, a long-standing identification between the soldier and the three feet he occupied when fully armed. The pun on *pedes* must have seemed an obvious one to Symphosius: the phrase is used by both Vegetius (*ternos pedes*, "three feet each") and (repeatedly) by Polybius (18.30.6, ἐν τρισὶ ποσί and 14.30.8, τρεῖς πόδας, "three feet"). Moreover, these three feet defined a soldier's duty. Part of the art and mark of being a good soldier in the later Roman Empire was the discipline to hold a formation with the correct spacing and so "maintain distinct battle lines."[13] Indeed, the assumption that formations will be held with absolute precision underpins all Roman military thinking and strategy of the period.

My reading of *Miles podagricus* brings it into line with the riddles on either side of it—an important consideration, given that Symphosius carefully ordered the riddles of the *Aenigmata* so that those with similar themes, images, concerns, or riddling strategies were grouped together.[14] *Miles podagricus* is framed by *Mulier quae geminos pariebat* (92) and *Luscus alium vendens* (94), both of which belong to a particular kind of riddle in which the riddle subject is described as possessing the attributes of whatever is associated with him.[15] Thus the woman in labor with twins (92) claims to have three souls, a claim she can make by counting the souls of her unborn children as her own, and the garlic seller (94) is described as having thousands of heads, because the garlic heads are attributed to him. This riddling strategy was common in the ancient world. Indeed, it is at the heart of the most famous ancient riddle, the riddle the Sphinx asks Oedipus: a human only goes on "three legs" if the object in his possession, the walking stick, is counted as a third "leg."[16] Crucially, in all these examples, the riddle derives its ambi-

---

[12] Several historians dispute Polybius' reckoning of six feet, for example, Daly 2002:159–160 and Sabin 2000.

[13] Phang 2008:55.

[14] Bergamin 2005:xxxii.

[15] Bergamin 2005:194.

[16] The earliest known version of this riddle is found in Asklepiades (fr. 21b 4–8): see Gantz 1993:496.

guity from the fact that the attribute is something the riddle subject has already—the woman's soul, the garlic seller's head, and Oedipus' legs—and, even more crucially, that these are counted in the final total. Indeed, in the case of the garlic seller where the number is not specified—there are *milia multa* ("many thousands") of heads—Symphosius goes out of his way to refer to the seller's own head by mentioning his eye. The solutions proposed by Bergamin and Shackleton Bailey which depend on the soldier's own feet being counted at line 3 but not in his original statement at line 2 contravene this convention of "riddle logic" and ought to be dismissed on that count alone.

Trinity College, Dublin

WORKS CITED

Barnes, T. D. 1979. "The Date of Vegetius." *Phoenix* 33:254–257.

Bergamin, M. 2005. *Aenigmata Symposii: La fondazione dell'enigmistica come genere poetico.* Florence.

Campbell, B. 2004. *Greek and Roman Military Writers: Selected Readings.* Abingdon.

Castalio, I. 1607. *Aenigmata Symposii poetae veteris: Cum scholiis auctioribus Iosephi Castalionis I. C. Romani; Elogiisque doctissimorum virorum de Symposio.* Rome.

Daly, G. 2002. *Cannae: The Experience of Battle in the Second Punic War.* London.

Gantz, T. 1993. *Early Greek Myth: A Guide to Literary and Artistic Sources.* Baltimore.

Glorie, F. 1968. *Variae collectiones aenigmatum Merovingiacae aetatis.* Turnholt.

Ohl, R. T. 1928. *The Enigmas of Symphosius.* Philadelphia.

Perionius (= Périon, J.). 1533. *Symphosii veteris poetae elegantissimi erudita iuxta ac arguta et festiua Aenigmata, nunc primum et inuenta et excusa: Accesserunt septem Graeciae sapientum sententiae, multo quam antehac emendatiores, et uersibus etiam aliquot auctiores.* Paris.

Phang, S. E. 2007. "Military Documents, Languages, and Literature." In *A Companion to the Roman Army*, ed. P. Erdkamp, 286–305. Oxford.

———. 2008. *Roman Military Service: Ideologies of Discipline in the Late Republic and Early Principate.* Cambridge.

Pithou, P. 1590. *Epigrammata et poematia vetera: Quorum pleraque nunc primum ex antiquis codicibus et lapidibus alia sparsim antehac errantia, iam undecumque collecta emendatiora eduntur.* Paris.

Sabin, P. 2000. "The Face of Roman Battle." *Journal of Roman Studies* 90:1–17.

Shackleton Bailey, D. R. 1979. *Towards a Text of "Anthologia Latina."* Cambridge.

Spallone, M. 1982. "Il Par. Lat 10318 (Salmasiano): Dal manoscritto altomedievale ad una raccolta enciclopedica tardo-antica." *Italia medioevale e umanistica* 25:1–71.

IMAGINARY ATHLETICS
IN TWO FOLLOWERS OF JOHN CHRYSOSTOM

CHRISTOPHER P. JONES

SCHOLARS OF ANCIENT ATHLETICS have devoted many excellent studies to *realia*, but have given somewhat less attention to "imaginary athletics," the athletics of simile and metaphor. By contrast, those with a primary interest in Jewish and Christian literature have long been interested in their authors' use of athletic imagery to convey moral and religious lessons.[1] The relation between reality and reflection, object and image, raises its own questions. What use can be made of these athletic images to recover ancient practice (since athletics not only changed with time but also differed from place to place)? How far are authors who use such images relying on their own experience, as opposed to concepts derived from their reading or plucked out of the air of shared culture? This question is particularly acute for Jewish and Christian authors who condemn participation in pagan events. For Christian writers the way was shown by the apostle Paul, who more than once draws on athletics to make his arguments.[2] The present article begins with an example in which the foremost preacher of the late fourth and early fifth centuries, John Chrysostom, exploits and develops an athletic image used by Paul; it then considers two authors closely connected with Chrysostom who similarly employ extended

---

I owe several suggestions and improvements to Glen Bowersock, Nathaniel Andrade, and the referee for *HSCP*.

[1] On athletic metaphor see now König 2005:132–139, "Athletics and Philosophical Virtue," with bibliography. For Jewish and Christian authors, e.g. Pfitzner 1967 (Paul); Harris 1976:51–91 (Philo); Sawhill 1928; Kertsch 1995; Kertsch 1999 (John Chrysostom).

[2] Important passages include 1 Cor. 4:9, 9:24–27; Gal. 2:2; Phil. 2:16, 3:13–14; 1 Tim. 4:7–10; 2 Tim. 2:5 (problems of authorship are not relevant to the present topic).

athletic metaphors; I end with some questions about the survival of traditional athletics in Late Antiquity.

In First Corinthians (4:9), Paul says: "God has made us apostles the most abject of people, like men condemned to death, since we have become a spectacle to the universe, both to angels and to humans" (ὁ θεὸς ἡμᾶς τοὺς ἀποστόλους ἐσχάτους ἀπέδειξεν ὡς ἐπιθανατίους, ὅτι θέατρον ἐγενήθημεν τῷ κόσμῳ καὶ ἀγγέλοις καὶ ἀνθρώποις). Chrysostom, preparing catechumens for baptism, expands this comparison as follows: "The time before this was a place of training and exercise (παλαίστρα καὶ γυμνάσιον), and our falls were pardonable. From this day forward the arena is open, the contest awaits, the audience is seated above, not only the human race but the multitude of the angels watches our struggles" (τὸ στάδιον ἀνέῳγεν, ὁ ἀγὼν ἐφέστηκε, τὸ θέατρον ἄνω κάθηται, οὐκ ἀνθρώπων φύσις μόνον ἀλλὰ καὶ ἀγγέλων δῆμος θεωρεῖ τὰ παλαίσματα). Paul goes on to explain his metaphor of Christians as "a spectacle to the universe" as follows: "The angels therefore are the spectators, the Master of the angels is the agonothete (ὁ τῶν ἀγγέλων δεσπότης ἀγωνοθετεῖ). This is not only an honor but also a security, for when the very one who gave his life for us judges our struggles (κρίνῃ τὰ παλαίσματα), what an honor that is! How great a security!"[3]

Martin Wallraff has recently produced an edition, with an Italian translation by Cristina Ricci, of an encomium on Chrysostom.[4] The work takes the form of a speech delivered in or near Constantinople soon after the saint's death in 407; there can be no telling how far it represents a text actually spoken, though it gives the impression of a high degree of orality. Four of the five manuscripts ascribe it to Martyrius, the bishop of Antioch from 459 to 471 or later, but he can hardly be the real author, and here he will be designated [Martyrius]. He writes in a classical style, with the use of the optative, Attic double tau, and "apodotic" δέ, and negotiates long and complex sentences without losing the syntactical thread. He several times uses athletic

---

[3]   1 Cor. 4:9; Chrys. *Huit catéch. bapt.* 3.8, SC 50.155.

[4]   Wallraff and Ricci 2007. See also Barnes 2001, though I do not accept all his conclusions.

imagery, notably in two long passages that make the work of interest to historians of ancient society and sport, though the first of them presents difficulties of text and interpretation.[5]

The background of the speech is as follows. Chrysostom was forced out of his position as patriarch of Constantinople by a coalition of his enemies, including the empress Eudoxia and Theophilus, the patriarch of Alexandria, in August 403. He was recalled because of popular outcry, then banished to the obscure Cucusos in the Taurus in 404; banished in 407 to a place even more remote, Pityus on the northeastern shore of the Pontus, he died on the way near Pontic Comana.[6] The speech, after an exordium (chs. 1–5), narrates Chrysostom's life in chronological order, with a number of long metaphors and digressions, for example on the Arian persecution of Athanasius (chs. 99–100).

In the first passage (ch. 22), [Martyrius] describes Chrysostom's tireless activity on behalf of his see of Constantinople, hinting only indirectly at the offense he gave by appearing meddlesome and overzealous. He then introduces a long athletic metaphor which seems intended to justify his hero's vigor by comparing him to an athlete who defeats all his competitors. Wallraff prints the passage as follows:

καὶ καθάπερ ἀθλητὴς ἄριστος ἐπὶ τὸν ἐξ Ὀλυμπίων
ἐληλυθὼς στέφανον, θαρρῶν τῇ τε τῶν μελῶν εὐεξίᾳ
καὶ τῇ περὶ τὴν πάλην ἐμπειρίᾳ, τὸν τῶν ἀγώνων ὑποβὰς
νόμον (ὁ δέ ἐστι τὸν κλῆρον ἀναμένειν διαιροῦντα
τοὺς ἀντιπάλους ἀλλήλοις) καί, τῶν προτέρων ὑπ'
ἀλλήλων καταβληθέντων ἐν ἑκάστῳ τῶν κλήρων, τὸν
καὶ τελευταῖον ὑπολειφθέντα καταγωνισάμενος οὕτω
λαμβάνει τὸν στέφανον,—αὐτὸς διά τε τὸ πλειόνως
ὀρέγεσθαι τῆς δόξης καὶ τῷ θαρρεῖν, ὅπερ ἔφθην εἰπών,
ἑαυτῷ καὶ ἑαυτὸν κατατάττοι τῷ κλήρῳ, μόνος τὸν πρὸς

---

[5]   Other passages not considered here are ch. 83, God re-opened the arena (στάδιον) so that the Devil could fight against Chrysostom; ch. 107, God lengthened the δίαυλος so as to make Chrysostom's crown more glorious.

[6]   Chrysostom: full and informative article by Brändle and Jegher-Bucher 1998; in English, Kelly 1995. For Cucusos, formerly in Cappadocia but since 371/372 in Armenia Secunda, Kelly 1995:254, *Barrington Atlas* 64 C 4; for Pityus, in modern Abkhazia, Kelly 1995:257–260, *Barrington Atlas* 87 F 1.

ἅπαντας ἀναδεχόμενος ἀγῶνα, ὡς ἂν καὶ μόνος τὴν
ἀπὸ τοῦ στεφάνου κληρονομήσοι δόξαν, μηδενὸς τῶν
καταβληθέντων ἔχοντος εἰπεῖν, ὡς ἄρα αὐτῷ συμβέβληταί
τι διὰ τῶν οἰκείων πόνων πρὸς τὴν ἀπὸ τοῦ στεφάνου τε
καὶ τῆς ἀναρρήσεως εὐδοκιμίαν—οὕτω δὴ καὶ ὁ θαυμάσιος
οὗτος, καίτοι τῶν ἄλλων μᾶλλον ἐπιστάμενος, ὡς ἄρα
ἐν ἐκκλησίᾳ οἱ μὲν ποιμαίνειν, οἱ δὲ διδάσκειν, οἱ δὲ
κυβερνᾶν, οἱ δὲ ἀντιλαμβάνεσθαι ἔλαχον, οὗτος τὰ ἐκ
πάντων ἑαυτῷ συντιθεὶς καὶ ἀποθησαυρίζων βραβεῖα,
διὰ πάντων ἵετο τῇ τε οἰκείᾳ σοφίᾳ καὶ τῇ τοῦ πνεύματος
τεθαρρηκὼς ἐνεργείᾳ.

Ricci renders the first part of this as follows:

E [Giovanni si comportava così:] come un ottimo atleta,
venuto per la corona delle gare olimpiche, confidente sia
nella prestanza delle sue membra sia nella sua esperienza
nella lotta [agonistica], si è sottomesso al regolamento
delle gare (e questo consiste nell'aspettare il sorteggio
che suddivide gli antagonisti [mettendo] gli uni contro gli
altri) e, mentre i primi sono sconfitti gli uni dagli altri in
ciascuno dei tiri a sorte, egli prevale anche contro l'ultimo
rimasto e così prende la corona; e lui stesso, poiché tende
alla gloria più del normale e, così che ho detto prima,
confida in sé, magari sostituirebbe se stesso alla sorte,
assumendosi da solo la lotta contro tutti, per poter otte-
nere da solo anche la gloria proveniente dalla corona, così
nessuno degli sconfitti avrebbe da dire di aver dato, con
gli sforzi personali, un qualche contributo a costui in vista
dell'onore derivante dalla corona e dalla proclamazione
pubblica [del vincitore].

This translation produces an illogicality. The use of the lot in
ancient athletics, at least before Late Antiquity, is known especially
from Lucian and a number of other authors, as well as from coins
and inscriptions. Its function was to pair off contestants one against
the other in the "heavy" sports of wrestling, boxing, and the pancration. Pairs of small stones marked alpha, beta, and so on through the

alphabet, making a total equal to the number of contestants, were placed in an urn, the contestants each drew one, and each of them was matched against the one who drew the same letter; if there was an uneven number of contestants, one unpaired stone was added, and the contestant who drew it received a "bye," and was called a "by-sitter" (*ephedros*); it is usually assumed that, if there was still an odd number of pairs in a later round, as could happen for example with an initial field of nine entrants ($[2 \times 4] + 1 = 9 \rightarrow [2 \times 2] + 1 = 5 \rightarrow 2 + 1 = 3$), the previous *ephedros* would be included in any subsequent drawing, and would only draw another bye by sheer luck.[7] With the text of Wallraff, the imagined athlete submits to the rule of having his name included in the lot, but gets a bye until the very end, when he defeats the last victor to emerge from the elimination process; he then undertakes to fight each of the contestants individually, in order that none of them can say that they have contributed to his victory by defeating their opponents in the previous rounds. A secondary problem is that Wallraff's text makes καί the first word after the parenthesis, thus in effect disguising the syntactical break.

A solution of the textual problem, even if it does not solve all the questions of the author's intention, is to read καταγωνισάμενον οὕτω λαμβάνειν with manuscript M (instead of καταγωνισάμενος οὕτω λαμβάνει), and to close the parenthesis at τὸν στέφανον rather than at ἀλλήλοις. I would translate the whole chapter thus:

> As an excellent athlete, having come in quest of the crown of Olympia, confident in his bodily fitness[8] and skill in wrestling, subjecting himself to the rule of the contest (and this is to submit to[9] the lot that separates the competitors from [i.e. matches them up against] each other and,

---

[7]   On the lot and the *ephedros*, Gardiner 1905:16–18; Jüthner 1905; Robert 1949b:106–112. The principal text is Lucian *Hermot.* 40–42.

[8]   εὐεξία: on this term, Crowther 1991a.

[9]   ἀναμένειν: Ritti translates 'aspettare', but since the corresponding phrase is ἑαυτὸν κατατάττοι, ἀναμένειν seems rather to mean 'be patient under', 'submit to.' Cf. the contemporary Palladius *Dialogus de vita Ioannis Chrysostomi* 8.235–236 (SC 341:178), ἀνεπίσχετον γὰρ τὸ δαιμονιῶδες ὅρμημα, οὐκ ἀναμένον σκέψιν, where Malingrey (1988) translates: "on ne peut arrêter l'élan du démon, il ne veut rien savoir."

when the previous ones have been floored by each other in each of the rounds, by defeating the last one left, thus to win the crown), he [our imagined athlete], because he aims at glory more than others and trusts in himself, as I have already said, subjects himself to the lot, alone undertaking the contest with everyone, so that alone he may inherit the glory of the crown, with none of those defeated being able to say that he contributed something by his own efforts towards the glory of the crown and the proclamation: so this wondrous man, though understanding more than all others that some in the church are assigned the task of shepherding, some of teaching, some of government, others of protection (?),[10] he, collecting for himself from all and storing away these prizes,[11] bypassed all of them by his own wisdom and trusting in the power of the Spirit.

It appears that [Martyrius] means the words, "alone undertaking the contest with everyone, so that alone he may inherit the glory of the crown," to indicate, not that the athlete undertakes to fight all the other entrants (since that would nullify the purpose of the lot): rather, that he "alone" both submits to the usual selection-process and emerges as the overall victor. The assertion that "none of those defeated [could] say that he contributed" to the athlete's victory need not imply that no one has been eliminated before the final, but only that the athlete has defeated all those against whom he was matched. Hagiographers not uncommonly claim surpassing sanctity for their heroes, and that may be [Martyrius'] meaning too, though he may be hinting at such adversaries of Chrysostom as Theophilus of Alexandria.[12]

---

[10] ἀντιλαμβάνεσθαι: Danker 2000:89 s.v. ἀντιλαμβάνω.

[11] For this sense of βραβεῖον, frequent in Christian texts after 1 Cor. 9:24, Danker 2000:183 s.v.; Lampe 1961:304 s.v.; Robert 1982:263–265 = *OMS* 5:826–828; the definition in LSJ s.v. II, 'wand, baton, given as a prize', is erroneous.

[12] Theophilus: Löhr 2002. For his role in Chrysostom's fall, references in Malingrey 1988:129–130. The author might also be thinking of some connection between κλῆρος in two senses, 'lot' and the Christian sense (LSJ s.v. III; Lampe 1961:757 s.v. 3) of 'clergy'.

That leads to a second question, the author's reference to "the crown from Olympia" (τὸν ἐξ 'Ολυμπίων ... στέφανον). At first sight this seems to imply a crown brought from the traditional site of the Olympics, Elis in the Peloponnese. That is not impossible, since the often-repeated statement that Theodosius I ended these Olympics in 393 has no basis in fact: there is some evidence that it was his grandson, Theodosius II.[13] But since the author in his second simile talks of a benefactor putting on a "spectacle of Olympic contests" (θέαν ... 'Ολυμπιακῶν ἀγώνων, 29), the phrase ἐξ 'Ολυμπίων may simply mean "deriving from." In later Greek the adjective *Olympikos*, as also the Latin *Olympicus*, tends to lose its association with the Olympia of Elis and to refer to important contests, or even to athletics generally.[14]

The second passage (chs. 29–30) occurs in the narration of Chrysostom's episcopate in Constantinople, when the author describes the formation of a conspiracy against him. By [Martyrius'] account, the true adversary was the Devil, who used Theophilus and others as his agents (s. 36): for the benefit of the angels, God wished to arrange a spectacle in which John, the spiritual champion, wrestled his fearsome adversary to the ground. The passage does not raise the same textual problems, and I begin with a translation, only giving the Greek terms that are relevant to the following discussion.

> Well, then, come, let us examine together, sir, whether constant tranquillity is always necessary or not. I ask you: suppose that there was once a rich man in a great city, called "Father of the People" by all, and (suppose that) later, moved by an overwhelming (impulse of) generosity (φιλοτιμία), he was also to promise the people to establish a spectacle of Olympic Games (θέα ... 'Ολυμπικῶν ἀγώνων), and was to send out much money to collect athletes; and when they had assembled he was to set over them an excellent trainer (παιδοτρίβης) practised in every kind

---

[13] See the excellent study of Weiler 2004.

[14] For this weak sense of ἐκ (ἐξ) see e.g. Danker 2000:296 s.v. ἐκ 3 c. 'Ολυμπικός: Lampe 1961 s.v. cites *Const. Apol.* 8.32.9 (SC 336:238), where Metzger translates 'athlète'. See further below, on John Cassian.

of wrestling (πάλη), and was to spare no expense on the nourishment (δίαιτα) that fed their bodies together with fitness (εὐεξία); and (suppose that) he made[15] the spectators themselves arbiters of the choice of antagonists; then, when they had chosen some barbarian who displayed a savage body and appearance, (and was) destined to defeat many competitors, being superior to them not through *his* strength but through *their* negligence, and yet destined to lose to many more of them through his cowardice and lack of technique, and when the time came, and the barbarian stripped (ἀποδυσάμενος) in the middle of the wrestling-ground (σκάμμα)[16] and denounced the benefactor (φιλότιμος) and challenged the athletes—would you then have wished the president of the contest (ἀγωνοθέτης), tell me, fearing the defeat of some, to dismiss those of exceptional bravery without a crown, and so waste the glory of the agonothete and the athletes together because of those who had not spent the past time as they should, and not given themselves over to the expertise of the trainer? I do not think so, for such an idea is full both of injustice and senselessness. (30) Well, then, follow the idea with me from the image to the truth, and you will see that the permission [given by God to the Devil to persecute John] is much more just and necessary. For consider: God, (though) being the most fearsome Master of All, takes pleasure in being called the Father of All because of his love of mankind, and has not ceased for all eternity from bestowing (φιλοτιμούμενος) many great things, surpassing all thought, on our nature. For he created the universe, having no motive for his creation other than his own goodness and our need. And he loves the angels, using them for the service of saving those who inherit the promise, but

---

[15] Wallraff follows the manuscripts in reading ποιεῖ, but the syntax requires an optative, ποιοῖ or ποιοίη, which could easily have been corrupted by itacism.

[16] For this term, properly denoting a patch of soil loosened for jumping, wrestling, etc., Jüthner 1927.

he hates the Devil who envies and wastes away over the prosperity of our race, seeing clay (i.e. humanity) in good repute with the Master, and it (i.e. humanity) being raised on high, while *he* is debased so far below his previous rank. He [God] has promised the angels from his great generosity (φιλοτιμία) to show him (the Devil) being defeated and floored (καταγωνιζόμενός τε καὶ καταβαλλόμενος) by this clay, him (the Devil) who is bodiless, swift, full of craft, and brimming with pride. He has collected many athletes, paying as the price the blood of the Firstborn, given them the pledge (ἀρραβών) of the Spirit,[17] [and] set aside nourishment (δίαιτα) for them inaccessible even to the angels.[18] As well as everything else, he set over them an excellent trainer for these purposes—this saint (i.e. Chrysostom).

The germ of this passage lies in the same passage of First Corinthians that Chrysostom developed in the *Baptismal Catechesis* quoted above. In [Martyrius'] treatment, two things deserve special note: the precision of his language, and the care with which he has worked out the relationship between the simile and its correlate in actuality. To begin with the first, he uses φιλότιμος and its cognates φιλοτιμία and φιλοτιμέομαι without any sense of "ambition" or "striving for honor," but in a sense well known in later Greek, "eagerly generous," or when used as a substantive "one who eagerly displays his generosity" by gifts to the public, so that it can be equivalent to the Latin *munerarius*.[19] The custom of calling such benefactors "Father" or "Mother of the City" goes back to the imperial period, and in Late Antiquity the "Father of the City" (πατὴρ τῆς πόλεως) is an important civic official, but I have found no other example of "Father of the People," though it might well have been used.[20]

---

[17] Borrowed from 2 Cor. 1:22: cf. Danker 2000:134 s.v. ἀρραβών. There does not seem to be any equivalent in ancient athletics.

[18] As Wallraff notes, the Eucharist: cf. ch. 94.

[19] For φιλότιμος and its cognates in the context of spectacles, Robert 1940:276–280.

[20] On such family terms in expressions of group identity, Harland 2007; in inscriptions the nearest parallel I have found is "Son of the People" (υἱὸς τοῦ δήμου) in three inscriptions of southwestern Caria: *Ilasos* 84.5–6 (υἱὸν / Δήμου), 616.3 (υἱὸν Δήμου), and

The tendency of benefactors to spend lavishly on their shows is too well attested to need much illustration, but the present passage is especially reminiscent of one in Dio Chrysostom's first diatribe on fame (δόξα). The lover of fame, says Dio, must not only provide a lavish meal for the populace, but "must collect flute-players and mimes and harpists and jugglers and, more than that, pugilists and pancratiasts and wrestlers and runners and all that tribe—at least unless he intends to entertain the mob in a cheap and beggarly manner ... [He has to seek] some Amoebeus or Polus [respectively a famous singer and actor] or hire some Olympic victor for a fee of five talents." An Oxyrhynchus papyrus of about 273 shows a gymnasiarch engaging a charioteer to compete in the city's forthcoming Capitoline Games.[21]

The author's image of a barbarian who deters the less stalwart of the contestants merely by stripping (ἀποδυσάμενος) recalls another known feature of ancient athletics. Inscriptions and coin-images show that certain athletes renowned for their strength and (perhaps) their ferocity could deter their competitors before the first drawing of the lots or later. An athlete at Pisidian Antioch claims that "when he stripped, his antagonists declined (to fight) him" (ὃν ἀποδυσάμενον παρῃτή[σ]αντο οἱ ἀντ[αγ]ωνισταί). Louis Robert has argued that the same circumstance lies behind those inscriptions that speak of athletes "stopping" (στῆσαι) their opponents: thus a great pancratiast of the later second century, M. Aurelius Asclepiades, says several times in his long inscription at Rome that he "stopped" his competitors, sometimes adding "after the first" or "second" lot.[22]

While Asclepiades was a pancratiast, the author imagines his athlete as a wrestler (πάλη). This was one of the three "heavy" categories of athletics together with boxing and the pancration, and, presumably because it was the least brutal and bloody of the three, was one

---

IKeramos 62.1–2 (δήμου / [υἱόν]). For "Father of the City" (πατὴρ τῆς πόλεως) as a civic title in Late Antiquity, Roueché 1979, Dagron and Feissel 1987:215–220.

[21] Dio Chrys. *Or.* 66.8, 66.11, tr. Crosby 1951:97, 99. On the practice of collecting entertainers and athletes, Robert 1930:115–116 = 1969:663–664, citing this passage. Papyrus: *P. Oxy.* 43.3135.

[22] For this explanation of στῆσαι, Robert 1949b:106–110, esp. 110 on the inscription of Antioch published by Anderson 1913:287 no. 12; Moretti 1957:234.

of the categories that Byzantine society, including church councils, continued to permit.[23] It also had the recommendation of being sanctioned by Scripture: in the Septuagint version, Jacob "wrestled" with the angel, and Paul similarly talks of "wrestling" with the powers of evil. Chrysostom expands this metaphor in one of his baptismal catecheses: "Therefore let us learn to overcome the wicked demon now, for we are about to strip (ἀποδύεσθαι) against him after baptism, and to box and fight against him. Let us therefore learn his holds (λαβαί), how wicked he is, how easily he can injure us, so that when the contests (ἀγῶνες) begin we may not feel out of place or be disturbed at the novel sight of wrestling-matches (παλαίσματα), but after having first practiced among ourselves and learned all his tricks, we may with confidence set about wrestling with him." Chrysostom's contemporary, Augustine of Hippo, in his sermon *Against the Pagans* compares Cyprian of Carthage, now in heaven, to an agonothete (*agonotheta*) who "not only watches (the faithful) wrestling but also helps them as they persevere" (*non solum spectat luctantes sed et adiuuat perdurantes*). Since agonothetes did not in real life intervene to help competitors, Augustine has somewhat stretched his simile.[24]

The reference to a trainer who exercises the athletes before the actual contest also has its correlate in reality, since it was a feature of the Olympics of Elis that entrants were required to train for thirty days before the actual event.[25] Philostratus makes Apollonius of Tyana give an "Olympic announcement" to his followers, and uses some expressions that recur in [Martyrius]: "If you have trained in a way worthy of your coming to Olympia, and have done nothing lazy (ῥᾴθυμον) or dishonorable, proceed with confidence (θαρροῦντες). But those of you who have not trained in this way may go wherever you please." Chrysostom is the only other author who refers to this thirty-day training-period, comparing the thirty days in which the catechumen awaits baptism to the regime of secular athletes: "thus, in your case

---

[23] Karpozilos and Cutler 1991.

[24] LXX Gen. 32:24; Eph. 6:12, cf. Pfitzner 1967:48–49. Chrysostom: *Trois catéch. bapt.* 1.16, SC 366:144–147 = Migne *PG* 49:228. Augustine: *Tractatus contra paganos* 3 (Dolbeau 1996:369).

[25] Crowther 1991b.

too, these thirty days are like a kind of wrestling, gymnasia, and practice (μελέτη)," again developing an image used by Paul.[26]

[Martyrius], a close follower of Chrysostom, had perhaps learned from him the art of fitting simile to *comparandum*, since this passage displays a series of such antitheses. The eager benefactor (φιλότιμος) is called "Father of the People" as God takes pleasure in being called "Father of All." The benefactor acts as president of the contest (ἀγωνοθέτης) and entertains the crowd by putting on an Olympic spectacle; God in his zealous generosity (φιλοτιμία) is a celestial ἀγωνοθέτης, and entertains the angelic audience with the spectacle of a contest between the clay of humanity and Satan. Many of the athlete's competitors, having failed to train properly, shrink from a barbarian, fearful in appearance; God has pitted his champion against the wiliest of opponents, Satan.[27] The secular benefactor nourishes his athletes with a special diet; God nourishes his athletes with the diet of the Eucharist. The benefactor sets the best of trainers over the athletes; God has appointed Chrysostom as the trainer of those in his care.

Another follower of Chrysostom uses a long athletic comparison that in several ways resembles that of [Martyrius]. John Cassian (Cassianus) was born about 360 in the Dobrudja, and after spending several years in Palestine and Egypt came to Constantinople, where Chrysostom ordained him deacon. After Chrysostom's deposition in 402, he traveled to Rome, and thence to Massilia, where he founded a monastery on the Egyptian model. The fifth book of his *De institutis coenobiorum* is devoted to the sin of gluttony, and in the twelfth chapter he takes as his text a verse of Paul's Second Letter to Timothy (2 Tim. 2:5), "one who contends in a contest is not crowned unless he has competed according to the rules" (*qui in agone contendit, non coronatur nisi legitime certauerit*). Cassian explains:

---

[26] Philostratus *Vita Apollonii* 5.43.2 (Jones 2005: vol. 2, 91); Chrys. *Trois catéch. bapt. 1.16*, SC 366:144–145) = Migne *PG* 49:228; 1 Cor. 9:25.

[27] Cf. Perpetua's dream of defeating Satan in the form of "some ugly-looking Egyptian" (*Pass. perp.* 10, Αἰγύπτιός τις ἄμορφος τῷ σχήματι), with the comments of Robert 1982:272–273 = 1989:835–836.

In those contests, which according to the same Apostle offer a "corruptible crown" to the winners, this practice is observed: one who strives to prepare himself for the crown that is glorious and is distinguished by the privilege of immunity (*immunitatis priuilegio decoratam*) must first display the nature of his young strength and the force of his training in Olympic and Pythian contests (*in Olympiacis et Pythiis certaminibus*). For in these, the younger ones who wish to profess these disciplines are tested as to whether they deserve or ought to be admitted to them by the judgment both of the person who presides over these contests and of the whole people. When someone, after careful examination, is first found not to have been besmirched by any infamy in his life; then has been judged not to have been degraded by the yoke of slavery and for this reason to be unworthy of this discipline or of contending with those who profess it; thirdly, if he gives proofs of his skill and courage, and has demonstrated his skill no less than his courage when competing against his juniors and his coevals; and if, proceeding from matches against ephebes, he is permitted after examination by the presiding judge to compete against men who are adult and tested by long experience, and proves himself not only their equal in courage by continual struggle, but also frequently attains the palm of victory even among these—only then will he deserve to arrive at matches in a glorious contest (*ad agonis praeclari*[28] *certamina*), in which the right to compete is granted only to victors and those who have been decorated by the reward of many crowns. If we have understood the example of earthly competition (*carnalis agon*), then we must understand by comparison with this what the discipline and order of spiritual competition is.

---

[28] *scripsi*: praeclara *codd.*

In the following chapters Cassian proceeds to work out the comparison point by point very much as [Martyrius] does, sometimes applying the word *Olympiacus* to the monk's "contest."[29]

A. H. M. Jones cited this passage as one of the latest references to the traditional athletic competitions, though he suggested that Cassian had drawn it "from a literary source and not from real life."[30] Certain elements in Cassian's account do roughly correspond to earlier practice: the division of athletes into age classes, selection (κρίσις) determining an athlete's fitness to compete in a particular age category, and the immunity granted to victors in the so-called "eiselastic" contests. Some form of this last appears to have continued until the sixth century, since (as again was noticed by Jones) Justinian reiterated a ruling of Diocletian on the immunity available to athletes if they could prove that they had competed for their entire life, and had won three crowns in a "sacred contest" (*certamen sacrum*) without cheating.[31] Other items in Cassian's description are more surprising: that both the "presiding judge" (presumably the official called the βραβευτής in Greek texts) and "the whole people" decide the fitness of youthful aspirants, and that these have to begin by competing in "Olympic and Pythian contests"; but since "Olympic" and "Pythian" are often used to refer to practices borrowed from the Olympia and Pythia, even this detail may be authentic, though not necessarily still true in Cassian's own day.

The traditional, recurrent Greek contests (ἀγῶνες) are only rarely mentioned after their enormous expansion in the Imperial period, but they did not immediately die out, and some survive as late as the sixth century. While the Olympia of Elis were suppressed either by Theodosius I or II, there had long been other Olympia modeled on them. Callinicus in his *Life of Hypatius* records how the saint organized a demonstration in the reign of Theodosius II to prevent the *praefectus urbi*, Leontius, from reviving the Olympia previously held in the theater of Chalcedon and suppressed by Constantine: but this may not have

---

[29] *De institutis coenobiorum* 5.12 (SC 109:208–211), also 5.13, 14, and 16.
[30] Jones 1964: vol. 3, 337n69.
[31] *Cod. Just.* 10.54.1.

been typical, since Constantinople across the water was the religious capital of the eastern empire. The Olympia of Antioch continued until their suppression by Justin I. At some time during the fifth century, a benefactor of Aphrodisias in Caria adapted the small theater-like *bouleutērion* to become a "wrestling-ground" (παλαίστρα), and graffiti on the seats suggest that competitions were still held here. Individual athletes appear as late as the sixth century, and a "circus program" from Oxyrhynchus, dated to the same century, advertises charioteers, vocalists, and an athletic troupe (ξυστός). [32]

Even before Theodosius I took steps to make Christianity the official religion of the Empire, the prevalence of athletic imagery in Christian thought, no doubt encouraged by the writings of Paul, had caused terms such as 'athlete' (ἀθλητής), 'contest' (ἀγών), and 'practice' (ἄσκησις) to acquire a specifically Christian meaning in Greek, from which they are borrowed in Latin and Syriac. [33] At the same time, the withering away of organized athletics made metaphors such as those used by Chrysostom and his imitators incomprehensible to most hearers and readers, for whom terms such as "Olympic" and "Pythian" had comparatively little meaning. The true "athletes" and "ascetics" were now monks and martyrs.

HARVARD UNIVERSITY

WORKS CITED

Ameling, W. 2004. *Inscriptiones Judaicae Orientis*. Vol. 2, *Kleinasien*. Tübingen.

Anderson, J. G. C. 1913. "Festivals of Mên Askaênos in the Roman Colonia at Antioch of Pisidia." *JRS* 3:267–300.

---

[32] Chalcedon: Callinicus *Vita Hypatii* 33 (SC 177.214–219); for Leontius, *PLRE* 2.669, Leontius 9. Antioch: Downey 1961:518. Aphrodisias: Roueché 1989: no. 43 with discussion, p. 79 (παλαίστρα); no. 80 (graffiti); no. 179 (remodeling of stadium when no longer needed for athletics). An athlete among Jewish proselytes in the fifth century: Ameling 2004, no. 14 B 54. A wrestler (λουκτάτωρ) in Georg. Mon. *Vita Theod. Syk.* 88 (Festugière 1970:73). Oxyrhynchus: *POxy* 34.2707.

[33] Lampe 1961 s.vv. ἀθλέω, ἄθλησις, ἀθλητής, ἀγών, ἄσκησις.

Barnes, T. D. 2001. "The Funerary Speech for John Chrysostom (*BHG3* 871 = *CPG* 6517)." *Studia Patristica* 37 (= M. F. Wiles et al., eds., *Papers Presented at the Thirteenth International Conference on Patristic Studies Held in Oxford, 1999*, vol. 4, 328–345).

Brändle, R., and V. Jegher-Bucher. 1997. "Johannes Chrysostomus I." *Reallexikon für Antike und Christentum* 18:426–503.

Crosby, H. L. 1951. *Dio Chrysostom*. Vol. 5, *Discourses 61–80, Fragments, Letters*. Cambridge, MA.

Crowther, N. B. 1991a. "Euexia, Eutaxia, Philoponia: Three Contests of the Greek Gymnasium." *Zeitschrift für Papyrologie und Epigraphik* 85:301–304.

———. 1991b. "The Olympic Training Period." *Nikephoros* 4:161–166.

Dagron, G., and D. Feissel. 1987. *Inscriptions de Cilicie*. Paris.

Danker, F. W., ed. 2000. *A Greek-English Lexicon of the New Testament and Other Early Christian Literature*. 3rd ed. Chicago.

Dolbeau, F. 1996. *Augustin d'Hippone. Vingt-six sermons au peuple d'Afrique*. Paris.

Downey, G. 1961. *A History of Antioch in Syria: From Seleucus to the Arab Conquest*. Princeton.

Festugière, A.-J., ed. 1970. *Georgius Monachus. Vie de Théodore de Sykéôn*. Vol. 1, *Texte Grec*. Brussels.

Gardiner, E. N. 1905. "Wrestling." *JHS* 25:14–31.

Harland, P. A. 2007. "Familial Dimensions of Group Identity (II): 'Mothers' and 'Fathers' in Associations and Synagogues of the Greek World." *Journal for the Study of Judaism* 38:57–79.

Harris, H. A. 1976. *Greek Athletics and the Jews*. Ed. I. M. Barton and A. J. Brothers. Cardiff.

Jones, A. H. M. 1964. *The Later Roman Empire, 284–602: A Social, Economic, and Administrative Survey*. 3 vols. Oxford.

Jones, C. P. 2005. *Philostratus. The Life of Apollonius of Tyana*. 3 vols. Cambridge, MA.

Jüthner, J. 1905. "Ἔφεδρος." *RE* 5:2747–2748.

———. 1927. "Σκάμμα." *RE* 3A:435–437.

Karpozilos, A., and A. Cutler. 1991. "Sports." *Oxford Dictionary of Byzantium* 3:1939–1940.

Kelly, J. N. D. 1995. *Golden Mouth: The Story of John Chrysostom—Ascetic, Preacher, Bishop.* London.

Kertsch, M. 1995. *Exempla Chrysostomica: Zu Exegese, Stil und Bildersprache bei Johannes Chrysostomos.* Graz.

———. 1999. "Der Ring- bzw. Faustkampf mit dem Sparringpartner oder auch mit dem Punchingball: Ein bildersprachliches Motiv in der griechischen Patristik." *Nikephoros* 12:231–241.

König, J. 2005. *Athletics and Literature in the Roman Empire.* Cambridge.

Lampe, G. W. H. 1961. *A Patristic Greek Lexicon.* Oxford.

Löhr, W. A. 2002. "Theophilus von Alexandrien." *Theologische Realenzyklopädie* 33: 364–368. Berlin.

Malingrey, A. M. 1988. *Palladios. Dialogue sur la Vie de Jean Chrysostome.* Vol. 2, *Histoire du texte, index et appendices.* Sources Chrétiennes 342. Paris.

Metzger, M. ed. 1987. *Les Constitutions Apostoliques.* Tome III, *Livres VII et VIII.* Sources Chrétiennes 336. Paris.

Moretti, L., 1957. *Olympionikai: I vincitori negli antichi agoni olimpici.* Rome.

Pfitzner, V. C. 1967. *Paul and the Agon Motif: Traditional Athletic Imagery in the Pauline Literature.* Leiden.

Robert, L. 1930. "Pantomimen im griechischen Orient." *Hermes* 65:106–122. = *Opera Minora Selecta: Épigraphie et antiquités grecques.* Vol. 1, 654–670. Amsterdam, 1969.

———. 1939. "Inscriptions grecques d'Asie Mineure." In *Anatolian Studies Presented to William Hepburn Buckler,* ed. W. M. Calder and J. Keil, 227–248. Manchester.

———. 1940. *Les gladiateurs dans l'Orient grec.* Paris.

———. 1948. "Les Hellénodiques à Éphèse." *Hellenica: Recueil d'épigraphie, de numismatique et d'antiquités grecques* 5:59–63.

———. 1949a. "Les boules dans les types monétaires agonistiques." *Hellenica: Recueil d'épigraphie, de numismatique et d'antiquités grecques* 7:93–104.

———. 1949b. "Inscription agonistique de Smyrne." *Hellenica: Recueil d'épigraphie, de numismatique et d'antiquités grecques* 7:105–113.

———. 1974. "Les femmes théores à Éphèse." *Comptes rendus des séances de l'Académie des Inscriptions et Belles-Lettres* 118:176–181.

———. 1982. "Une vision de Perpétue martyre à Carthage en 203." *Comptes rendus des séances de l'Académie des Inscriptions et Belles-Lettres* 126:228–276. = *Opera Minora Selecta: Épigraphie et antiquités grecques.* Vol. 5, 791–839. Amsterdam, 1989.

Roueché, C. 1979. "A New Inscription from Aphrodisias and the Title πατὴρ τῆϲ πόλεωϲ." *Greek, Roman, and Byzantine Studies* 20:173–185.

———. 1989. *Aphrodisias in Late Antiquity: The Late Roman and Byzantine Inscriptions.* JRS Monographs 5. London.

Sawhill, J. A. 1928. *The Use of Athletic Metaphors in the Biblical Homilies of St. John Chrysostom.* Princeton.

Wallraff, M., and C. Ricci. 2007. *Oratio funebris in laudem sancti Iohannis Chrysostomi: Epitaffio attribuito a Martirio di Antiochia (BHG 871, CPG 6517).* Spoleto.

Weiler, I. 2004. "Theodosius I und die Olympischen Spiele." *Nikephoros* 17:53–75.

THE STERLING DOW ARCHIVE

PUBLICATIONS, UNFINISHED SCHOLARLY WORK, AND EPIGRAPHICAL SQUEEZES

WILLIAM T. LOOMIS

AND

STEPHEN V. TRACY

S TERLING DOW was a member of the Departments of the Classics and of History at Harvard University from 1936 until his retirement as John E. Hudson Professor of Archaeology in 1970.[1] To carry out wishes that Dow expressed frequently during his lifetime, his scholarly legatee

---

[1] Dow was born November 19, 1903, and died January 9, 1995. There is a biography in *Studies Presented to Sterling Dow on His Eightieth Birthday* (Greek, Roman, and Byzantine Monographs 10. Durham, NC, 1984) ix–xi. At Dow's memorial service in Harvard's Memorial Church on April 8, 1995, talks were given by his colleagues Zeph Stewart and Donald H. Fleming, his student Alan L. Boegehold, and his grandson Bradley M. Lown; the program for the service, bound with the texts of these talks, is available in the Harvard University Archives. For other obituaries, see Alan L. Boegehold, *American School of Classical Studies at Athens Newsletter* 35 (Spring 1995) 13, 15; Alan L. Boegehold and Mortimer Chambers, *CW* 88 (1995) 473; W. M. Calder III, *Gnomon* 68 (1996) 572–574; Michael J. Elliott, *New York Times* (January 14, 1995) 30; Donald H. Fleming, Mason Hammond, Emily D. T. Vermeule and Zeph Stewart, *Harvard University Gazette* (May 31, 2001) 21; Tom Long, *Boston Globe* (January 13, 1995) 41; William T. Loomis, *Tavern Club Memorials* (May 15, 1995) 5–7 (available in the Harvard University Archives); William T. Loomis, *CB* 72.2 (1997) 2–3; Bradley M. Lown, *The Exeter Bulletin* 90.4 (Spring 1995) 25; Zeph Stewart, *American Philological Association Newsletter* 18.2 (April 1995) 16–17; Stephen Tracy, *Association of Ancient Historians Newsletter* 66 (April 1995) 3; Emily Vermeule, *AJA* 99 (1995) 729–730; William H. Willis, *Greek, Roman and Byzantine Studies* 36 (1995) 3; no author stated, *AIA Newsletter* 10.3 (Spring 1995) 3; same, *Boston Herald* (January 17, 1995) 47; same, *The Exeter Bulletin* 90.4 (Spring 1995) 61; same, *Harvard Magazine* 97.5 (May–June 1995) 88; same, *Harvard University Gazette* (February 2, 1995) 2, 14; same, *Portland* [ME] *Press Herald* (January 11, 1995) 7B; same, *York County* [ME] *Coast Star* (January 11, 1995) 12A.

has given a nearly complete set of his publications,[2] his unfinished scholarly work, and his epigraphical squeezes to the University.

The publications and unfinished scholarly work are housed in the Depository of the Harvard University Archives. The publications consist of 5 books and 246 articles, reviews, and other items.[3] On many of these Dow recorded his subsequent thoughts, and he also attached letters from other scholars who commented on the particular publication. The unfinished scholarly work is organized as Dow organized it, in 397 (almost entirely loose-leaf) notebooks, whose titles (as given by Dow) are listed in Appendix 1.[4] Anyone wishing to examine a particular item should notify the Archives' Reference Department at least two business days in advance, so that the item may be brought in from the Depository to the Archives Reading Room.[5]

The squeezes are housed in the Depository of the Houghton (Rare Book) Library. Most of them were made by Dow and his wife, Elizabeth Flagg Dow, during their first visit to Greece, from 1931 to 1936. Numbering approximately 5,000, they constituted the largest private squeeze collection in the world prior to their donation to Harvard. The squeezes are an important scholarly resource, for three reasons. First, unlike many squeezes in large collections, which were made by museum guards or other persons who were not themselves concerned with the text of the inscriptions, these squeezes were made by a scholar who was

---

[2] The very few omissions are those for which no offprint ever was supplied, or for which none was preserved in Dow's files.

[3] To the list of publications in *Studies Presented to Sterling Dow on His Eightieth Birthday* (above, n1) xix–xxxvi, add the following: "The Cult of the Hero Doctor," *Bulletin of the American Society of Papyrologists* 22 (1985) 33–47; "Life in the Hooper-Lee-Nichols House: The Emerson and Dow Years," *Proceedings of the Cambridge Historical Society* 44 (1976–1979) [published 1985] 29–39; "Opportunities in Classical Studies," *CB* 64 (1988) 67–69; "Father Schoder and *Ancient Greece from the Air*," in Robert F. Sutton Jr., ed., *Daidalikon: Studies in Memory of Raymond V. Schoder, S. J.* (Wauconda, IL, 1989) 13–28.

[4] Additional explanatory details are enclosed in square brackets, with Dow's own words in quotation marks. Dow did publish on some of the subjects listed in Appendix 1, but his notebooks on those subjects are of interest in showing the development of his thinking prior to publication and his thoughts subsequent to publication.

[5] All communications with respect to Dow's memorial service, obituaries, publications, and notebooks should be directed to the Reference Department, Harvard University Archives, Pusey Library, Harvard University, Cambridge, MA 02138; telephone: 617-495-2461; fax: 617-495-8011; web: http://hul.harvard.edu/huarc/contact.shtml.

acutely aware of the problem areas in each inscription, and therefore particularly careful to get good impressions of faint letters and broken letters on the edges of stones, often by means of multiple squeezes. Second, in contrast to most squeezes, which are made with a single sheet of paper, these double-thickness squeezes (sometimes more than double) have retained a stiff and durable impression of the underlying letters. Finally, because many of the stones have been lost or damaged since the 1930s, the squeezes are now our best or only witness to a number of epigraphical texts. Appendix 2 contains a summary description of the squeeze collection, including a link to the electronic list of inscriptions represented by one or more squeezes.[6] Anyone wishing to examine a particular squeeze should notify Houghton's Reference Department at least two business days in advance, so that the squeeze may be brought in from the Depository to the Houghton Reading Room.[7]

As the first fruits of the squeeze collection from its new home, we offer the following:

I. *IG* II² 641 + 818 (FIGURES 1–2)

A squeeze that Dow labeled "Nat Mus Room 8" joins with each of his two squeezes of *IG* II² 641 (described by Kirchner as *tabula marmoris Pentelici, olim aetomate ornata*) to provide the missing ends of lines 1–3 on the upper right part of the stone, just outside and above the sloping gable. (Figure 1 shows the two squeezes placed as close together as the squeeze margins permit, while in Figure 2 the margins have been cropped to produce the effect of an actual join.) The line-ends had been read by Köhler for his 1877 edition (*IG* II 297), but Kirchner reported

---

[6] In compiling this list, we enjoyed the hospitable assistance of William P. Stoneman (Florence Fearrington Librarian of Houghton Library and Acting Curator of Early Books and Manuscripts), Susan C. Pyzynski (Associate Librarian for Technical Services), Rachel Howarth (Associate Librarian for Public Services), and the staff of the Houghton Reading Room. We also thank Kevin Clinton for help in identifying a fragmentary Eleusinian squeeze.

[7] All communications with respect to Dow's epigraphical squeezes should be directed to the Reference Department, Houghton Library, Harvard University, Cambridge, MA 02138; telephone: 617-495-2440; fax: 617-495-1376; e-mail: houghref@help.hmdc. harvard.edu.

that they had been broken off and lost by the time of his 1913 edition (*IG* II² 641). As Tracy recently observed,[8] the fragment bearing these letters is probably what Kirchner published separately as *IG* II² 818 (*pars superior tabulae marmoris Pentelici aetomate superatae*); Kirchner's description of it as non-stoichedon is inaccurate and in fact its letter-spacing precisely matches that of stoichedon *IG* II² 641. Tracy reported that he had "been able to locate neither the stone nor a squeeze" of *IG* II² 818, and that "[t]here is no EM number for it listed in the files at the Epigraphical Museum in Athens and it is not joined to *IG* II² 641 or indicated as part of it." Now, at the very least, we have a squeeze, and Dow's label suggests that we should look for the stone in the National Archaeological Museum, where he made his squeeze in the 1930s.

II. *IG* II² 3783 (PART) = AGORA I 851 (FIGURES 3–4)

First discovered in 1861 in excavations at the church of St. Demetrios Katiphori (c. 470 meters east of the Stoa of Attalos), the stone may already have been lost by the time of Dittenberger's 1878 edition (*IG* III 779), which was based on Lüders' hand-copy.[9] In 1935, Kirchner reported (*IG* II² 3783) that its whereabouts were unknown, but by then its left and right sides had broken off and the remaining fragment had been brought into the area of the Agora Excavations and inventoried as Agora I 851.[10] Until now, it has not been recognized as the middle portion (letters that are not underlined) of all eight lines of *IG* II² 3783:

---

[8] Stephen V. Tracy, *Athens and Macedon: Attic Letter-Cutters of 300 to 229 B.C.* (Berkeley 2003) 38.

[9] St. Demetrios Katiphori was located on the eastern flank of the Post-Herulian Wall (*Agora* XXIV 136–138, 140 and Plate 5). Presumably, Lüders' hand-copy was made sometime between the first publication of the inscription in *Philistor* [Φιλίστωρ] 1 (1861) 198–199, no. 11, and Dittenberger's 1878 edition.

[10] John McK. Camp II, Field Director of the Agora Excavations, reports as follows (by email to Loomis on May 22, 2009): "I 851 has an unsatisfactory provenience. We have a series of notebooks (ΚΤΛ, standing for καὶ τὰ λοιπά), dedicated to things that get into the collection from elsewhere. I 851 is #2 in that series. Provenience is given as 'Brought in from outside the excavations' and the date is given as 'May 1933'. So it may well have been found at or near its 19th century locale." We thank Camp for furnishing these details, for advising us that the letter traces on the stone (Figure 3) are substantially the same as those on the squeeze (Figure 4), and for giving us permission to publish this information.

εἴ τι π[άρ]ος μερόπων γεραὸς <u>νόος εὗρ' ἐνὶ τέχναι</u>,
<u>φαμί σε [πᾶ]ν κατιδεῖν εὐξυνέτοις πραπίσι</u>,
<u>κρίνανθ' ἰητρῶν σοφὰ δόγματα καὶ τὸ περισσὸν</u>
ἐκ βύβλων <u>ψυχῆς ὄμματι δρεψάμενον</u>,
5 <u>εὐιάδος</u> τ', Ἀργαῖε, πορεῖν <u>γάνος ἀμερίοισιν</u>
<u>οἴνας γυιοπαγεῖς</u> ῥυόμεν<u>ον καμάτους</u>.
<u>ἀνθ' ὧν σοῦ</u> τέχνας ἐρατ<u>ὸν κλέος οὔποτ' ὀλεῖται</u>,
<u>λαμπρότερον</u> δ' ἄστρων <u>ἔσσεται οὐρανίων</u>.

If in the past the venerable mind of mortals discovered any skill, I say that you grasped all of it with perceptive understanding, after you had evaluated the wise teachings of physicians and with your mind's eye had plucked the best from books, and, Argaios, you furnished the refreshment of Bacchic wine to mortals, warding off limb-stiffening pains. In recompense for these things, the lovely glory of your skill will never perish and will be brighter than the heavenly stars.

III. JOINS AND ASSOCIATIONS

Dow's labels suggest seven joins or associations which, to our knowledge, have not yet been published. Because the publication of new or revised texts should be based on the stones as well as the squeezes, we here merely record Dow's labels:

(a) *IG* II² 797 + "²830 belongs with ²797."

(b) *IG* II² 2005 (= EM 8519) + EM 3841. On the right side of a single squeeze, the three lines of EM 3841 are aligned with, but not joined to, the first three lines of *IG* II² 2005, resulting in a text different from that published in *IG* II² 2005.

(c) *IG* II² 2014, frs. a (= EM 3860), b (= EM 3856), c (= EM 3701) + an unlabeled 21-line fragment (fitting above and to the right of fr. a), all joined on a single squeeze.

(d) *IG* II² 2449 + "EM 4421 file with ²2449."

(e) *IG* II² 2471b + "EM 4646 unpub? file with ²2471b."

(f) "Eleus EM 4573" + two different squeezes labeled "Eleus with EM 4573."[11]

BOSTON AND INSTITUTE FOR ADVANCED STUDY

APPENDIX 1

Titles of Notebooks Containing
Sterling Dow's Unfinished Scholarly Work

AGORA CONSTITUTION, Rev[iew of] Thompson–Wycherley [Thompson, Homer A., and R. E. Wycherley. 1972. *The Agora of Athens: The History, Shape and Uses of an Ancient City Center*. Volume 14 of *The Athenian Agora: Results of Excavations Conducted by the American School of Classical Studies at Athens*. Princeton.]

[Agora] I 72

AGORA I 286 [2 notebooks]

Ag[ora] XV [Merritt, Benjamin D., and John S. Traill. 1974. *Inscriptions: The Athenian Councillors*. Volume 15 of *The Athenian Agora: Results of Excavations Conducted by the American School of Classical Studies at Athens*. Princeton.] [13 notebooks with detailed comments on individual inscriptions, including a review labeled] TRAILL

Ag[ora] XVII [Bradeen, Donald W. 1974. *Inscriptions: The Funerary Monuments*. Volume 17 of *The Athenian Agora: Results of Excavations Conducted by the American School of Classical Studies at Athens*. Princeton.] [3 notebooks with detailed comments and a] Rev[iew]

ΑΓΡΙΠΠΕΙΝΙΛΛΑ [*IGUR* I 160]

ΑΓΡΙΠΠΕΙΟΝ

Alexander [J. R., 2 notebooks, one labeled "Lecture"]

---

[11] We thank Bob Zinck, of Harvard College Library Digital Imaging and Photography Services, for Figures 1, 2, and 4, and Craig Mauzy, of the Agora Excavations, for Figure 3.

A[lphabetization in Antiquity and the Middle Ages] [7 notebooks relating to a projected book by Dow and Lloyd W. Daly]

AMPHIPOLIS LION

Ἀμφίθεος [3 notebooks]

Andania [*IG* V.1 1532, 2 notebooks]

ANDREWS [Eugene P.]

ARCHAIC [Period]

Archaic Grave Monuments

[ARCHERY]

Architecture

ARCHIVES [2 notebooks]

Askl[epieion] Records [*IG* II]² 839 [+ *IG* II² 840–842, 878, 1532–1539]

ΑΣΚΛΕΠΙΟΣ

ΑΘΕ/ΑΘΗΝΑΙ [2 notebooks on "The Greatness of Athenai, Extent and Causes"]

ATHENS, FOUR LECTURES 1964–1966

ATHLETIC [Inscriptions]

ΑΘΛΟΘΕΤΑΙ

ΑΘΠ [17 notebooks on Aristotle's *Athenaion Politeia*, including discovery, chronology, early scholarship, bibliography, editions, translations, topics, etc.]

ATTIC GRAVE MONUMENTS [3 notebooks]

AUGUSTUS AND AGRIPPA IN ATHENS

ΑΥΤΟΛΥΚΟΣ [*SEG* XXIII 78]

Βατή [Deme]

BOULE

BOUSTROPHEDON INSCRIPTIONS FROM THE ELEUSINION [draft article with this title building on "L H JEFFERY *Hesp[eria]* 1948. 86–111", 2 notebooks][12]

BRIT[ain, Romanization of]

BRONZE AGE [2 notebooks]

Brothers

CALDER REV[iew of Briggs, Ward W., and William M. Calder III. 1990. *Classical Scholarship: A Biographical Encyclopedia.* New York.]

[Calligraphy]

CAMBRIDGE INSCRIPTIONS [Greek and Latin inscriptions and papyri in private collections in Cambridge, Massachusetts]

CATS Inscrs [i.e., *Catalogi generis incerti* (*IG* II² 2364–2489), 2 notebooks]

CHAMBER TOMBS

ΧΑΡΙΤΕΣ

ΧΙΟΣ

CIT[izenship]

C[ode, i.e., Athenian Law Code] [25 notebooks including] Commentary on [individual] Lines, EPITHETS, HIEROSYNA, APOMETRA, HERALDS, FRAGMENTS, GENESIA, ΚΥΡΒΕΙΣ ΑΞΟΝΕΣ, LECTURES, ΛΥΣΙΑΣ, MARA-THONIAN CODE, Negatives, OUTLINES, PHOTOGRAPHS, RUBRICS, PRICES, VICTIMS, FESTIVALS, SCRIBES AND MASONS, TEXT

COLONIZATION

CRETE AND EGYPT

CROWNS

---

[12] Jeffery's article is entitled "The Boustrophedon Sacral Inscriptions from the Agora."

Cult of Meter

DARK AGE PHOENICIANS

DECREES BY BOULE

Delos

DEMESMEN OF KEKROPIS [*IG* II]² 2385

DEMOTICS, Theories about

DIAITs [i.e., διαιτηταί]

ΔΙΚΑΣΤΗΡΙΑ Articles

DIOGENES [2 notebooks]

DISCOVERERS [of the Bronze Age]

DRAKON

Egyptian Papers

ΕΙΚΑΔΕΙΣ [*IG* II]² 1258, 2631, 2632 [2 notebooks]

EKKL[esia]

ΕΚΛΕΚΤΟΣ [Athletic Victor, *IG* II² 3169/70]

ENVIRONMENT

ΕΦΗΒΟΙ [15 notebooks on all aspects and periods]

Epidauria

ΕΠΙΚΟΥΡΟΣ [3 notebooks, including one on] PROSOPOG[graphy]

ΕΠΙΜΕΛΣ [i.e., ἐπιμεληταί] [2 notebooks]

EPITAPHIOS

EPSILON [Delphic] [3 notebooks]

ERETRIA

FOLLET 15 [Follet, Simone. 1976. *Athènes au iie et au iiie siècle:* Études *chronologiques et prosopographiques.* Paris. No. 15 (pages 443–450) in Appendix 1, "Édition ou réédition de fragments" = *IG* II^2 2242 + 2486]

GAPS [in Inscriptions]

GAR[risons in Attike, *IG* II^2] 1958

GARRISONS [at Eleusis]

GENESIA

GORTYN CODE

GRAVE MONUMENTS

GREATNESS OF ATHENS

GR[eek] REL[igion]

HAD[rianic Attic Grave Monuments, Harvard University 1905.8, Rhode Island School of Design 5230, 4 notebooks]

HATHERTON [Monument, i.e., *IG* II^2 3145, *SEG* XXI 698]

HDT [i.e., Herodotos] Bridges, Xerxes' Advance

ΗΡΩΣ ΙΑΤΡΟΣ

ΗΣΙΟΔΟΣ [2 notebooks]

Hesp[*eria*]. 1978 266–268

Hesp[*eria*]. 1978 [269–331], 1982 [197–235]

HISTORY of ATHENIAN CODES

HIST[ory] OF CULT OF BENDIS/THRAIKS

HOLBORN Roman Grave Monu[ment, British Museum 1961. 7–4]

H[omer] [10 notebooks on various aspects of the *Iliad* and *Odyssey* including] Battle, [*Iliad*] 1 [and] 23, Embassy, KAT[alogue of Ships], MERIONES, *ODYSSEY*, PERSONNEL, SPECIAL OPERATIONS

HONORS

HOROI

HUM[an] SAC[rifice] [3 notebooks]

HYM[ettos, Sanctuary of Zeus on] [3 notebooks]

IG I² 1

[*IG*] I² 77

[*IG* II]² 948, 990

[*IG* II]² 1035 [3 notebooks]

[*IG* II]² 1043

[*IG* II]² 1961

[*IG* II]² 1969, 1970, 1971 Jointly [2 notebooks]

[*IG* II]² 1973. 2–6, 1973a, 1973b, 1989, 1990, 1998 [2 notebooks]

[*IG* II]² 2051, 2191

[*IG* II]² 2119

[*IG* II]² 2160 + 2159 + 2136

[*IG* II]² 2245

[*IG* II]² 2333

[*IG* II]² 2344

[*IG* II]² 2362

[*IG* II]² 2366

[*IG* II]² 2470

[*IG* II]² 2679

[*IG* II]² 2875, 1945

[*IG* II]² 3193

[*IG* II]² 11606a

INTRODUCTION of the PHOENICIAN ALPHABET

ΙΟΒΑΚΧΟΙ [*IG* II² 1368, 3 notebooks]

ΙΣΘΜΙΑ [2 notebooks]

Jones [Nicholas F., "The Civic Organization of Corinth," *TAPA* 110 (1980) 161–193, unpublished appendix by Dow on "The Size of the Casualty List (Korinthos Inv. No. I 734)"]

KALKANI [vase]

KAN[ephoroi] [2 notebooks]

Κήρυκες

KINGSHIP

Ki[rchner, Johannes]

ΚΛΗΡΩΤΗΡΙΑ [7 notebooks on all aspects, including discovery, catalogue of fragments, etc.]

KOP [i.e., Corinth, 3 notebooks on] AIDS [to the study of] KOR INSCRS, Cor VIII 1 108, ΦΥΛ[ΑΙ]

ϘΟΡ [i.e., Corinthian tribes and inscriptions] [4 notebooks]

ΚΟΣΜΗΤΗΣ, [*IG* II]² 1990

Lectures St. Paul's C[lassical]A[ssociation of]N[ew]E[ngland] on "England and the Great Papyrus Treasure" and "The Discovery of the Aristotelian Constitution of Athens"]

Letters about Article MINOAN WRITING [Dow, Sterling. 1954. "Minoan Writing." *American Journal of Archaeology* 58:77–129]

LIONS Essay

LIONS IN GREECE

Longevity

Lowell [Lectures on] MYK[enaians] IN KNOSSOS, MYK[enai] 1400–1100, DARK AGE, ILLITERACY, HOMER, THOUKYDIDES [4 notebooks]

ΛΥΚΕΙΟΝ

LYNCH [J. P., 1972. *Aristotle's School: A Study of a Greek Educational Institution*. Berkeley.], Rev[iew of]

Μελίστω [Grave Relief, Harvard University Art Museums 1961.86]

ΜΕΛΛS [i.e., Μελλέφηβοι]

MHN [Cult of, Manissa Inv. No. 5414] [3 notebooks]

MEN NAMED FROM GODS

Menodoros [2 notebooks]

METHODS OF ALLOTMENT

Metroon, etc.

MIN[oan]-MYK[enaian] SEALS

MIN[oan] THAL[assocracy]

MINOAN WRITING

Mondo *BCH* 1949 [i.e., archon Mondo, *Hesperia* 11 (1942) 71, no. 37; M. T. Mitsos, *BCH* 73 (1949) 351–360, "Inscriptions d' Athènes"]

MOULDINGS

NAMES

NAMES [ending in] -ας, HISTORY

NERO AND ATHENS

NOTABLE ATH[enian]S

ΩΔΕΙΟΝ [2 notebooks]

ΟΛΥΝΘΟΣ

Onomastics/Prosopography

ΟΣΤΡΑΚΙΣΜΟΣ [6 notebooks]

ΠΑΝΑΘ [i.e., *Panathenaic Games Inscriptions*]

ΠΑΡ[ΕΔΡΟΙ] [2 notebooks]

M Parry [3 notebooks]

Περικλῆς

PERSIA

ΦΑΡΟΣ [at Alexandria]

ΦΙΛΟΙ [3 notebooks, including one on *IG* II]^2 2002, 2471

ΠΥΛΑΙ ΑΘΗΝΩΝ [4 notebooks]

ΦΥΛΟΒΑΣΙΛΕΙΣ

Πλαταιαί

ΠΛΑΤΩΝ ["The Sacred Calendar in Platon's *Phaon*"]

Plotina

ΠΟΛΙΣ

Precedence, Games

Princeton Encyclopedia of Classical Sites [Review of, 3 notebooks]

ΠΡΟΓΟΝΙΟΝ [apron]

PROSOPOG[raphie]S

Πρυτσ [i.e., Prytaneis]

ΡΗΤΩΡ

Roofs [3 notebooks]

THE ROMAN EMPEROR AND ATHENS

SABAZ[IOS, Cult of, 2 notebooks]

ST. PAUL [2 notebooks]

ΣΑΛΣ [i.e, Salaminioi] [4 notebooks]

ΣΑΜΟ [i.e., Samothracian Inscriptions]

Sathers [i.e., Sather Lectures in 1964 at the University of California at Berkeley, on "Knossos and Mykenai: the Great Powers in the Bronze Age" (unpublished)] [3 notebooks]

SAYCE [Archibald Henry]

SCHLIEMANN

Seattle [i.e., Marble Lekythos in the Seattle Art Museum]

SECURITY AREA AT KNOSSOS

SEG III 122

SHIPS

SITES II [there is no notebook "SITES I"]

ΣΙΤΟΦΥΛΑΚΕΣ

ΣΩΦΡΩΝ

SPARTA

SPHERES

STAFF [of the Ephebeia]

STATE CULTS

SUFFECTI

ΣΥΜΠΡΟΕΔΡΟΙ, ΑΝΑΓΡΑΦΕΙΣ

ΣΥΝΟΙΚΙΣΜΟΣ II [there is no notebook "ΣΥΝΟΙΚΙΣΜΟΣ I," but see "UNION OF ATTIKE" below]

T[ables, Cult] [6 notebooks]

ΤΕΙΘΡΑΣ [Calendar]

Terms of Bouls [i.e., Bouleutai]

ΘΕΟΙ

THEOPHORIC NAMES

THEOR[odokoi at] NEMEA

THERA

THOLOI [2 notebooks]

THOUKYDIDES [4 notebooks]

Θραικές

TOPICS/PROJECTS [2 notebooks]

TRAILL [J. S., 1986. *Demos and Trittys: Epigraphical and Topographical Studies in the Organization of Attika*. Toronto.] Rev[iew]

TRANS-ISTHMIAN WALL

ΤΡΟΙΖΗΝ

UNION OF ATTIKE

Vapheios

Ventris and Bronze Age Greek [2 notebooks]

Walker-Ames Lectures I–III [in 1972 at the University of Washington, on "The People and the Kings of Mycenae in the Bronze Age"]

Xenophon's *Anabasis* [11 notebooks on such topics as] ΚΟΥΝΑΞΑ, Μεταφέρνης, Ἴσσοι

ΞΕΝ ΣΥΜΠ [i.e., Xenophon's *Symposium*]

) [2 notebooks on the use of this sign in Attic Inscriptions]

APPENDIX 2

Sterling Dow's Epigraphical Squeezes

The squeezes are stored in 49 numbered boxes, organized pretty much as Dow organized them, as follows:

Inscriptiones Graecae I[3]	Boxes 1–3
Inscriptiones Graecae II[2]	Boxes 4–29
Inscriptiones Graecae III	Box 29
Agora	Boxes 30–33
Attic Inscriptions in Other Corpora	Box 34
Hesperia	Boxes 35–36
Attic Inscriptions in *Supplementum Epigraphicum Graecum* and Journals other than *Hesperia*	Box 37
EM (Athens Epigraphical Museum) Numbers	Box 38
Agora I(nscription) Numbers	Box 39
Attic Squeezes Not Yet Identified	Box 40
Corinth	Box 41
Aegina and Peloponnese (other than Corinth)	Box 42
Central and Northern Greece	Box 43
Aegean Islands (other than Euboea), Asia Minor, Ostia	Box 44
Euboea	Box 45
Res Gestae Divi Augusti	Box 46
Diocletian's Price Edict	Box 47
Dow Epigraphical Aids	Box 48
Odds & Ends	Box 49

A list of the inscriptions represented by squeezes is accessible at http://nrs.harvard.edu/urn-3:FHCL.Hough:hou02042. Scholars seeking the squeeze of a published inscription are advised to search by its earlier as well as later places of publication (including *SEG*), and also by its museum inventory number (which is usually given in the publication). A list of publication places of all Agora I(nscription) numbers is available at the Houghton Library.

Figure 1: Squeezes of *IG* II[2] 641 (below) and 818 (above). Photo Credit: MS Gr 39, Houghton Library, Harvard University.

Figure 2: Squeezes of *IG* II² 641 (below) and 818 (above); margins cropped to produce the effect of an a join. Photo Credit: MS Gr 39, Houghton Library, Harvard University.

Figure 3: *IG* II² 3783 = Agora I 851. Photo Credit: American School of Classical Studies at Athens—Agora Excavations.

Figure 4: Squeeze of *IG* II² 3783 = Agora I 851. Photo Credit: MS Gr 39, Houghton Library, Harvard University.

SUMMARIES OF DISSERTATIONS
FOR THE DEGREE OF PH.D.

Isabel Katharina Köster—*Roman Temple Robbery*

In this dissertation I study temple robbery in the Roman world from the third century BCE to the second century CE. In the Roman world, the safety of a city was based on a contract with the gods: the gods protected the city, if the people in turn guarded the sanctuaries and the gods' possessions within them. The protection of sacred property was therefore vital, and law, literature, inscriptions, and the architecture of temples all address the unauthorized removal of objects from a sacred space. This is the first extensive study of temple robbery in the Roman world. As I argue, the crime posed significant social and religious challenges and shows how important the concept of sacredness was to the Romans.

The first chapter focuses on attempts to establish a legal definition of temple robbery. It shows that the sparse attention given to temple robbery in the legal sources is at odds with the rich discussions of the crime in non-legal texts. Despite the existence of some legal regulations and penalties, temple robbery was primarily conceived of as a crime against the gods that was punished by divine powers. The second chapter examines the sacred space and asks what temple robbers would be interested in stealing. Greek and Roman sanctuaries were depositories for many precious objects, but these were not the only things that became the targets of thefts. Instead, everything from a precious cult statue to the manure of sacred animals could be subject to temple robbery. The third chapter looks at the most widely recognized aspect of Roman temple robbery: plundering during military campaigns. It argues that there was a widespread concern with treating foreign deities properly. The final chapter examines temple robbery as a motif in invective, focusing especially on Cicero's Verrines as an example of a text in which a temple robber is seen to put his entire society at risk by arousing the anger of the gods through his robberies.

Degree in Classical Philology 2011

PETER ALFRED O'CONNELL—*Prose as Performance: Seeing and Hearing in the Forensic Speeches of Antiphon, Andokides and Lysias*

THE TEXTS OF ATHENIAN FORENSIC SPEECHES preserved in papyri and medieval manuscripts are records of oral performances before hundreds of jurors in the fifth and fourth centuries BCE. Litigants used voice, words, gestures, and appearance to try to convince the jurors to accept their version of events. This is the first comprehensive study of the relationship between the surviving forensic speeches of Antiphon, Andokides, and Lysias and their original performances. I focus on the language of seeing as the nexus of text and performance. I show how litigants' words work together with their physical appearance, how litigants plant images in their jurors' minds, and how litigants bring their speeches to life by referring to people in the lawcourt.

In the first half of the dissertation, I compare forensic performances with performances in the assembly and the theater, and, in the second half, I look closely at the relationship of the texts of forensic speeches to their original performance contexts. I demonstrate that the theater, the lawcourts, and the assembly do not fit into a pattern which equates looking with judging. Forensic speakers consciously manipulate their jurors' sight rather than subject themselves to it. Furthermore, I show how they use the vocabulary of eyewitnessing, internal audiences, quoted speech, and deictic pronouns to suggest that the jurors are seeing what they are really only hearing and to bridge the gap between the past time of the narratives and the here-and-now of the lawcourts.

I discuss legal, rhetorical, and performative aspects of numerous speeches, including Antiphon 5, Lysias 7, Lysias 24, and Lysias 32. I propose a more nuanced understanding of the term *enargeia*, which Dionysios of Halikarnassos applies to Lysias' style. I also compare the overlap of ritual and rhetorical uses of the language of sight in

Andokides 1 and Lysias 6, two speeches which address Andokides' alleged profanation of the Eleusinian Mysteries in 415 BCE.

Degree in Classical Philology 2011

ARIANE SCHWARTZ—*Horace and His Readers in Early Modern Europe*

THIS DISSERTATION EXPLORES THE VERSE OF HORACE through its afterlives in Europe between 1550 and 1650, a period in Horatian scholarship when educators began to package Horace's text differently for consumption by their students. Horace's moral standards were put in sharp contrast with those of early modern Christian society during this period. My contribution shows how, through particular commentaries and textual editing, his poetics and philosophy had to be sanitized and stripped of their characteristically pagan elements, and how that kind of manipulation helps us understand the ancient world.

The introduction considers Horace's journey from his origins in the first century BCE down to 1550, and looks at how the way his text was read explains how it was transformed. The first chapter, through a discussion of a 1592 Latin commentary on *Odes* 2.16, a 1652 edition of English translations, editions of *Odes* 4.7, and Pierre Gassendi's *Lettres latines* and *Vie et moeurs d'Epicure*, traces the dialogue between the recovery and response to Epicurus and Lucretius in the sixteenth and seventeenth centuries and the interpretation of Horace. The second chapter explores why Horace's *Epistles* 1 was attractive and adaptable to the educational reformer Peter Ramus' philosophical method, which emphasized the ordering of knowledge to bridge the gulf between theory and practice in education in the middle of the sixteenth century.

The final chapter, discussing the fates of material from the *Odes* and *Epodes* in Jesuit editions printed between 1569 and 1630, looks closely at the repackaging of Horace's text in the hands of instructors and editors who did not want their readers to be exposed to his erotic verse. My conclusions based on these case studies show how educators in early modern Europe faced challenges in offering for study an ancient poet with moral standards very different from those in their world. They let us see as well the kind of reading experience early modern students were supposed to have. Horace is revealed as an author who could be, with suitable manipulation, moral enough for almost any purpose.

A survey of editions until 1650 concludes the dissertation.

Degree in Classical Philology 2011

This volume was edited by Kathleen M. Coleman and
composed by Ivy Livingston
(Department of the Classics, Harvard University).

It was manufactured by Sheridan Books (Ann Arbor, MI) and printed on
recycled paper.

The typeface is GentiumAlt, designed by Victor Gaultney
and distributed by SIL International.